TEXTILE
Analysis, Quality Control & Innovative Uses

3ⁿᵈ Edition

Usha Chowdhary, Ph.D.

Published by Linus Learning
Ronkonkoma, NY 11779

Copyright © 2022 Linus Learning
All Rights Reserved.

ISBN 10: 1-60797-967-5

ISBN 13: 978-1-60797-967-8

No part of this publication may be reproduced, stored in a retrieval system, or transmitted, in any form or by any means, electronic, mechanical, photocopying, recording, or otherwise, without the prior permission of the publisher.

Printed in the United States of America.

This book is printed on acid-free paper.

Print Number   5   4   3   2   1

ACKNOWLEDGMENTS

This task of creating second edition would not have been possible without the help of several people and organizations. I am grateful to the following.

1. My past and present students who inspired me for making this course what it is today. My future students will get it in new and improved form.

2. My textile teachers who helped me understand the basics of textiles.

3. My administrators at the University of Missouri – Columbia and Central Michigan University who trusted me with developing and/or teaching a textile analysis course. Additionally, CMU supported me with seeking funding for updated equipment and development of an Environmental chamber with standardized settings.

4. I am also indebted to my colleagues for their support and trust.

5. Special gratitude is extended to Eldrick Jeremiah Murphy for diligently reviewing every chapter for its ease of readability and careful editing.

6. Several organizations and journals that offered opportunities for professional development and recognition, and shared textile materials for teaching, research, and development.

7. I also want to extend my gratitude tothe publisher who agreed to produce second edition of two books in the same year.

8. Finally, I extend special thanks to my husband Dr. Sarvjit Chowdhary who has supported me all along with his companionship, money, and time; my children (Abhineet and Neha) for being my extended wings and introducing me to the updated uses of various textiles in their personal and professional lives; and my grandchildren (Ronan, Ishika, and Alex) who taught me about the functionality of the new and improved merchandise in contemporary times.

This Herculean job would not have been possible without the help of several people from every walk of life. I thank you all for your contributions so that I could realize my goal of upgrading this book. I hope that future students and faculty will find it useful for teaching the importance of textile analysis for determining appropriateness for end-use and compatibility between various layers of the garment.

PREFACE

Overall, the second edition has been updated with latest references, new examples, removal of materials that are redundant for today's times, new content, addition of relevant textile attributes, use of websites, and innovative practice activities. A special effort was made to bridge the gap between academia and industry for effective use of textile analysis in personal and professional lives. Special editing was done to enhance the readability of materials.

Global perspective and glossary of terms are added in chapter 1. Chapter 2 has updated tests and problems. Chapter 3 has new examples and removed information on the Analysis of Variance (ANOVA). Chapter 4 has new examples of images and problems. Chapter 5 is reorganized to enhance understanding of dry performance attributes for aesthetic, comfort, durability, safety, and sensory functions of textiles. ASTM standards are added for selected end-uses. Information of air permeability, bursting strength, and stretch and recovery are expanded with applied research from the latest literature. Chapter 6 is reorganized within the context of aesthetic, care, and comfort functions. New attributes are added or expanded. Antimicrobial and wicking behavior are just two examples. Additionally, AATCC and ASTM standards are included in the reorganized format.

Chapter 7 includes some examples of damage from laundering, updated laundering procedures and storage. Chapter 8 is revamped for establishing connection between what is taught in academic settings and what is practiced in industry. Concept of color is presented using scientific and artistic principles and their use by industry to understand personal differences and industrial practices in merchandising and retailing. Examples are used to demonstrate the impact of type of four dyes on selected fiber contents as a special addition. Chapter 9 refines the roe of textile and apparel for enhancing comfort of individuals with special needs as well as sports activities.

Chapter 10 incorporates innovations in several areas of interest in addition to retaining the basic innovations in textiles. Additions focus on ballistic protection, digital printing, military apparel, moisture management, Phase Changing Materials (PCM), smart textiles, space clothing, and sustainability, Chapter 11 uses new examples of technical data sheets and fabric layout. Chapter 12 offers 350 questions on different aspects of textiles with answers. It incorporates the current research in the applied areas. Examples applied research are integrated in the text rather than having a separate chapter in the first edition. Finally, chapter 13 continues to focus on globalization, cross application, quality assurance and control, and special treatments to understand the importance of textile analysis for several end uses because bot appropriateness for various end-uses and compatibility of different layers used in a garment are of critical importance for consumer, manufacturers and retailers.

Usha Chowdhary, Author

TABLE OF CONTENT

Acknowledgments iii
Preface iv

CHAPTER 1
Textile Testing: An Overview 3 1

CHAPTER 2
Textile Standards and Organizations 19

CHAPTER 3
Data Analysis and Interpretation 35

CHAPTER 4
Structural Attributes 53

CHAPTER 5
Performance Attributes: Dry Tests 75

CHAPTER 6
Performance Attributes: Wet Tests 109

CHAPTER 7
Textile Care and Upkeep 139

CHAPTER 8
Color, Theory, Evaluation, Measurement and Use 157

CHAPTER 9
Comfort and Textiles 185

CHAPTER 10
Innovative Treatment and Uses 207

CHAPTER 11
Textile Analysis & Development of Technical Data Sheets 223

CHAPTER 12
Textile Analysis: A Summative Reservoir 249

CHAPTER 13
Quality Assurance, Quality Control, and Special Applications 285

APPENDIX
Appendix A - Purposeful Collaboration Between Academia and Industry 299

Appendix B - Reference Styles for Various Publications That Publish on Textiles 300

Appendix C - Author Index 301

Appendix D - Subject Index 308

TEXTILE TESTING: AN OVERVIEW

1 CHAPTER

INTRODUCTION

This chapter focuses on definition and reasons for textile testing, as well as structural and performance attributes of textiles with definitions, examples, and function. It also covers the indicators used by consumers while purchasing textile materials and apparel. Additionally, it covers information on types of testing and distinction between quality assurance and quality control. Finally, it provides summary, study questions and activities along with references.

WHAT IS TEXTILE TESTING?

Textile testing refers to the evaluation of textile materials with standardized tests to determine appropriateness for intended use and compatibility of competing materials used in the apparel and/or industrial products. Testing is conducted for both structural and performance attributes to ensure quality control.

There are three important organizations worldwide that are responsible for developing the testing standards for textile materials. **American Society for Testing and Materials** (ASTM) is engaged in developing dry or physical tests as well as evaluation criteria for men's and women's apparel, and linens, upholstery and window coverings. It also provides information on several types of stitches and seams to bridge the gap between textile and apparel projects. ASTM provides standards for several materials beyond textiles. However, volumes 7.01 and 7.02 focus exclusively on textiles. D-13 committee of the organization continually focuses on new, old, and revised methods. They are examined every five years for their reapproval or discarding decisions. Many of the developed tests are used internationally exclusively, as well as in conjunction with **ISO** (International Organization of Standardization) that is responsible for overseeing the quality of materials as well as environment worldwide. The **American Association of Textile Chemists and Colorists** (AATCC) is responsible for developing standards for wet tests to determine quality of textile and apparel.

As recognized previously that testing is executed for both structural and performance attributes. Therefore, it is imperative to understand their definitions and examples for best use. **Structural attributes** are the properties that are necessary for the textile product to exist at fiber, yarn, and fabric levels. Examples of structural attributes include fiber content, fiber diameter, fiber length, yarn crimp or twist, yarn size, fabric construction, fabric count, fabric flaws, fabric thickness and fabric weight. The knowledge about the structural attributes provides preliminary ideas about the quality of fabrics under consideration. For example, filaments are stronger than staple fibers and yarns. Higher fabric count yields better quality than lower count. Yarns with higher number of twists are stronger than the lower twist levels. Synthetic yarns with higher crimp have higher stretch than those with lower crimp. Fabric flaws such as bow and skew impact the drape of resulting garments. Fabrics with knit construction have higher stretch than woven materials.

Performance attributes are those properties of textiles that result from various pressures during wear-and-tear of textile materials. Examples of the performance attributes are abrasion resistance, air permeability, breaking/bursting/tensile strength, colorfastness to laundering/light/water, dimensional stability, elongation, fabric drape/hand, flame resistance, pilling resistance, porosity, seam efficiency/strength, stretch, tear resistance, water repellency, and wrinkle recovery. Performance tests determine if the textile material will meet the needs of the intended uses effectively or not. For example, we can allow more dimensional change for towels than wearable apparel. Likewise, flame- resistance is of critical importance for children's sleepwear, firefighter's clothing, apparel for race-car drivers, and airplane interiors. Formal attires should have higher wrinkle resistance and appearance retention than casual apparel. Breaking and tear strength, abrasion resistance and stretch are important for athletic wear. Water repellency is important for rainwear and swimming. Stretch is important for aerobic apparel.

WHY DO TEXTILE TESTING?

Textile testing has special role in both academia and industry. In academia, students learn from using standardized tests to pass or fail the fabrics for intended use. In industry, knowledge of the test outcomes helps with choosing fabrics for the intended end-uses and making decisions for care labels. Chowdhary (2009) identified thirteen reasons for conducting textile testing. Fourteen reasons are described for textile testing below as adherence to government regulations; apparel product development; assist designers, manufacturers, retailers and consumers of apparel from textiles; analysis of fabric failures; building ties between academia and industry; confidence building; cost reduction; enhancing predictability; expediting communication among various stakeholders; forensic testing; learning about the textile analysis process; product evaluation; quality control; and quality promotion.

1. **Adherence to Government Regulations**

    The **Rules and Federal Trades Commission (FTC)** is charged with the responsibility of reinforcing the Textile Fiber Products Identification Act -1960 (Collier, Bide & Tortora, 2009). The Act requires that all textile items should include a generic name if they represent at least 5% of the fiber content. It should also include Registration Number (RN#) or WPL (Wool Product Labeling #). The legislation requires that the fiber content with highest percentage should be listed first and the lowest percentage as last. Chowdhary (2009, p.2) provided five examples to understand application of the legislation in industry. Example 1 below lists rayon first because its percentage is more than acetate. It is important to list the generic name of the fiber (Example 2). If the content is less than five percent but it impacts the overall character of the textile material, it can be listed rather than writing other textile materials (Example 3). For wool products, RN number is replaced with WPL number (Example 4). In 1984, the law was amended to include country of origin (Example 5). On July 8, 2013, USA-ITA, now USFIA, filed comments in response to the FTC's request. On the first point, we suggested that the FTC eliminate the disclosure requirement in the first point unless there is a demonstrable danger of deception. On the second point, we suggested that the Section 303.45(b)(4) be revised by adding ", including articles or wearing apparel", so as to read: "Secondhand household articles, including articles of wearing apparel." The act is also known as the "Textile Labeling Rules" (2013). https://www.usfashionindustry.com/policy/archive/textile-fiber-products-identification-act). USFIA (2013) requested that requirements for hang tags and other non-permanent attachments used for point of sales should not be upheld to the similar disclosure standards. This act excludes "Secondhand household articles, including articles of wearing apparel" (p.1).

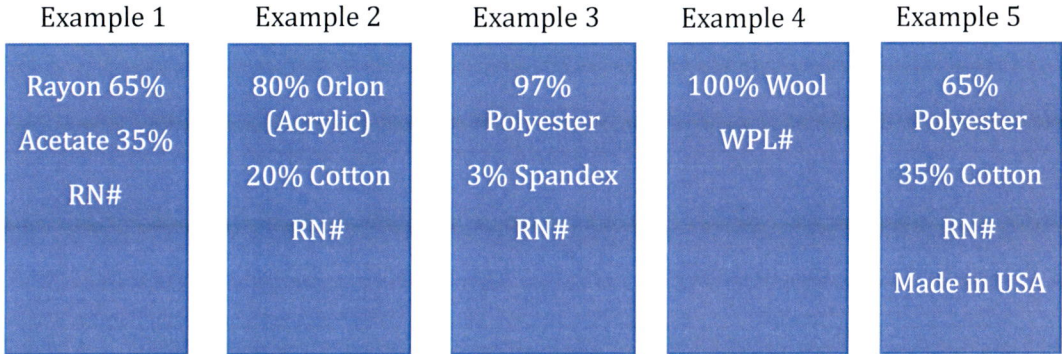

Example 1	Example 2	Example 3	Example 4	Example 5
Rayon 65% Acetate 35% RN#	80% Orlon (Acrylic) 20% Cotton RN#	97% Polyester 3% Spandex RN#	100% Wool WPL#	65% Polyester 35% Cotton RN# Made in USA

The Permanent Care Labeling Act needs to be implemented for all wearable apparel except the one that costs less than three dollars, footwear, headwear, and gloves (Chowdhary 2009). The law requires that the label should include one safe method of washing and drying, as well as ironing. It should also provide information on use of bleach. This Act is regulated by FTC and was first introduced in 1972. The label is generally placed at the back neckline or side seams. One example is provided below.

Wash Warm
Use color safe bleach
Tumble Dry Low
Iron Warm

Based on the Federal regulation, children's sleepwear must meet the flammability standards, and the treatment should last for at least 50 launderings. Bozok and Reczek (2016) discussed several agencies and tests that are necessary for textile materials and uses. **Consumer Product Safety Commission** (CPSC) is associated with flammability, children's products and hazardous materials. **Customs and Border Protection** (CBP) agency regulates origin of imported products. **Environmental Protection Agency** (EPA) regulates use of pesticides and toxic substances. The FTC focuses on labeling requirements fiber content, permanent care, environmental and country of origin labeling, as well as advertising. (USDA) **United States Department of Agriculture** focuses on "organic claims" (p.2). Some of the highlights provided by the authors were as follows.

a. Surface coating on children's apparel should not exceed 90 00m and lead 100 00m.

b. Children's sleepwear and bibs should have <.1 % of the six phthalates and be certified.

c. For children 12 years and under, tracking labels should be used.

d. Do not use drawstrings for the upper garment of infants.

e. For flammability standard levels 1 and 2 should be accepted and 3 be rejected in general.

f. Tight fitting sleepwear must have a hang tag with additional information to prevent hazards.

g. Antimicrobial clothing and household items must be registered with EPA prior to distribution.

h. Fur Product Labeling Act (FPLA) labeling requires the following.

- h.1 If fur is natural, pointed, bleached or dyed
- h.2 Name of animal
- h.3 if surface area is >10% from the pieces
- h.4 Country of origin
- h.5 If used or damaged
- h.6 RN #
- h.7 Other

For additional details, access the original source free from: http://dx.doi.org/10.6028/NIST.IR.8115.

Carp (2021) reported that labelling is a critical tool that can be used to inform consumers about 'social responsibility'. The author provided fourteen examples of eco-labeling used in several different countries. There are several voluntary certifications and initiatives that should not be mixed with governmental regulations. The author also provided the "environmental claims" guidelines (45-46) from UK and the Federal Trade Commission of the United States. Educating the consumers was highlighted by the author.

2. **Apparel Product Development**

In industry time is money. Therefore, every effort is made to accomplish this goal by optimizing the manufacturing processes to allow sustainability and appropriateness for end-use of the textile materials for enhanced performance and sale. Testing the materials prior to production minimizes the chances of producing a poor quality or non-functional apparel product. Companies perform critical standardized tests to confirm the appropriateness of the fabric for its end-use. For example, if appearance is important, appearance retention, pilling resistance, and wrinkle recovery are relevant tests. If care is important, dimensional stability will be a good choice. If comfort is important, go for wicking behavior, thermal insulation, stretch and recovery, and air permeability. For durability, abrasion resistance, breaking strength, seam strength and efficiency, and tear resistance/strength are of critical importance. Flammability testing helps with safety determination. Appropriate test selection is important for developing quality merchandise. Making textile testing part of the apparel product minimizes the risks of failure of the product.

3. **Assist Designers, Manufacturers Retailers and Consumers of Apparel from Textiles**

   Standards provide a common platform for textile and apparel manufacturers, retailers and consumers both in apparel and interior design (Chowdhary, 2009). Standardized testing alleviates the confusion resulting from procedural differences. Designers can use the information to choose appropriate textile that is compatible with the needs of their design. Manufacturers can select manufacturing processes that are compatible with their fiber content and construction. For example, while cutting synthetic fibers, one should consider the heat generated by various cutting procedures. Otherwise, synthetic materials may plasticize. Likewise, knits as well as bias cut materials tend to shrink during the spreading process. The ignored variabilities have more adverse impacts in mass production than home sewing. Retailers can use the information for promotion as well as persuasion of consumers. Consumers can use the information for appropriate selection with regard to appearance, care. comfort, durability and safety.

4. **Analysis of fabric Failures**

   Consumer satisfaction is important for repeated use of the garments made from textile materials. Inadequate performance results in increased returns. In such cases, it is important to examine what resulted in poor performance of the product so that future productions do not have the same issues. **International Fabricare Institute** (IFI) now called **Dry cleaning and Laundering Institute** (DLI) use analytical approach for the returned merchandise to determine who was responsible for problems of unsatisfactory colorfastness, dimensional stability, tearing etc.? Was it textile manufacturer, dyer, consumer, or apparel manufacturer?

5. **Building Ties Between Academia and Industry**

   To enhance compatibility in student learning and industry needs, enhance efforts have been made since the 1990s to bridge gaps between the two contingents. This is accomplished by having ties with industry through Advisory Boards or via internships to provide on the job training. Additionally, offering courses to teach students about conducting standardized tests and interpreting results for selected end-uses can prepare them better for the future jobs. **Center for Design Merchandising and Technology** (CMDT) testing center at Central Michigan University involves students in such testing. Some of these affiliations have resulted in jobs for the graduates. See Appendix A for details by Wroblewski.

6. **Confidence Building**

   Each standardized test has specific requirements for testing that offers it repeatability. Use of standardized tests improve confidence building between buyers and sellers. It can also assist with building of the legal contract. Buyer and seller can relax some of the tolerance set by standards with mutual consent.

7. **Cost Reduction**

   Cost reduction is an important consideration for any successful business. With use of Cost is an important consideration in the merchandising process of any product. With use of standardized criteria and parameters to determine quality, as well as perform and interpret tests for the intended end-uses, predictability increases. The increased confidence results in reduced waste and thereby cost. Freiman and Quinn (2001) identified threefold benefits of standardization as cost saving, accelerated acceptance by regulatory agencies, and purchase facilitation. ISO 9000 was reported to yield cost reduction as one of the several benefits by Scott and Collins (1998).

8. **Enhancing Predictability**

    Passing of the standardized tests for the intended end use(s) results in enhanced predictability and confidence. Consistency in conducting standardized tests enhances this predictability at all levels of manufacturing, retailing, and consumption. Enhanced predictability increases the chances of success for all stakeholders.

9. **Expediting Communication among Various Stakeholders**

    Textile testing ensures quality control by providing standard parameters for apparel manufacturers, retailers and consumers. Consequently. Grey areas are minimized and reliability of claims is substantiated between and among various stakeholders. Borland (2004) reported the Spectrophotometer analyzes reflectance of light to measure color. Color difference of 1.25 was believed to be acceptable. Thiry (2006) asserted that one should use standardized conditions while testing and communicate about color. She noted that temperature and humidity have a significant impact on color. One can experience so while using the ironing process also. Precise color communication (2007-2013) mentioned that the L*a*b* color space is used in a variety of disciplines to understand saturation, lightness and color. Numerical values from the standardized process allows us to determine even subtle differences more easily than the naked eye.

    Speer (2002, 2003) reported that we should use standardized color systems so that professionals from different areas speak the same language worldwide. Pantone and Scotdic were mentioned as two such systems.

10. **Forensic Testing**

    Use of textile materials as evidence for civil and criminal lawsuits is called forensic testing. The evidence could include fiber content, flame resistance, fabric damage, brand names and more. Davies (2021) asserted that fabric analysis for forensic evidence assists with determination of guilt or innocence in criminal cases. Davis made her point with examples of specific cases.

11. **Learning About the Textile Analysis Process**

    In educational institutions, textile analysis via quality standards is taught to students so that they can make better judgement on appropriateness and compatibility of textile materials for its intended end-uses. The learning process prepares them with the ability to perform standardized tests and interpret them as consumer as well as budding professional in industry.

12. **Product Evaluation**

    Product evaluation is an integral part of textile testing. It involves both structural and performance attributes. Structural attributes focused on the properties that make the textile. They render certain characteristics to the textile material. For example, higher count enhances the strength and quality of the fabric. Higher twist offers greater strength than the lower twist in yarns. Fibers provide different character than the filament yarns. Fiber and stock dyeing provides better color than yarn or fabric dyeing. Performance attributes refer to the impact of a process or treatment on the appearance, care, comfort, durability and safety. A more durable fabric should break, erode and tear less than the less durable fabric. Fabric with less defects will drape and look better. Colorfast material neither bleeds when laundered or fades on exposure to light for long hours. Table 1 provides specifications for rainwear and all-purpose water- repellent coat fabrics based on ASTMD 7017 – 2014 (ASTM 2019, *7.02*, pp. 782-783).

Table 1: "Standard Performance Specifications for Rainwear and All-Purpose Water- Repellent Coat Fabrics" (ASTM 2019, 7.02, p. 782).

#	Attribute	Minimum/Maximum Requirements
1.	Breaking Strength (Woven)	40 psi minimum
2.	Bursting Strength (Knits)	50 psi minimum
3.	Tearing Strength	3 psi Minimum
4.	Resistance to Yarn Slippage	25 psi minimum
5.	Dimensional Change Pressing and Finishing Laundering Dry Cleaning	2% Maximum 3% Maximum 2% Maximum
6.	Colorfastness to Laundering Shade change Staining	4 Minimum 3 Minimum
7.	Colorfastness to Dry Cleaning Shade Change	4 Minimum
8.	Colorfastness to Crocking Dry Wet	4 Minimum 3 Minimum
9.	Colorfastness to Chlorine Bleach Shade change	4 Minimum
10.	Colorfastness to Nonchlorine Bleach Shade change	4 Minimum

11.	Colorfastness to Water	
	Shade change	4 Minimum
	Staining	4 Minimum
12.	Colorfastness to Perspiration	
	Shade change	4 Minimum
	Staining	3 Minimum
13.	Colorfastness to Light	4 Minimum
	Frosting	4 Minimum
14.	Water Repellency	
	Smooth Textured Fabrics (Original)	90 Minimum
	After 5 launderings or 3 dry cleanings	70 Minimum
	Rough Textured Fabrics	80 Minimum
	After 5 launderings or 3 dry cleanings	70 Minimum
15.	Water Resistance (Time-based with maximum weight gain at the following head pressures)	
	Shower 600 mm (2ft) for 30 seconds	1gram Maximum
	Rain 600 mm (2ft) for 2 minutes	1gram Maximum
	Storm 915 mm (3ft) for five minutes	1gram Maximum
16.	Fabric Appearance	3.5 Minimum
17.	Flammability	Class 1

As evident through table 1, for the selected end-use there are 17 possible standards that can be used for determining appropriateness of textile material for thorough determination. Yarn slippage, breaking and bursting strength and tearing strength determine durability. Dimensional stability, and colorfastness test care related performance. Fabric appearance (Appearance retention) and colorfastness impact looks after use. Flammability provides data on safety. Water repellency and water resistance are more function related textile attributes. Choices of tests can be based on the price and quality level of the merchandise. Generally, abrasion resistance and pilling are not as relevant for the selected end-use. Therefore, they are not included in this list. Personally, I see dry cleaning important for coats but not rainwear as some of the rainwear should not be dry cleaned.

13. **Quality Control**

One of the critical functions of textile testing is quality control for consistency (Chowdhary, 2009). Performance of tests in conformance with standard specifications provides assurance that the produced product will meet the requirements of the intended end-use. These indicators include acceptable tolerances, colorfastness, durability, defect free fabric, overall appearance and performance, seam quality and uniform color distribution. Failing to meet the quality standards could result in return of merchandise for unsatisfactory performance, increased cost for redoing the below quality features, selling the merchandise at lower price than the regular price through different outlets, as well as waste of time and energy of every involved member of the company and decreased motivation.

14. **Quality Promotion**

The apparel and textile manufacturers use standardized tests to back up their guarantee of the product quality. Doing so gives them a competitive edge against their rivals. Several companies use quality indicators as a basis for backing their merchandise even when they use flexibility in using the standards and provide relaxations for consumers. Defective or below quality merchandise is either replaced with quality product of similar price range or sold at lower price than marked. Several manufacturers restrict the use of their trademark only for the quality merchandise.

Borland (2006) reported the use of better moisture transfer management, odor control, thermal regulation, antibacterial effect, as well as protection from ultraviolet rays in textiles as indicators of quality. Several companies offered antibacterial yarns to offer odor neutralization as well as moisture management. A Switzerland based company offered silver-coated nylon for antibacterial effect to be used for socks, pajamas, underwear, and children's gloves. A French company introduced becool nylon to be used for sportswear (Nike) and underwear (Victoria Secret). Pozzi Electa company of Italy sold Carbon yarns for potential use in the dermatitis treatment, socks for diabetes as well as sunburn treatment. Dow Fiber Solutions has partnered with Calvin Klein to introduce boxer's briefs, trunks and V-neck tops that have flexible fit.

Stretch fibers were mentioned very often by several companies to provide comfort. Invista was noted for developing innovations in knitwear by blending commercial yarns such as Lycra, Tactel, Coolmax, Thermolite, and Teflon for flexibility, comfort, and stain repellence. Belgium based UCO textiles in collaboration with India, Romania and the United States created high-end images with stretch and comfort. Knitwear was mentioned the most for casual and classic looks.

Chowdhary and Mathews (2018) suggested to develop technical data sheets to make quality determination and promotion of textiles used for garments for appropriateness, compatibility. The determination was based on the standards set by ASTM. Based on structural attributes, fashion fabric and lining discussed in the study were compatible for yarn type, fabric construction, fabric count and fabric weight. However, they were not compatible for the fiber content. Fashion fabric was cotton and lining was acetate. Results for the performance attributes revealed that two fabrics were compatible for pilling resistance but not compatible for appearance retention, dimensional stability, horizontal wicking and tear strength. Creating technical data sheets makes interpretation transparent for all stakeholders.

15. **Advancing Knowledge Base Through Testing Research**

Textile testing and analysis through scholarly work results in advancing the reservoir of knowledge by making new discoveries and inventions. Research projects allow scholars to optimize products and processes by testing them in labs as well as with stakeholders. Consequently, industry can use the improved quality of product and environment along with enhanced cost and time effectiveness. Lee and Chen-Yu (2018) found that consumers perceived highly discounted merchandise as reduced quality products. Scholarly work can compare the differently priced items for their quality through textile testing for performance. For example, Chowdhary (2002) noted that price did not directly relate to the quality for three types of Gap jeans in different price ranges and fabric counts. Retailers can use the results from research for bringing new and improved merchandise for consumers and offer new promotional strategies. Consumers can enjoy products at reduced cost, and enhanced variety and improved quality.

HOW DO CONSUMERS DETERMINE APPAREL PURCHASE?

It is important to understand the criteria used by the consumers in purchase of apparel to ensure that industry's decisions are in line with its ultimate purchaser of the merchandise. Several scholars have provided information on the criteria used by consumers for the selection of textile products. Chowdhary (2009) used aesthetics, care, comfort, durability, purchase price, safety and serviceability as seven criteria used by consumers for the purchase of textile products. Saricam and Erdumlu (2017) noted product information as one of the 13 criteria of website sales. Glasheen (2019) reported that fast fashions are out and consumers are looking for better quality that has resale value. Industry is considering the cost per wear value model. Checking the label for care and cotton versus polyester is important to today's consumer. Sustainability and lifetime warranty are picking up. Some companies that offer such warranties are Columbia, Eddie Bauer, L. L. Bean. North Face, and Patagonia. *Quality Assurance* is substantiated by the companies that offer warranties and have consumer savvy return policies.

Quality assurance refers to standing behind a company's products. Some companies use higher tolerances than provided by standards to reduce their costs and maximize their profits. Defects resulting from liberal use of standards should be compensated by quality assurance for repeat purchases of the product.

Considering the changing expectations of consumers, it is important to complement their expectations with quality parameters important to them. Textile testing can help with identifying such indicators and determine high quality merchandise based on the structural and performance attributes.

TYPES OF TESTING

Ideally, there are two types of textile testing: Labe and wear or service. **Lab testing** conducts standardized tests with set size and number of specimens. Results are then compared against the industry standards to accept or reject the textile materials. This type of textile testing requires a lab facility with a conditioned environment for standardized testing. Once the lab is in place, recurring costs are relatively less than the wear test. Merkel (1991) also called it accelerated testing. **Wear or service test** entails wearing the actual garment to determine if the garment meets the standard and consumer satisfaction. This test is more expensive than the lab test. ASTM D3181-2015 provides a standard guide for conducting this test on textiles (ASTM 2017, *7.01,* 754-759. One must set the evaluation parameters that may vary for different end uses. Table recommended by ASTM (2017, *7.01,* 756) is provided below.

Textile Testing: An Overview

Attributes and levels can be adjusted for different garments. For example, abrasion might be of more critical importance for jeans than t-shirts. Pilling resistance may be of less importance for flannel pajamas than dress shirts, and flammability for children's sleepwear than playwear. Even for one textile attribute, requirements may be different for different garments. For example, in case of abrasion resistance, collars, cuffs, elbows, underarms, pockets, front and back may be considered for dresses and blouses (ASTM 2019, 7.01). Front pocket, fly, knee, crotch, back pocket, seat, cuffs/hems and crease could be important for trousers and slacks.

Table 2: Evaluation of the refurbishing cycle.*

Wear test identification number: _____

Wear Level: _____

Fabric Identification: _____

Item	1	2	3	4	5	6	7	8	9	10	etc.
Evaluation Date											
Times worn											
Hours worn											
Times Refurbished											
Abrasion											
Bagging											
Color Change											
Crease Retention											
Dimensional Stability											
Fabric Smoothness											
Holes											
% Length Change											
% Width Change											
Pilling											
Seam Puckering											
Snagging											
Hand											
Wear Wrinkling											
Etc.											

*One can add or delete attributes depending on the end-use.

GLOBAL PERSPECTIVE

Today, we live in the global world. Textile industry is an integral part of the supply chain management. It will add additional insight to look at the data that helps us understand the global aspects. Supply Chain Insights (2014) reported that the consumers from the United Kingdom valued quality as the important factor in their apparel. However, they received less than the expected value in the existing merchandise. They related cotton to sustainability and performance issues made them to move away from cotton. Italian consumers valued quality. However, they experience decline in quality and durability of the apparel. Sixty percent of Italians were bothered by substituting cotton with other fiber contents. *Global Consumer Insight* (2017) reported increase in apparel expenditure in the United States, Europe, Italy and China. Seventy nine percent Italians were willing to buy cotton and blends and 76% looked for fiber content on the labels. Globally, 56% of the consumers looked for the fiber content.

With Pandemic COVID-19, consumer demand has taken a twist. Barrie (2021) reported the perspectives of several leaders such as CEOs, academicians, and industry professionals from Hong Kong, United Kingdom and United States. Several of them emphasized that consumers are getting interested in casual wear because they send more time indoors than ever before. Comfort and durability are becoming the norm. They are shunning away from cheap products. Secretary General of the International Apparel Federation (IAF) also asserted that collaboration and flexibility will be the key factors in the supply chain. Several leaders consented with the importance of innovations, new labelling, product safety and sustainability. Many identified that E-Commerce will be on the rise due to closing of several Brick-and-Mortar stores.

Cotton Incorporated (2020) conducted surveys for the United States, Mexico, Italy, and China and found that a majority of the consumers valued comfortable apparel, cotton as fiber content, and feel scared to make purchases (Table 3). Women were noted to be more apprehensive than men in all four countries. Other preferred fiber contents were spandex, polyester and rayon.

Table 3: Supply Chain Dimensions to Impact Textile Products.

Country	Comfortable Apparel	Cotton as the most safe and comfortable	Feel Afraid	More Women Than Men
China	69%	67%	57%	Yes
Italy	76%	72%	80%	Yes
Mexico	66%	72%	59%	Yes
United States	80%	70%	66%	Yes

A survey regarding the demand and fiber content of face masks in the second wave revealed that a large majority wanted to wear masks in China, Mexico, and the United States. Consumers preferred to buy cotton face masks in the later two countries more so than in China (Table 4). Additionally, intention percentage to buy online also rose for all three countries.

Textile Testing: An Overview

Table 4: Face Masks and Details

Country	Wear Face Mask	Wear Cotton Face mask	Limit Expenditure	Online Shopping Change (up) Wave 1	Wave 2
China	89%	60%	72%	62%	64%
Mexico	84%	89%	85%	26%	37%
United States	71%	75%	84%	32%	44%

The third wave data were available only for the United States. It addressed the expenditure on apparel, shopping intentions and practices and the type of clothing preferred.

Table 5: Consumer intentions on purchase and expenditure of apparel in the third wave.

Item	First Wave (March 20, 2020)	Second Wave (April 27, 2020)	Third Wave (September 9, 2020)
Consumer Spending Level			
Less	34%	43%	33%
Same	30%	26%	33%
More	36%	31%	34%
Clothing Expenditure since pandemic	14%	14%	31%
Plan to purchase in next three months	-	-	63%
Comfortable Clothing (t-shirts, loungewear, and clothing made in cotton.	-	-	43%
Athletic Clothing (activewear, athleisure)	-	-	37%
Feel comfortable shopping in stores	-	-	64%

The preceding discussion reveals that comfort, durability quality and sustainability were the most valued factors by the consumers. It is critical that professionals from academics and industry use tests and criteria that address consumers' expectations and provide quality products with comfort, durability, and sustainability. Global data further confirms the need of textile testing for developing the quality products. Even though pandemic has changed the retail environment some of the basic requirements of the textile and apparel products stay the same.

SUMMARY

Quality control and assurance are of critical importance to win consumer's confidence. Textile testing can serve as one of the tools to accomplish this goal. Knowledge of both structural and performance attributes is essential to fully understand the strengths and weaknesses of the textile. Reasons for textile testing and criteria used by consumers should be clearly understood. One can do so by either lab or wear test. Standardized tests provide reliability, confidence, and credibility in the quality control process. Outcome from the standardized tests can be used for making informed decisions for the products to be sold, purchased, and promoted. Pilot testing from target population further offers verification of its serviceability for the intended end-uses(s).

REFERENCES

Annual book of ASTM standards. (2020). *7.01,* West Conshohoken, PA: ASTM International.

Annual book of ASTM standards. (2019). *7.02,* West Conshohoken, PA: ASTM International.

Barrie, L. (2021, January 14). Outlook, 2021 – Apparel industry Challenges and opportunities. https://www.just-style.com/analysis/outlook-2021-apparel-industry-challenges-and-opportunities_id140471.aspx

Benson, L. M., $ Reczek, K. (2016). *United States apparel and household textiles compliance requirements.* http://dx.doi.org/10.6028/NIST.IR.8115 N

Borland, V. S. (2004, January). Color works. *Textile World, 48-50.*

Borland, V. S. (2006, November/December). Function joins fashion for 2007-2008. Textile World, 48-51.

Carp, B. (2021, January/February). Labelling sustainability *AATCC Review, 21*(1), 40-46. DOI: 10.14504/ar.21.1.3.

Chowdhary, U. (2002). Does price reflect emotional, structural, or performance quality? *International Journal of Consumer Studies, 26,* 128-133.

Chowdhary, U. (2009). Textile analysis, quality control and innovative uses. Deer Park, NY: LINUS.

Chowdhary, U., & Mathews, S. (2018). Textile analysis and interpretation for decision making. *Trends in Textile Engineering and Fashion Technology, 4*(4), 1-3.

Collier, B. J., Bide, M., & Tortora, P. G. (2009). *Understanding textiles.* Upper Saddle River, NJ: Prentice Hall.

Davies, N. (2021, January/February). Solving crimes: When textiles come to the fore. *AATCC Review, 21*(1), 34-39. 10.14504/ar.21.1.2.

Freiman, S. W., & Quinn, G, D, (2001, October). How property test standards help bring new materials to the market. *ASTM Standardization,* 26-31.

Glasheen, J. (2019, November 17). Consumers use new criteria to evaluate apparel. *therobinreport.com.*

Global lifestyle monitor: Italy. (2014). Lifestylemonitor.cottoninc.com.

Global lifestyle monitor: Italy. (2017). *Global Consumer Insight.* https://www.cottoninc.com/market-data/supply-chain-insights/global-lifestyle-monitor-italy/

Global lifestyle monitor: The United Kingdom (2014). Lifestylemonitor.cottoninc.com.

Lee, J. E., & Chen-Yu, J. H. (2018). Effects of price discount on consumers' perceptions of savings, quality, and value of apparel products: mediating effect of price discount affect. *Fashion and Textiles,* 5(13), DOI: https://doi.org/10.1186/s40691-018-0128-2

Merkel, R. S. (1991). *Textile product serviceability.* New York: Macmillan.

Precise color communication (2007-2013). Japan: Konica Minolta. http://konicaminolta.com/instrments/network.

Saricam, C., & Erdumlu, N. (2017). Determination of priorities in apparel purchasing from private sales websites *AUTEX Research Journal, 17,* No 4, December 2017, DOI: 10.1515/aut-2016-0038 © AUTEX

Scott, I., & Collins, P, (1998). Evaluation of the ISO 9000 series. Benefit and problems of implementation and maintenance in production companies. *The Journal of Textile Institute, 89*(1), 90-109.

Speer, J. K. (2002, December).AATCC tackles color communication. *Bobbin, 6.*

Speer, J. K. (2003, August). Taking the color challenge. *Apparel,* 30-34.

Ten Things to know about COVID-19 and consumer concerns (2020, March). Supply Chain Insights, *Cotton Incorporated.* https://www.cottoninc.com/market-data/supply-chain-insights/

Ten Things to know about COVID-19 and consumer concerns in the U.S. Second Wave . (2020, April 27). Supply Chain Insights, *Cotton Incorporated.* https://www.cottoninc.com/market-data/supply-chain-insights/

Ten Things to know about COVID-19 and consumer concerns in the U.S. (2020, September 9). Supply Chain Insights, *Cotton Incorporated.* https://www.cottoninc.com/market-data/supply-chain-insights/

Ten Things to know about COVID-19 and consumer concerns in China, (2020, March). Supply Chain Insights, *Cotton Incorporated.* https://www.cottoninc.com/market-data/supply-chain-insights/

Ten Things to know about COVID-19 and consumer concerns in China, (2020, April 27). Supply Chain Insights, *Cotton Incorporated.* https://www.cottoninc.com/market-data/supply-chain-insights/

Ten Things to know about COVID-19 and consumer concerns in Italy. (2020, March). Supply Chain Insights, *Cotton Incorporated.* https://www.cottoninc.com/market-data/supply-chain-insights/

Ten Things to know about COVID-19 and consumer concerns in Mexico (2020, March). Supply Chain Insights, *Cotton Incorporated.* https://www.cottoninc.com/market-data/supply-chain-insights/

Ten Things to know about COVID-19 and consumer concerns in Mexico (2020, April 27). Supply Chain Insights, *Cotton Incorporated.* https://www.cottoninc.com/market-data/supply-chain-insights/

Textile Fiber Products Identification Act (2013). Retrieved on January 6, 2021 from https://www.usfashionindustry.com/policy/archive/textile-fiber-products-identification-act).

Thiry, M. C. (2006, March). Condition. *AATCC Review, 6,* 21-24.

GLOSSARY OF TERMS

Evaluation refers to assessing materials for their positive and negative attributes.

Fabric Failures refers to the unsatisfactory performance of the fabrics for necessary attributes.

Forensic Testing refers to the science of learning how and when the crime was committed.

Government Regulations refers to the rules that set interpretation boundaries.

Lab Testing refers to the standard procedures used to determine quality and appropriateness of the products under investigation.

Performance attributes are those properties of textiles that result from various pressures during wear and tear of textile materials.

Product Development refers to the steps involved in movement of product from concept to consumption.

Quality Assurance refers to backing of a product by manufacturer for quality and consumer satisfaction.

Quality Control refers to maintaining appropriate standards with set parameters for consistency in production.

Refurbishing is the process used to make the used product new again. For example, dry cleaning and laundering on a regular basis.

Structural attributes are the properties that are essential for the textile product to exist at fiber, yarn, and fabric levels.

Textile Testing refers to the evaluation of textile materials with standardized tests to determine appropriateness for intended use and compatibility of competing materials used in the apparel and/or industrial products.

Wear Test refers to testing the textile product through wear trials to examine the appropriateness of the product for the expected life cycle for vital characteristics.

STUDY QUESTIONS AND PRACTICE ACTIVITIES

1. Select ready-to-wear (rtw) apparel items from the market. Identify appropriate structural and performance tests for different end-uses. Make a comparison chart to identify similarities and distinctions between and/or among various end uses.

2. Review reasons for textile testing. Expand/contract the list using your personal experiences and/or literature readings.

3. Examine your wardrobe purchases. Identify the criteria used by you for the purchase of the apparel items. Rank order the criteria and compare with your peers.

4. Conduct a wear test project using attributes from table two. Wear the item for two weeks and wash for at least five times. Record the observations for washed and unwashed stages. Write a comparison account between washed and unwashed merchandise for selected performance attributes. Later, you can use t-test for scientific comparison.

5. Identify two salient structure attributes and provide rationale for your choice.

6. Identify two most important attributes for the chosen end-use and provide rationale for your choice.

ADDITIONAL RESOURCES

https://url.linuslearning.com/E3Ac6

CHAPTER 2
TEXTILE STANDARDS AND ORGANIZATIONS

TEXTILE STANDARDS

Textile standards refer to the organized procedures established for measuring and reporting information on various textile attributes in a systematic manner. They are used for efficiency, effective exchange of information, quality control, and reliable work ethics by all sectors of the textile industry. The standardized tests help the textile manufacturers with creation of textiles for the intended end-use. Apparel designers use information for creating styles with function appropriateness. Apparel manufacturers use information to optimize the steps involved in the manufacturing process. Apparel retailers use the resulting information for promoting and selling the merchandise. Finally, apparel consumers benefit with informed decision-making. American Association of Textile Chemists and Colorists (AATCC), American Association for Testing and Materials (ASTM), and International Organization of Standardization (ISO) are three standardizing organizations used worldwide for developing textile standards (Chowdhary, 2009).

ANATOMY OF A STANDARDIZED TEST

Anatomy of the test details various essential elements of a test. The number of categories range from test to test as well as one organization to another. For example, AATCC TM 8 2016e, titled, "Test Method for Colorfastness to Crocking: Crockmeter" has 13 items. Whereas AATCC TM 22 2017a titled, "Test Method for Water Repellency: Spray" has 11 categories (Table 3). The crocking test was first developed in 1936. It is partially equivalent to ISO 105-X12. The water repellency rest was initially developed in 1941 and is technically equivalent to ISO 4920.

Description of the categories of the colorfastness to crocking standard follows the comparison chart in table 3.

Chapter 2

Table 3 A comparison table for AATCC TM 8 2016e, titled, "Test Method for Colorfastness to Crocking: Crockmeter" and AATCC TM 22 2017a titled, "Test Method for Water Repellency: Spray"

#	Category	AATCC TM 8 2016e	AATCC TM 22 2017a
1	Purpose and Scope	x	x
2	Principle	x	x
3	Terminology	x	x
4	Safety Precautions	x	x
5	Uses and Limitations	x	x
6	Apparatus and Materials	x	x
7	Verification	x	-
8	Test Specimens	x	x
9	Conditioning	x	-
10	Procedures	x	x
11	Evaluation and Report*	x	x
12	Precision and Bias	x	x
13	Notes	x	x

*Some tests list evaluation and report separately.

Description of Categories for AATCC TM 8 2016e (*Manual of international test methods and procedures* (2021, pp. 21-23).

1. **Purpose and Scope:** The test uses white dry and wet crock squares to determine color transfer from the colored surface.

2. **Principle:** Color transfer via rubbing under controlled conditions is measured using Gray Scales of color change and staining and/or 9-step Chromatic color scale.

3. **Terminology:** Two terms crocking and colorfastness are defined.

4. **Safety Precautions:** Safe laboratory practices should be used. Occupational Safety and Health Standards (OSHA) standards should be followed.

5. **Uses and Limitations:** Use AATCC crock squares and test before and after treatments. It is not recommended for carpets and printed materials.

6. **Apparatus and Materials:** It requires Crockmeter, evaluation scales, Specimen holder and clip.

7. **Verification:** Make verification checks periodically with a fabric that is predictable and has repeatable readings.

8. **Test Specimens:** Use at least one bias cut specimen for dry and wet conditions of 50 x130 mm (2" x 5"). Sample size could be increased for enhanced precision.

9. **Conditioning:** Condition both crock squares and test fabric at temperature between 10-23⁰C (66-74⁰F) and 63-67% relative humidity.

10. **Procedures:** Follow procedure for dry and wet testing fully.

11. **Evaluation and Report:** Back the crocked square with three layers of crock square and report dry and wet ratings separately to the first decimal place.

12. **Precision and Bias:** Inter laboratory evaluations revealed that differences were nonsignificant for dry crocking but significant for wet crocking.

13. **Notes:** Some points were discussed about use of different equipment and fabrics to help with enhancing precision and bias

ASTM D5035-11 (Reapproved 2019) has 15 categories. This test is titled. "Standard Test Method for Breaking Force and Elongation of Textile Fabrics (Strip Method)". However, ASTM D7017 – 14, titled, "Standard Performance Specifications for Rainwear and All-Purpose, Water-Repellent Coat Fabrics" has only six categories Table 4).

Table 4: A comparison table for "Standard Test Method for Breaking Force and Elongation of Textile Fabrics (Strip Method)" ASTM D5035-11 (Reapproved 2019) and "Standard Performance Specifications for Rainwear and All-Purpose, Water-Repellent Coat Fabrics" ASTM D7017 – 14.

#	Category	ASTM D5035-11 Reapproved 2019	ASTM D 7017-14
1	Scope	x	x
2	Referenced Documents	x	x
3	Terminology	x	x
4.	Summary of Test Method	x	-
5	Significance and Use	x	x
6	Apparatus, Reagents, and Materials	x	-
7	Sampling	x	-
8	Conditioning	x	-
9	Preparation of Specimens	x	-
10	Verification and Calibration of Apparatus	x	-
11	Procedures/Test Methods	x	x (Test Methods)
12	Calculations	x	-
13	Report	x	-
14	Precision and Bias	x	-
15	Keywords	x	x

Description of Categories for "Standard Test Method for Breaking Force and Elongation of Textile Fabrics (Strip Method)" ASTM D5035-11 (Reapproved 2019), *Annual book of ASTM standards.* **(2019).** *7.02,* **pp. 181-188.**

1. **Scope:** The test is recommended for dry and wet testing of woven fabrics and is not recommended for the knitted fabrics.

2. **Referenced Documents:** The test offers a list of relevant standardized tests.

3. **Terminology:** The manual asks referring to D123, D4848, D4849, and D4850 for relevant terminology.

4. **Summary of Test Method:** The test gives information on using three types of machines and four types of specimens.

5. **Significance and Use:** Possibilities of comparison of machines and other suggestions are provided. It is not recommended for the knitted fabric due to high stretch.

6. **Apparatus, Reagents and Materials:** Details of machines are provided The Carriage should move at the speed of 12+.5 inches per minute and use loads to break between 17-23 seconds.

7. **Sampling:** The test provides information on lot samples, laboratory samples and test specimens. It recommends that one should use 2-3 extra specimens for unfamiliar fabrics.

8. **Conditioning:** Use D1776 test for the duration and parameters of conditioning.

9. **Preparation of Specimens:** The test describes allowable variations for different number of yarns per inch.

10. **Preparation, Calibration and Verification of apparatus:** Set the machine and clamp system. Make sure that machine is calibrated.

11. **Procedure:** Follow machine operation instructions carefully. Distilled water should be used for wetting the specimens for wet testing.

12. **Calculations:** Calculate average of breaking strength and elongation.

13. **Report:** Report average of each variable as well as number of specimens used and special treatments if any.

14. **Precision and Bias:** Interlaboratory differences were observed by type of machine and fabrics.

15. **Keywords:** woven and nonwoven fabrics, elongation and breaking strength were identified as the key words.

Anatomy of two tests described above from two different organizations provides documentation of subtle differences. It also reflects careful attention to detail for facilitating reliability. Using conditioning creates normalizing situations for comparing results from multiple locations for a variety of textiles.

ENVIRONMENTAL CONDITIONS

The test "Standard Practice for Conditioning and Testing Textiles" (D1776-1776/D1776M -16) provides parameters for different fiber contents used for textiles. It emphasizes that one should pay attention to using metric and inch-pound units because they are not equivalent. Bringing fabrics to moisture equilibrium is of critical importance in textile testing. Chowdhary (2017) reemphasized the importance of standard conditions in textile testing.

Conditioning refers to bringing the test specimens within the standard atmospheric conditions. It is also known as bringing the material to moisture equilibrium. **Moisture equilibrium** refers to the stabilized condition of the textile material at which it neither gains nor loses moisture. **Preconditioning** refers to bringing the specimen between 3-25% humidity prior to conditioning. **Moisture content** refers to the water content I total mass of material represented in percentage. It is the ratio between the sorbed water (difference between oven dry weight and the moisture equilibrium weight) and the moisture equilibrium weight. **Moisture regain** refers to the ratio between the sorbed water and the oven dry weight represented in percentage. Textiles that have higher moisture regain require longer time to reach the moisture equilibrium than those with lower moisture regain (Table 5).

Table 5: Standard Table for Conditioning Hours by Fiber Source (*Annual Book of Standards*, 7.01, 2017, 432), Merkel (1991, p.65 for Rayon)

Fiber Source	Recommended Minimum Hours
Animal fibers and regenerated proteins	8
Rayon	8
Vegetable fibers	6
Acetate	4
Textiles with moisture regain of <5% at 65% relative humidity.	2

STANDARD ATMOSPHERIC CONDITIONS (D1776 – 16)

Standardized conditions for textile testing are important to consider for reliability of results. Otherwise, one may pay the price of water for wool or have different test results for different sites on rainy days. Therefore, it is important to control the temperature and humidity of the environmental chambers that are used for conditioning and testing.

Table 6: Standard Atmospheric Conditions for Testing Textiles (*Annual Book of Standards*, 7.01, 2014, p. 420)

Material	Temperature	Relative Humidity
Textiles	21±1°C (70± 2°F)	65±2 %
Aramid	20±2°C (70± 2°F)	65±5%
Nonwovens	23±2°C (73± 4°F)	50±2%

COMPUTATION EXAMPLES OF MOISTURE REGAIN

$$\text{Moisture Regain \%} = \frac{100 \,(\text{Equilibrium weight} - \text{oven dried weight})}{\text{oven dried weight}}$$

Example:

Equilibrium weight = 10 grams

Oven dried weight = 9.2 grams

Sorbed water = 10-9.2 = 0.8 grams

Moisture Regain % = 100 (0.8/9.2) = 8.70%

Compare your value with Appendix 1. Based on the moisture regain value, your textile will be either mercerized cotton or Linen. From a quantitative reasoning standpoint, moisture regain percentage helped you to determine that your fiber content is either cotton or linen. To further confirm the fiber content, do a microscopic test. If there is a twist, it will be cotton. If there is bark like structure then it will be linen.

CONVERSION OF CELSIUS TO FAHRENHEIT AND VICE VERSA

Same units of temperature are not used worldwide. Therefore, it is important to know the conversion technique especially when WIFI is not available even in the digital world of today. One time I thought of dropping it from the environment. I was flying from overseas and got in the need to use the thermometer. The thermometer measured the temperature in Celsius and I was more familiar with Fahrenheit system. The air hostess had no idea about the conversion factor. No WIFI was available for easy conversion. My knowledge of how to convert paid off. I chose not to exclude this activity from the revised version.

Celsius = 5/9 (Fahrenheit temperature -32)

For

Examples:

5/9 (212-32) 100°C

Fahrenheit = (1.8 x Celsius temperature) + 32

(1.8 x 100) + 32 = 212°F

Textile Organizations: Consumer Protection

Acronym	Expansion	Function
ACI (Name changed in 2010)	The American Cleaning Institute	It was founded in 1926 as the Association of American Soap and Glycerine Producers that was founded to advance the public's understanding of the safety issues and benefits of the cleaning products and their ingredients. (https://www.cleaninginstitute.org/about-aci/history-aci, 2/2/ 2021) It was formerly known as SDA (Soaps and Detergent Association) from 1960s-2010. It focuses on the development and growth of cleaning products in the United States. It represents the manufacturers of commercial, household, industrial, and institutional cleaning supplies.
CPSC	Consumer Product Safety Commission	It enforces several federal legislations to protect consumers from injuries and risks. It is responsible for administering the Flammable Fabrics Act for wearing apparel, and children's sleepwear.
FTC	Federal Trade Commission	FTC enforces labeling regulations. RN numbers, Wool Product Labeling (WPL), and Textile Fiber Product Identification Act (TFPIA) are some of the means of authentication.

Textile Organizations: Government Bodies

Acronym	Expansion	Function
DOC	Department of Commerce	The National Institute of Standards and Technology (NIST) division of DOC has played a role in the textile industry. They play an important role in making the industry globally competitive. They oversee the standardization of weights used in several standardized tests. Additionally, it supports the new technologies used in the industry.
DOD	Department of Defense	It consumes 8000 textile items, and 31,000 line items annually for all four (air force, army, marines, and navy) military services http://www.ncto.org/facts-figures/textiles-and-our-military/). Some examples include bullet proof vests, chemical protective suits, floatation devices, helmets, interfacings and linings, masks, parachutes, uniforms, and wetsuits.

EPA	Environmental Protection Agency	EPA is responsible for regulating air, noise and water pollution as well as waste disposal.
		"The Environmental Protection Agency is a United States federal government agency whose mission is to protect human and environmental health. The EPA regulates the manufacturing, processing, distribution, and use of chemicals and other pollutants (Jul 19, 2020)." See the website below for additional details. https://www.epa.gov/aboutepa/our-mission-and-what-we-do.
OSHA	Occupational Safety and Health Administration	It was created to offer safe and healthy working conditions for men and women of the workforce. Recommended temperatures are 68-76°F.
		Uses of ear plugs in the textile industry and wearing of dust masks to cover the nose are two examples of safety measures that protect workers from hearing loss and asthma. Even visitors at the textile manufacturing sites are required to wear ear plugs to prevent potential hearing loss.
		Likewise, ergonomics use to improve worker's health through optimum adjustments of work stations are another example. Splint use for Carpal Tunnel Syndrome (CTS) problem, tilting of worker's table, providing standing modules with feet mattresses, ergonomic flow of construction operations, adjustable heights of the fabric defects viewing operations, and providing air floatation tables for moving large lengths of several layers of fabrics while spreading are few other examples of worker's safety.

Textile Organizations: Interior Design

Acronym	Expansion	Function
ACT	Association for Contract Textile	ACT is a non-profit trade organization that addresses several issues related to the contract textiles for interiors. It was established in 1985.
		It also provides performance guidelines of ASTM and AATCC standards with five symbols. The symbols represent abrasion resistance, colorfastness to crocking and light, flame resistance, and physical properties. These standards are voluntary but used for quality promotion. Several merchants use these symbols in their sampling books to inform architects, consumers and designers. Use link below for those symbols. https://contracttextiles.org/

Textile Standards and Organizations

UFAC	Upholstered Furniture Action Council	This organization was established in 1978. Its original purpose was to prevent fires from the smoldering cigarettes which were the leading cause (90%) of the household fires. Today, it is 79.3% down since the conception of UFAC. The council created special gold hangtag with message in English, French and Spanish. The hangtag confirms that the material meets the UFAC criteria. For current information, go to https://ufac.org/

Industrial Associations/Councils

Acronym	Expansion	Function
AFMA	American Fiber Manufacturers Association	Supports textile producers in the United States.
ATMA	American Textile Machinery Association	This professional trade association was founded in 1933. It focusses on " ----the advancement of the textile machinery, parts and accessories in the textile industry." (www.atmanet.org) The headquarter of ATMA® is located in Washington D. C. The organization sets up exhibitions to bring diverse manufacturers with innovative products.
DLI	Dry Cleaning and Laundry Institute	It is an international organization of garment care professionals that was established in 1883. It represents 10,000 facilities in the United States. The activities include performance evaluations, garment analysis and educational training and seminars. They offer information and solutions to provide competitive edge to its members. Go to https://www.dlionline.org/about for the latest details.
IFAI	Industrial Fabrics Association International	IFAI represents the international marketplace for specialty fabrics. It is claimed to be the largest non-profit trade association that serves the industry through multiple ways. For recent details go to www.ifai.com. It has published *Specialty Fabrics Review* as "flagship magazine" since 1915. Its sixteen divisions represent several product categories as well as countries.
NCC	National Cotton Council	The council addresses the needs of seven segments of the industry and attempts to build consensus. The seven segments are cooperatives, cottonseed, ginners, manufacturers, merchants, producers, and warehousers, it participates in policy decisions to enhance competitiveness of the industry. For the latest information, go to www.cotton.org.

Chapter 2

NCTO	National Council of Textile Organizations	It is a conglomeration of four councils: fiber, yarn, fabric, and supplier industries. It was founded in 2004 to lobby for the survival and preservation of the textile industry of the United States in the global economy. An attempt is made to create strong international alliances. For the latest details, go to www.ncto.org.
NTC	National Textile Center	This a consortium of eight universities, and is engaged in innovative cooperative research. The universities represented are: Auburn, Clemson, Cornell, Georgia Institute of Technology, North Carolina State University, UC – Davis, University of Massachusetts - Dartmouth, and Philadelphia.

Standard Test Development

Acronym	Expansion	Function
AATCC	American Association of Textile Chemists and Colorists	AATCC is responsible for the development of standards to test the chemical properties and wet tests of textiles. The research committees develop standards through rigorous procedures. The new tests are reviewed every year for three years and then every five years. AATCC is actively involved in organizing several workshops to disseminate knowledge to industry professionals and educators. It also holds an annual conference for scholarly exchange of information. Additionally, it publishes *AATCC Review* and *AATCC Journal of Research*. AATCC annually publishes a manual of standards, offers evaluation and testing tools, scholarships, and research and service awards. Several technical committees are formed to develop, revise and approve the standards. The developed tests are used internationally. The following symbols should be used for the interpretation of test numbers and related designators. TM Test Methods LP Laundering Procedure EP Evaluation Procedure M Monographs t Additional changes within the same year e Editorial changes

Textile Standards and Organizations

ASTM	American Society for Testing and Materials	ASTM is predominantly responsible for the development of physical or dry tests. Additionally, it has included body measurements, various types of seams and stitches, and performance criteria for several end uses. Volumes 7.01 and 7.02 focus specifically on textiles. D-13 committee works with approval of new and revised tests on an ongoing basis. Old standards are reviewed every five years for reapproval to ensure their continued relevance.
ISO	International Organization of Standardization	ISO was founded on February 23, 1947 and has its headquarter in Geneva Switzerland. Currently, it has 165 members. Individuals and companies cannot become its members. Each country has one nominee. They have three membership categories: Full/member, correspondent and subscriber. Full members participate in development of standards and policies and have a voting right. American National Standards Institute (ANSI) represents the United States on ISO. Correspondent members participate as observers. Like full members, they can sell and adopt the ISO standards. Subscriber members just stay updated but cannot buy/sell the standards. The major function of ISO is to promote quality in worldwide exchange of goods. Its 9000 series focusses on quality assurance and management of products and processes, and 14000 series concentrate on the environmental management.

Textile Industry Liaisons/Advocate

Acronym	Expansion	Function
AAFA	American Apparel and Footwear Association	It represents apparel, footwear and sewn products and the group strives for achieving and maintaining global competence. For the latest information, contact https://www.aafaglobal.org/.
ANSI	American National Standards Institute	It represents the United States on ISO.

SUMMARY

This chapter focused on the importance of standardization and anatomy of the test, examples of textile standards from AATCC and ASTM, environmental conditioning, temperature conversion, moisture equilibrium and moisture regain. The chapter information stressed the need to use standard environmental conditions for testing for enhancing the generalization ability of the work. Additionally, the role of various organizations in developing standardized tests and their evaluation lobbying or consulting for the textile industry, offering consumer protection, and textile care is discussed. Collectively, the information should allow comprehensive understanding of the role of textile testing in quality control.

PRACTICE ACTIVITIES

A. Anatomy of Standard Test

1. What does ASTM D5034 -09 (2017) represent?
2. What does AATCC TM19.3-2020 represent?
3. What does AATCC TM198-2011e3(2020)?
4. What does AATCC EP1-2020 represent?
5. What does AATCC EP2-2020 represent?
6. What does AATCC LP2-2018 (2020) represent?
7. What does AATCC M12-2020 represent?

    TM   Test Methods

    LP   Laundering Procedure

    EP   Evaluation Procedure

    M   Monographs

    t   Additional changes within the same year

    e   Editorial changes

B. Standard Conditions

1. What is the standard temperature for the woven textile?
2. What is the standard temperature for Aramid?
3. What is the standard temperature for the nonwoven textile?
4. What is the standard relative humidity for the woven textile?

Textile Standards and Organizations

5. What is the standard relative humidity for Aramid?
6. What is the standard relative humidity for an Aramid?
7. What is the standard relative humidity for the nonwoven textile?
8. What do you understand by conditioning?
9. What is the importance of conditioning?
10. For how long should polyester be conditioned before testing?
11. For how long should cotton be conditioned before testing?
12. For how long should wool be conditioned before testing?
13. For how long should acetate be conditioned before testing?
14. For how long should rayon be conditioned before testing?

C. Moisture Regain

1. What is moisture equilibrium?
2. What is the importance of moisture equilibrium in textile testing?
3. What is the difference between moisture content and moisture regain?
4. If the oven dried weight of the fibers is 4.8 grams and that of the environmentally conditioned fabric is 5 grams, respond to the following.

    4.1 What will be the percentage of the moisture regain?

    4.2 Based on the data under Appendix I, what will be the possible fiber contents?

    4.3 Which test will you use to conform the fiber content?

5. If the oven dried weight of the fibers is 5 grams and that of the environmentally conditioned fabric is 5.06 grams, respond to the following.

    5.1 What will be the percentage of the moisture regain?

    5.2 Based on the data under Appendix I, what will be the possible fiber contents?

    5.3 Which test will you use to conform the fiber content?

6. If the oven dried weight of the fibers is 10 grams and that of the environmentally conditioned fabric is 11.1 grams, respond to the following.

    6.1 What will be the percentage of the moisture regain?

    6.2 Based on the data under Appendix I, what will be the possible fiber contents?

    6.3 Which test will you use to conform the fiber content?

7. If the oven dried weight of the fibers is 4.8 grams and that of the environmentally conditioned fabric is 5 grams, respond to the following.

   7.1 What will be the percentage of the moisture regain?

   7.2 Based on the data under Appendix I, what will be the possible fiber contents?

   7.3 Which test will you use to conform the fiber content?

8. If the oven dried weight of the fibers is 7.8 grams and that of the environmentally conditioned fabric is 8.7 grams, respond to the following.

   8.1 What will be the percentage of the moisture regain?

   8.2 Based on the data under Appendix I, what will be the possible fiber contents?

   8.3 Which test will you use to conform the fiber content?

9. If the oven dried weight of the fibers is 10 grams and that of the environmentally conditioned fabric is 11.3 grams, respond to the following.

   4.1 What will be the percentage of the moisture regain?

   4.2 Based on the data under Appendix I, what will be the possible fiber contents?

   4.3 Which test will you use to conform the fiber content?

D. Temperature Conversion

1. Convert 40 degrees Celsius to the Fahrenheit temperature.

2. Convert 90°F to Celsius temperature.

3. In Sydney, Australia, it showed 18°C. What will it be in Fahrenheit?

4. In San Francisco, California, the temperature was 100°F. What will it be in Celsius?

E. Role and Use of Textile Organizations

1. If durability and appearance are of utmost importance to John, which tests should he select and which manuals should he use?

2. Which organizations play an important role in protecting the textile industry of the United State and why? Give two appropriate examples.

3. Which organization is responsible for developing dry test standards?

4. Which organization is responsible for developing wet test standards?

5. Which organization has developed 9000 and 14000 series for quality and environmental management?

6. Which organization represents the United States at ISO?

7. Which organization is developed for consumer protection?

8. Which organization is responsible for overseeing the cleaning products in the United States?

9. Which government organization is responsible for administering the Permanent Care Labelling Act?

10. Which organization plays a significant role for the employee's safety.

11. Which organization is responsible for regulating air and water pollution as well as waste disposal?

REFERENCES

Annual book of ASTM standards. (2020). *7.01,* West Conshohoken, PA: ASTM International.

Annual book of ASTM standards. (2019). *7.02,* West Conshohoken, PA: ASTM International.

Chowdhary, U. (2009). Textile analysis, quality control and innovative uses. Deer Park, NY: LINUS.

Chowdhary, U. (2017). Comparing three brands of cotton t-shirts. *AATCC Journal of Research, 4*(3), 22-33. DOI: 10.14504/ajr.4.3.3

Federal Trades Commission Protecting America's Consumers (2018). https://www.ftc.gov/tips-advice/business-center/selected-industries/clothing-and-textiles

Our mission and what we do (2020. September). EPA: U. S. Environmental Protection Agency. https://www.epa.gov/aboutepa/our-mission-and-what-we-do

Manual of international test methods and procedures (2021). Research Triangle Park, NC: American Association of Textile Chemists and Colorists.

Merkel, R. S. (1991). *Textile product serviceability.* New York: Macmillan.

MOISTURE REGAIN CHART

Source: Annual Book of Standards (2017, p. 455); ASTM D1909-13.

Fiber	Commercial Moisture Regain %	Commercial Allowance %
Acetate	6.5	9
Acrylic	1.5	2

Aramid
    High Modulus
    Standard
	
	3.5
	7.0
		
		3.5
		7.0

Cotton
    Raw
    Natural
    Dyed
    Mercerized
	
	8.5 Syrian
	7.0
	8.0
	8.5	

Flax
    Raw
    Linen
	
	12.0
	8.75	

Fluorocarbon	0	
Glass	0	2/3.0
Hemp	12.0	
Jute	13.75	
Metallic	0	2

Modacrylic
    Class I
    Class II
    Class III
	
	0.4
	2.0
	3.0	

Nylon	4.5	
Olefin	0	
Polyester	0.4	1.5
Ramie	7.6	
Rayon	11	13
Rubber	0	
Saran	0	
Silk	11	
Spandex	1.3	
Triacetate	3.5	7.0
Vinal	4.5	
Vinyon	0	
Wool	13.6	

DATA ANALYSIS AND INTERPRETATION

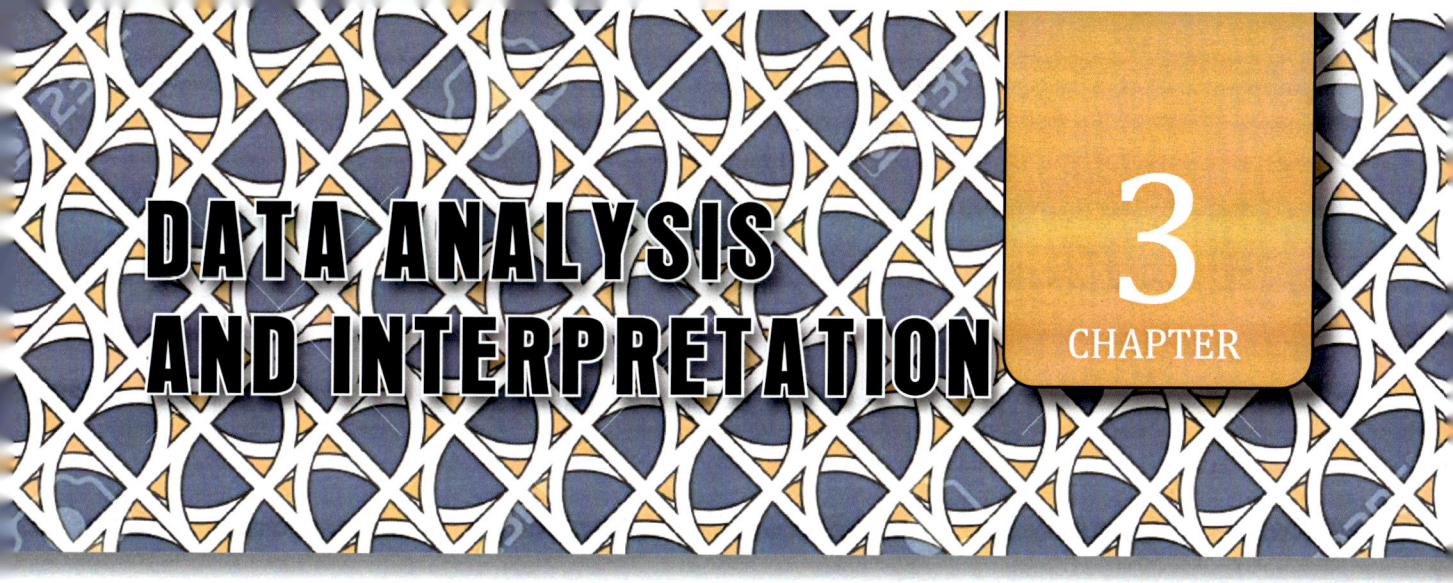

CHAPTER 3

Data analysis is the process of applying and interpreting descriptive and inferential statistical procedures by meaningful description and extraction from the data. This procedure allows the users to extrapolate from the numerical data through quantitative reasoning in a cohesive and concise manner within the chosen level of confidence. ASTM accepts 95% level of confidence aka p<.05. Data are generated from the standardized experiments for testing hypotheses and explaining relationships.

It is of critical importance to follow the test procedures accurately so that reliability is improved. A sound sampling procedure should be used for reliable results. Merkel (1991) described the universe of sampling as the production lot. One should randomly select 10% of the total lot for best results. If the production lot is 200, select 20 rolls/pieces for laboratory testing. Specimens are dimensions of material that are used for actual testing. For example, 15" (38 x 38 cm. x 15" specimen is used for dimensional stability and apparel retention. For statistical significance, one should select the number of specimens based on the following formula (Merkel, 1991, p. 100). Otherwise use of 5 observations for most tests is a common practice used in textile research.

$k = (tv/A)^2$ or $k = (ts/E)^2$

k = Number of tests   k = Number of tests

v = Coefficient of Variation   s = Calculated Standard Deviation

t = The desired confidence level   t = The desired confidence level

A = Allowable difference   E = Allowable difference

The number of specimens required will be more for the higher level of confidence than the lower level. Table 7 shows the values of confidence level in relation to the standard deviations (t).

Table 7: Confidence level for Standard Deviations. (Merkel, 1991).

Confidence Level (Percent)	Standard Deviation (="t")
66.27	1.00
90.00	1.645
95.00	1.96
95.45	2.00
99.00	2.576
99.73	3.00

EXAMPLES TO DETERMINE # OF SPECIMENS

The recommended range of allowable difference by Merkel (1991) is 2% to 7%.

Data Information

Example 1:

$s = 1.338$ $v = 2.46$ E or A = Allowable Difference = 2%

$k = 1.645$ (90%) $k = 1.96$ (95%) $k = 2.576$ (99%)

Using Coefficient of Variation

# of Specimens 90% Level of Confidence

$k = (tv/A)^2$ $k = (1.645 \times 2.46/2)^2 = 4.129 = 4$

# of Specimens 95% Level of Confidence

$k = (tv/A)^2$ $k = (1.96 \times 2.46/2)^2 = 5.813 = 6$

# of Specimens 99% Level of Confidence

$k = (tv/A)^2$ $k = (2.576 \times 2.46/2)^2 = 10.036 = 10$

Using Standard Deviation

# of Specimens 90% Level of Confidence

$k = (ts/E)^2$ $k = (1.645 \times 1.338/2)^2 = 1.21 = 1$

# of Specimens 95% Level of Confidence

$k = (ts/E)^2$ $k = (1.96 \times 1.338/2)^2 = 1.719 = 2$

# of Specimens 99% Level of Confidence

$k = (ts/E)^2$ $k = (2.576 \times 1.338/2)^2 = 3.161 = 3$

Data Analysis and Interpretation

Example 2:

s = 4.567   E or A = Allowable Difference = 2%

k = 1.645 (90%)   k = 1.96 (95%)   k = 2.576 (99%)

# of Specimens 90% Level of Confidence

k = (ts/E)²   k = (1.645 x 4.567 /2)² = 14.281 = 14

# of Specimens 95% Level of Confidence

k = (ts/E)²   k = (1.96 x 4.567 /2)² = 19.963 = 20

# of Specimens 99% Level of Confidence

k = (ts/E)²   k = (2.576 x 4.567 /2)² = 34.598 = 35

The preceding examples reflect that the data with higher consistency requires less number of specimens than the data with lower consistency as determined by the standard deviation. Likewise, the number of specimens needed should be larger for the higher level of confidence than the lower confidence level. The number of specimens required by different textile standards varies. Those numbers may be sufficient for simple testing. However, the method above provides higher reliability than using the minimum suggested in various tests. It is good to use structural attributes like fabric count, yarn size, or fabric weight for determining the number of specimens required. Chowdhary and Poynor (2006) used fabric count to determine the number of specimens required for their study. They found that fewer numbers of specimens were needed for warp direction than the weft direction based on the same criteria. It is consistent with the common belief that the lengthwise direction is stronger than the crosswise direction of the fabrics.

While cutting specimens, it is important that certain rules are followed to make sure that the specimens fairly represent the material. Merkel (1991, 82-84) identified five rules of cutting the specimens for best results. Collier and Epps (1999), 54) also reiterated them in a modified form. The author has used them in teaching for over twenty years and agrees with the assertions of Merkel (1991) and Collier and Epps (1999). The rules are presented below in paraphrased form with specific examples.

1. **Do not Use Selvage Edges of Fabrics for Specimens.**

   Selvage has closely woven edges that make fabric stronger than the most of the fabric. Collier and Epps (1999, p. 54) purported that ideally, 10% of the width from the selvage should not be used for specimens. Based on this rule, only 36" of the 45 inches wide fabric can be used for cutting the specimens. You do not use 4.5 inches (10%) from each selvage end. Likewise, if the fabric width is 58", you can use only 46.4 inches for cutting the test specimens. Merkel (1991) reported that people have used 2.5 inches on both sides to avoid wastage. Collier and Epps (1999) noted that even avoiding use of 2 inches on both sides could suffice for the economic reasons. Despite the option chosen, selvage edges should be excluded from inclusion. Example below is from Chowdhary (2009).

Chapter 3

[Diagram: Usable area between two arrows]

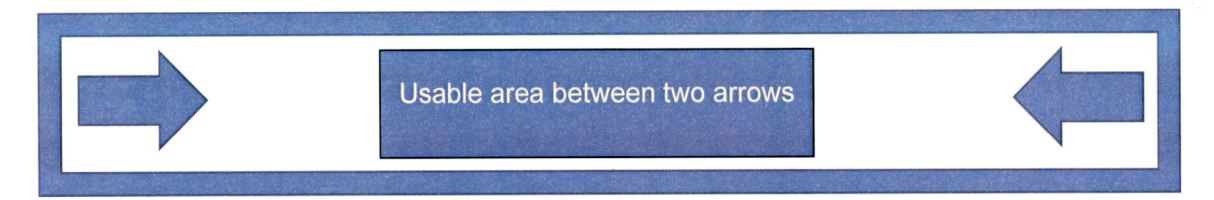

2. **Do not Take Specimens for One Test from the Same Set of Yarns.**

    Of the two rectangles below, the one on the right is correct because it covers the entire width of the fabric. However, the one on the left has white area between two blue squares that will not be part of the test.

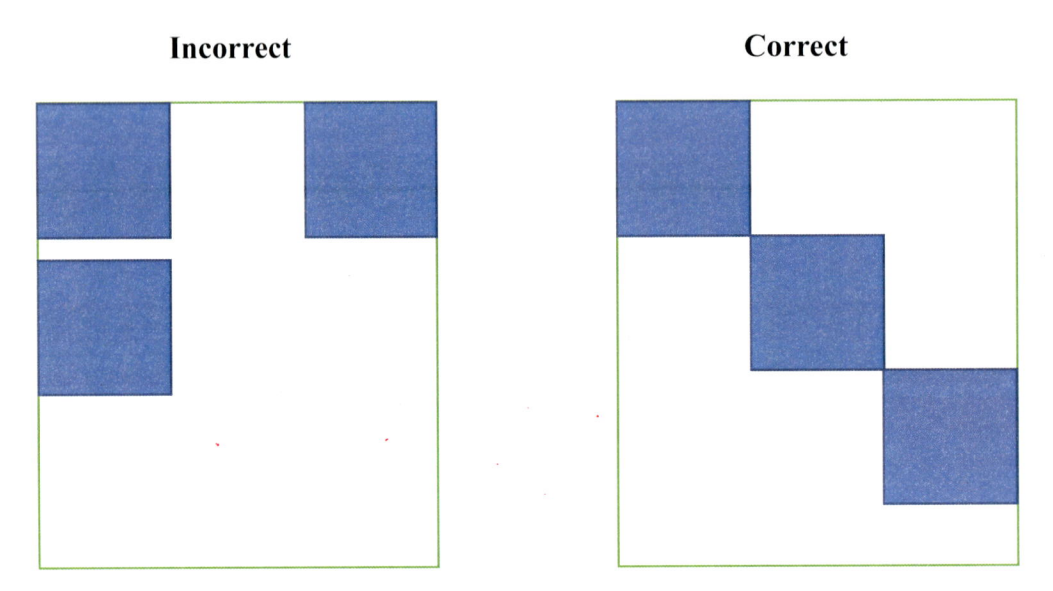

    Incorrect   **Correct**

3. **Mark only Lengthwise Grain of All Specimens Before Cutting the Specimens.**

    After the specimens are cut, marking lengthwise grainline serves as a guide for identification of the direction of the fabric. It is a critical step because fabric responds differently in length and width directions. For example, warp is generally stronger than the weft direction. Likewise, for unbalanced weaves, the number of warp yarns are more than the crosswise yarns. Unless the direction is marked, you will not know what you are testing. Picture below shows marking of the lengthwise grain.

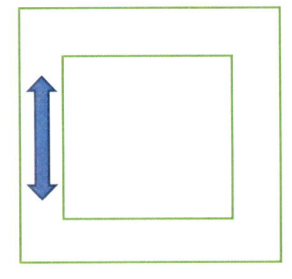

4. **Cut specimens accurately and on grain.**

   Fabrics cut on bias impact the readings of textile attributes. Therefore, they should be cut on straight of the grain. It means that warp and weft should make an angle of 90^0 in a woven fabric. Otherwise, it will result in a measurement error. For the tests that require raveling in both directions, the specimen will have a distorted look. Square on the left is cut on the grain. However, on the right is not.

5. **Keep Grainline and other Markings on the Specimens Small and in Areas that will not be Affected during Testing.**

   It is necessary to keep marking small and away from the testing area so that they do not obstruct the experimenter's measuring ability due to losing them in the torn areas by losing or covering up the area to be used. For the example below, B is a better choice than A.

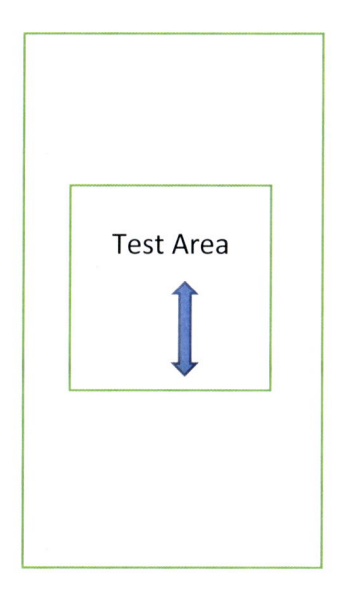

IMPORTANT TERMS AND PROCESSES

Table 8 provides important terms for quantitative reasoning along with their definitions and examples. Intent is to bring reader and writer at the same wavelength of understanding.

Table 8: Definitions and examples of various terms.

Term	Definition	Example
Accuracy	Closeness of the computed value to the true value.	If the standard temperature is between 68-72°F, the calculated value of various readings should fall within this range for the conditioning rooms.
Average or Mean	Ratio between some of all observations divided by the number of observations.	65+68+70+72+75 =350/5 = 70
Coefficient of Variation (CV)	Ratio between the standard deviation and mean that is represented in percentage.	SD = 2.767 Mean = 120 CV= 100(2.7667/120) = 2.31%
Experimental/ Method Error	Variable due to mistakes made by the experimenter while conducting the experiment.	Not following the guidelines of the standard fully and collecting biased data.
Hypothesis	An educated guess or expectation derived from literature or theory.	*Wet strength of cotton is higher than dry strength. *Fabric with higher thread count is stronger than the lower thread count. *No difference will exist between dimensional stability of polyester and polyester/cotton blend.
Instrumental Errors	Sample collected from the malfunctioning instrument as a measurement tool.	Getting differentials reading while testing the same fabric for the same test using the same instrument under the same conditions. It can happen when instruments are not calibrated.
Laboratory sample	Original material used for testing from the production lot.	The fabric is one yard long and the entire width of the fabric is used for flat bolts Collier and Epps, 1999). For circular knits, at least one foot band is chosen.
Lot Sample	Using materials from more than one mode of shipment (bolts, cartons, cases).	Using various fiber contents or vendors for choices.
Median	Middle value of the series of observations arranged in ascending or descending order.	**Data Set 1:** 65 68 70 72 75 Median = 70 **Data Set 2:** 65 68 70 72 75 76 Median will be average of the two middle numbers. 70+72 = 142/2 = **71**

Data Analysis and Interpretation

Term	Definition	Example
Mode	Most frequently used number in the data set.	60, 65, 67, 67, 67, 68, 68, 70, 70, 70, 70, 70, 72, 74, 74 In the above data set, 70 has been used more often than any other number in the data set. Therefore, mode will be 70.
Personal Errors	They occur at the experimenter's level due to carelessness, ignorance, lack of experience, or physical conditions.	With aging one may see more yellowness or have vision problems. Being unfamiliar with equipment or methodology can yield erroneous data.
Precision	Closeness of values to each other	**EXAMPLE 1** **Set 1** 110+112+112+114+115 **Set 2** 105 + 110 +115+120+125 Of the two data sets above, the data set 1 is more precise than the data set 2 because numbers are only 5 units apart as opposed to the data set 2 where the range is 20. **EXAMPLE 2** Imagine that there are two weighing scales. One measures it to the second decimal place (.01) and the other one to the third decimal place (.001). When you weigh one meter yarn, the results will be affected as follows. | Obs.	Tex	Obs.	Tex
---	---	---	---
.02	20	.017	17
.02	20	.016	16
.02	20	.018	18
.03	30	.026	26
.03	30	.031	31
	24		21.6 Mean	 In this example, the second set will be more precise than the first one. Because it takes away the rounding up error and offers more conservative estimate than the first set.

Term	Definition	Example
Range	Difference between the highest and the lowest number.	7, 9, 10, 12, 15 15-7 = 8, or 7-15.
Reliability	Repeatability of the results	A cotton shirt fabric received the same readings in Australia, China, Hong Kong, India, Italy, Japan, Korea, New Zealand, Switzerland, Taiwan, United Kingdom, and United States under standard conditions. It will be interpreted as reliable performance or tests.
Replicate	Repeating the experiment or test.	Computing yarn size test for same yarn in India, Korea, and United States.
Sample	A portion of material used for testing or cutting specimens.	
Specimen	Material with specific dimensions that is used for actual testing.	5" x 5" for fabric weight 15" x 15" for dimensional stability and appearance retention of woven fabrics. 8" x 8" for horizontal wicking
Standard Deviation	Dispersion of values in the data set from the mean and is measured by taking square root of the variance. Or By taking square root of the sum of the squared differences of observations from the mean divided by the number of observations -1.	Obs d d^2 4 0.9 0.81 4 0.9 0.81 4 0.9 0.81 5 0.1 0.01 5 0.1 0.01 5 0.1 0.01 5 0.1 0.01 5 0.1 0.01 5 0.1 0.01 6 1.1 1.21 6 1.1 1.21 4.9 4.90 Mean $\sum d^2$ S = Square root of $\sum d^2/n-1$ = 0.738
Standard Error of the Differences between Means	SE = Square root of $$\frac{N_1 S_1^2 + N_2 S_2^2}{N_1 + N_2 - 2} \times \frac{N_1 + N_2}{N_1 \times N_2}$$	$N_1 = 10$ $N_2 = 10$ $S_1^2 = .544$ $S_2^2 = ..667$ SE = .367

Data Analysis and Interpretation

Term	Definition	Example
t-test	Compares differences between the means of two groups. It is ratio of difference between two means divided by the standard error of the differences between two means.	$$\frac{\text{Mean 1} - \text{Mean 2}}{\text{standard error}}$$ Mean 1 = 11.9 Mean 2 = 15 Standard error = .367 $$\text{t-value} = \frac{11.9 - 15}{.367} = .3.1/.367 = -8.447$$ If hypothesis is "No difference will exist between two variables," **accept** if the calculated value is less than ± 2.101 and **reject** if it is ± 2.101 or higher. If hypothesis is "Mean 2 will be higher than Mean 1," **accept** if the calculated value is more than ± 1.734 and **reject** if it is less than ± 1.734. + or − of the t-value only tells the direction of the relationship. Negative value does not mean below zero interpretation.
Variance	The ratio of the sum of the differences squared divided by the number of observations -1. In other words, it is the square of the standard deviation.	Obs d d^2 4 0.9 0.81 4 0.9 0.81 4 0.9 0.81 5 0.1 0.01 5 0.1 0.01 5 0.1 0.01 5 0.1 0.01 5 0.1 0.01 5 0.1 0.01 6 1.1 1.21 6 1.1 1.21 4.9 4.90 Mean Σd^2 Variance = $\Sigma d^2/n-1$ 4.9/9 = 0.544

Source used: Chowdhary (2009).

Chapter 3

EXAMPLES OF T-TESTS

Example 1: Null Hypothesis

Hypothesis: No difference will exist between fabric count of wool and acetate.

Data

#	Wool			Acetate		
	Obs.	d	d²	Obs.	d	d²
1	90	-2.5	6.25	118	-1.2	1.44
2	90	-2.5	6.25	118	-1.2	1.44
3	90	-2.5	6.25	118	-1.2	1.44
4	90	-2.5	6.25	119	-.2	0.04
5	90	-2.5	6.25	119	-.2	0.04
6	92	-0.5	0.25	119	-.2	0.04
7	92	-0.5	0.25	119	-.2	0.04
8	92	-0.5	0.25	119	-.2	0.04
9	92	-0.5	0.25	119	-.2	0.04
10	92	-0.5	0.25	119	-.2	0.04
11	92	-0.5	0.25	119	-.2	0.04
12	92	-0.5	0.25	119	-.2	0.04
13	94	1.5	2.25	119	-.2	0.04
14	94	1.5	2.25	120	0.8	0.64
15	94	1.5	2.25	120	0.8	0.64
16	94	1.5	2.25	120	0.8	0.64
17	95	2.5	6.25	120	0.8	0.64
18	95	2.5	6.25	120	0.8	0.64
19	95	2.5	6.25	120	0.8	0.64
20	95	2.5	6.25	120	0.8	0.64
$\sum d^2$			67.0			9.2

Mean	92.5		119.2
Mode	92		119
Median	92		119
Range	90-95 or 5		118-120 or 2
Standard Deviation	1.878		.696

Variance	3.526	.484
Coefficient of Variation	2.03%	0.58%
Standard Error		.459
Degrees of Freedom:		38
Calculated Value		-58.170*

Table t-value for null hypothesis: ± 2.042 for 30 df and ± 2.021 for 40 df

Conclusion: Null hypothesis is rejected. Acetate had significantly higher fabric count than wool with 95% level of confidence.

Example 2: Alternate Hypothesis

Hypothesis: Tear strength of satin weave is higher than the plain weave.

Data

#	Satin Weave Pounds per square inch (psi)			Plain Weave Pounds per square inch (psi)		
		d	d^2		d	d^2
1	20.8	1.7	2.89	10.7	1.22	1.489
2	19.0	0.1	0.01	10.2	0.72	0.518
3	18.8	0.3	0.09	9.7	0.22	0.048
4	18.5	0.6	0.36	8.5	-0.98	0.960
5	18.4	0/7	0.49	8.3	-1.18	1.392
Mean	19.1			9.48		
Σd^2			3.84			4.407
SD			1.857			1.834
Variance			3.448			3.363

Degree of Freedom 8

Critical t-value for Alternate hypothesis = 1.86

Calculated t-value = 7.372*

Conclusion: Null hypothesis is accepted. Satin weave has significantly higher tear strength than the plain weave at 95% level of confidence.

OTHER USEFUL HINTS

1. **Rounding Up**: As a rule of thumb, values higher than .5 should be rounded up to the higher number and less than .5 to the lower number. For example, 17.5-17.9 should be rounded up to 18.0, and 17.1-17.4 to 17.

2. **Decimal Places:** For percentages, report to the second decimal place. For standard deviation, t-test, Analysis of Variance (ANOVA}, etc. compute to the third decimal place. For example, elongation could be written as 9.75% but breaking strength should be written as 58.752 pounds per square inch (psi).

3. **Loss through Abrasion**: Abrasion is measured through visual inspection, strength loss and weight loss. Visual inspection reveals thinning of fabric and counting of pills. Strength and weight loss are measured in percentages. It can occur by rubbing of two surfaces. Rubbing could be between two textile materials, textile material and dust or sand, or material and other surfaces like metal, wood, etc.

    3.1 Strength Loss: It refers to the ratio between the weight difference of abraded and unabraded material divided by unabraded strength and multiplied by 100.

    ### Example 1

    Strength of unabraded specimen = 78 pounds per square inch (psi)

    Strength of abraded specimen = 75 psi

    Strength loss = 78-75 = 3 psi

    % Loss = 100(3/78) = 3.85%

    Interpretation: Abraded specimen had lower strength than the unabraded specimen.

    ### Example 2

    Strength of unabraded specimen = 90 pounds per square inch (psi)

    Strength of abraded specimen = 82 psi

    Strength loss = 90-82 = 8 psi

    % Loss = 100(8/90) = 8.89%

    Interpretation: Strength loss was 8.89% . Strength loss of second examples was higher than the first example.

    3.2 Weight Loss: It refers to the ratio between the weight difference of pre and post abrasion weight divided by unabraded weight and multiplied by 100.

    ### Example 1

    Weight of unabraded specimen = 5 grams

    Weight of abraded specimen = 4.5 grams

Weight loss = 5.0-4.5 = 0.5 grams

% loss = 100 (0.5/5) = 10%

Interpretation: Abrasion resulted in 10% weight loss. Or, the weight of the abraded specimen was 90% of the original weight.

Example 2

Weight of unabraded specimen = 9 grams

Weight of abraded specimen = 8 grams

Weight loss = 9-8 = 1 gram

% loss = 100 (1/9) = 11.11 %

Interpretation: Unabraded specimen was heavier than the abraded specimen. Percentage of weight loss from abrasion was 11.11%.

SUMMARY

It is important to follow certain rules while cutting specimens for optimizing the results of comparisons and preventing careless mistakes from happening. Information in this chapter confirms the importance of data analysis for meaningful quantitative reasoning for clear interpretation of the data. One can use both descriptive and inferential statistics for data analysis. Data analysis can be as simple as means and percentages for efficiency or more sophisticated and use t-tests, analysis of variance and regression analysis. The chapter provides examples of t-test only.

REFERENCES

Chowdhary, U. (2009). Textile analysis, quality control and innovative uses. Deer Park, NY: LINUS.

Chowdhary, U., & Poynor, D. (2005). Impact of stitch density on seam strength, seam elongation and seam efficiency. *International Journal of Consumer studies, 30* (6), 561-568. https://doi.org/10.1111/j.1470-6431.2005.00479.x.

Collier, B. J. (1999), & Epps, H. H. (1999). *Textile testing and analysis.* Upper Saddle River, NJ: Prentice Hall.

Merkel, R. S. (1991). *Textile product serviceability.* New York: Macmillan.

Chapter 3

PRACTICE ACTIVITIES

1. Use data below and calculate mean, mode, median, range, coefficient of variation and standard deviation.

#	Observation	Data arranged in the ascending order	d — Difference between mean and observation	d^2	$\sum d^2$
1	105				
2	106				
3	107				
4	106				
5	106				
6	105				
7	107				
8	105				
9	106				
10	106				

Mean =

Mode =

Median =

Range =

Variance =

Standard Deviation =

Coefficient of Variation =

2. Use data below to test a hypothesis, "Vinal and Nylon will not differ for their moisture regain %."

#	Vinal	#	Nylon
1	4	1	4.3
2	4	2	4.3
3	4	3	4.4
4	4.2	4	4.5
5	4.2	5	4.4
6	4.2	6	4.3
7	3.9	7	4.3
8	4.2	8	4.4
9	4.1	9	3.4
10	4	10	4.5

Data Analysis and Interpretation

Item	Vinal	Nylon
Mean		
Mode		
Median		
Range		
Variance		
Standard Deviation		
Coefficient of Variation		
Standard Error		
Degrees of Freedom		
Calculated t-value		
Table t-value (p<.05)	±2.101 1.734	

Check one.

    Hypothesis accepted: _____

    Hypothesis Rejected: _____

Interpretation:

3. Use data below to test a hypothesis, "Acrylic and polyester will differ for their moisture regain %"

#	Acrylic	#	Polyester
1	1.2	1	.3
2	1.2	2	.3
3	1.3	3	.4
4	1.3	4	.5
5	1.2	5	.4
6	1.2	6	.4
7	1.2	7	.3
8	1.3	8	.4
9	1.3	9	.4
10	1.2	10	.5

Item	Vinal	Nylon
Mean		
Mode		
Median		
Range		
Variance		
Standard Deviation		
Coefficient of Variation		
Standard Error		
Degrees of Freedom		
Calculated t-value		
Table t-value (p<.05)	±1.734	

Check one.

    Hypothesis accepted: _____

    Hypothesis Rejected: _____

Interpretation:

4. What do you understand by the 10% rule of usable fabric width for cutting specimens? Provide two examples.

5. Why do some recommend using less than 10% from the selvage? What are those values?

6. How many rules of cutting specimens are there?

7. What is the significance of following the rules of cutting specimens?

8. Which of the two grainlines should be marked on the specimens before cutting it?

9. What is the difference between a specimen and a sample?

10. What are the indicators of abrasion of textile material?

11. What do you learn from computing standard deviation?

12. When do we use t-test?

13. What do we learn from t-test?

14. What is the null hypothesis?

15. What is an alternate hypothesis?

16. What is the difference between calculated and table t-values?

17. What is the commonly used number for testing in textiles?

18. Use data below to determine the number of specimens needed for a tear resistance research?

    Confidence level = 95%

    Allowable difference = 2%

    Coefficient of variation = 10%

19. What is the standard deviation "t" for the 95% confidence level?

20. What is reliability?

STRUCTURAL ATTRIBUTES

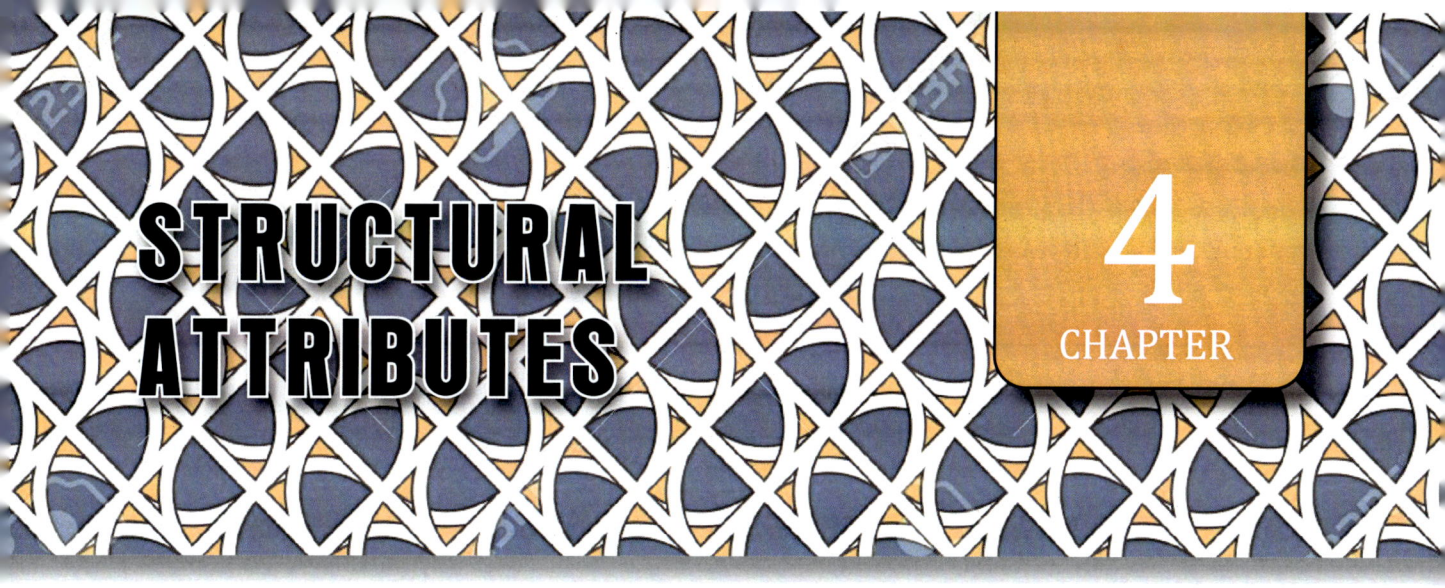

4 CHAPTER

Structural attributes provide physical status to textiles and are essential to the existence of materials. They provide inherent character to textile that could impact their performance. They are the foundation to offer quality that could later be improvised with mechanical and chemical finishes to render additional properties for meeting the requirements of the intended use. The examples of the structural attributes are length and diameter at the fiber level; yarn crimp/twist and yarn size at the yarn level; and fabric construction, count, defects, thickness, and weight at the fabric level.

A. AT THE FIBER LEVEL

A.1 Fiber-Content

Fiber content refers to the raw materials used for making the textiles. It can be tested by microscopic, burning, and chemical testing. Some textile is 100% of natural fibers and blends. Examples of natural fibers are 100% cotton, flax, jute, silk, rayon, lyocell, and acetate as regenerated fibers, and synthetic fibers as nylon, polyester, acrylic, olefin, and aramid. Blends can be exemplified by polyester/cotton (65/35 percent), rayon/acetate (70/30 percent), cotton/Lycra (97/3 percent), etcetera.

Microscopic structure is used to distinguish different natural fibers and determine distinctions between natural and synthetic fibers (*2021 Manual of International Test Methods and Procedures*). Both longitudinal and crosswise sections of fibers are performed using AATCC 20 standard. Longitudinal structure of cotton shows twist under the microscope. For mercerized cotton, the twist is softer. Scales are seen for wool under the microscope and gum spots for silk. Linen appears like bamboo like structure and jute like tree bark. For rayon and acetate, one sees striations under the microscope. Synthetic fibers appear like tubular structures with or without speckles. Spandex is dark with dull luster. When viewing the **cross-sectional** view of different fiber contents, cotton looks like kidney or bean shape for mature and raw cotton but oval shaped for mercerized cotton, It is polygonal for jute. Acetate and rayon are serrated, and nylon is trilobal.

Burning test is good to differentiate between natural, regenerated, and synthetic fibers. Cotton, rayon, linen and other cellulosic fibers form ash when burned. Wool and silk form crushable beads. Acetate and synthetic fibers form plasticized mass. It is worth noting that both nylon and aramid are polyamides. However, nylon melts but the aramid does not burn but just scorches. Standardized test *AATCC - TM 20 2013(2018) provides a table on page 65* which offers information on burning behavior of different fiber contents including the appearance of ash (*2021 Manual of International Test Methods and Procedures*).

Chemical testing is needed to confirm the fiber content the best for synthetic fibers (*2021 Manual of International Test Methods and Procedures*, p. 67*)*. Acetate is the only fiber that dissolves in acetic acid. Acrylic dissolves only in dimethyl formamide and so does Spandex. When viewed under microscope, acrylic fiber shows lots of speckles but Spandex shows dark colored appearance. Cotton, linen and rayon dissolve exclusively in sulfuric acid. However, one can follow this test with microscopic structure for verification. Wool and silk dissolve completely in Sodium hypochlorite. Silk also dissolves in sulfuric acid. Spandex fully dissolves in dimethyl formamide. Only polyester dissolves in m-cresol. Modacrylic dissolves totally in cyclohexane. For detail on other fiber contents, refer to the *2021 Manual of International Test Methods and Procedures.*

A.2 Diameter (ASTM D 2130 - 2013)

Fiber diameter refers to the distance between two extremes of the circle of its width. It is measured in the micron system. One **micron** equals 1/1000 of a millimeter and it is expressed in µm (Cohen and Johnson, 2010, 41-42). The authors provided an average micron range for cotton from 12-20 µm, flax from 12-16 µm, wool from 17-40 µm, and silk from 11-12 µm. Binding is better in the fiber with lower than higher values. *McGregor,* Stanton, Beilby, Speijers, & Tester (2014) found that fine fabrics with lower diameter were associated with the lower fabric sensation. Diameter impacted the feeling of clinginess, dampness, mugginess, and sweatiness.

A.3 Length (ASTM D 1234 - 2013, ASTM D 4031 – 07 (Reapproved 2018)

Fiber lengths are of two types: staple and filament. Staple fibers are measured in centimeters and inches. Filaments are measured in kilometers and miles. Filaments are stronger than the staple fibers. Manufactured and synthetic fibers are made as filaments. Later, they are cut into small staples if such benefits are needed than of filaments. *ASTM Manual of Standards* (2020) defines staple fiber as "natural fibers or cut lengths from filament" (p. 55), and filament as "a continuous fiber of extremely long length" (p. 27). All natural fibers except silk are staple. However, all manufactured fibers are filaments. Even-though the filaments are strong, their negatives of being slippery and hydrophobic have forced the textile manufacturers to cut them to staples so that positive properties of the staple fibers could be incorporated for added comfort. ASTM D 1234 – 2013 is designed to measure fiber length for greased wool and ASTM D 4031 – 07 (Reapproved 2018) is developed for the bulk property of the textured yarn,

A.4 Moisture Content (AATCC 20A -2020)

This test contains several different tests. This chapter will focus only on moisture content and fiber content distribution. Procedure is slightly modified for ease of understanding. **Moisture content** refers to the amount of water that is held by the textile without making the wearer feel wet. For moisture content, use at least one gram of the fibrous structure. Weigh in a petri dish. Add the weight of the petri dish to the weight of the fiber. Heat it for 1.5 hours in the oven at 105-110⁰F, and weigh. Continue he process and weigh every 30 minutes until eight becomes constant. Record the weight after it does not change any more. Calculate percentage as follows.

$$\text{Moisture Content} = \frac{\text{Original weight} - \text{Oven dried weight}}{\text{Original weight}} \times 100$$

Original weight = weight of the fiber + weight of the container

Oven dried weight = constant weight of the fiber + weight of the container

This process is opposite of moisture regain. For fiber content analysis. In moisture regain, we begin with oven dried material and keep it under standardize conditions. Weight it periodically, until it stops gaining any weight. Formula changes for that as follows. Due to change in the denominator moisture regain value will be higher than the moisture content value.

$$\text{Moisture Regain \%} = \frac{100 \,(\text{Equilibrium weight} - \text{oven dried weight})}{\text{oven dried weight}}$$

For **fiber content analysis,** weigh blend. Add solvent that will dissolve one of the two fiber contents. Take out the remaining fiber content and let it dry. Weigh the dried fiber. For example, if you have rayon and acetate in a blend, use acetone for dissolving the acetate. Dry the left-over fiber that will be rayon. If your original weight is 1 gram, and weight of the left-over fiber is .40 grams, percentage of each fiber content will be as follows.

1-.40 = .6   100 (.6/1) = 60% Acetate   100(.4/1) = 40% Rayon

For solvent refer to page 67 of the *Manual of international Test Methods and Procedures* (2021). This test works better for fabrics that have warp in one fiber content and weft in different fiber content, or if it is used in the blended fibrous forms.

B. AT THE YARN LEVEL

B.1 Yarn Crimp (ASTM D 3883 – 04 (Reapproved 2020), ASTM D 3937 – 2013; ASTM D 4031 – 07 (Reapproved 2018)

Yarn crimp refers to " – the undulations, waviness, or succession of bend, curls, or waves induced either naturally, mechanically, or chemically." (*2019 Annual Book of Standards,* 7.01, 82). Yarn crimp is an important textile attribute. It renders texture to a straight filament and enhances bulk, comfort, resiliency, stretch, and warmth. Yarn crimp is induced in manufactured fibers to make them flexible and stretchy. It can be done by knitting processes and de-knitting processes or heat settings. It naturally exists in wool.

ASTM D 3883 – 04 (Reapproved 2020) measures yarn crimp and yarn take-up in woven fabrics. This test uses ten specimens in each direction. **ASTM D 3937 – 2013** measures number of crimps and extra length required for each crimp. Number of crimps is determined by marking each crimp (one peak and one valley) for unstretched one inch yarn length. Formula below was used to calculate extra length required for each crimp.

Extra length needed for each crimp = $\dfrac{\text{Extended length of inch} - 1\text{inch}}{\text{\# of crimps/inch}}$

For Example: $\dfrac{4.5 - 1}{22} = 3.5/22 = 0.159"$

Table 9: Classification of number of crimps per inch. (Chowdhary (2018).

Classification	Range/Inch
Low	2-12
Medium	13-20
High	20-30

Matsudaira, Kawabata, & Niwa (1984) reported that fibers from good quality have high crimp. They stressed that fiber crim impacts yarn's extensibility and compressibility as well as fabric extensibility. They further argued that smoothness and softness are also impacted by the fiber crimp. Behery (2010) found that crimp impacts abrasion resistance. Maqsood, Hussain, Nawab, Shaker, & and Umair (2014) developed prediction models and found that an increase of crimp in weft yarns decreased it in the warp direction. Findings of Ezazshahahi, Mousazadegan, Varkivani, and Saharkhiz (2014) were also similar to Maqsood et al. (2014) Strength and stiffness decrease with increase in yarn crimp (Stig and Hallstrom, 2019).

B.2 Yarn Number/Size (ASTM D1059 - 2017; ASTM 6612 - 2016)

Yarn number refers to the linear density of yarn measured in "mass per unit length" (*2020 of Standards, 7.01,* 2020, 68). ASTM D 1059 – 2017 is based on short-length specimens. It is used for yarns that stretch less than 5% with tension increase of .25-.75 gf/Tex. ASTM D 6612 – 2016 requires one specimen for filament yarns and five specimens for spun yarns. It uses computer software for calculations. Chowdhary (2007) recommended ten specimens of one meter length in both directions. Their weight is then multiplied by 1000 to get Tex. Nine Tex can make one denier. This method is called the direct method. In this method length stays the same but weight varies. **Tex** is weight in gram of 1000 meters of yarn. **Denier** is weight in gram of 9000 meters.

In the indirect system of yarn numbering, weight is kept constant but length varies. It is defined as yards per pound and is not based on the metric system. Based on this system cotton count has 840 yards per pound. Worsted count is 560 yards per pound. Based on this example, cotton is lighter than wool because it has a higher number of yards in one pound weight than wool.

ASTM D2260 – 03 (2018) offers conversion factors to bring equivalence of numbering achieved from different numbering systems. Even industry uses sliding rulers with the (*2020 of Standards, 7.01,* 2020, 68). conversion tables because everyone in industry does not use the same numbering system. One Tex is 1/9 of the denier. In contrast, denier is nine times of the Tex. One example from ASTM D2260 – 03 (2018) from ((*2020 of Standards, 7.01,* 2020, 583-593) is provided below. 40 decitex is equal to 36 Deniers, 4 Tex, 6.774 American Grain Count, 250.0 Metric Count, 413.4 Linen Woolen Cut, 77.51 Woolen Run, 221.4 Worsted Count and 147.6 in Cotton Count (p. 84). The example above shows values from 9 different numbering systems. Increase in yarn size based on the indirect system reflects that the yarn is finer than decrease in number. However, in the direct numbering system, it is just the opposite. Deci Tex is the term used for 10 Tex.

Kadolph (1998) reported that yarn size is an important consideration for sewing threads. Cohen and Johnson (2010, p. 80) documented that **18-30 Tex** (fine)is good for light articles such as blouses, dresses, lingerie, sleepwear and swimwear. **30-60 Tex** (medium) is good choice for aprons, athletics, caps, foundation garments, jeans, pants, rainwear, shorts, and windbreakers. **60-105 Tex** (heavy) is best for workwear, parkas, protective clothing, overcoats, and footwear. Finally, **105-135 Tex (extra heavy)** is great for decorative stitching with bold design, luggage, and golf bags. It is obvious from Cohen and Johnson's classification that finer thread should be used for light weight garments and extra heavy thread should be used for the objects that take extra heavy load.

ASTM D1683 – 2007 was discontinued in 1999 and reinstituted in 2007. It suggested that for **high density construction** with fine yarns, use 35 Tex sewing thread for cotton and 40 Tex for polyester for fabrics that weighed up to 8 ounces per square yard or 270 g/m^2. Those over 270 g/m^2 should use 70 Tex for cotton and 60 Tex for polyester. For **medium density construction**, use 70 Tex for cotton and 60 Tex for polyester for fabrics that are up to 270 g/m^2 and 105 Tex for cotton and 90 Tex for polyester if they are more than 270 g/m^2. Finally, **for low density construction** with coarser yarns, use 70 (cotton) and 60 (polyester) Tex for under 8 ounces and 105 and 90 Tex respectively for over 8 weight fabrics. Chowdhary (2009[a]) used 32 Tex for a premium cotton muslin. Chowdhary and Wentela (2018) used varying values of Tex for different fiber contents in their study. It ranged between 23.9 to 29.8 Tex. Chowdhary (2019) used sewing thread with a yarn size of 29.7 Tex for a knitted wool fabric.

B.3 Yarn Twist (ASTM D 1422/1422M – 13 (Reapproved 2020)

The ASTM test uses the untwist-retwist method to determine the number of stitches per inch. The *2020Annual of ASTM Standards* (2020, page 63) defines twist as "the number of turns about the axis per unit of length in a yarn or other textile strand." The manual provides its classification as follows on page 312 of the volume 7.1. They can be labeled as low, medium, and high even though ASTM did not specify so. All scholars have not used the same numbers. Table 9 shows the distinctions.

5 or less	Low
Over 5-15	Medium
Over 15	High

Table 10: Classification of Yarn Twist.

Category	ASTM	Kadolph and Langford, 2002	Cohen and Johnson, 2010
Low	5 or less	2-3	2-12 (soft)
Medium	Over 5-15	-	20-30 (hard)
High	Over 15	-	-
Napping	-	Warp 12 Filling 6-8	-
Average	-	Warp 25 Weft 20	-
Crepe	-	40-80 singles plied with ply 2-5	Combines high and low twist.

Chowdhary (2009) reported that yarn twist is measured as twists per inch (TPI) 0r 25 mm based on the metric system. The higher number of twists per inch create stronger yarn than the lower twists per inch. The convolution is created by twisting the fibers or filaments in S or Z direction. Most yarns have a Z twist. However, if the twist of a single yarn has a Z twist, the plied yarn made from it will have a S twist.

Merkel (1991) reported that twisting operations strengthen the staple fibers more so than the filament yarns. Twist also reduces bulkiness due to the spiral effect. Collier, Bide and Tortora (2009) testified that low twist yarns have less luster, strength and abrasion resistance than the yarns with high twist yarns. Twisting either uneven slub yarns or low twist yarns with high twist yarns create rough surfaces. Varying twist level impacted light reflectance for three basic weaves (Omerglu, Mine, Behcet, 2015). Atalie, Ferede, and Rotich (2019) asserted that twist level impacts mechanical and sensorial comfort.

B.4 Yarn Type

Yarn is created by two or more fibers or yarns to create single, plied, cord or novelty yarns. **Single** yarn is produced by twisting fibers and they are the result of one twisting operation. **Ply** yarns are created by twisting single yarns together. They are the result of two twisting operations. **Cord** yarns are created by twisting ply yarns together. They are the result of the third twisting operations. Cord yarns are used for curtain's tie backs as well as decorating children's hats. Ply yarns are stronger than the single yarns. Most of the yarns used for knitting are ply yarns and can be used for weaving also. Novelty yarns are fancy yarns that are used for decorative purposes. They can be created to make yarns loopy, thick and thin, flat, or combination of all three, and introduction of metallic yarns or using both staple and filament yarns. Tweed is an example of novelty yarn made from single yarns. However, boucle and chenille are examples of ply yarns.

C. AT THE FABRIC LEVEL

Fabric construction, fabric count, fabric defects, fabric thickness and fabric weight are integral fabric attributes that determine fabric quality for different end uses. Each attribute makes a unique contribution for essential purposes of aesthetics, care, comfort and durability.

C.1 Fabric Construction

C.1.1 Weaving

Fabric construction processes consist of weaving, knitting and several nonwoven techniques. **Weaving** uses interlacing of yarns. **Knitting** connects loops horizontally, vertically, or diagonally with needles. **Bonding, laminating, crocheting, fusing, and tatting** are some other techniques of creating fabrics. Woven fabrics are stronger than knits and the knitted fabrics are more stretchy than woven fabrics. Laces are used as decorative textiles and the nonwoven textiles are used for interfacings (called interlining in industry).

Woven fabric is created by interlacing of warp and weft yarns at ninety degrees angle. **Selvage** edges are closely woven edges of the fabric that anchor the fabric during the weaving process on the loom. They run parallel to the length of the fabric. There are three basic weaves (plain, twill, satin). Other weaves are just variations of these weaves. **A plain weave,** a repeat of 1x1 is used. It means the filling yarn goes over and under the warp yarns (Figure 1). Dark square shows the warp, and the light square represents the weft. Each repeat requires two warp and two weft yarns that can be repeated as many times as necessary depending on the fabric width and length desired.

Row 1   1O1U

Row 2   1UIO

Repeat the pattern in both directions for the desired length and width.

O = Over

U = Under

Figure 1: An example of plain weave with 4 repeats in each direction.

Basket weave is a simple variation of plain weave. The repeat for this weave could be 2x2, 3x3, 4x4 and so on. **Oxford** weave is also a variation of plain weave. The repeat is 2x2 in the warp direction and 1x1 in the weft direction.

Twill weave shows the diagonal pattern with displacement of one or two yarns. It has repeat of 2x1, 2x2, or 3x1. Figure 2 shows the pattern for 2x1 repeat. Each repeat requires three yarns in the warp and three yarns in the weft direction.

Row 1   2O1U

Row 2   1O1U1O

Row 3   2U1O

Repeat the pattern in both directions for the desired length and width.

Figure 2: An example of twill weave with two repeats in each direction.

Satin Weave Has longer floats than plain and twill weave. It displaces more than one yarn in the diagonals. It means that the diagonal line made through this pattern is not continuous. This weave uses floats of 4 and higher number of yarns. Figure 3 shows 4x1 repeat. Each repeat is completed in five rows.

Row 1   4O1U

Row 2   1O1U3O

Row 3   3O1U1O

Row 4   1U4O

Row 5   2O1U2O

Repeat the pattern in both directions for the desired length and width.

Figure 3: An example of satin weave with two repeats in each direction.

Each weave has its own advantages and disadvantages. Plain weave ravels and snags less, and wrinkles more than the two other basic weaves. Additionally, it has low tearing strength. Twill weave is strong and wrinkle resistant but ravels easily. Satin weave is most vulnerable to snagging, pliable, and lustrous. Satin weave has the highest tearing strength.

Several specialty weaves evolve from the weaving concept of basic weaves. Selected examples include dobby, jacquard, and pile weaves. **Dobby weaves** have figurative designs with less than 25 warp arrangements. Some examples are heart and diamond shapes. They are used for blouses, curtains, and shirt materials. Jacquard weave uses more than 25 warp arrangements because figures are larger in size than the dobby weave. They are used for bedspreads, drapes, shawls. upholstery, and wall hangings.

Pile weaves are created by adding an extra set of yarns for creating the pile in warp as well as weft directions. Pile is inserted in a warp direction for velvet and towels. The pile can be cut or uncut. Velvet has a cut pile that gives it a shaded effect. Fabric looks darker in one direction and lighter in the other. It is important to layout in the same direction. Otherwise, garments will have light and dark shades. It is inserted in the weft direction for velveteen and corduroy. Towels generally have an uncut pile that adds to its absorbing power. For weft insertion of piles, both corduroy and velveteen are cut type. The removed pile from the piled fabrics shows the V or W shape of the pile.

C.1.2 Knitting

Knitted fabrics are created by interlooping the yarns. In knitted fabrics, the terms used are wales and courses. **Wales** are the columns formed by stitches and **courses** are the rows formed by the stitches. When the stitches are joined horizontally, it is called the weft knit. Examples of the weft knit are plain jersey, rib, and purl knit. When they are joined diagonally and vertically, they are called the warp knits. Example of the warp knit is tricot. Two basic stitches are knit and purl. The knit stitch looks like a V and a purl stitch looks like relaxing C. Front of the jersey knit looks like a knit and back like the purl stitch (Figure 4). Image of purl knit is shown in figure 5. Purl knit shows the raised effect of purl stitch on both front and back. Rib knit is created by alternating the repeat of knit and purl stitches. Figure 6 shows a rib knit created by alternating two knit and two purl stitches.

Figure 4: An example of Jersey knit.

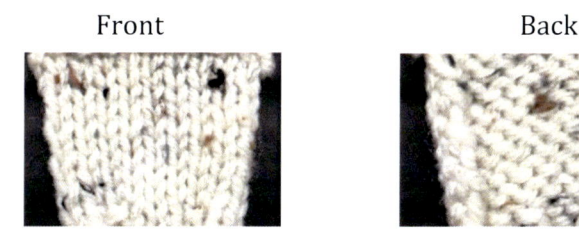

Front   Back

Figure 5: An example of purl knit.

Figure 6: An example of rib knit.

C.1.3 Nonwovens Other than Knits

Crocheting is also created by inter looping with a hooked needle that is available in several different sizes like the knitting needles. It is used for making laces and accessories. Likewise, lace can be made by **tatting** that uses a shuttle. Figure 7 shows fabric from crochet in beige and tatting shuttle in pink and turquoise. **Spunbonded and melt blown nonwovens as well as felts** are not as strong as the woven and knitted fabrics. They are mostly used as support fabrics, medical supplies and household wipes.

Figure 7: An example of crochet and tatting products.

C.2 Fabric Count (ASTM D 3775 - 17)

Fabric count refers to the number of warp (ends) and weft (pick) yarns per inch. Fabric should be tension free form. The convention of reporting the fabric count is Warp x Weft = Warp + Weft. For example, 100 x 75 = 175. The test requires five observations unless the coefficient of variation is more than 5%. In that case, one should use 10 specimens. For fabrics with five inches or less width, use ends for the entire width and picks for one inch at five spots. One can use linen tester as well as raveling technique for the fabric count. One can also use the repeats of weave for counting warp and filling yarns. Of course, digital methods can also be used via image analysis for enhanced efficiency.

ASTM D8007-2015 (2019) is developed for fabric count of weft knit fabrics. Wales and courses per inch are measured. The method can be used for jersey, rib, interlock, and pique knits. Wales are measured horizontally, and the courses are measured vertically. For reporting, it is written as wales x courses = wales + courses. For example, 35 x 51 = 86. No classification is provided in the standard. In general fabric count of knitted fabrics is lower than the woven fabrics.

Fabric count can be classified as low, medium, and high (Collier and Epps, 1999) for the practical purposes even though the standard does not specify so. There are between classification gaps. While interpreting, on needs to go to the closest number from the table. For example, if your values are 42 x42, label it as low rather than medium. Likewise, if your reading is 70 x 70, it can be classified as medium or high. However, if it is 71x72, label it as high. If it is 67 x70, then classify it as medium. Sometimes, it might be advantageous to look at the fabric count rather than ends and picks for this determination.

Table 11: Fabric Count Classification

Type	Classification
Low	10x10 to 40x40
Medium	45x45 to 65x65
High	>75x75

Fabric count is used to determine its quality. Higher fabric count is associated with better quality than the low fabric count. Chowdhary (2017) compared three brands of 100% cotton t-shirts for fabric count within the context of frequency of washing with commercial detergent. Fabric count increased significantly for all three brands between 5th and 25th wash. Differences were significant for two of the three brands for wales and all three brands for the courses. Originally, ASTM D3887 – 2004 was used for knitted fabrics. It is not presented in the 2020 issue of the manual.

C.3 Fabric Defects (ASTM D 3990 – 12 (Reapproved 2020)

This test identifies terminology and its definitions. Some examples of the defects of structural dimension are bow, broken filament or pick, float, seam mark, skew, slub, and snag. **Bow** refers to the nature of the fabric when warp and weft do not make an angle of 90 degrees but form an ark. **Broken filament** refers to the breaking of one or more filaments. **Float** refers to the part of the yarn that is not looped. **Seam mark** is the pressure mark that shows the seam thickness through the fabric when pressed. **Skew** refers to the state when warp and weft make an angle of less or more than 90 degrees. **Slub** refers to the bumpiness created in the yarn. **Snag** refers to the "pulled or plucked" from the flatness of the surface.

ASTM D3882 08 (Reapproved 2020) offers methods to determine bow and skew in woven and knitted fabrics. **Bow** can be of five different types: bow, double bow, double hooked bow, double reverse bow, and hooked bow. The bow should be ≤2% to pass for the woven fabrics and ≤5% for the knitted fabrics. Use the following steps for determining the bow of the fabric.

1. Straighten the woven fabric by either pulling a thread across the entire width or by tearing along the entire width.

2. Align the fabric along the straight lines of a table or the floor tiles.
3. Measure the distance between two selvages for the fabric width.
4. Draw a straight line between two ends of the selvages in a contrasting color pen.
5. Measure the diversion distance and identify the bow pattern as bow, double bow, hooked bow, double hooked bow, or double reverse bow.
6. Calculate the bow percentage by using the formula 100(bow depth/fabric width). For example, if ark height is .7" and fabric width is 45". The bow will be 100(.7/45) = 1.56%.
7. Compare the computed percentage against the standard. The value is less than 2%. Therefore, you will pass the material. If the bowed ark or diversion was 1.3" for 45" width, the bow % will be 2.89%. This fabric will fail.

Skew can be left-handed (S) and right-handed (Z). The passing grade for skew is ≤2.5% for the woven fabrics and ≤5% for the knitted fabrics

Follow the following steps for measuring and calculating skew.

1. Straighten the woven fabric by either pulling a thread across the entire width or by tearing along the entire width.
2. Align the fabric along the straight lines of a table or the floor tiles.
3. Measure the distance between two selvages for the fabric width.
4. Draw a straight line between two ends of the selvages in a contrasting color pen.
5. Measure the diversion distance and identify the skew pattern as Left Hand ("S') or Right Hand ("Z") type skew. Left hand moves upward to the left from the straight edge of the fabric. The Right hand moves downward from the straight edge of the fabric.
6. Calculate the skew percentage by using the formula 100(skew length/fabric width). For example, if ark height is .5" and fabric width is 45". The bow will be 100(.5/45) = 1.11%.
7. Compare the computed percentage against the standard. The value is less than 2.5%. Therefore, you will pass the material. If the skewed ark or diversion was 1.5" for 45" width, the bow % will be 3.33%. This fabric will fail because it is more than 2.5%.

Worth Street Textile Market Rules (1986) used penalty points to classify fabrics as first or second class. The penalty points are assigned based on the length of the defect. The table 12 shows the penalty point for each length of the defect.

Structural Attributes

Table 12: Assignment of penalty points for lengths of defect.

Length of Defect	Penalty Points Assigned
<3″	1
3″ – 6″	2
>6″-9″	3
>9″	4

Table 13 provides parameters for classifying fabrics based on their width and penalty points assigned. It gives information on different types of fabrics: Woven, coated and laminated, knitted, and Novelty.

Table 13: Classification and parameters of penalty points

Type of Fabric	Maximum number of Penalty Points/100 yards	Width of the Fabric	Classification
Woven	<41	≤50″	<41 = First
			≥41 = Second[c]
	<45	>50″	<45 = First
			≥41 = Second[c]
Circular Knits			
Basic	40	60/62″	<40 First
Surface Finished	50	60/62″	
Novelty Fabrics	43	60/62″	A
	47	60/62″	B
	50	60/62″	C
	53		D
Coated and	<7 Major[ab]	≤60″	6 or lower = First
Laminated	<8 Major[ab]	>60″	7 or higher = Second
Knitted Pile Fabrics	40	58/60	First = <50
Raschel Knit	40	60/62	
Tricot Knit	100	60/62″	≤3 = 1
			>3-9= 5
			>9 = 10

a   Major defects include smash, washed out oil spots, starchy places, group floats, heavy filling, shuttle marks, heavy warp, hard crease, kinky filling, crayon marks, and two missing threads over 9 inches.

b   Four defects that should not be present at all.

C   Tweaked slightly for better interpretation. For example, ≥41 rather than >40

Two examples of woven fabrics are provided below for the woven fabrics using the above-mentioned criteria. Example indicates defects of different dimensions for 100 yards. For less than 50" width and more than 50" width. The decision will be made for classifying first and second Class.

Example 1 For Woven Fabric

Fabric Defect Length	Frequency Fabric A	Penalty Points Fabric A	Frequency Fabric B	Penalty Points Fabric B	Fabric Width " <50
<3"	8	8	10	10	
3'-6"	5	10	7	14	
6"-9"	5	15	6	18	
>9"	1	4	2	8	
Total		37		50	
Decision		First Class		Second Class	

Example 2 for Woven Fabrics

Fabric Defect Length	Frequency Fabric A	Penalty Points Fabric A	Frequency Fabric B	Penalty Points Fabric B	Fabric Width " >50
<3"	8	8	19	10	
3'-6"	7	14	5	10	
6"-9"	5	15	5	15	
>9"	3	12	2	8	
Total		49		43	
Decision		Second		First	

C.4 Fabric Thickness (ASTM D 1777-96, Reapproved 2019)

Fabric thickness refers to the distance between the upper and lower surface of the fabric under controlled pressure. The test ASTM D 1777-96, Reapproved 2019 gives presser foot diameters, pressure applied, and readability for fabrics with different fabrics. Fabric thickness plays an important role in thermal insulation. Thicker materials provide higher level of warmth than the thinner fabrics from one viewpoint. Thermal insulation comes from the dead air points available in the fabric. Based on the Physics, two layers of thin materials can offer better insulation than one thick layer of the similar dimension. Thinning of fabric from abrasion over extended wear can result in weight and strength loss. Additionally, thicker fabrics are supposed to be less flexible and have poor drape. Additionally, they are bulkier than the thinner materials (Kadolph, 2007). It is measured in inches and mm.

Kundu and Chowdhary (2020) found that thinner jersey knit showed higher air permeability but lower horizontal wicking and evaporative resistance than thicker and heavier fabric. Whereas, specimens were not significantly different for thermal resistance, bursting strength and horizontal wicking. Thicker and heavier interlock knits exhibited higher bursting strength and evaporative resistance but lower air permeability than thinner and lighter fabrics. Thinner fabrics showed higher horizontal wicking than the than the thicker fabrics. Chowdhary (2017) compared three brands of 100% cotton t-shirts for fabric thickness within the context of frequency of washing with commercial detergent. Fabric thickness changed significantly for all three brands between 5th and 25th wash. However, it increased for two brands and decreased for the third brand.

Akgun (2015) reported when fineness of filaments increased roughness of the surface decreased. Increase in fabric density from use of fine fibers decreased fabric's porosity but increased cover. Fabric thickness and porosity significantly impact the moisture transport processes (Li, Zhu, Yeung, 2002). An increase in thickness of the angle interlock structure boosted the elongation (Chen, Spola, Gisbert, and Sellabona, 1999). In study by Mackay, Anand, and Bishop (1996), fabric thickness stayed the same after laundering.

C.5 Fabric Weight (ASTM D 3776/3776M - 2020)

Fabric weight refers to the mass per unit area expressed in ounces pe square yard or grams per square meter. The test standard ASTM D 3776/3776M – 2020 provides several formulae on pp 854-855 as follows.

1. **Option A - Full piece or rolls**

    $g/m^2 = 10^3 M/LW$

    M = Mass of fabric in kg

    L = Length of the fabric in yard

    W = Width of the fabric in yard

    $oz/yd^2 = 576\ M/LW$

    M = Mass of fabric in pounds

    L = Length of the fabric in meters

    W = Width of the fabric in meters

2. **Option B - Full Width Sample (at least 10" long)**

    $g/m^2 = 10^6 G/LW$

    G = Mass of specimen in grams

L = Length of the fabric in mm

W = Width of the fabric in mm

oz/yd² = 1296 G/LW

G = Mass of specimen in ounces

L = Length of the fabric in inches

W = Width of the fabric in inches

3. **Option C - Small Swatch of Fabric**

Specimen area = 100cm² or 15.5 inch²

g/m² = 10⁶G/A

G = Mass of specimen in grams

A = Area of the specimen mm²

W = Width of the fabric in mm

oz/yd² = 1296 G/LW

G = Mass of specimen in ounces

A = Area of the specimen in²

W = Width of the fabric in inches

Converting Ounces Per Square Yard to g/m²

g/m² = 33.906 x oz/yd²

Converting g/m² to oz/yd²

oz/yd² = (g/m²)/33.906

Structural Attributes

Table 14: Fabric weight classification by three authors. (Chowdhary 2009)

Classification	Collier and Epps, 1999	Kadolph and Langford, 2002	Cohen and Johnson, 2010
Very Light Weight	<1	-	<1
	(<25)	-	(<25)
Light Weight	2-3	<4	2-4
	(70-100)	-	(50-96)
Medium Weight	5-7.5	4-6	5-7
	(170-240)	-	(120-170)
Heavy Weight	9.5-12	>6	9-11
	(300-375)	-	(215-260)
Very Heavy Weight	>15	-	>14
	(>475)	-	(>350)
# in parentheses is g/m²			

As evident from the table, there are differences in three classifications. The categories range from three to 5. Additionally, there ar missing numbers between two classifications by the same author. It should not confuse the reader. They should reason out to determine the classification that your reading is closer to. For example, if your fabric weight is 400 g/m², classify it as heavy. However, if it is 450 g/m², classify it as very heavy. You will have to make that judgment because cuts are not crystal clear.

Kundu and Chowdhary (2020) examined the influence of fabric thickness and fabric weight on performance attributes of jersey and interlock knits. The researchers found that the differences were significant for the light and heavier fabrics for air permeability, evaporative resistance, bursting strength, and horizontal wicking. Heavier fabrics had high bursting strength and horizontal wicking but lower air permeability for both types of knits. Chowdhary (2017) compared three brands of 100% cotton t-shirts for fabric weight within the context of frequency of washing with commercial detergent. Fabric weight increased significantly for all three brands between 5th and 25th wash.

Rahman, Biswas, Mitra and Rakesh (2014) examined pilling resistance of jersey with Lycra, plain single jersey, 1x1 rib, single Lacoste, double Lacoste and interlock knit for grey fabric, with and without enzyme. Enzyme treatment smoothened the fabric and reduced pilling. Rahman et al. (2014) found that fabric weight reduced due to removal of pills and fuzziness after enzyme treatment.

SUMMARY

As evident from the preceding information, structural attributes provide infrastructure and impact quality and performance of textile materials. Microscopy helps with the fiber identification. Yarn crimp and twist are related to flexibility and strength. Yarn size is related to fabric weight. Fabric quality helps with determining the quality of fabrics. Fabric weight is related to intended end-uses. Fabric defects help with ensuring flawlessness of the material. Fabric thickness is associate with abrasion resistance and thermal insulation. Fabric construction helps with ascertaining of abrasion resistance, flexibility, raveling, snag resistance, and strength for the textile material. Collectively, this knowledge helps with educated decision making for intended end-uses.

REFERENCES

Akgun, M. (2015). Effect of yarn filament fineness on the surface roughness of the polyester woven fabric. *Journal of Engineered Fibers and Fabrics, 10*(2), 121-128.

Annual book of ASTM standards. (2020). *7.01,* West Conshohoken, PA: ASTM International.

Annual book of ASTM standards (2008). *7.01,* West Conshohoken, PA: ASTM International

Annual book of ASTM standards. (2019). *7.02,* West Conshohoken, PA: ASTM International.

Atalie, D., Ferede, A. & Rotich, G.K. Effect of weft yarn twist level on mechanical and sensorial comfort of 100% woven cotton fabrics. *Fashion and Textile,* **6**(3) (2019). https://doi.org/10.1186/s40691-018-0169-6

Behery, H. M. (2010). Yarn structural requirements for woven and knitted fabrics. *Advances in Yarn Spinning Technology,* 155-189.

Chen, M. Spola, J. Gisbert, P. and Sellabona, M. (1999). Experimental studies on the structure and mechanical properties of multi-layer and angle-interlock woven structures. *The Journal of Textile Institute, 90.1* (1), 91-99.

Chowdhary, U. (2019). Impact of interfacings and linings on breaking strength, elongation, and duration of the test for knitted wool. *International Journal of Textile Science and Engineering, 3*(1), 125. DOI:29o11/IJTSE-125/100025.

Chowdhary, U. (2017). Comparing three brands of cotton t-shirts. *AATCC Journal of Research, 4*(3), 22-33. DOI: 10.14504/ajr.4.3.3

Chowdhary, U., & Wentela, C, (2018). Impact of Support Fabrics on Breaking Strength, Elongation and Time Taken for the Test for Woven Fabrics in Different Fiber Contents. SSRG International Journal of Polymer and Textile Engineering (SSRG - IJPTE), 5(3), 1-6.

Chowdhary, U. (2009[a]). Seam strength, elongation, and seam efficiency of surged and un-surged seams. In Usha Chowdhary (Ed.) *Textile analysis, quality control and innovative uses.* (pp. 191-195). Deer Park, NY: LINUS.

Cohen, A.C., & Johnson, I. (2010). *Fabric Science.* New York, NY: Fairchild.

Collier, B. J., Bide, M., & Tortora, P. G. (2009). *Understanding textiles.* Upper Saddle River, NJ: Prentice Hall.

Ezazshahahi, N., Mousazadegan, F., Varkivani, S. M., & Saharkhiz, S. (2014). Crimp analysis of worsted fabrics in the terms of fabric extension behaviour. *Fibers and Polymers, 16*(6), 1211-1220.

International manual of test methods and procedures. (2021). *96,* Research Triangle Park, NC: American Association of Textile Chemists and Colorists.

Kadolph, S. J. (2007). *Quality assurance for textiles and apparel.* New York, NY: Fairchild.

Kadolph, S. J. (1998). *Quality assurance for textiles and apparel.* New York, NY: Fairchild.

Kundu, S. K., & Chowdhary, U. (2020). Comparison of comfort properties of jersey and interlock knits in polyester, cotton/spandex, and polyester/Rayon/Spandex. *International Journal of Polymer and Textile Engineering (SSRG - IJPTE), 7*(1), 6-22.

Li, Y., Zhu, Q., & Yeung, K. W. (2002). Influence of thickness and porosity on coupled heat and moisture transfer in porous materials. *Textile Research Journal, 72*(5), 435-446.

Mackay, C., Anand, S. C., & Bishop, D.C. (1996). Effects of laundering on sensory and mechanical properties of 1x1 rib knitwear fabrics. *Textile Research Journal, 66*(3), 151-157.

Maqsood, M., Hussain, T., Nawab, Y., Shaker, K., & Umair, M. (2014). Prediction of warp and weft yarn crimp in cotton woven fabric. *The Journal of Textile Institute,* DOI: 10.1080/00405000.2014.981041

Matsudaira, M., Kawabata, S, & Niwa, M. (1984). 29 - The effect of fibre crimp on fabric quality. *The Journal of Textile Institute, 75*(4), 273-277. https://doi.org/10.1080/00405008408631702

McGregor, A., Stanton, J., Beilby, J., Speijers, J., & Tester, J. (2015). The influence of fiber diameter, fabric attributes and environmental conditions on wetness sensations of next-to-skin knitwear. *Textile Research Journal, 85(*9), 912-928. https://doi.org/10.1177/0040517514555800

Omerglu, S., Mine, A., & Behcet, B. (2015). Effect of yarn twist levels on percentage reflectance of cotton fabrics woven with various construction parameters. *AATCC Journal of Research, 2*(1), 1-10. DOI: https://doi.org/10.14504/ajr. 2.1.1

Rahman, H., Biswas, P. K., Mitra, B. K., Rakesh, M.S.R. (2014). Effect of enzyme wash (cellulase enzyme) on properties of different weft knitted fabrics. *International Journal of Current Engineering and Technology, 4*(4), 4242-4248.

Stig, F., & Hallstrom, S. (2019). Effects of Crimp and Textile Architecture on the Stiffness and Strength of Composites with 3D Reinforcement *Advances in Material Science and Engineering, 1-8.* https://doi.org/10.1155/2019/8439530

Worth Street Textile Market Rules (1986). Retrieved document from *Worth Street Textile Market Rules* on

PRACTICE ACTIVITIES

1. Anne wanted to use polyester for lining her jacket. She had a pile of some leftover fabrics from a previous construction project. However, she did not label her left over projects. When she tested her fiber content under the microscope, one showed striations, and the other one showed speckles in a tubular structure. Which of the two is likely to be a polyester fabric?

2. What should you see under the microscope for polyester/cotton blend?

3. What should you see under the microscope for wool/cotton blend?

4. Yarn A has 15 crimps per inch and Yarn B has 20 crimps per inch. Which of the two yarns is likely to have higher flexibility?

5. If yarn A has five twists per inch and Yarn B has 12 twists per inch. Which of the two is likely to be stronger?

6. If you have to select a sewing thread between 12 and 24 Tex for jeans and t-shirts, which one will you choose for the jeans?

7. Of the two percale sheets with a fabric count of 100x100 = 200 and 300x300 = 600, which one will you buy for the silky feel and better quality? Justify your response with convincing explanation.

8. You purchased 100% cotton denim for jeans with twill view. When tested for skew, it had 3% skew. Based on the ASTM standard, will you pass/fail the fabric?

9. A 100% cotton t-shirt fabric had a skew of 4%. Will you accept or reject this fabric? Provide rationale for your decision.

10. A polyester knit fabric had a bow of 6%. Will you pass or fail the fabric and why?

11. For a knitted polyester/cotton golf shirt, what will you accept as the maximum bow and skew?

12. Name the units of yarn size by direct method.

13. What are the units of fabric weight?

14. What are the units used for bow and skew?

15. What are the units used for count, crimp, and twist?

16. What are some of the common end uses of plain, twill and satin weaves?

17. What is the difference between dobby and jacquard weave?

18. What is the difference between the construction of plain and oxford weave?

19. Will lower or higher count fabric have higher potential for shrinkage from laundering.

20. Will plain or satin weave snag more? Justify your choice.

21. What is the difference between single and ply yarn?

22. What is the direction of most yarns used in industry?

23. What is the unit for the repeat of the weaves?

24. Calculate penalty points for each fabric and classify as first or second class.

Structural Attributes

Fabric Defect Length	Frequency Fabric A	Penalty Points Fabric A	Frequency Fabric B	Penalty Points Fabric B	Fabric Width " <50
<3"	10		7		
3'-6"	6		8		
6"-9"	7		4		
>9"	2		1		
Total					
Decision					

25. Use data below to calculate Tex value and calculate mean and standard deviation for the Fabric B. Calculations are shown as example for Fabric A.

Fabric A #	Weight	Weight x 1000	Fabric B #	Weight	Weight x 1000
1	.008	8			
2	.008	8			
3	.008	8			
4	.009	9			
5	.009	9			
6	.009	9			
7	.009	9			
8	.010	10			
9	.010	10			
10	.010	10			

Mean   9.0 Tex

Standard Deviation   .817

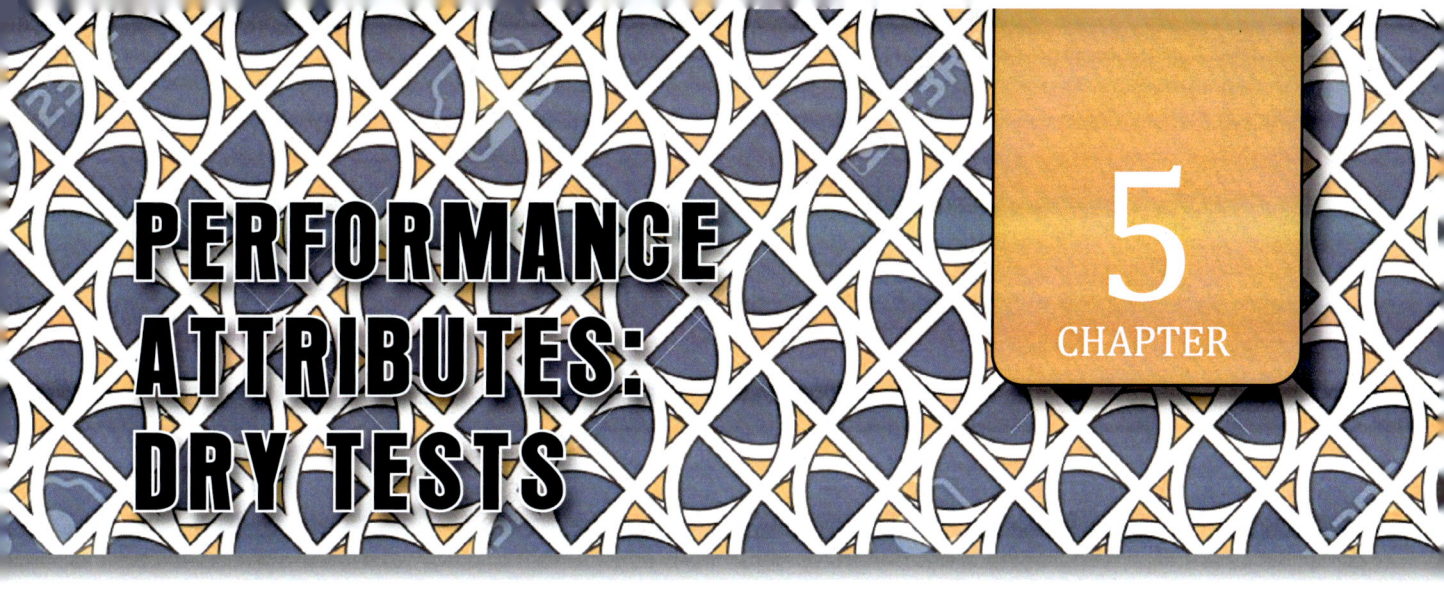

PERFORMANCE ATTRIBUTES: DRY TESTS

CHAPTER 5

Structural attributes make the fabric. However, performance attributes test the appropriateness of the textiles for the intended use by testing their ability to withstand wear and tear resulting from care, storage, and use. The resented set of tests focus on aesthetics, comfort, durability, and safety. These attributes are of important in everyday life for physical protection, psychological satisfaction, and social approval. This chapter covers the following performance tests that were predominantly developed by the ASTM members. The chapter discusses four functions of textiles as Aesthetic (abrasion, pilling and wrinkle resistance), comfort (air permeability, elongation and stretch and recovery), durability (abrasion resistance, breaking/bursting strength, and tear strength), safety (flame resistance), and sensory (fabric hand). Figure 8 shows five function related categories of the dry performance tests.

Aesthetic Attributes

This section focuses on abrasion resistance, pilling resistance and wrinkle resistance. Abrasion can change the appearance by making the fabric lighter in color, thinner from rubbing, and snags and holes from wear and care.

Comfort Attributes

This section includes air permeability, elongation, stretch and recovery, and thermal insulation. Air permeability enhances comfort by improving the breathability of the fabric. Elongation improves it by providing give and ease of movement. Stretch and recovery offers comfort through growth and flexibility. Thermal insulation refers to the ability of textile to offer warmth. It is opposite of thermal transmittance (*Annual book of ASTM standards*, 2020, p.66)

Figure 8: Classification of dry performance tests.

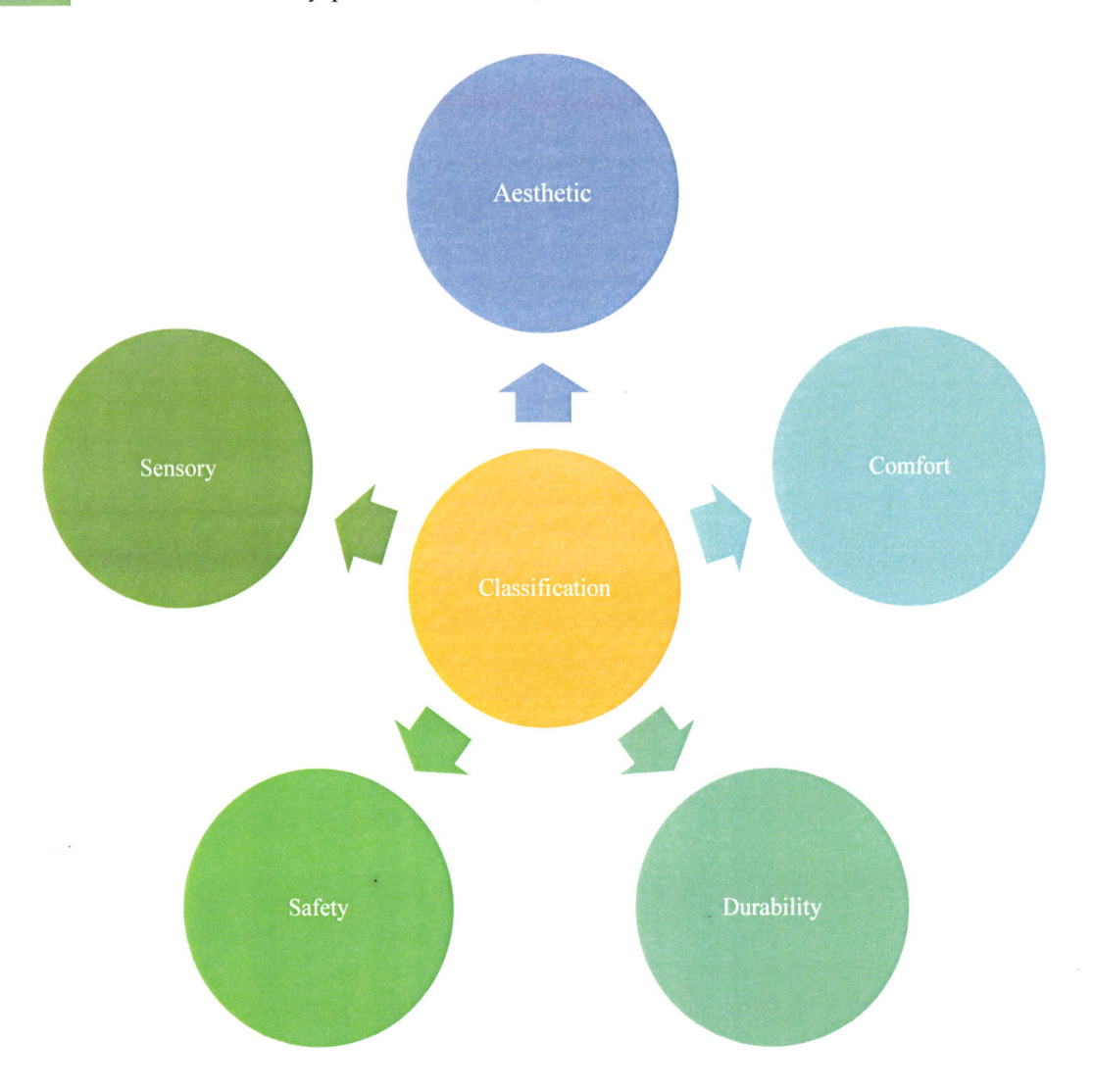

Durability Attributes

This set of characteristics includes abrasion resistance, breaking strength, bursting strength, seam strength and tear strength. Abrasion resistance prevents fading, thinning, and excessive wear and tear. Breaking strength provides protection from stresses of everyday wear for woven fabrics. It is measured in pounds per square inch (psi). It varies from one end-use to another. For example, it is 25 psi minimum for linings and 50 psi minimum for fashion fabrics. Bursting strength is the best choice for the knitted materials. Tear strength resists spread of tear.

Tear strength also has different standards for different end uses. For example, ≥1.5 psi for lining and ≥2.5 psi for the fashion fabrics. Seam strength is also measured in pounds per square inch. However, seam efficiency is reported in percentage. Seam strength is important for sewn products.

Safety Attribute

Flame resistance is the safety attribute that offers protection for the wearer if certain standards are met. It is tested by vertical and 45 degrees angle method.

Sensory Attribute

Fabric hand is the sensory characteristic. It is rated based on touch.

AESTHETIC ATTRIBUTES

(Abrasion Resistance, Pilling Resistance and Wrinkle Resistance)

Abrasion Resistance refers to the ability of resisting wearing away when rubbed against other surfaces (ASTM D3884-09, Reapproved 2017). Abrasion is a function of friction and impact on appearance and comfort of textiles. Ahmed and Slater (1989) reported that abrasion caused disintegration of fiber, yarn, and fabric. For cotton, polyester, silk, and wool, it also increased softness and reduced thickness for all but polyester. Wyzenbeek methods tests with rubs and warp and weft direction. However, Martindale test moves in the figure 8 direction. Wyzenbeek test continues until two yarns break. In Martindale test, it continues until there is a yarn break, pilling, and holes. In double head abrasion, a number of cycles after the formation of hole are recorded.

    ASTM does not provide specific values for passing or failing the fabric. Kadolph (2007) reported that regular apparel should withstand at least 750 cycles. Specifically, Kadolph (2007) reported 750 cycles minimum for shirts and 1000 cycles for pants and shorts using the Tabor Abraser Method. For light upholstery, she recommended 3000 via use of the oscillatory cylinder method test (ASTM D4157-13, Reapproved 2017). Based on the Martindale test (ASTM D4966-12, reapproved 2016), it should be 20.000 double rubs.

    Previous research shows that type of spinning of yarns, finishes, and alumina particles impact the abrasion resistance of fabrics. Omeroglu and Ulku (2007) found that the 100% combed cotton made from conventional or compact ring spun yarns from compact ring spun yarns had higher abrasion than the fabrics made from conventional yarns. Terry fabric had the worst surface appearance after 40000 rubs (Emirhanova, & Kavusturan, 2008). The coating in the study improved both abrasion and pilling resistance. "PET/CO (67:33)" improved the abrasion resistance by 38% (Rosace, Canton, &Colleoni, 2010; Brzezinski, Kowalczyk, Borak, Jasiorski, & Tracz, 2011). Alongi and Mallucelli (2013) found that the presence of alumina particles increased abrasion resistance greatly.

Pilling Resistance

Pilling resistance refers to the prevention of ball formation on the fabric surface from tangled fibers resulting from abrasion Chowdhary, 2009, p. 82). The random Tumble Pilling Tester is used for testing pilling resistance (ASTM D3512/3512M – 2016). Pilling is an important characteristic because the pilled garment impacts appearance, color, hand and weight (Figure 9). Pills are the formation of balls from the fuzz due to friction between two surfaces. The specimens are rated on a five-point scale. One represents the worst performance (worst pilling) and 5 represents the best performance (least pilling). Recommended performance specification for regular apparel is 3.5 minimum (Chowdhary, 2009, p. 82). Pills do not have any unit of analysis. Their readings range from 1-5. However, if it is found to be between two ratings, it is suggested to record as 2.5, 3.5, etc.

Figure 9: Pilled specimen of a knitted fabric.

Quality of fabrics is a function of its ability to retain its original appearance even after wear and care over time. The friction experienced by garments during wear and care can create the pills on the garment. Pilled garments take away from the aesthetics of the garment and give them a used look. Pills refer to bunches or balls of tangled fibers held on the fabric surface by one or more fibers temporarily or permanently (Annual Book of ASTM Standards, 2008, *7.01*; Chowdhary, 2007; Merkel, 1991). Merkel (1991) described pill formation as a three-step process consisting of development of fuzz, tangling of fuzz into pills, and breaking away of pills.

Soft-finished staple fibers and blends with polyester were reported to pill more than the filament and textured yarns (Kadolph & Langford, 1998; Collier and Epps, 1999). Kadolph (2007) reported that the abrasion resulting from the agitation during the cleaning process could cause the textile to snag, pill and get distorted. Pilling can adversely affect the appearance, feel, texture and service of the textile material (Goswami, Duckett, and Vigo, 1980). Chowdhary (2007) presented annotations on pilling that could be categorized in the following three sections: Textile's mechanical structure and pilling, subjective and objective measurement of pills, and performance-driven pilling.

Mechanical Properties and Pilling

This section reports on the research studies that discussed pill formation in general as well as for selected fiber contents, yarn types, fabric constructions, bio-polishing, and textile care processes. Goswami, Duckett, & Vigo (1980) provide literature to describe pill formation due to mechanical action of rubbing, laundering, and drying during the wear and cleaning process. Fuzz formation (first stage) was reported as the function of friction and bending stiffness of fibers. The second stage of entanglement of fibers was attributed to the linear density of fiber, and shape of cross-section. The third stage of pill formation was reported to be the influence of abrasion resistance. The scholars used cotton/polyester shirt that had been washed six times as the specimen. The authors found that polyester fibers were entangled in active manner and cotton fibers played a passive role. However, polyester was flaked and cracked which activated the entanglement process. The authors concluded that Torsional fatigue process was responsible for interlocking of fibers and formation of pills.

Ruppenicker & Russell (1981) reported that knit structures from high cotton content blends with polyester showed some problems with pilling. Candon and Onal (2002) reported that pilling was higher for plain jersey than lacoste and two-thread fleece. McCloskey and Jump (2005) asserted that bio-polishing of polyester and polyester-cotton blend enhanced their pilling 3 resistance. Srinivasan, Ramakrishnan, Mukhopadhyay & Manoharan (2005) reported that the pilling resistance of the polyester microdenier and normal denier fibers did not differ significantly in their study. Akgun, Becerir, & Alpay (2006) reported that fuzz was observed for the filament yarns, and pill was noticed for the staple yarns. Hearle & Wilkins (2006) focused on the role fiber movements during fiber assemblies on forms of entanglements that can make the fibers and yarns knotted. Kretzschmar, Özgüney, Özçelik, & Özerdem (2007) reported that jersey, rib and interlock knits made from compact yarns had higher pilling resistance than those made from ring spun yarns.

Can (2008) tested three plain weave fabrics that had same fabric count but three different yarn types: ring carded, ring combed, and open-end rotor spun yarns. Findings revealed that the fabric woven from the open-end rotor spun yarns showed highest pilling and the ring combed spun yarns had the lowest pilling. They also noted that abrasion resistance and pilling were related to each other. Knowledge about one can help one predict the other. Wang and Jin (2008) reported that attaching a reducing hairiness nozzle on a winding machine resulted in less pilling and smoother surface than without such attachment. Emirhanova and Kavusturan, (2008) evaluated 14 different structures of 80/20 blend of lambswool and polyamide outerwear fabric in knit structure for abrasion resistance, air permeability, bending rigidity, bursting 4 strength, and dimensional stability. Findings revealed that moss and seed stitch fabrics had the best pilling resistance. Akaydin (2009) also found that compact yarns had higher bursting strength and lower pilling. Akaydin and Can (2010) reported that interlock knits have better pilling resistance than jersey knits and compact yarns offer higher pilling resistance than the ring spun yarns. A study by Li, Zhu, & Wei (2014) revealed that mule yarn pilled more than the ring spun yarn. However, 'worn off weight' was less for mule yarn than the ring spun yarn. Smriti and Islam (2015) found that fabrics with higher weight pilled more than with lower weight. Addition of polyester to cotton increased pilling. Singed fabrics pilled less than the unsigned fabrics. Telli and Ozdil (2015) found that pills were more likely to be formed with PET blends versus cotton blends. Adding 30%r-PET could enhance bursting strength and reduce pilling. As evident from the preceding information, pilling can be a function of several factors. These factors that influence pilling resistance could be fiber content, fiber length, yarn type, fabric construction, bio-polishing, and rubbing action.

Measurement of Pills

Literature review provided mixed results from various subjective and objective instruments used by the previous researchers. The methods used consisted of image analysis, comparison of image analysis to the photographic images, and measurement of height, width, intensity and frequency of the pills. Some researchers recommended use of multiple methods to 5 enhance objectivity of interpretation. A brief account of various instruments used by the researchers of the reviewed literature is provided below.

Amirbayat and Alagha (1994) did objective assessment of fabric pilling for fifty knitted fabrics going beyond the number of pills alone. They examined the total projected area, the total number, the maximum projected area of the largest pill within the sample, and maximum height of the tallest pill. The authors asked for further investigation of the topic. Hsi, Breese, & Annis (1998a, 1998b) used image-analysis techniques for pill detection as well as comparison with the visual pill ratings. Authors developed software to accomplish the task. Recommendation was made to eliminate the specimens with uneven pilling. Pill detection was found to be easier with the wear test rather than the laboratory test. In the comparison study of 122 fabrics that used both visual and image analysis methods, no correlations were found. The authors concluded that subjective visual rating by using ASTM photographic standards was found to be both convenient and familiar instrument that could be applied to a vast variety of fabrics as opposed to the image analysis software. However, visual comparison considers the number of pills as the only factor. However, several other details could be observed through image analysis software that could not be used effectively for dark colored and textured fabrics.

Collier and Epps (1999) reported that fabrics with staple fibers and low twist are more likely to pill than the filament and high twist fibers. Ukponmwan, Mukhopadhyay, & Chatterjee (1999) reported that lack of reproducibility was one of the problems with pilling measurement test methods. Latifi, Kim, & Pourdehimi (2001) used cylindrical lighting to assess fabric pilling for 100% combed cotton and polyester (Coolmax). They found that it was easier to observe pills by this method than the visual inspection with the naked eye. They were similar with pilling up to 2000 cycles. However, after 2000 cycles, polyester was found to pill more than cotton.

Goktepe (2002) used three different methods for what their sensitivities and tested three different fabrics under normal and wet conditions. The author stressed that in the raw form three methods differed for their sensitivities. The pilling box test is sensitive to blend ratio, weave type, and fabric stretch direction (single or double). The pilling drum method was noted to show similar tendency except it does not pick-up the weave type as readily. Martindale test is sensitive only to the stretch direction and yarn count. In the finished stage, the pill box as well as the Martindale tests showed sensitivity to yarn count and twist along with the direction of the stretch. The Pilling drum performed similar in raw and wet forms. The author noted that the Martindale test graded lower than the other two tests. Because all tests did not show sensitivity toward same mechanical structures of the textile, the author recommended to use more than one method.

Xin, Hu, and Yan (2002) also used image analysis technique for plain knitted wool. The authors asserted that illumination technique helped with seeing of pills better than the naked eye approach. Omerglu and Ulku (2007) examined 100% combed cotton made from conventional or compact ring spun yarns for abrasion, pilling and tensile strength. Results revealed that fabrics made from compact ring spun yarns had higher abrasion and pilling resistance, and breaking strength than the fabrics made from conventional yarns. Chowdhary (2007[a]) reported that several researchers are involved with development and testing of the objective methods to measure pilling. However, comparison between the subjective and objective methods is still ongoing. Mendes, Fiadeiro, Miguel, and Lucas (2009) proposed an alternative/complementary approach for quantifying pilling based on optical triangulation that they claimed, "to be precise, robust, and 7 systematic." (p. 410). Chowdhary, Hoque, Hutson, Thurston, Vanderploeg, and Zfenix (2016) found that even though several objective and subjective measurement techniques were used in the reviewed literature, each warranted further investigation to allow generalizing of the technique used. They also found that objective method showed higher number of pills than were seen by the human eye. The objective pilling tester used in the study was developed by Dr. Thamil Periyaswamy at Central Michigan University. The objective analyzer records number of pills as well as the ASTM based rating from 1-5. Image for woven and knit structure with outcome from the objective pill classifier is provided below (Figure 10). Currently, the classifier is being updated by the developer for bringing it closer to the visual observation than in its existing form.

Figure 10: Image of woven fabric with rating of 1.

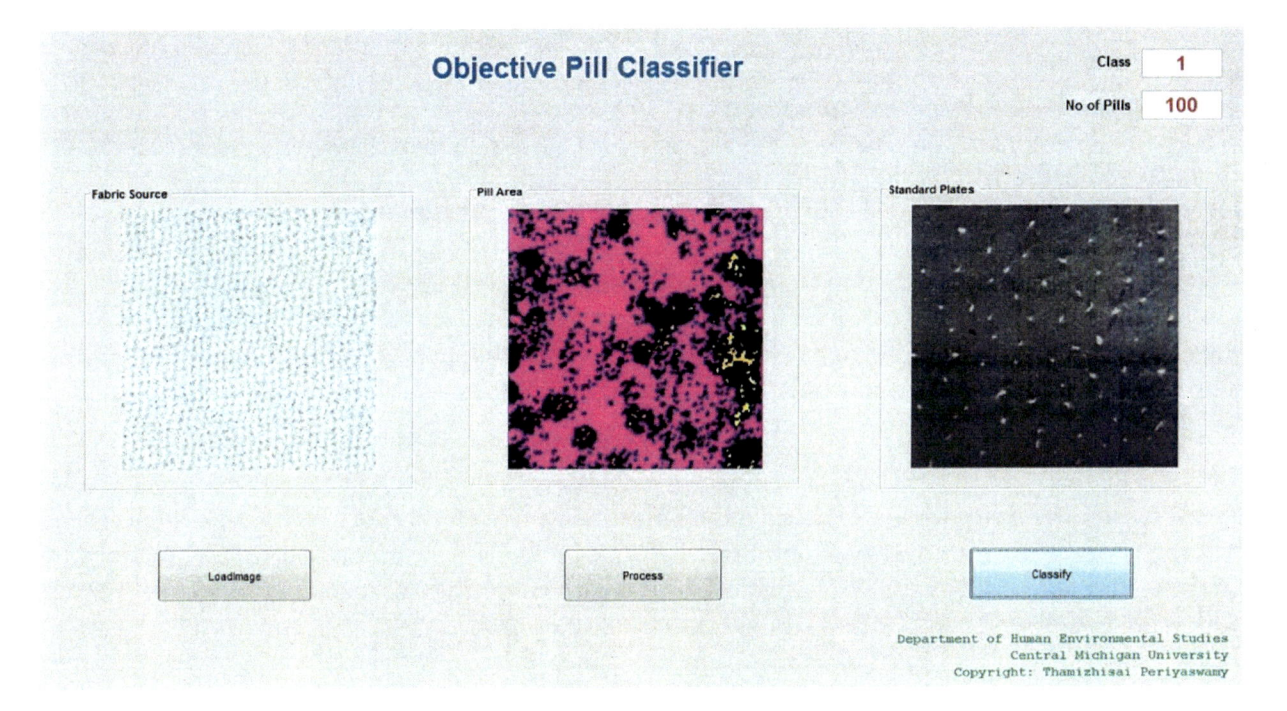

Previous scholars who talked about the objective measurement techniques did not provide comparison of the specimen, process evaluation and the pilling structure. All investigations did not use the same instruments in their scholarly work. Therefore, it was hard to compare different methods.

Performance-Driven Pilling

This section reports the studies that reveal the impact of care on pilling. Candon and Onal (2002) reported that pilling increased with successive launderings. Chiweshe & Crews (2000) reported that wet fabric softeners caused higher pilling for shirts, pajamas, and sleepwear made from the flannel. Cellulase enzymes were found to be effective in reducing fuzziness and pilling of some of the cotton fabrics. Collier, Bide, and Tortora (2009) reported that pilling is more of a problem with stronger than weaker fabrics because the pills do not break away easily and stay on the fabrics. Ibrahim, Khalifa, Hossamy, & Twafik (2010) examined the impact of knit structure and finishes on their four finishes were applied and three structures were used. Light Melton, single jersey and single pique. The four finishes were Soft-Finish, Bio-Finish, antibacterial and water repellent finish. The scholars examined absorbency, air permeability, bursting strength, fabric weight, heat transmittance, pilling rate, roughness, stain release, shrinkage, and 8 stiffness. Findings revealed that fabric with Bio-finish shrank the least and with soft finish shrank the most. Unfinished fabric pilled the most and fabric with Bio-finish pilled the least.

Brzezinski, Kowalczyk, Borak, Jasiorski, & Tracz (2011) reported that the coating improved pilling resistance. Pilling resistance was measured using the Martindale test. Pilling resistance of the finished fabric was 5 with "PET/CO (67:33)" finish (p. 83) on a rating scale of 1 (worst pilling) to 5 (No pilling). Chowdhary (2017) compared three brands of 100% cotton t-shirts for pilling resistance within the context of frequency of washing with commercial detergent. Pilling resistance decreased significantly between 5th and 25th wash for all three brands of t-shirts.

Wrinkle Recovery (AATCC TM128-2017e)

Wrinkle recovery to the ability of the fabric to free itself from the folding deformations over time. The test method recommends the use of 6" x 11" specimens. The test simulates wrinkling by placing the specimen between two flanges with a set weight of 3500 grams on the top flange. Weights are removed after 20 minutes and the specimen is hung for 24 hours before evaluation. The specimens are then evaluated against the standard wrinkle recovery replicas from four feet away under the fluorescent light. The specimens are rated from 1-5. Five indicates the best performance (least wrinkling), and 1 as the worst performance (most wrinkling). To pass the fabric, a rating of 3.5 minimum is needed. Standards should be raised for the better quality apparel.

In Baumert and Crews' study (2000), fabric softeners improved the recovery from wrinkles for all fabrics but the polyester/cotton blend. Kang and Kim (2001) reported that silicone treatment improved the wrinkle recovery but also increased the yellowness in the treated fabric. Kuzuhara and Hori (2002) mentioned that increase in moisture regain enhanced hydrogen bonding and improved the wrinkle recovery. Yang, Zhou, Lickfield, and Parachura (2003) informed that cellulose treatment of durable press finish cotton did not make any difference for wrinkle resistance. Yatagai & Takahashi (2005) stated that use of citric acid treatment with particulate soil improved the wrinkle recovery of cotton fabric. Doty and Easter (2009) reported that active wear received slightly higher ratings for smoothness retention than the workwear after 20 launderings.

The newly developed measurement system was noted to have three important changes: removed bias, recorded complete change, and yields more accurate and efficient readings (Wang, Liu, Pan, & Gao, 2014). Dyeing enhanced wrinkle recovery of the fabric (Hazavehi, Shahidi, & Zolgharnein (2015). Both mercerization as pretreatment and use of sol-gel application enhanced the wrinkle resistance of the linen fabrics. (Arik, 2020)

COMFORT RELATED ATTRIBUTES

(Air permeability, Elongation, Stretch and Recovery, Thermal Insulation)

Air Permeability

Air permeability refers to "the rate of air flow passing perpendicular through a known area under a prescribed air pressure differential between the two surfaces of a material." via test standard ASTM D737-18 (*2020 annual Book of ASTM Standards,* p. 10). It is measured as in inch-pound units as $ft^3/min/ft^2$ and SI units as $cm^3/s/cm^2$.

Fahmy and Slater (1977) identified air permeability, fabric thickness, fabric weight, and thermal resistance as factors that can be controlled to enhance the body comfort. Ahmed and Slater (1989) reported that increased abrasion enhanced air permeability. Zhang, Gong, Yanai, and Tokura (2002) added that air permeability of fabrics with high cover is low. Ogulata (2006) found that fabric count impacts air permeability. Increase in number of decreases air permeability. So is true for the number of twists. Increase in number of twists decreases the air permeability. The author also reported that permeability and porosity are related to each other strongly. Air permeability was noted as one of the three attributes related to comfort. Its measuring units were noted as cm3/s/cm2 and ft3/m/ft2. Lee and Obendorf (2007) found that nonwovens had higher air permeability than the woven fabrics. Majumdar, Mukhopadhyay and Yadav (2010) reported that air permeability is higher for the plain than rib and interlock fabrics.

Air permeability was defined as the ability of air to flow through the fabric. Coruh (2015) examined 4 blends (cotton/viscose, cotton/polyester (40/60, and 30/70), and cotton/poly as single jersey knit. Results revealed that increase in the loop length decreased in loop length increased the air permeability and wearer's comfort. Increase in thickness reduced the air permeability.

Wroblewski (2017) conducted a research to determine a relationship of quilting to air permeability and thermal insulation. Air Permeability (l/m2/m3) was measured using the TexTest FX 3300 Labair permeability machine. Following ASTM 737 -04 (2012) and ISO 9237. The test head surface area of 5 cm2 was used with a pressure differential of 125 Pascals. Findings revealed that three quilting structures did not differ for air permeability. Additionally, air permeability was not found to be related to fabric thickness and weight either.

Air permeability differences existed between knitted t-shirts from 100% cotton and 50/50 cotton/polyester blend. Both fabrics also differed in washed and unwashed forms (Marsha and Chowdhary, 2018). Kundu and Chowdhary (2018) found that air permeability was highest for polyester followed by rayon and cotton. Spandex was common fiber content in all blends. Filiz (2018) uncovered that the towels with longer pile had lower air permeability. However, those with bamboo in towels had higher air permeability. Kundu and Chowdhary (2020) found that lighter and heavier fabrics had higher air permeability than heavier and thicker fabrics for both jersey and interlock knits.

Elongation

Elongation refers to the ability of fabric to extend or stretch before it breaks. Based on the ASTM standard, it is represented in percentage (ASTM D5035-11, Reapproved 2019). An output from the Instron machine's output gives elongation both in inch/inch as well as percentage. Chowdhary (2007) suggested a minimum of 5% for the regular apparel. Elongation is affected by several structural fabric attributes.

Elongation of Kenaf/cotton blend increased after mercerization (Ramaswamy and Wang, 1999). Increased thickness of the angle-interlock structure enhanced the elongation (Chen, Spola, Gisbert, and Sellabona, 1999). It was higher for warp than weft in their study. Kislak (1999) asserted that the pivoting areas of the body like knees and elbows in a garment go through cyclical stresses that cause spherical deformation of the fabric. Therefore, linear testing may not justify the complex impact of bagging optimally. Sular and Seki (2018) provided an extensive review of fabric bagging, its definition and measurement.

Liquid ammonia treatment increased the elongation of linen fabrics Csiszar and Dornyi, 2006). Jersey, rib, and interlock knits made from compact yarns had higher bursting strength, elongation and pilling resistance than those made from ring spun yarns (Kretzschmar, Özgüney, Özçelik, & Özerdem, 2007). Serged seams elongated more than the unserged seams for both directions (Chowdhary, 2009). So was true for serged and unserged seams inclusively. Seam efficiency was highest for weft serged seam followed by warp unserged, weft unserged and warp serged. The extension and bursting strength of "denim viewed knitted fabrics" (Degirmenci, Celik, Ghaziantep and Cukurova, 2016). They argued the importance of these parameters for quality. Chowdhary and Wentela (2018) had the lowest elongation for linen. Additionally, it was less for acetate than polyester.

Stretch and Recovery

In the era of casual lifestyle and extensive use of the knitted materials, it is of critical importance to pay attention to the measurement and interpretation of stretch and recovery. **Stretch** refers to the growth of fabric with mechanical pressure and recovery refers to its return to the original position. 2020 Annual Book of *ASTM Standards* (2020, p. 57) defined woven stretch fabric as material that can expand at least 20%. Depending on the type of knit, it stretches in both directions as well as diagonally. However, woven fabrics stretch the most in the diagonal direction the most unless they are a blend of spandex. Cao, Branson, Peksoz, Nam, & Farr (2006) stated that fabrics with 100% polyester and 20% spandex were rated the best because of their knit structure, wicking. Moisture management and stretch property. Tamanna, Suruj-Zaman, Mondal, & Saha (2017) reported that stretch of weft knit is influenced by fabric count, thickness, and weight.

Chowdhary (2018) compared jersey and interlock knits by the industrial and BS4294-1968 methods. Findings revealed that % of spandex did not impact stretch % proportionately. The stretch was 120% for the 5% and 9% spandex and 84% for the 12% spandex in the crosswise direction. For jersey knits, it was similar for the lengthwise direction. Two interlock knits with the same fiber content performed differently. Two blends with different fiber contents did not have similar performance either. Poly/cotton blend stretched more than rayon/nylon/spandex interlock knit. Fabric counts also impacted the stretch of the tested knits. However, results did not differ for two methods: BS4294 and the industrial.

Fabric thickness was not significantly related to stretch but fiber content was. Rayon/spandex blend had the highest stretch (175%) followed by polyester (155%) and cotton (153%). So was true for the recovery that was 94.91% for poly/spandex, 91.93% for rayon/spandex, and 89.52% for cotton/spandex. However, differences were not significant between cotton and polyester. They differed significantly between cotton/spandex and rayon/spandex as well as polyester/spandex and rayon/spandex. (Kundu and Chowdhary, 2018) Stretch was highest for medium weight/low count, poly/acrylic blend for the interlock knits, heavy weight/low count bamboo/spandex (95/5%) for jersey knit and light weight/light count 100% cotton for pique knits (Chowdhary and Adnan, 2019). The authors used the industrial method for measuring stretch.

Thermal Insulation

Thermal insulation provides body comfort by providing warmth to the wearer. It is an important consideration during cold weather to prevent hypothermia. Designing strengthens it through layering or introduction of different fillers like cotton or polyester fibers and feathers.

Fahmy and Slater (1977) identified thermal resistance as one of the four important factors of body comfort. Chen, Fan and Zhang (2003) asserted that the clothing thermal insulation of the sweating body is 2-8% less than the non-sweating body. Lapitsky and Dickey (2006) reported that women wore pants the most to keep warm indoors. The other above average mean choices were jackets, layered clothing, sweaters, vests, and warm pajamas for thermal comfort. Layered clothing explained the highest variance (44.3%) of the fourteen choices. The socks, heavy socks, high neckline, and thermal underwear collectively accounted for 83.9% of the variance. Responding participants valued comfort the most. It was followed by a tie between easy care, economics, and warmth.

Heat loss was significantly reduced through improved ventilation designs (McQuerry, Emiel, & Roger, 2016). Atasagun, Okur and Psikuta (2019) reiterated the importance of layered clothing on thermal comfort. Raw material of undershirt had higher impact on the chest and fit influenced back the most. Kavitha, & Gokarneshan (2019) reported that engineered protective clothing can people with creation of optimum heat balance between human body and environmental condition for enhanced body comfort. Teyeme, Malengier, Tesfaye, Vasile, & Langenhove (2020) asserted that fabric choice for cyclists impact their thermophysiological responses.

DURABILITY ATTRIBUTES

(Abrasion resistance, breaking strength, bursting strength, seam strength and tear strength)

Abrasion Resistance

Thinning of fabrics reduces the strength of the fabrics. Treating with special finishes improves the abrasion resistance, Abrasion, strength, and weight are related with each other. AATCC 93 – is known as the accelerotor method of determining abrasion resistance. The specimens for one method are cut based on the fabric weight. In everyday wear, abrasion can occur between two fabric parts, between the human body and the fabric, between fabric and other objects like wooden or metal chairs, and other materials like dirt, grass, and sand. Specimen size is smaller for the bulky fabrics than the lightweight fabrics (*Manual of International Test Methods and Procedures,* 2021, p.156). Table 15 below shows the details.

Table 15: Fabric weights and the corresponding specimen sizes.

Fabric Weight in g/m^2	Specimen Size in mm	Fabric weight in oz/yd^2	Specimen size in inches
300-400	95	9-12	3.75
200-300	115	6-9	4.5
100-200	135	3-6	5.25
Less than 100	150	Less than 3	6

For the first method cut a square of appropriate dimensions. Edges should be cut with the pinking shears. Apply adhesive to prevent fraying when in the accelerotor. Dry the adhesive before weighing. For option B, cut 4 x 12" specimen and cut in half in length that will give you two pieces of 6' x 4".

Use one for test and leave one as control. Measure pre- and post- treatment pieces for percentage of strength and weight losses. The formulas for weight and strength loss are as follows.

Weight Loss % = 100 (A-B)/A

A = Original (pre-treatment) weight

B = Post-treatment weight

Example

Pre-weight = 5 grams

Post weight = 4.7 grams

Weight Loss % = 100(0.3/5) = 6%

Strength Loss % = 100 (A-B)/A

A = Original (pre-treatment) strength

B = Post-treatment strength

Example

Pre-strength = 90 psi

Post-strength= 84 psi

100(6/90) = 6.67%

Breaking Strength

Breaking strength is an important variable that impacts the durability of fabric. Ahmed and Slater (1989) reported that wool and silk lost strength with increased abrasion in their study. Breaking strength refers to the maximum ability of the fabric to withstand the tensile load or force before the specimen ruptures (*2020 Annual book of ASTM standards*, p. 13). Unit of analysis for breaking strength is pounds per square inch. It is measured by three types of machines: CRE (Constant Rate of Extension), CRL (Constant Rate of Load), and CRT (Constant Rate of Traverse). For example, a CRE machine has carriage speed set at 12 inches per minute ±.5 minutes for the breaking strength and 2 inches per minute for the tearing strength. CRE is the most commonly used machine for breaking strength (ASTM D5034-2017 and 5035-2017), bursting strength (ASTM D6797-2015) seam strength (ASTM D1683 –2018) and tear strength (ASTM D2261–2018). Breaking strength of fabrics is measured by two methods: Strip method and grab methods. Fabric specimen is unraveled along the longer direction for quarter inch on both sides. The specimen size used for this test is 6" x 1.5" for the woven fabrics and 6" x 1" for the knit fabrics. For grab method, the specimen size is 6" x 4" (Figures 11a and 11b) and figures 12a and 12b show specimens of breaking strength by strip methods. Rupture in general refers to the breaking or tearing of the fabric. Rupture in the seam strength includes breaking of threads of the seam, as well as breaking of the fabric before the seam.

Figure 10a: Warp specimen by grab method

Figure 10b: Weft specimen by grab method

Figure 11a: Warp specimen for strip method. Untested (L) Tested (R)

Figure 11b: Warp specimen for strip method. Untested (L) Tested (R)

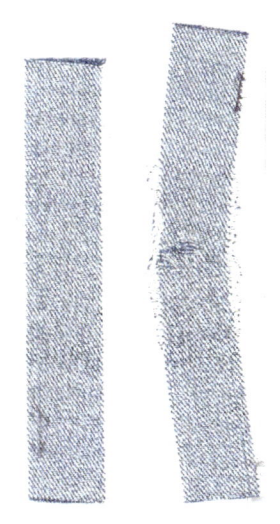

Table 16: Requirements of breaking strength for various end uses by ASTM.

.#	End Use	Minimum Requirement
1.	Lining (Woven) ASTM D3783, 4114-14	25 psi
2.	Women's Sportswear ASTM D4155 - 14	Worsted cotton warp 35 psi Worsted cotton warp 30 psi Woolen 25 psi
3.	Woven Dry Cleanable Coat for Men's and Boys' ASTM D3562-14	30 psi
4.	Woven Dry Cleanable Coat for Women's and Girls ASTM D3562 -14	25 psi (Napped Length) 20 psi (Napped 30 psi Width)
5.	Woven Swimwear ASTM D 3994 - 14	Non-Stretch 30 psi Stretch 20 psi
6.	Umbrella Fabrics ASTM D4112	35 psi (Dry) 20 psi (Wet)
7.	Rainwear ASTM D7017 -14	40 psi
8.	Men's and Boy's Knitted and woven beachwear and sports shirt ASTM D4154 - 2014	25 psi (Woven)
9.	Corset-Girdle combination fabrics ASTM D4116-2020	70 psi (Woven) CRT
10.	Bras, Slips, Lingerie, and Underwear ASTM D7019-14	Sheer 15 psi Non-Sheer 25 psi
11.	Blouse, Dress, Dress Shirt and Sport Shirt ASTM D7020-14	Sheer 15 psi Non-Sheer 25 psi Dress and Sport Shirt 25 psi
12.	Bathrobe, Dressing Gown, Negligee, Nightgown, & Pajamas ASTM D7021-14	Sheer 15 psi Non-Sheer 25 psi
13.	Women's and Girls' Knitted and Woven Dress Gloves ASTM D4115-20	50 psi

Ramaswamy and Wang (1999) reported that elongation of Kenaf/cotton blend increased after mercerization. Fabric softeners reduced the breaking strength (Chiweshe, 2000, Kang & Kim, 2001). The stretch breaking process of wool resulted in lower elongation and higher breaking strength. Modulus of the broken fiber was higher than the unbroken one (Kwak, Lee, Lee, & Jeon, 2007). Omeroglu and Ulku (2007) found that the fabrics made from compact ring spun yarns had higher breaking strength than the fabrics made from conventional yarns. Chowdhary (2009) reported that in the study of serged seams tensile strength was higher in weft than warp direction. However, it was consistent with convention for the men's shirt fabrics.

Fabric with modal weft had higher tensile and tear strength than the fabrics with bamboo weft (Zubair, Maqsood, and Neckar, 2016). Polyester/Cotton blends also had high tear and tensile strength in their study. Plain weave was stronger than the twill weave (Jahan, 2017). Addition of interfacing did not always add to the strength of the fashion fabric that was knitted wool in this case. Polyester was found to be stronger than acetate that has been traditionally used for lining (Chowdhary and Wentela, 2018).

Bursting Strength

Bursting strength refers to the force required to rupture the knitted fabric under controlled conditions (ASTM D-6797-2015) by ball bursting method. The apparatus is CRE type. For breaking strength, the carriage moves upward and ruptures the specimen. However, for the bursting strength, it moves downwards for bursting the fabric Figure 12). It is measured in pounds per square inch to be compatible with the breaking strength unit. Table 17 below shows the minimum standards for various end uses.

Figure 12: Instron 5544 with bursting strength attachment.

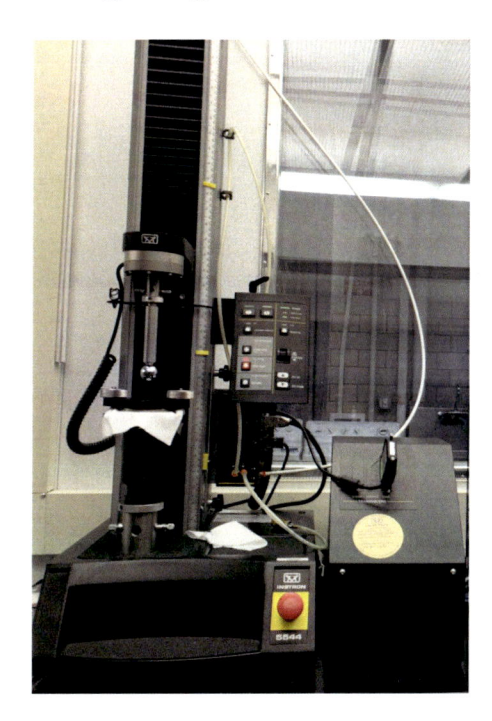

Plain and half Milano had strong bursting strength. (Emirhanova, & Kavusturan, 2008) Akaydin (2009) found that compact yarns had the higher bursting strength than the combed ring yarns. Addition of Lycra enhances the bursting strength (Sadek, El-Hossini, Eldeeb, & Yassen, 2012). Yesmin et al. (2014) examined single jersey, Lacoste and double pique knit in relation to their bursting strength. Their findings revealed that bursting strength was the highest for single Lacoste and lowest for double pique knit. The team did not study interlock knits. The tested fabrics of their research were manufactured with 100% cotton and five different stitch lengths.

Table 17: Requirements of bursting strength for various end uses.

#	End Use	Minimum Requirement
1.	Knitted Career Dress Apparel ASTM D3995 - 14	60 psi
2.	Knitted Career Vocational Apparel ASTM D3995 - 14	60 psi
3.	Knitted Swimwear ASTM D 3996 -14	30 psi
4.	Men's and Boy's Knitted and woven beachwear and sports shirt ASTM D4154 - 2014	25 psi
5.	Seamless Knitted Garments ASTM D 7268-14	30 psi
6.	Sliver knitted overcoat and jacket for men and women ASTM D3655 – 14	70 psi
7.	Corset-Girdle combination fabrics ASTM D4116-2020	70 psi
8.	Women's and Girls' Knitted and Woven Dress Gloves ASTM D4115-20	50 psi

Increase in polyester content enhanced the bursting strength (Coruh, 2015). It was highest for 70/30 polyester cotton (Coruh, 2015, Telli & Ozdil, 2015). Increase in stitch length decreased the bursting strength. Kevlar and linen did not differ from each other for the bursting strength (Ciobanu, Ciobanu, Dumitras, & Bogdan, 2016). Increase in stitch length as well as the wax removal from the dyeing process reduced the burking (Uyanik & Degirmenci, Topalbekiroglu, & Geyik, 2016). Bamboo and modal fabrics were reported to have the lowest bursting strength (Degirmenci, Celik, Ghaziantep, & Cukurova, 2016).

Chowdhary, Adnan, & Cheng (2018) examined seventeen knitted fabrics for pique, interlock, and jersey. Among interlock knits, the bursting strength was highest for polyester /spandex and lowest for rayon/Lycra. Among jersey knit fabrics. It was highest for cotton/polyester 60/40, and lowest for the rayon/spandex (95/5). Of the three pique knit fabrics, 100% cotton had the lowest bursting strength, and 100% polyester had the highest.

Seam Strength and Efficiency

Seam strength refers to the breaking load required for the seam to rupture. ASTM D1683/D1683M-17(2018) is used to measure seam strength and efficiency. **Seam efficiency** is the ratio between seam strength and fabric strength represented in percentage. For seam strength, use 6"x4" specimens. For seams, use 8" x 4" specimens for making seamed specimen of 6"x4" with ½" seam allowance in both directions. Seam allowance can range from ½ inch to 1.5 inches depending on the fabric count of the fabric. The seam allowance should be half inch for the high-count fabric, 1" for the medium count fabric and 1.5vfor the low count fabric.

Seam efficiency of less than 100% suggests that fabric is stronger than the fabric. When it is more than 100%, it means that the seam is stronger than the fabric. When seam efficiency is less than 70%, change stitch density, sewing thread, stitch type, seam type, and yarn size.

Fabric and seam strength were not impacted by the type of treatment to three (antique stonewashed and sand blasted) denim jeans Chowdhary, 2002). Seam strength was the highest for 10-12 stitches per inch and the lowest for 6-8 stitches per inch (Chowdhary & Poynor, 2006). Seam efficiency and strength were impacted by the stitch density. Serged and unserged seam comparison study of 100% cotton for seam strength, and seam efficiency examined by Chowdhary (2009, 191-201). 34 warp and 54 weft specimens were tested for 95% level of confidence using the formula $k=(tv/A)2$. Findings revealed that the un-serged warp was stronger than the serged warp. In the weft direction, the serged seam was stronger than the unserged seam. For serged seams, the weft seam was stronger than the warp. For unserged seams, warp was stronger than weft.

In another study, Chowdhary (2009, 201-203) examined breaking strength of fashion fabric with five sew-on and fusible interfacings. All interfacings enhanced breaking strength of fashion fabric in warp direction. However, differences were significant for JoAnn's sew-on, JoAnn's sew-on and heavy weight, fashion fabric and JoAnn's feather weight, JoAnn's sew-on and light weight fusible and fashion fabric and fusible shirt, and light-weight fusible and fusible shirt. For weft direction, breaking strength increased with all interfacings except for JoAnn's feather weight sew-on. However, differences were significant only for JoAnn's feather weight sew-on and light-weight fusible, and fusible-shirt. Findings for elongation were similar to the breaking strength. Addition of interfacing improved elongation for all combinations with fashion fabric in warp and all but light weight fusible for weft direction. The highest increase was observed for lightweight sew-on in warp and heavy weight sew-on in weft direction. Five significant differences were found in warp and eight in the weft direction. Findings suggest that type of interfacing can impact both strength and elongation and deserve the attention of the apparel designers.

A third study (Chowdhary, 2009, 203-212) The researcher investigated six fabrics appropriate for men's shirts. Instron 1011 was used to measure both fabric and seam strength. Six fabrics represented

Madras cloth (100% cotton), blue 100% cotton, striped flannel, knit flannel, blue polyester, and white polyester. Seam efficiency was higher for warp than filling direction for both lapped seam (LS) and superimposed seam (SS) seams. However, overall values were higher for the lapped than superimposed seams. For two lapped seams (LSb-1 and LSb-m) seam efficiency was higher for warp than weft in cotton. Reverse was true for polyester for both lapped seams. It is worth noting that several comparisons for seam and stitch types could not be made because fabric broke bit seam did not. It is important to select seam and stitch type carefully because they impact performance of the garments.

Unfinished polyester/cotton blended fabrics were stronger than the finished fabrics (with silicone fabric softener), and seam strength was higher for plain than twill and satin weaves (Bharani & Gowda, 2012). Stitch density of five stitches per inch was found to be best for sewing leathers. Lock stitch performed better than the chain stitch for seam strength, elongation, Seams sewn with the COREP had better seam efficiency than the seams stitched with MERC. Sewing thread was reported to impact seam strength. Warp showed higher seam efficiency than weft. Polyester had lowest seam strength in the weft direction (Sular, Mesegul, Kefsiz, & Seki, 2015). and efficiency (Aaron and Chandrasekran, 2014). Stitch density higher than 5 per inch damaged the fabric that was demonstrated by cuts in leather and decreased strength. Increase in stitch density resulted in higher seam strength than decrease in stitch density when tested with bound, lapped and superimposed seams (Ali, Rehan, Ahmed, Memon, and Hussain, 2014).

Stitch density increased with the tightness factor. Additional stretch in the rib knit also gave it higher tensile strength (Choi, Kim, & Powell, 2015). Seam strength increased with increase in the stitch density. Crease resistance enhanced appearance, seam efficiency, and sewing ability of seams (Illeez, Dallabast, and Ozelik, 2017). Fiber content influences breaking strength, elongation and time taken to break the fabric for woven fabrics (Chowdhary and Wentela, 2018). Addition of lining enhanced the strength. However, results from interfacing were mixed for different fiber contents. Increase in strength did not always result in decreased elongation. Chowdhary (2019) replicated the study for knitted wool and found that both fusible and non-fusible interfacings did not increase strength of the fabric. However, fusible interfacing lost its strength less than the non-fusible interfacing. Addition of polyester lining increased strength but reduced elongation.

Tear Strength

Tear strength refers to preventing spread of tear after it has been initiated (ASTM D 2261-2017) Tear strength is always less than the breaking or bursting strength. For academic purposes one specimen of 8" x 3" in each direction should be cut for dry testing and one for wet testing. 3.5" plot is used for selecting five readings every half an inch. Mean is reported and used for interpretation. As evident from figures 13-14, tear strength is higher for warp than weft direction (Figure 13 and14). Denim is a twill weave. Outcome is different for different fiber contents and weaves, It is highest for the satin weave than twill and plain weaves.

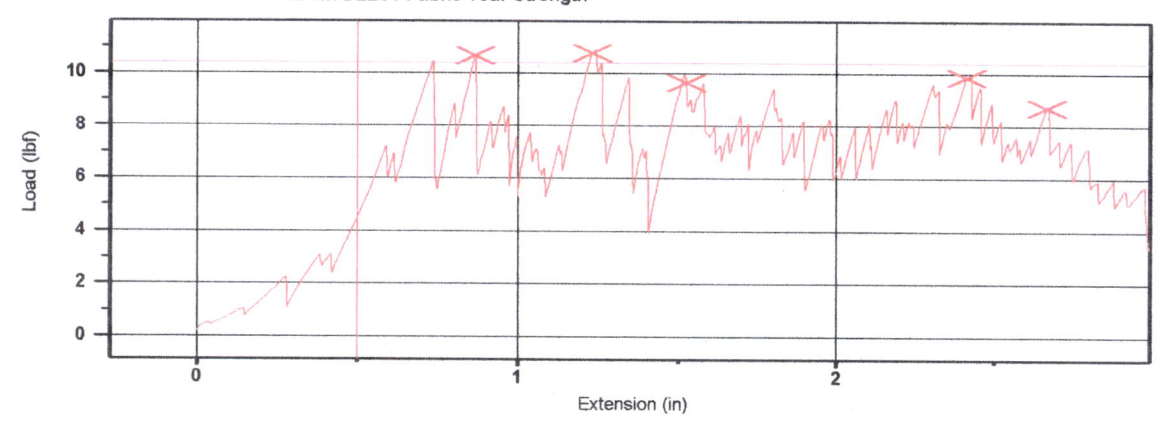

Figure 13: Tear strength of Denim in warp direction.

Instron Application Laboratory

Company:	Instron ASTM Method Set	Name:	denim warp
Course Number:	355	Number of specimens:	1
Operator ID:	uc	Temperature:	70
Test date:	2/28/2022	Humidity:	65%
Note 1:		Speed:	2.00 in/min

Results

	Tearing Force (lbf)	Average of cursor (lbf)	Specimen Info	Fabric Direction
1	10.368	9.91	Filling Dry	Filling
Mean	10.368	9.91	0.00	0.00
S.D.	0.000	0.00	0.00	0.00
C.V.	0.000	0.00	0.00	0.00
Range	0.000	0.00	0.00	0.00

Curves

ASTM D2261 Fabric Tear Strength

Chapter 5

Figure 14: Tear strength of Denim in weft direction.

Instron Application Laboratory

Company:	Instron ASTM Method Set		Name: denim weft	
Course Number:	355		Number of specimens:	1
Operator ID:	uc		Temperature:	70
Test date:	2/28/2022		Humidity:	65%
Note 1:			Speed:	2.00 in/min

Results

	Tearing Force (lbf)	Average of cursor (lbf)	Specimen Info	Fabric Direction
1	5.560	5.12	Warp Dry	Warp
Mean	5.560	5.12	0.00	0.00
S.D.	0.000	0.00	0.00	0.00
C.V.	0.000	0.00	0.00	0.00
Range	0.000	0.00	0.00	0.00

Curves

ASTM D2261 Fabric Tear Strength

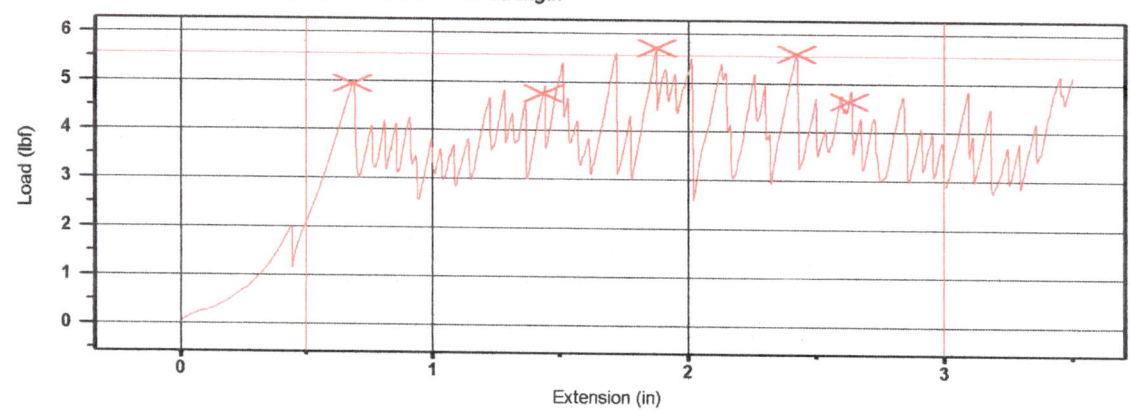

It varies for different end uses. Kadolph (2007) mentioned 2.5 psi for the regular apparel including women's pants. and 3.0 psi for men's pants and shorts. Chowdhary (2007[a]) reported a range of 1 psi to 6 psi for different end uses based on the ASTM standards. However, the values range between 1-3 psi for the latest *Manual of ASTM Standards*. See Table 18 for the minimum recommended values by the ASTM for various end-uses.

Table 18: Minimum recommended for tear strength of several end-uses by ASTM for tear strength.

.#	End Use	Minimum Requirement
1.	Lining (Woven) ASTM D3783, 4114 -14	1.5 psi
2.	Women's Sportswear ASTM D4155 - 14	2 psi
3.	Woven Dry Cleanable Coat for Men's and Boys' ASTM D3562 – 14	3 psi
4.	Woven Dry Cleanable Coat for Women's and Girls ASTM D3562 -14	3 psi
5.	Woven Swimwear ASTM D 3994 - 14	1.5 psi
6.	Rainwear ASTM D7017 - 14	3 psi
8.	Men's and Boy's Knitted and woven beachwear and sports shirt ASTM D4154 - 2014	1.5 psi (Woven)
9.	Corset-Girdle combination fabrics ASTM D4116-2020	3 psi (Woven) CRT
10.	Bras, Slips, Lingerie, and Underwear ASTM D7019-14	Sheer 1 psi Non-Sheer 1.5 psi
11.	Blouse, Dress, Dress Shirt and Sport Shirt ASTM D7020-14	Sheer 1 psi Non-Sheer 1.5 psi Dress and Sport Shirt 1.5 psi
12.	Bathrobe, Dressing Gown, Negligee, Nightgown, & Pajamas ASTM D7021-14	Sheer 1 psi Non-Sheer 1.5 psi
13.	Women's and Girls' Knitted and Woven Dress Gloves ASTM D4115-20	Woven 2.5

Treatment of fabrics with silicone improved the tear strength of woolen fabrics (Kang & Kim, 2001). The fabric with modal weft had higher tensile and tear fabrics with bamboo weft. Polyester/Cotton blends also had high tear and tensile strength. (Zubair, Maqsood, and Neckar, 2016). Fabric construction impacts tear strength. Plain fabrics were found to have low tearing strength. Tearing strength was higher for ribbed fabrics than plain fabrics. Fabrics with filament yarns had higher tearing strength than those with textured yarns (Eryuruk and Kalaoglu, 2018).

SAFETY PROPERTY

(Flame Resistance)

Flame resistance refers to the ability of the fabric to prevent, terminate and inhibit burning from the source of ignition (ASTM D4391-18 in *2020 Annual Book of ASTM Standards). ASTM 4391 – 18a* provides definition for the terms used in the burning behavior. The residue left from incomplete combustion is called **charring**, and the resulting change to the textile material is called the **burning behavior. Combustion** refers to the oxidation process that produces both heat and light. One can see light as a glow or flame. When a material is not inherently flame resistant it is treated with a chemical and called **flame retardant. Smoldering** refers to scorching or burning without flame but with smoke.

Flammability can be tested by vertical (ASTM D6413 – 2015) or 45 degrees angle ASTM D1230 – 17) tests. For vertical flammability testing, ten specimens are cut in 12" x 3" for D6413 and 10" x 3.5" dimension for ASTM 6545. Acceptable passing grade requires that none of the ten specimens should burn the entire length and mean of the char length should not exceed 7". ASTM 6545-18 is used for the children's sleepwear. Fabric is tested after it has been washed for 50 times.

Specimen size for the 45^0 angle tester is 2" x 6". In this case time taken to burn the specimen from one end to the other is recorded. Five or ten specimens can be used for this test. For the **plain** surfaces, it should take at least 3.5 seconds or more (≥ 3.5) to be classified as Class I If the fabric has the raised surface, the average of seven seconds or more (≥ 7) is needed to be classified as Class I. For class II, it should be between 4-7 seconds and for class three it should be less than 4 seconds. *2020 Annual Book of ASTM Standards (7.01,* p. 258*)* reports that class three is not considered appropriate for the apparel products.

The danger of polyester-cotton blends (1986) reported that loose clothing spreads flame faster than the tight fitted clothing. Polyester/cotton blend burns 25% faster than 100% cotton because melting of polyester speeds up the burning process by enhancing the wicking speed. It also stated that rayon/polyester blend burns faster than the polyester/cotton blend. Fiber content, yarn count, yarn twist, fabric structure, and fabric thickness had a general effect on flammability. Air permeability and stitch density did not have any effect on flammability (Candan, Dayioglu, & Ozcan,1999).

Phosphorous-based polycarboxylic acids enhanced the flame resistance of cotton/polyester fleece (Blanchard and Gravens, 2005). Flame-retardant's concentration, curing time and temperature are critical parameters in creating effective FR finishes (Ozcan, Dayioglu, and Candan, 2006). Chang, Condon, and Nam (2020) found that casein coated flame-resistant fabrics can be used effectively for commercial and industrial use of textile materials.

SENSORY ATTRIBUTES

(Fabric Hand)

Fabric Hand refers to the sensory feeling of the material through touch. Chowdhary (2007[b]) provided some examples as hard/soft, rough/smooth, cool/warm, stretchy/non-stretchy. ASTM D6828 – 02 (Reapproved 2019) is the only test found for stiffness. AATCC EP 5-1996e2(2020) also provides the evaluation procedure for fabric hand. AATCC EP5-1996e2 (2020) noted that one may or may not view specimens while judging. For fabric hand However, test, the author of the book suggests that one should not see the fabric that is being evaluated so that the subjectivity may be minimized.

At Central Michigan University, the lab uses booths like food tasting stations. The fabric is fed from the booth that has small opening evaluator to slide his/her hand for feeling the fabric and judging the fabric for the selected bipolar adjectives. Reason that the specimen should be felt with hand only and not seen with eyes is to make sure that red/yellow fabric may not be rated warmer and blue/green cooler than what it should be.

Evaluators can be asked to evaluate each fabric on a Likert type scaling. Descriptive and inferential statistics should be used to evaluate the sensory performance. The Textile Protection and Comfort Center of the North Carolina University uses the AATCC 5 procedure. They use 30 to 40 subjects for evaluating the textile materials. They have also added thick and thin, stretchy and non- stretchy, and loose and dense. If necessary other bipolar attributes can be added to the list. AATCC EP5-1996e2(2020) provides list of eleven physical attributes for compression, nine for bending, eight for shearing, and fifteen for the surface (p.465). Appropriate attributes that are consistent with the study can be selected. One example is provided below.

Evaluation Form for fabrics hand.

Attribute	1	2	3	4	5	6	7	Attribute
Rough								Smooth
Stiff								Flexible
Soft								Hard
Warm								Cool

Li, Holocombe, and Dear (1996) reported that coolness was found to be higher for the hygroscopic fibers. Increase in humidity enhanced the coolness. Marooka, Seto and Marooka (1996) reported that smoother fabrics had higher real contact than the textured fabrics. Degumming of silk made the touch bulkier, fabric elegant, drape good, and resilient than the gummed silk (Youngjoo, & Chunjeong, 2001). An, Gam, and Cao (2002) compared stiffness as sensorial property for organic cotton, bamboo-blended and soybean blended fabrics. Their results revealed that bamboo-blended fabric performed the best for children's sportswear and sleepwear. An addition of 5-15% silk to cotton made the fabric softer than its absence (Tyndall, 2006).

Jeguirim et al. (2010) reported that finishes in their study improved the hand of the fabrics. In a study by Halleb, Sahnoun, & Cheikhrouhou, (2015), evaluators rated denim lower on tenderness, silkiness, sleekness, and slipperiness. However, they rated it higher for suppleness and the wrinkly effect after rinsing. However, stone finishes enhanced softness, bulkiness, and made it less wrinkly. Kawamura et al. (2016) analyzed thirteen fabric hand properties for the raw, US, Japan, and spa jeans: cool/warm, damp/dry, heavy/light, hard soft, itchy/non-itchy, non-fullness/fullness, prickle/non-prickle, rough/smooth, sticky/non-adhesive, scratchy/non-scratchy, stiff/pliable, and thick/thin. Results revealed that Raw and USA fabrics were hard and rough. However, the Japanese and SPA fabrics were soft and smooth.

Summary and Conclusions

The preceding information in this chapter reveals that the dry performance tests are important in determining the quality of the textile materials. They help with evaluation of aesthetics, comfort, durability, safety, and sensory attributes. These can be considered inclusively and exclusively depending on the chosen end-use. For example, safety attributes are more important for children's sleepwear than children's sportswear. Likewise, comfort and care related attributes are more important for casual and sportswear than formal wear. The standardizing organizations provide methodologies with tools. However, interpretations are based on the end-use and careful reasoning when results fall between two categories.

REFERENCES

Aaron, K. P., & Chandrasekran, B. (2014). Studies on influence of stitch density and stitch type on seam properties of garment leathers. Retrieved on 8/28/2016 from https://www.researchgate.net/publicaton/273290807_Studies_on_In...

Adnan, M. M. & Chowdhary, U. (2021). Color measurement and colorfastness of different weaves and dimensional forms. *Journal of Textile Science and Fashion Technology, 8*(1), 1-9.

Akgun, M., Becerir, B., & Alpay, H. R. (2006). Abrasion of polyester fabrics containing staple weft yarns: Color strength and color difference values. AATCC Review, 6(3), 40-43.

Akaydin, M. (2009, March). Characteristics of fabrics knitted with basic knit structures from combed ring and compact yarns. Indian Journal of Fiber and Textile Research, 34, 2, 30.

Akaydin, M., & Can, Y. (2010). Pilling performance and abrasion characteristics of selected basic weft knits. Fibres and Textiles in Eastern Europe, 18 (2), 51-54.

Ali, N., Rehan, A. M., Ahmed, Z., Memon, H., & Hussain, A. (2014). Effect of different types of seam, stitch class and stitch density on seam performance. Journal of Applied Emerging. Science, 5(1), 32-43.

Alongi, J., & Malucelli, G. (2013). Thermal stability, flame retardancy and abrasion resistance of cotton and cotton-linen blends treated by sol-gel silica coatings containing alumina micro- or nanoparticles. Polymer degradation and Stability, 98, 1428-1438.

Amirbayat, J. & Alagha, M. J. (1994). The objective assessment of fabric pilling Part II Experimental work. Journal of Textile Institute, 85, 397-400.

An, S. K., Gam, H. J., & Cao, H. (2002). Evaluating thermal and sensorial performance of organic cotton, bamboo-blended, and soyabean blended fabrics. *Clothing and Textiles Research Journal, 31*(3), 157-166.

Annual book of ASTM standards. (2020). 7.01, West Conshohoken, PA: ASTM International.

Annual book of ASTM standards. (2019). 7.02, West Conshohoken, PA: ASTM International.

Arik, B. (2020). Characterization and wrinkle resistance enhancement by sol-gel method of variously pretreated linen fabrics. *Fibers and Polymers, 21*, 82-89.

Aston, P.V. (1994). Pilling of sweatshirts that are a 50/50 blend of polyester and cotton. Textile Research Journal, 64, 592-596.

Atasagun, H. G., Okur, A., & Psikuta, A. (2019). The effect of garment combination on thermal comfort of office clothing. *Textile Research Journal,* https://doi.org/10.1177/0040517519834609 First Published March 11, 2019 Research Article

Baumert, K. J., & Crews, P. (2000). Influence of household fabric softeners on properties of selected woven fabrics. *Textile Chemist and Colorist,* 32(9), 41-47.

Bharani, M., Gowda, R. V. M. (2012). Characterization of seam strength and seam slippage of pc blend fabric with plain woven structure and finish. Research Journal of Recent Science, 1 (12), 7-14.

Brzezinski, S., Kowalczyk, D., Borak, B., Jasiorski, M., & Tracz, A. (2011). Nanocoat finishing of polyester/cotton fabrics by sol/gel method to improve their wear resistance. Fibres and Textiles in Eastern Europe, 19 (8), 83-89.

Can, Y. (2008). Pilling performance and abrasion characteristics of plain-weave fabrics made from open –end and ring spun yarns. Fibres and Textiles in Eastern Europe, 16(1), 81-84.

Candan, C., & Onal, L. (2002). Dimensional, pilling, and abrasion properties of weft knits made from open-end and ring spun yarns. Textile Research Journal, 72, 164-169. 13.

Candon, C., Dayioglu, H. & Ozcan, G. (2003). Effect of gray fabric properties on flame resistance of knitted fabrics. Textile Research Journal, 73(10), 883-891.

Cao, H., Branson, D. H., Peksoz, S., Nam, J., & Farr, C. A. (2006). Fabric selection for a liquid cooling garment. *Textile Research Journal, 76*, 587-595.

Chang, S., Condon, B. Nam S. (2020). Development of flame-resistant cotton fabrics with Casein using pad-dry-cure and supercritical fluid methods. Journal of Material Science and Applications, 9(4), 53-61.

Chen, Y. S., Fan, J., & Zhang, W. (2003). Clothing thermal insulation during sweating. *Textile Research Journal, 73*(2), 152-157.

Chen, M., Spola, J., Gisbert, P., & Sellabona, M. (1999). Experimental studies on the structure and mechanical properties of multi-layer and angle-interlock woven structures. *The Journal of Textile Institute, 90.1*(1), 91-99.

Chiwese, A., & Crews, P. C. (2000). Influence of household fabric softeners and laundry enzymes on pilling and breaking strength. Textile Chemist and Colorist and Dye Stuff Reporter, 32(9), 41-47.

Choi, W., Kim, Y., & Powell, N. B. (2015). An investigation of seam strength and elongation of knitted-neck edges on complete garments by binding-off processes. The Journal of the Textile Institute, 106(3), 334-341.

Chowdhary. U. (2002). Does price reflect emotional, structural or performance quality? International Journal of Consumer Studies, 26(2), 128-133.

Chowdhary, U. (2007[a]). Textile analysis: An annotated bibliography. Deer Park, NY: LINUS.

Chowdhary, U. (2007[b]). Textile analysis laboratory manual. Deer Park, NY: LINUS.

Chowdhary, U. (2009). Textile analysis, quality control and innovative uses. Deer Park, NY: LINUS.

Chowdhary, U. (2017). Comparing three brands of cotton t-shirts. AATCC Journal of Research, 4(3), 22-33. DOI: 10.14504/ajr.4.3.3.

Chowdhary, U. (2018). Stretch and recovery of jersey and interlock knits. International Journal of Textile Science and Engineering, vol. 112(1), 1-8. DOI: 10.29011/ IJTSE-112/100012

Chowdhary, U. (2019). Impact of interfacings and lining on breaking strength, breaking strength, elongation and duration of the knitted wool. International Journal of Textile Science and Engineering, 3(1), 1-6.

Chowdhary, U., & Adnan, M. M. (2019). Knit structure and its relationship to dimensional stability, appearance retention, industrial stretch, pilling resistance and colorfastness to crocking. International Journal of Polymer and Textile Engineering, 6 (2), 1-8.

Chowdhary, U., Adnan, M. M., & Cheng, C. (2018). Bursting strength and extension for jersey, interlock and pique knit. Trends in Textile Engineering and Fashion Technology, 1(2), 1-9.

Chowdhary, U., Hoque, M., Hutson, C., Thurston, J., Vanderploeg, A., & Zfenix, R. (2016). A comparison of three pilling measurement methods for knitted and woven fabrics. Paper presented in Daejeon, South Korea from July 31, 2016 – August 6, 2016 at the congress of International Federation of Home Economics.

Chowdhary, U., & Islam, M. R. (2019). Pre-post wash wicking behavior, moisture transfer, and water repellency of plain, twill and satin weaves. *Journal of Textile Science and Fashion Technology, 2*(3), 1-13.

Chowdhary, U., & Poynor, D. (2006). Impact of stitch density on seam strength, seam elongation and seam efficiency. International Journal of Consumer Studies, 30 (6), 561-568.

Chowdhary, U. & Wentela, C. (2018). Impact of support fabrics on breaking strength, elongation, and time taken for the test for woven fabrics in different fiber contents. SSRG International Journal of Polymer and Textile Engineering, 5 (5), 1-6.

Ciobanu, A. R., Ciobanu, L., Dumitras, G. G., & Bogdan, S. (2016). Comparative analysis of the bursting strength of knitted sandwich fabrics, *Fibers and Textiles in Eastern Europe, 24*(2):95-101. DOI:10.5604/12303666.1191432

Collier, B. J., Bide, M. J., & Tortora, P. G. (2009). Understanding textiles. Upper Saddle River, NJ: Merrill.

Collier, B. J., & Epps, H. H. (1999). Textile testing and analysis. Upper Saddle River, NJ: Merrill.

Coruh, E. (2015). Optimization of comfort properties of single jersey knit fabrics. Fibres and Textiles in Eastern Europe, 23, 4 (112), 66-72. DOI: 10.5604/12303666.1152728.

Csiszar, E. and Dornyi, B. (2006). Liquid ammonia treatment of the linen fabrics, *AATCC Review, 6*, 43-48.

Degirmenci, Z., & Celik, N., (2016). Relation between extension and bursting strength properties of the denim viewed knitted fabrics produced by cellulosic fibers. Fibres and Textiles in Europe, 24, 101-106.

Doty, K. C., & Easter, E. (2009, May). An analysis of the care and maintenance of performance textiles and effects of care on performance. *AATCC Review,* 37-42.

Emirhanova, N., & Kavusturan, Y. (2008). Effect of knit structure on the dimensional and physical properties of winter outerwear knitted fabrics. Fibres and Textiles in Europe,16(2), 69-74.

Eryuruk, S. H. & Kalaoglu, F. (2018). The effect of weave construction on tear strength of woven fabrics. AUTEX Research Journal, 15(3), 207-213.

Fahmy, S. M., & Slater, K. (1977). The use of the acoustic test to predict body comfort properties. In Hollies, N. R. S., and Goldman, R. F. (Eds.) *Clothing comfort: Interactions of thermal ventilation, construction and assessment factors (pp. 19-30).* Ann Arbor, MI: An Arbor Science.

Filiz, S. (2018). A study on comparison of air permeability properties of bamboo/cotton and cotton towels. *Scientific Research and Essays, 13*(13), 143-147.

Ghalachayan, A. (2010). How heat and humidity affect fabric stretch and recovery properties. Student Research and Creative Endeavors Exhibition, 19.

Goktepe, O. (2002). Fabric pilling performance and sensitivity of several pilling testers. Textile Research Journal, 72, 625-630. 14.

Goswami, B. C., Duckett, K. E., & Vigo, T. L. (1980). Torsional fatigue and initiation mechanism of pilling. Textile Research Journal, 50(8), 481-485.

Halleb, N. A., Sahnoun, M., Cheikhrouhou, M. (2015). The effect of washing treatments on the sensory properties of denim fabric. *Textile and Research Journal, 85*(2), https://doi.org/10.1177/0040517514542971

Hazavehi, E., Shahidi, S., & Zolgharnein, P. (2015). Effect of dyeing on wrinkle properties of cotton cross-linked by butane tetracarboxylic acid (BTCA) in presence of titanium dioxide (TIO_2) nanoparticles. *AUTEX Research Journal, 15*(2), 104-111. DOI: 10.2478/aut-2014-0039 © AUTEX.

Hearle, J. W. S., & Wilkins, A. H. (2006). Movement of fibers in assemblies. Journal of the Textile Institute, 97, 1-9.

Hsi, C. H., Bresee, R. R., & Annis, P. A. (1998a). Characterizing fabric pilling by using Image analysis techniques Part II: Comparison with visual pill ratings. Journal of Textile Institute, 89, Part 1 (1), 96-104.

Hsi, C. H., Bresee, R. R., & Annis, P. A. (1998b). Characterizing fabric pilling by using image analysis techniques Part I: Pill detection and description. Journal of Textile Institute, 89, Part 1 (1), 80-94.

Ibrahim, N. A., Khalifa, T. F., EL-Hossamy, M. B., & Twafik, T. M. (2010). Effect of knit structure and finishing treatments on functional and comfort properties of cotton knitted fabrics. Journal of Industrial Textiles, 40(1), 49-64. DOI: 10.1177/1528083709357975.

Illeez, A. A., Dallabast, E.S., Ozelik, K. G. (2017). Seam properties and sewability of crease-resistant shirt fabrics. AATCC Journal of Research, 4(1), 28-34. DOI: https://doi.org/10.14504/ajr.3.3.2

Jeguirim, S. E., Dhouib, A. B., Sahnoun, M., Cheikhrouhou, M. Njeugna, N., Schacher, L., & Adolphe, D. (2010). The tactile sensory evaluation of knitted fabrics: Effect of some finishing treatments. *Journal of Sensory Studies, 25*(2), 201-215.

Jahan I. (2017). Effect of Fabric Structure on the mechanical properties of woven fabrics. Advanced Research in Textile Engineering.2(2), 1018.

Kawamura, A., Zhu, C., Peiffer, J., Kim, K., Li, Y. & Takatera, M. (2016), Relationship between the physical properties and hand of jean fabric. *AUTEX Research Journal, 16*(3), 138-145. DOI: 10.1515/aut-2015-0043 © AUTEX

Kadolph, S. J. (2007). Quality assurance for textile and apparel. New York, NY: Fairchild.

Kang, T. J., & Kim, M. S. (2001). Effects of silicone treatments one the dimensional properties of wool fabric. Textile Research Journal, 71(4), 295-300.

Kavitha S, & Gokarneshan N. (2019). A Review of Some Significant Research Trends in Thermophysiological Comfort of Fabrics to Suit Varied Areas of Applications and Weather Conditions. *Current Trends in Fashion Technology and Engineering,* 5(5): 555673. DOI: 10.19080/CTFTTE.2019.05.5673.

Kisilak, D. (1999). A new method of evaluating spherical fabric deformation. T*extile Research Journal,* 69(12), https://doi.org/10.1177/004051759906901204

Kretzschmar, S. D., Özgüney, A. T., Özçelik, G., & Özerdem, A. (2007). The comparison of cotton knitted fabric properties made of compact and conventional ring yarns before and after the dyeing process. Textile Research Journal, 77(4), 233-241

Kujuhara, A. & Hori, T. (2002). Reducing wrinkle formation in wool with 2-Iminotheranehydrochloride. *Textile Research Journal, 72*(4), 285-289.

Kundu, S.K., & Chowdhary, U. (2020). Effect of fiber content on comfort properties of cotton/spandex, rayon/spandex, and polyester/spandex single jersey knitted fabrics. *SSRG International Journal of Polymer and Textile Engineering, 5*(1), 33-39.

Kundu, S. K. and Chowdhary, U. (2018). Effect of Fiber Content on Comfort Properties of Cotton/Spandex, Rayon/Spandex, and Polyester/Spandex Single Jersey Knitted Fabrics. *SSRG International Journal of Polymer and Textile Engineering, 5*(3), 33-39.

Lapitsky, M., & Dickey, L. E. (1986). Textile clothing in thermal energy conservation. *Home Economics Research Journal, 14,* 314-325.

Latifi, M., Kim, H.S, & Pourdehimi, B. (2001). Characterizing fabric pilling due to fabric-to-fabric abrasion. Textile Research Journal, 71, 640-644.

Lee, S., & Obendorf, S. K. (2007). Barrier effectiveness and thermal comfort of protective clothing materials. *The Journal of Textile Institute, 98*, 87-97.

Li, L., Zhu, M., & Wei, X. (2014). Pilling performance of cashmere knitted fabric of woolen ring yarn and mule yarn. Fibers and Textiles in Eastern Europe, 22 (1), 74-75.

Li, Y., Holocombe, B. V., and Dear, R. (1996). Enhancement of coolness to te touch of the hygroscopic fibers Part I. Physical mechanisms. Textile Research Journal, 66(9). 587-594.

Majumdar, A., Mukhopadhyay, S., and Yadav, R. (2010). Thermal properties of knitted fabrics made from cotton and regenerated bamboo cellulosic fibres. *International Journal of Thermal Sciences, 49*(10), 2042-2048.

Marooka, H., Seto, T., & Marooka, H. (1996). Morphology of cloth surfaces of panty hose in real contact with a rigid plate., Textile Research Journal, 66(2), 73-82.

Marsha, S. S. & Chowdhary, U. (2018). Comparison of selected structural and performance attributes of cotton and C/P blend of t-shirts. International Journal of Polymer and Textile Engineering (SSRG - IJPTE), 5(3), 40-49.

McQuerry, M., Emiel, D., & Roger, B. (2016). Garment ventilation strategies for improving heat loss in structural firefighter clothing ensembles. *AATCC Journal of Research, 3*(3), 9-14. **DOI:** https://doi.org/10.14504/ajr.3.3.2

Mendes, A.D. O., Fiadeiro, P.T., Miguel, R. A. L., & Lucas, J. M. (2009). Optical estimation of set of pilling coefficients for textile fabrics. Textile Research Journal, 79, 410-417.

Merkel, R. S. (1991). Textile product serviceability. New York, NY: Macmillan.

Ogulata, R. T. (2006). Air permeability of woven fabrics. Journal of Textile and Apparel Technology and Management. 5 (2), 1-10.

Omeroglu, S., & Ulku, S. (2007). An investigation about tensile strength, pilling and abrasion properties. of woven fabrics made from conventional and compact ring-spun yarns. Fibres and Textiles in Eastern Europe, 15 (1), 57-63.

Oner, E., & Okur, B. A. (2014). The effect of different knitted fabrics' structures on the moisture transport properties. *The Journal of Textile Institute, 104*(11), 1164-1177. DOI:10.1080/00405 000.2013.782214.

Ozcan, G., Dayioglu, H., Candan, C. (2003. Effect of gray fabrics properties on flame resistance of knitted fabrics.

Ozcan, G., Dayioglu, H., Candan, C. (2006). Application of flame-retardant products to knitted fabrics. Indian Journal of Fibre and Textiles Research, 31, 330-334.

Ramaswamy, G. N., & Wang, J. (1999). Mercerization and dyeing of Kenaf/Cotton blend fabrics. *Textiles Chemist and Colorists, 31*(3), 27-31.

Rosace, G., Canton, R., & Colleoni, C. (2010). Plasma enhanced CVD of SiOxCyHz thin film on different textile fabrics: Influence of exposure time on the abrasion resistance and mechanical properties. Applied Surface Science, 256, 2509-2516.

Ruppenicker, G. F. (1981). Properties of yarns and fabrics produced from high cotton content blends with polyester. Textile Research Journal, 51, 590-596.

Smriti, S. K., & Islam, M.A. (2015). An exploration on pilling attitudes of cotton polyester blended single Jersey knit fabric after mechanical singeing. Science Innovation, 3(1), 18- 21.

Srinivasan, J., Ramakrishnan, G., Mukhopadhyay, & Manoharan, S. (2005). A study of knitted fabrics from polyester microdenier fibres. Journal of the Textile Institute, 98, 31-35.

Subjective evaluation of fabric hand (2021). Retrieved on 2/23/2021. https://textiles.ncsu.edu/tpacc/comfort-performance/subjective-evaluation-of-fabric-hand/

Sular, V., & Seki, Y. (2018). A review on fabric bagging: The concept and measurement methods. *The Journal of Textile Institute, 109*(4), 466-484. https://doi.org/10.1080/00405000.2017.1354450

Sular, V., Mesegul, C., Kefsiz, H., & Seki, Y. (2015). A comparative study on seam performance of cotton and polyester woven fabrics. The Journal of the Textile Institute, 106(1), 19-30.

Tamanna, T. A. Suruj-Zaman, N. M., Mondal, B. V. & Saha, P. K. (2017). Investigation of stretch and recovery property of weft knitted regular rib fabric. *European Scientific Journal 13*, 400-412.

Telli, A. & Ozdil, N. (2015). Effect of recycled PET fibers on the performance properties of knitted fabrics. Journal of Engineered Fibers and Fabrics, 10(2), 47-60.

Textile abrasion test: Wyzenbeek vs Martindale. Retrieved 2/20/2021 from https://www.josephnoble.com/inspiration/textile-abrasion-test-wyzenbeek-vs-martindale/

The danger of polyester-cotton blends. (1986) Science News, 129, 297.

Teyeme, Y., Malengier, B., Tesfaye, T., Vasile, S., & Langenhove, L. V. (2020). Comparative analysis of thermophysiological comfort-related properties of elastic knitted fabrics for cycling sportswear. *Materials, 13(18),* doi:0.3390/ma13184024

Tyndall, M. (2006, November/December). The Luxe for lee: Cotton blends offer a hand to textile. Textile World, 39.

Ukponmwan, J. O., Mukhopadhyay, A., & Chatterjee, K. N. (2002). Pilling: Measurement of pills. Journal of Textile Institute, 28(3), 16-27.

Uyanik, S., Degirmenci, Z., Topalbekiroglu, M., & Geyik. F. (2016). Examine the relation between the number and location of tuck stitches and bursting strength in circular knitted fabrics. Fibres and Textiles in Europe, 1(115), 114-119.

Wang, L., Liu, J., Pan, R., & Gao, W. (2014). Dynamic measurement of fabric wrinkle recovery angle by video sequence processing. *Textile Research Journal, 84*(7), 694-703.

Wroblewski, S. M. (2017). Quilting structure: Impact of air permeability and thermal properties of a non-woven, a two-fold study. Unpublished research project, Central Michigan University.

Xin, B., Hu, J., & Yan, H. (2002). Objective evaluation of fabric pilling using image analysis technique. Textile Research Journal, 72, 1057-1064.

Yang, C. Q. Zhou, W., Lickfield, G. C., & Parachura, K. (2003). Cellulose treatment of durable press finished cotton fabric: Effects on fabric strength, abrasion resistance and handle. *Textile Research Journal, 73*, 1057-1062.

Yatagai, M., & Takahashi, Y. (2005, January). Effect of citric acid DP finishing with particulate soil of cotton fabric. *AATCC Review, 5,* 17-21.

Yesmin, S., Hasan, M., Miah, M.S., Momotaz, F., Idrish, M.A., & Hasan, M. R. (2014). Effect of stitch length and fabric constructions on dimensional and mechanical properties of knitted fabrics. World Applied Sciences Journal, 32(9), 1991-1995.

Youngjoo, N., & Chunjeong, K. (2001). Quantifying the handle and sensibility of woven silk fabrics. *Textile Research Journal, 71*(8), 739-742.

Zhang, P., Gong, R. H., Yanai, Y., & Tokura, H. (2002). Effect of clothing on thermoregulatory responses. *Textile Research Journal, 7*(1), 83-89.

Zhu, C., & Takatera, M. (2015). Effects of hydrophobic yarns on liquid migration in woven fabrics. *Textile Research Journal, 85*(5), 479-486. DOI: 0.1177/004051751454998.

Zubair, M., Maqsood, H. S., & Neckar, B. (2016). Impact of filling yarns on woven fabric performance. Fibers and Textiles in Eastern Europe, 24(5), 50-54.

PRACTICE ACTIVITIES

1. Select the articles of apparel in your wardrobe that have been laundered for at least five times. Examine them for abraded areas. Identify reasons for abrasion for both location and intensity.
2. If the weight of the unabraded fabric was 5 grams and the abraded specimen was 3.9 grams, what will be the percentage of weight loss?
3. If the weight of the unabraded fabric was 7 grams and the abraded specimen was 6 grams, what will be the percentage of weight loss?
4. If the strength of the unabraded fabric was 70.8 psi and the abraded specimen was 65 psi, what will be the percentage of strength loss?
5. If the strength of the unabraded fabric was 60 psi and the abraded specimen was 53 psi, what will be the percentage of strength loss?
6. What is the unit of abrasion resistance based on the Taber abrader?
7. What is the unit of abrasion resistance based on the accelerotor method?
8. What is the unit of pilling resistance?
9. What is the unit of breaking strength?
10. What is the unit of elongation?
11. What is the unit of bursting strength?
12. What is the unit of tear strength?
13. What is the unit of seam strength?
14. What is the unit of seam efficiency?
15. What is the unit of air permeability?
16. What is the unit of vertical flammability test method?
17. What is the unit of 45 degrees angle flammability test method?
18. What is the unit of measurement for the wrinkle recovery?
19. List five bipolar combinations of attributes for fabric hand.
20. Compare woven and knitted fabrics for pilling resistance.
21. In your study of determining seam efficiency, the seam strength was 99.75 psi and the fabric strength of 85.25 psi. What will be the seam efficiency? Will seam be stronger than the fabric? What will you do to improve the quality of your seam?

Performance Attributes: Dry Tests

22. In your study of determining seam efficiency, the seam strength was 99.75 psi and the fabric strength of 105.5 psi. What will be the seam efficiency? Will seam be stronger than the fabric? What will you do to improve the quality of your seam?

23. Compare wrinkle recovery of 100% cotton, 100% polyester, and polyester/cotton (50/50) blend.

24. What are the flame resistance standards for plain and raised surfaces?

25. If a fabric has a flame spread time of 5 seconds for plain surface, will you pass or fail the fabric.

26. If average char length of all 10 specimens is 8.5 inches, will you pass or fail the fabric for flame resistance?

27. If average char length of all 10 specimens is 6 inches, will you pass or fail the fabric for flame resistance?

28. If a fabric has a flame spread time of 3 seconds for the raised surface and it was classified as class III, will you use it for the apparel purposes?

29. Which of the dry performance tests will you use for the fabric selection for jeans?

30. List three tests that you will select for swimwear?

31. How can you use the knowledge of the performance tests as fashion design and fashion merchandising majors?

32. Complete the decision column of the chart below as pass or fail based on the ASTM standards for women's sportswear.

#	Attribute	Standard	Your Reading	Decision
1	Breaking Strength	30 psi Minimum	28 psi	
2	Tear Strength	2 psi Minimum	4 psi	
3	Flammability	Class 1	Class I	
4	Pilling Resistance	≥ 4	3	
5	Elongation	5% Minimum	8%	

PERFORMANCE ATTRIBUTES: WET TESTS

CHAPTER 6

Most of the wet tests for performance attributes are found in the *AATCC Manual of International Test Methods and Procedures* (2021). Except for the wrinkle recovery all need use of water. They are used to examine the performance for aesthetics, care, and comfort (Figure 20). Aesthetic related tests include appearance retention, crease retention, frosting, seam smoothness, and wrinkle recovery in fabrics. Care related standards include colorfastness to various conditions, dimensional stability, skew change, and stain removal, Comfort related tests are antibacterial, electrical resistance, mercerization, moisture transfer, water repellency, weather resistance, and water vapor transmission.

Figure 20: Classification of wet performance tests.

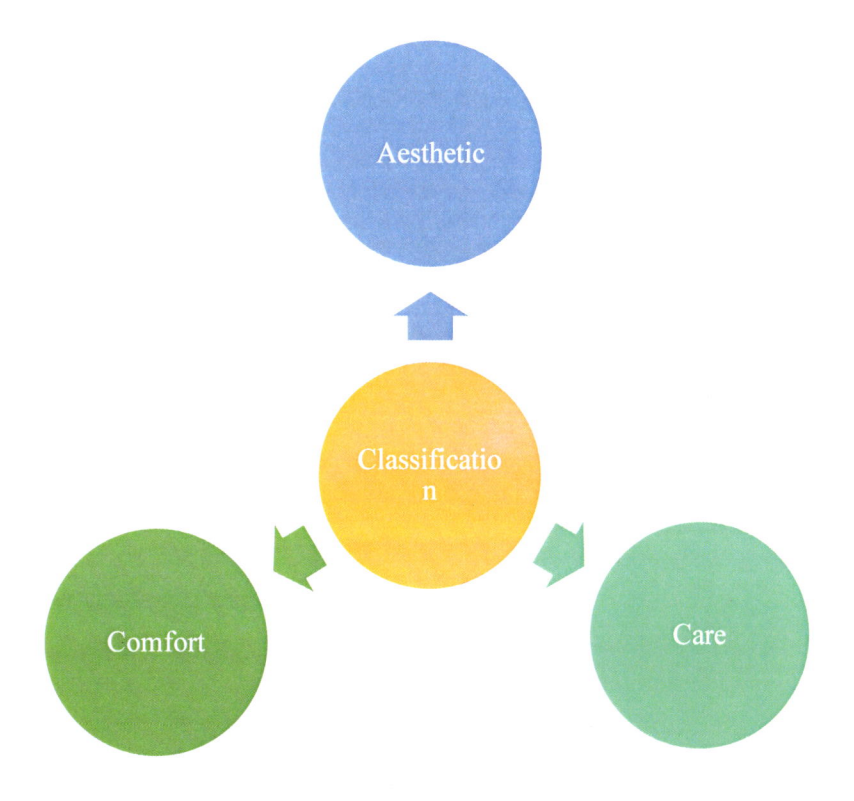

AESTHETIC

Aesthetic tests enhance the appearance, texture, or hand of the textile material. Textile materials change in many ways during wear and tear. Because tests create simulations to expedite the process, an attempt is made to allow the retention of original appearance as best as possible. Therefore, it is important that attention is paid to the aesthetics that can be spoiled by color changes, pill formation, snagging, staining, thinning, worn out look, and wrinkling.

Antibacterial (AATCC TM100-2019)

This test focuses on the quantitative evaluation of the activity of bacterial growth. It is used for assessing the antibacterial finishes. It is designed on the belief that quantitative appraisal provides a clear picture about the functionality and quality of the applied finish.

Literature has information on the importance of antimicrobial finishes from several different perspectives. Innovations in advanced textiles (2021, March, p. 15) reported that Sclessent tested Agion® antimicrobial treatment and found that it achieved "99.99 percent inactivation of SARS-Cov-2, the virus that causes COVID-19". The effectiveness was tested after 20 launderings. It noted that this finish is effective on both woven and knitted textile used for medical purposes. Melt blown process was used for nonwoven materials, and mixed in the polymer for the synthetic material.

Ketema & Worku (2020) asserted that natural fabrics are vulnerable to the microbial attack and damage the quality of the fabric. They used a native plant from Ethiopia for finishing a cotton fabric. The authors premised their study on the fact that microbial growth results in appearance changes, discoloration, and loss of strength and elongation. They chose cotton because natural fibers are vulnerable to the microbial attack. They tested the application of new finish for 40 washes and found the finish to be a cheap substitute for Ethiopia. For assessment of the finish, they used the AATCC TM 100-2004 version.

Shalini and Anitha (2016) conducted a review of antimicrobial textile. They identified six methods of finishing as using additives in the spinning solution of synthetic materials, padding with crosslink binders, exhaustion application, spraying, microencapsulation, and polymer modification. Chowdhary (2007) reported on 17 articles with several different foci. Collectively, they focused on new techniques of finishing, role of microbial finishes in multiple disciplines and multiple uses, medicinal value of silver used for antimicrobial finishes, and effectiveness treating fabric with hydrogen peroxide. Both sweat and water were responsible for microbial growth that impacted the integrity of the fabric.

Menezes and Choudhari (2007) asserted that antimicrobial finishes can be used in apparel, home furnishings and sportswear. Examples used for apparel were undergarments, socks, shirts, pants, and handkerchiefs. For athleticwear, they listed athletic shows, batting gloves, soccer equipment, and socks. Menthoglycol was noted as an insect repellent that could be stabilized by micro-capsulating it with Phenolbenzotriazole to enhance its effectiveness from UV protection also.

Hofer (2006[a]) discussed the complexity resulting from the interaction between textiles, sweat, and skin. Hofer (2006[b]) emphasized the use of antimicrobial finishes in domestics, medicine, sports, and leisure, outdoor, and technology. Examples of domestics presented by the author were carpets, coverings, curtains, fabrics, and underwear. Medicine field included bedding, filling, implants, incontinence liners, pillows, and support stockings. For outdoors, it listed Astro turfs, awnings, jackets, sunshades, tents, and uniforms. Sports and leisure were represented by the bike-wear, jogging suits, shoes, socks, team kit, and t-shirts. Technology examples used were air filters, automotive, geotextiles, roof coverings, and wall hangings. One can clearly see that areas that presence of moisture enhances the vulnerability of microbial attack the most.

Kut, Orhan, Gunesoglu and Ozakin, C. (2005) examined the antibacterial activities of S. Aureus and E. Coli. Results revealed that the fabrics bleached with hydrogen peroxide had higher antibacterial activity than the unbleached fabric. Microbial resistance was better on the bleached than unbleached fabric. Additionally, the test environment with acidic, basic, and urine presence reduced the antibacterial activity.

This topic has gained impetus since the beginning of the twenty-first century. Microbial growth is highest in the presence of water. In everyday life, you can see it on the shower curtains, wet laundry that is not washed immediately, shoes in snow times, etc. Health and fitness have taken people to gyms more and exercising makes people sweat more than the sedentary lifestyle. It can be identified by discoloration, unwanted spots, and bad odor. Antibacterial finishes help with prevention of their growth. S. Aureus affects the textile. Moisture is the leading cause of microbial attack and silver has been used the most for antimicrobial finishes on ships for a long time.

Appearance Retention (AATCC TM124 – 2018t)

This method is developed to determine smoothness appearance of fabrics after standard home laundering procedures. Any material than can be laundered is qualified to be tested by this method in any fabric construction. The test provides directions for normal, delicate and permanent-press cycles with details on water level, agitation speed, washing time, spin speed and time, and wash temperature. Three-dimensional replicas of appearance retention are used to assess the textiles from 1 (the most wrinkled or least smooth) to 5 (the least wrinkled or most smooth). A minimum rating of 3.5 is used to pass the specimen on this test. Ideally, three observers should evaluate the specimens from 4 feet distance for objectivity of evaluation. Chowdhary and Adnan (2019) found that appearance retention was best for medium count and heavyweight polyester/spandex 96%/4% blend and worst for 100% cotton in low count and medium weight for interlock knits. 96/4% blend performed better than the 95%/5% blend of polyester/spandex. For jersey knit, results were best for 60/40 polyester/cotton blend and worst for 100% cotton. For pique knit, low count light weight material performed better than medium weight/low count pique knits. Light weight and low count polyester performed better appearance retention but worst for pilling resistance and stretch. For pique knit, polyester performed better than cotton for appearance retention.

Despite the move to casual lifestyle, appearance retention is still important consideration in consumers' lifestyle. Base on the standard 3.5 is the minimum rating required to pass the tested fabric. Care label can include ironing or dry-cleaning option if there are issues with this consideration.

Crease Retention (AATCC TM88C, 2018t)

This method is used to examine crease retention after laundering using three-dimensional crease replicas of AATCC. Grades range from 1 (least retention) to 5 (sharpest crease retention. The same process of three observers and 4 feet distance is used for the evaluation process as appearance retention is used. No minimum standard is established. Average of the ratings is reported. Traditionally, garments required it for both casual and formal wear. In today's world of casual lifestyle, this test is more important in formal wear.

Electrostatic Charge: Fabric to Metal (AATCC TM115– 2000 e 2011e)

The test examines the clinging tendency of materials. It is based on the physics principle that positively and negatively charged materials attract each other because of instantaneous induction. Metal plate is used to represent the human body. Electrostatic cling differs from person to person. This method was reported to be useful for lightweight fabrics. Record the time taken by the fabric to decling. If it takes more than ten minutes, record it >10 minutes and discontinue the test. Use three specimens and report individual readings for both warp and weft as well as averages. This test is important for synthetic materials. Using blends or finishes or use of fabric softeners in laundering can alleviate this problem.

Frosting (AATCC TM120 – 2019)

This test evaluates the color change in textile material that is caused by flat abrasion. Color change is reported from 5-1. 5 means no color change and 1 means the most color change. Frosting creates lighter streaks that result from wearing away of color from abrasion and are seen on pants close to the edges of the creases made by the pleats. They are more readily visible when two different colors are used for warp and weft.

Mildew and Rot Resistance (AATCC TM30, 2017e)

This test evaluates the deterioration of material as well as unpleasant sight and bad odor. It is used for sandbags, tarpaulins, and tents. Tests are buried in soil for a certain length of time. Then, it is tested for strength.

Oil Repellency (AATCC TM118 – 2020); (AATCC TM130 – 2018t) test focuses on release of the oily stains from laundering. The washed stains are evaluated by a five-point scale with 1 as the poor performance and 5 as the best performance. *AATCC Manual of International Test Methods and Procedures* (2021) talks about the oily Stains only. Chowdhary and Mock (2009) in Chowdhary (2009) also emphasized the importance of studying stain removal and examined the cleaning efficiency of 12 stains with 13 cleaners followed up by laundering. Sample size used was 4"x4" rather than 15" x 15" recommended for the oily stains. AATCC did not give any on a five- point scale.

Bueno, Laso, Amador and Bakalis (2019) reported that the mechanical action and detergent concentration could be adjusted depending on the solid present in the stain. This helps with preventing fabric damage. Jhatial, Khatri, Ali, and Babar (2019) found that Sol-gel treatment got 3-4 stain release rating for bamboo fabric. Zhong et al. (2019) claimed that by installing a UV light source in the washing machine, one can achieve better stain removal for cross-linked cotton fabrics.

Bao and Yun Jun (2018) found that increasing temperature from 140-170⁰C improved soil release. Silicone softener did not help with stain release. Hassan (2018) Stated that stain resistance against acid dye stains was improved with increase in the coating percentage for wool. Moiz, Padhye, and Wang (2018) unveiled that coating helped with removal of oil and chemicals without staining the materials' surface only if their surface tension was different from the un-finished fabric. Suna, Zhaoa, Liua, Chena, and Xhoua, (2018) had similar findings for polyester.

Eladwi, Shaker, and Abdelrahman (2017) were examined oil, tea and roselle stains for 10, 20, and 30 washes. AATCC 130 was used to evaluate oil release. Hassan and Leighs (2017) found that treatments worsened the stain repellence for red wine and mustard. Kabbari and Liouane, Fayala, and Ghith (2017) reported that water and oil repellency can be improved with fuzzy modeling better that the surface response methodology. Miranda, Santos, and Soares (2017) learned that use of chemical modification was effective with soil release. Their study examined the soil-release behaviour of polyester fabrics after they were treated with polyethylene glycol. Murphy (2015) asserted that even though sales have gone up for softeners, their role in reducing costs is yet to be determined. In their investigation, they found that STRUKTOL VP 5417 was found to be effective on 100% cotton and 65/35 poly/cotton blend.

Stains impact the aesthetics of a garment. Oily stains are hard to be removed from the synthetic fibers due to their oleophilic tendency. Therefore, it is important to establish and use stain removal strategies. Some stain removal products are available in the market that can be used before laundering the garments. This topic will be further expanded in chapter 7.

Seam Smoothness (AATCC TM88B, 2018t) in fabrics can be examined by standard replicas after laundering. The replicas were designed to evaluate woven fabrics with durable finish after laundering. It is done for both single needle and double needle seams. The evaluation procedure is like appearance retention and crease retention reported earlier. The author believes that Minimum rating of 4 is a safe choice to go for. The replicas can be purchased from AATCC.

Hati and Das (2011) contended that seam puckers are not perceived indicators of a high-quality clothing construction and should be examined. They discussed several objective and subjective methods of evaluation. The authors recommended that it may be impossible to get pucker free seams and it may be necessary to accept slight puckering. Pan, Gao, Li, and Xu (2017) developed an objective system to counter the subjectivity of the replica evaluation of today and found it to be more effective than the method described in 88B.

This test is more critical for formal wear that expects polished look and aesthetic experience than casual apparel. Nevertheless, a person with clothes that have smooth single and double thread seams is perceived more positively than the one in puckered seams. The value of these tests is subject to consumer expectations and industry responds accordingly.

Wrinkle Recovery (AATCC TM66, 2017e) measures recovery angle of the simulated wrinkle under controlled conditions. It is recommended for woven fabrics. The Wrinkle Recovery Angle tester is used with accessories. The specimen size is 40x15 mm. Six specimens are cut I the warp direction and six in the weft direction. The conditioned specimen is folded face to face and placed between two leaves with a tweezer. A weight of 500 grams is applied for 5 minutes. The specimen is removed and transferred on the circular holder with loose end aligned at 90 degrees angle. Record the recovery angle after five minutes. Repeat the process with three specimens folded face-to-face and three with back-to-backfolding. Repeat the same process for the weft specimens. If the difference between the two averages of back-to-back and face-to-face specimens are higher than 15 degrees for warp and/or weft specimens, report averages of all sets of three specimens separately. The recovery angle can range from 90-180 degrees. A recovery angle of 120 degrees is believed to be the same as the 3.5 of the AATCC TM 128-2017c test. For wrinkle recovery. **(AATCC TM128 – 2017e)** standard see under Chapter 5 and *Annual Manual Manual of International Test Methods and Procedures* for details.

Wang, Liu, Pan, & Gao (2014) developed a system to objectify the process. The authors developed a video capturing and processing system for dynamic measurements of fabric wrinkle recovery angle. They videotaped the whole process and compared it with AATCC TM 66 method and found it to be equally effective. Their adapted version had three advantages: 1) human interference was eliminated, 2) The also records the change in angle, and 3) use of video sequences for calculating the recovery angles that enhanced the accuracy and efficiency of measurement.

Doty and Easter (2009) reported that active wear in their study had higher ratings than workwear after twenty washes. Yatagai and Takahashi (2005) stated that citric acid treatment with specific soil improved the wrinkle recovery. Yang, Zhou, Lickfield, and Parachura (2003) found that treating cellulose (cotton) with durable press finish impacted wrinkle resistance. Kuzuhara and Hori (2002) observed that increase in hydrogen bonds improved the wrinkle recovery.

CARE

Care predominantly deals with colorfastness to different conditions, dimensional stability including growth and shrinkage, seam twist and skew. The colorfastness can be tested for bleaching, burnt gas fumes, crocking. laundering, perspiration. Water of chlorinated pool, and sea water.

Colorfastness to Bleaching (AATCC TM101 – 2019) refers to the ability of the textile materials to resist color change when exposed to bleach during processing as well as care. It is important that textile is colorfast to the commonly used chemicals because the faded and distorted colors are perceived adversely. This standard uses hydrogen peroxide for all textiles except polyamide that is damaged more readily by the Clorox bleach. This test requires stitching of white and colored specimens of 4" x 1.5" dimensions. One can use the multi-fiber strip for multifiber testing. The specimens are soaked in bleach bath for 1-2 hours. Remove the specimens and rinse under cold water for ten minutes. Remove the stitching and flatten the specimen. Dry it at less than 60 degrees Celsius. Evaluate colored piece using gray scale for color change and white piece using gray scale for staining using rating scale of 1-5. Rating of 1 represents the worst performance and rating of 5 represents the best performance. One can also use spectrophotometer to determine color change between original and bleached material.

Colorfastness to Burnt Gas Fumes (AATCC TM23-- 2015e, 2020) assesses resisting of material's color change to nitrogen bound oxides found through combustion of natural gas via atmosphere. They can come in open air as well as home cooking. The author noticed so at the stomach level from the cooking heat from the gas range. The color change is evaluated using the standard gray scale of color change.

Colorfastness to Chlorinated Water (AATCC 188-2010e3(2017) e assesses colorfastness to sodium hypochlorite/chlorine bleach of 4-6% concentration with pH between 9.8-12.8. It is also known as the chlorine bleach. This test is designed for the home laundering situations. The evaluation of color change is recommended after five home launderings. For reporting, numerical averages should be used. No specific values for passing were listed in the standard. **Colorfastness to powdered nonchlorine bleach** (AATCC 172-2007) is also tested through five home launderings using weight-based (100-120 grams) specimens specified in the test. The procedure is very similar to AATCC 188. For both these tests, 3 and higher rating is recommended for colorfastness to staining and 4 and higher for the color change.

Sarkar and Khallil (2014) examined fading and characteristics loss for denim. People use bleach to intentionally fade the 100% denim jeans. They found in their investigation that doing so, resulted in shrinkage of 6% in length and 1% width. Structurally, weight reduced 2.9%, ends by 1.9% and picks by 7.1%. Tensile strength decreased by 2.6% in warp and 4,5% in weft. Seam strength reduced by 21.79%. Color change was rated as 3.0 on the 5-point scale.

Colorfastness to Crocking (AATCC TM8--016e) assesses the color transference through rubbing on other surfaces. A crock meter is used as an instrument for rubbing in this test. The test is a 2" x 5.1" bias cut piece that is rubbed against the white crock square in dry and wet conditions for ten complete turns or 20 back and forth movements. The crocked crock squares are then compared against the gray scales of color change as well as staining established and sold by AATCC. The specimens are rated from 1-5. For most fabrics ≥3 is the passing grade for wet crocking and ≥4 for the dry crocking. Exceptions can exist. Crock test square is made of 100% combed cotton which is de-sized and bleached. It uses a yarn size of 15 Tex (40/1 cotton count), and twist with z direction, and approximately 15 twists per inch. Thread count is 33 ± 3 in the warp and 32 ± 3 in the weft direction. It has ½ plain weave, 6.5-7.5 pH, and 108-118 grams per square meter for greige good and 97-107 grams per square meter for the finished material. Its whiteness ranges from 78-82.

Colorfastness to Laundering has several different methods and include both accelerated and home laundering methods of specimens and garments. Some of those tests and procedures are described below.

Accelerated Method (AATCC TM61, 2013e, 2020) is designed to determine if textile can withstand frequent laundering. This test is timed for 45minutes. For this test wear and tear of five laundering is simulated by using steel balls. Number of steel balls changes from 10 – 100 for different purposes. The original test provides this information.

This test uses an accelerated laundering machine. This test has five options. For option 1A, the specimen size is 2"x4"and 2A-5A is 2"x6". Multifiber strip is used for the first two methods and both bleached cotton and multifiber strip can be used for 5A option. 2A is no bleach option for the 5A option, and 3A is no bleach option for the 4A option. Wool fiber can absorb bleach for tests 4A and 5A. Test recommends removing wool if multifiber strip is used. Multifiber strips are stapled or sewn on the fabric to be tested (Figures 21-23). Figures 21-23 are in the post-laundered stage. Use gray scales of rating color changes and staining for assessment from 1-5. 1 represents the worst performance and 5 means the best performance. The passing grade of 3 or higher rating is recommended for colorfastness to staining and 4 or higher for the color change. Doty and Easter (2009) found that garments showed some color change after the first wash. However, they did not have any color change for the next nineteen washes in their study.

Figure 21: Cotton fabric with cotton crock square sewn with long running stitch.

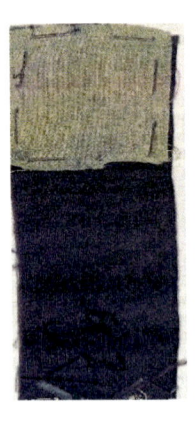

Figure 22: Cotton fabric with multifiber strip sewn with long running stitch.

Figure 23: Cotton fabric with multifiber strip sewn with run and back stitch.

Figure 21 shows that laundering resulted in loss of colored material and gain of the crock square. The rating is between 1-2 of color change and 1 of staining. Because the base fabric was cotton, transfer is very intense. Figures 22-23 have multifiber strips attached to the same cotton fabric. It is worth observing that different fiber contents got color transferred at different levels. Color has transferred only on 2nd, 4th, sixth, tenth, and 13th strips. They are modacrylic, cotton, Dacron 54, spun silk, and wool. However, no color transferred on diacetate, triacetate, Creslan, Dacron 64, Nylon 66. Orlon 75, polypropylene, and viscose rayon. Disperse dyes were first developed for acetate and later recommended for other synthetic fibers. Chemical composition of fiber contents impact staining during laundering. This observation has implications for laundering of clothes.

Home Laundering (AATCC TM135 – 2018t) is based on machine parameters for home laundering. It suggests four washing procedures, three agitation cycles, and four drying procedures for home care options. One should use standard machines, AATCC detergent and laundering ballast if needed. Specimen size is 15" x 15" with a 10" x 10" square inside. The test provides washing and drying parameters. Average % of dimensional change (DC) is calculated using the formula below.

Average DC % = 100 (B-A)/A

DC = Average Dimensional Change

A = Average Original Dimension

B = Average Dimension After Laundering

Home Laundering Garments (Home Laundering (AATCC TM150 – 2018t) This test has similar processes as AATCC 135 in several ways except it is designed for laundering garments. Both lengths and widths of the garments are measured. In addition to providing other parameters for washing, drying, and ballasts, the test suggests benchmark locations for thirteen garments. Those 13 locations are blouse, boxer shorts, coveralls, overalls, pajama bottom, pajama top, shirt, shorts, skirt, slip, sweater, trousers, and uniform/dress (*AATCC Manual of International Methods and Procedures*, 2021, p. 296).

Colorfastness to Light (AATCC TM16.1, 2013e) provides general principles for determining colorfastness to light. Test options include Xenon Arc Lamp. Gray scales of color change and Blue Wool Lightfastness Standards. For latest details, refer to the latest manual.

Colorfastness to Perspiration (AATCC TM125-2013e2, 2020) tests 2.0 x 2.75" specimens. Weigh it and soak in a petri dish that has a diameter of 9 cm and depth of 2 cm. To prepare the reagent, use water, sodium chloride, lactic acid, disodium hydrogen phosphate and histidine monohydrochloride in the amount provided in the manual. Fill to 1.5 cm depth with the perspiration solution and soak for 30 minutes. Agitate and squeeze occasionally. Squeeze it through the wringers press through two blotting papers so that its weight is almost double of the original weight. For example, if the original weight is 6 grams, the weight should range between 11.5-12.5 grams. Then mount it on the exposure frame following directions from AATCC TM 16.3. Use gray scale of color change or instrumental measure for assessment. Pass if the rating is ≥3 for staining an ≥4 for the color change.

Colorfastness to Water

Impact of different waters varies for dyeing, printing, and caring for textile materials. **AATCC TM107 – 2013e2** is designed to assess how colored, dyed, and printed textile resists to the distilled or deionized water. Distilled water is used to accommodate for the variation of its composition in different geographic area. The specimen (6 x 6 cm ±2 cm) in the test is backed by the multifiber strip ((5 x 5 cm ±2 cm). The specimen is soaked in the solution for fifteen minutes and agitated occasionally. Remove the specimen from the solution and pass it between squeezes rolls. Continue until the wet weight is 2.5-3 times of the dry weight. Insert the specimens in the perspiration tester to produce 4.5 kg or 10 pounds pressure. Heat the specimen at 100^0F +2^0F for 18 hours. Evaluate using AATCC Gray Scale of Color Change and Staining. Manual dos not give the passing standard. The author of this text believes that ≥4 is the safest. Additional tests are provided below to further understand the effects of water.

Colorfastness to Water: Chlorinated Pool (AATCC TM162 – 2011e2) has different reagent preparation. Following OSHA standards is recommended. While mixing the chemicals, use safety glasses, gloves, and apron. Eyewash safety water should be easily accessible. The reagent includes distilled or deionized water, chlorine, and hardness concentrate. In 800 cc water, 8 grams Calcium Chloride and 5 grams of Magnesium Chloride are added, and solution is made 1 liter. The test gives other options of making solution and accelerated and dry cleaning options. Gray scales of color change and staining are recommended for evaluation for each fiber content on the multifiber strip. **AATCC TM188-2010e3(2017) e** is recommended for determining the colorfastness of sodium hypochlorite bleach in home laundering.

Sea Water (AATCC TM106– 2009e, 2013e3) test is same as AATCC TM107 – 2013e2. The only difference is about the test solution that is simulated as sea water. The solution requires 30 grams of sodium chloride and 5 grams of magnesium chloride in 1000 cc water solution. A rating of ≥4 is the safest to use for passing the specimen.

Thiry (2009) reported that swimwear fabrics should have colorfastness to ultraviolet rays, chlorinated water seawater, perspiration, suntan oils, and sunscreens in addition to being stretchy. It is also important to think of the wet sag when making the selection of the yarn for swimwear. It is worth knowing that stretch fabrics require special type of stitching. One should also pay attention to seam type and stitch density (Chowdhary, 2009).

Devanand and Parthiban (2019) contended that sea water will be a good choice for dyeing cotton fabrics despite salt level of 35 grams per litter. In their study, results exhibited similar performance to the ground water use. Ferreira, Medeiros, Steffens, & Oliveira (2019) reported that the whiteness index was good when bleached with seawater than distilled water. Additionally, tensile strength and 'hydrophilicity' was also better with seawater. Authors purported that it will be possible to use seawater for cotton fabrics in future. Zerin, Foisal, Datta, and Rana (2017) found that cotton dyed in sea water produced lighter shades than the ground water. Other quality parameters were no impacted adversely.

Thiry (2009) reported that swimwear fabrics should have colorfastness to ultraviolet rays, chlorinated water seawater, perspiration, suntan oils, and sunscreens in addition to being stretchy. It is also important to think of the wet sag when making the selection of the yarn for swimwear. It is worth knowing that stretch fabrics require special type of stitching. One should also pay attention to seam type and stitch density (Chowdhary, 2009).

Dimensional Stability refers to the "ability of the fabric to resist growth (increase) or shrinkage (decrease) in length and/or width after exposure to laundering (Chowdhary, 2009, 96). It could vary from one fabric construction to another as well as one refurbishing technique to another. Number of washes can also make an impact. There are several different standards provided in the *AATCC Manual of International Test Methods and Procedures*. Four of the standard tests are provided below.

Laundering of Woven and Knitted Fabrics ((AATCC TM196 – 2012e3) is designed to determine dimensional changes of all fiber contents except wool when exposed to the commercial launderings. For drying five procedures are established. The one appropriate for the tested materials should be selected. It is different from the accelerated method. Procedure is repeated if impact of multiple launderings is to be determined. The test gives six tests with corresponding washing temperatures and time used, five drying methods and three restoration methods. It also provides washing test conditions for all six methods. The percentage of dimensional change is calculated using formula below.

Average DC % = 100 (B-A)/A

DC = Average Dimensional Change

A = Average Original Dimension

B = Average Dimension After Laundering

If the percentage is in negative, the fabric shows growth. If the difference between 5%B and a is positive, it shows shrinkage. For example, if average after laundering was 38 cm and it was 40 cm originally. The percentage will be 100(2/40) = 5% shrinkage. If the dimensions after laundering were 42 cm, the resulting 5% will be growth. Recommended maximum dimensional change is 2-3% for woven dress apparel and 5% for the knitted apparel. To interpret the response from the example provided above, the fabric will be accepted for the knitted material and rejected for the woven materials. Tables 19-20 below provides standards for various end uses from the ASTM volumes 7.01 and 7.02.

Home laundering – Machine washing (AATCC LP1 – 2018e) is designed consistent with the parameters used for other laundering procedures. It uses automatic washing machine, standard detergent, and ballast. It gives details for normal, delicate, and permanent press. It provides information on both traditional as well as high efficiency machines.

Table 19: Requirements of dimensional change for various end uses by ASTM.

.#	End Use	Maximum Requirement in %
1.	Lining (Woven) ASTM D3783, 4114-14	3 (After five launderings) 2 (After 3 Dry Cleanings)
2.	Women's Sportswear ASTM D4155 – 14	3 (After five launderings) 2 (After 3 Dry Cleanings)
3.	Woven Dry Cleanable Coat for Men's and Boys' ASTM D3562-14	2 (After 3 Dry Cleanings)
4.	Woven Dry Cleanable Coat for Women's and Girls ASTM D3562 -14	2 (After 3 Dry Cleanings)
5.	Woven Swimwear ASTM D 3994 – 14	3
6.	Umbrella Fabrics ASTM D4112	3

.#	End Use	Maximum Requirement in %
7.	Rainwear ASTM D7017-14	3 (Laundering) 2 (Dry Cleanings)
8.	Men's and Boy's woven beachwear and sports shirt ASTM D4154 – 2014	3 (After 5 washes) 3 (After 3 Dry Cleanings)
9.	Corset-Girdle combination fabrics ASTM D4116-2020	Length 5 Width 3
10.	Bras, Slips, Lingerie, and Underwear ASTM D7019-14	3 (Laundering) 2 (Dry Cleanings)
11.	Blouse, Dress, Dress Shirt and Sport Shirt ASTM D7020-14	3 (After 5 washes) 2 (After 3 Dry Cleanings)
12.	Bathrobe, Dressing Gown, Negligee, Nightgown, & Pajamas ASTM D7021-14	3 (Laundering) 2 (Dry Cleanings)
13.	Women's and Girls' Woven Dress Gloves ASTM D4115-20	3

Table 20: Requirements of dimensional change in knitted fabrics for various end uses Source: ASTM

.#	End Use	Maximum Requirement in %
1.	Career Dress Apparel (ASTM D3995-14)	3 (After 5 washes) 3 (After 3 Dry Cleanings)
2.	Career Vocational Apparel (ASTM D3995-14)	3 (After 5 washes) 3 (After 3 Dry Cleanings)
3.	Women's Sportswear ASTM D4156 – 14	3 (After five launderings) 3 (After 3 Dry Cleanings)
4.	Woven Dry Cleanable Coat for Men's and Boys' ASTM D3562-14	2 (After 3 Dry Cleanings)
5.	Woven Dry Cleanable Coat for Women's and Girls ASTM D3562-14	2 (After 3 Dry Cleanings)
6.	Woven Swimwear ASTM D 3994 – 14	3
7.	Men's and Boy's Knitted beachwear and sports shirt ASTM D4154 – 2014	3 (After 5 washes) 3 (After 3 Dry Cleanings)

.#	End Use	Maximum Requirement in %
8.	Corset-Girdle combination fabrics ASTM D4116-2020	Length 5 Width 5
9.	Bras, Slips, Lingerie, and Underwear ASTM D7019-14	5 (Laundering) 5 (Dry Cleanings)
10.	Bathrobe, Dressing Gown, Negligee, Nightgown, & Pajamas ASTM D7021-14	5 (Laundering) 5 (Dry Cleanings)
11.	Women's and Girls' Knitted Dress Gloves ASTM D4115-20	5

Home laundering – Hand washing (AATCC LP2 – 2018e, 2020) includes hand washing and line and flat drying methods. Like other laundering methods, it uses the AATCC's standard detergent. One of the limitations is that it may not replicate exactly between and among individuals and households. The test lists temperatures for very cold to hot. The test suggests that the experimenter should give temperature of wash and rinse cycles. Number of completed cycles of washing and drying methods should also be specified.

Seam Twist (AATCC TM207 – 2019) This is a relatively new standard and was first developed in 2017 and revised in 2019. IT is believed to be function of the direction of fabric, garment assembly, and skewness. It is worth checking the garment twist before and after laundering. Ideally, it is developed for the garments with vertical seams that are found in tops and pants. However, its use could be extended to interiors such as curtains, drapes, and pillowcases. **Seam twist** refers to the lateral rotation that occurs when different panels of a garment by a seam. They are the most applicable to the vertical seams such as outer and inseams, and center seams of the pants. It is not applicable to the curved seams. If the twist numbers for left and right side are different, take an average.

The test illustrates with examples of pants and shirts. It also provides laundering parameters. Pictures are used to mark and measure distances before and after laundering. Percentage of each seam should be calculated using the formula below (*Manual of International Test Methods and Procedures, 2021*, 430).

Before Laundering

$X_0 = 100 \times (AA'/AB)$

X_0 = Seam twist before laundering

AA' = Twist distance before laundering (mm or inches)

AB = Seam length before laundering (mm or inches)

After Laundering

$X_n = 100 \times (AA''/AB)$

X_n = Seam twist after n laundering cycles (%)

AA" = Twist distance before laundering (mm or inches)

AB = Seam length before laundering (mm or inches)

You should average percentage of all seams before and after laundering. Also calculate percentage change after laundering. Remember that this test is for garments and not fabric. Seams can create a tension that could act differently after laundering than the fabric. Fiber content, seam type, stitch type, as well as stitch density in a seam impact the garment twisting.

Skew (ATCC TM 179-2019) refers to "a fabric condition resulting when filling yarn or knitted courses are angularly displaced from a line perpendicular to the edge or side to side of the fabric." (ASTM D123-19) It is a fabric defect that can impact the fit of the garment if it exceeds 2.5% for woven materials and 5% for the knitted fabrics. The test method shows two methods of marking a fabric and a garment. It also provides laundering guideline along with marking guidelines after laundering. The test suggests calculating percentage to 0.1%. The formula is given below.

X = 100 (AA'/AB)

X= % change in skew

AA' = Displacement after laundering

AB = original length

Stain Removal (AATCC TM 130) test method focuses on the release of oil stain from the fabric. This method can be used on garments also. Standard laundering procedure is used. Ballast should be used if necessary. The test describes the soiling and laundering procedures. It provides stain remove replica for evaluation from 1-5. 1 means the worst performance and 5 means the best performance. Average rating of ≥4 cab used as the passing grade.

Bueno, Laso, Amador, and Bakalis (2019) found that mechanical action and detergent concentration could be adjusted depending on the solid present in the stain. This helps with preventing fabric damage. Jhatial, Khatri, Ali, Babar (2019) asserted that s sol-gel treatment got 3-4 stain release rating for bamboo fabric. Zhong et al. (2019). Asserted that by installing a UV light source in the washing machine, one can achieve better stain removal for cross-linked cotton

Bao and Yun-Jun (2018) reported that increasing temperature from 140-170°C improved soil release. However, silicone softener did not help with stain release. Hassan (2018) mentioned that the stain resistance against acid dye stains was improved with increase in the coating percentage for wool. Moiz, Padhye, and Wang (2018) claimed that coating helped with removal of oil and chemicals without staining the materials' surface. When surface tension of the coated surface was like the uncoated stage the stain removal was not good. Suna, Zhaoa, Liua, Chena, and Zhoua, (2018) iterated that the fluorinated polyacrylate treatment helped with the release of oily stains from polyester.

Eladwi, Shaker, and Abdelrahman (2017) used AATCC 130 replica of oil release to evaluate the stains of oil, tea and roselle after 10, 20, and 30 washes. Hassan and Leighs purported that surface treatments worsened the stain repellence for red wine and mustard. Kabbari, Liouane, Fayala, and Ghith, A (2017) asserted that water and oil repellency could be improved with fuzzy modeling better that the surface response methodology. Miranda, Santos, and Soares (2017) found that use of chemical modification was effective with soil release. Murphy (2015) reported that STRUKTOL VP 5417 is effective on 100% cotton and 65/35 poly/cotton blend.

Doty and Easter found that mineral and oil stains were hard to remove from the workwear. Active wear did not show any trend. Chowdhary (2008) Shout, Spray'n Wash, and Oxy wash were not effective for removing the motor oil stains. The same three were used on different colored permanent markers. The best efficiency was seen for the yellow stain and the worst for the black stain. Repeated trials lightened the stain for all colors. Chowdhary (2007) reported several articles on stain removal with six key findings. 1) Vinegar was effective on basic stains. 2) Clorox worked good on the acidic stains. 3) Woolite removed ketchup and pudding stains better than tide. 4) Powdered detergents performed better than the liquid detergents. 5) Didiseven was not effective on mustard and oily stains. However, it removed chocolate, coffee, ink, and wine stains completely. 6) Muriatic acid removed the rust stains effectively.

Evaluation Procedures for color change include the gray scales of color change and staining. They are recommended to evaluate the colorfastness of textiles because they offer neutral colors with light and chroma variations.

Gray Scale of Color Change (AATCC EP1 – 2020) provides gray chips for examining the color changes after treatments such as light exposure, laundering abrasion, and crocking etc. It measures loss pf color from the colored material after a treatment. For most cases, minimum of 4 rating on a five-point scale is recommended for passing. 1 represents the worst performance and 5 the best performance. Figure 24 shows its picture for visualization (*AATCC Manual of International Methods and Procedures*, 2021, 459). This scale is available from AATCC headquarters at Research Triangle Park in North Carolina.

Figure 24: Gray scale of color change.

Gray Scale of Staining (AATCC EP2 – 2020) is used to assess the amount of color picked up by the crock square or multifiber strip. This test is used for assessing the colorfastness of colored materials to crocking, dry cleaning, laundering, and light. It is also rated between 1 and 5. The rating of 1 represents the worst performance and 5 the best performance. In general, a minimum rating of 3 is acceptable for the wet staining and 4 for the dry staining. Figure 25 shows its picture for visualization (*AATCC Manual of International Methods and Procedures*, 2021, 461). This scale is also available from the AATCC headquarters.

Figure 25: Gray scale of staining.

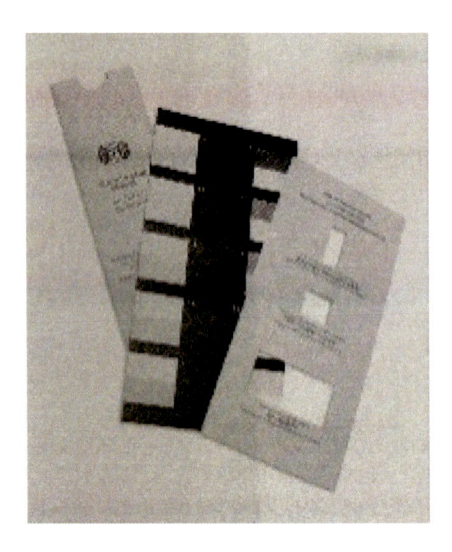

    Chowdhary and Adnan (2019) The findings revealed that dimensional stability was best for 100% polyester was best for medium count 96/4 polyester/spandex blend for interlock knits. Among jersey knits, 50/50 cotton/poly in wales and 85/15 cotton polyester blend performed the best in the course direction. In pique knit low count light weight cotton had the best performance for dimensional stability than cotton for appearance retention.

    Chowdhary (2017) compared three brands of 100% cotton t-shirts for frequency of washing and dimensional stability with standard and commercial detergents. Results revealed that one of the brands reduced significantly for chest width between 11-15 and 21-25 wash cycles with standard detergent. All differences were less than 5% and acceptable. For the other two brands, dimensional change was highest for the neck opening. A significant reduction in dimensional percentage was noticed between 11-15 and 21-25 wash cycles for both brands, and between 16-20 and 21-25 wash cycles for one of those two brands using standard detergent.

    With commercial detergent, one t-shirt revealed progressive shrinkage for front length for all three brands. Shrinkage was more than 5% and increased significantly from 11-15 to 21-25 wash cycles for brand 1, 1-5 through 16-20 and 21-25 for brand two, and 1-5 through 21-25 for brand Three t-shirts differed significantly when they were laundered with standard detergent rather than the commercial detergent. Fabric count and fabrics weight also increased after laundering.

    Marsha and Chowdhary (2018) compared cotton and cotton/polyester blend t-shirts for dimensional stability before and after was laundering for six body parts, as well as air permeability, bursting strength, and horizontal wicking. Comparisons were also made in washed and unwashed forms for fabric count, thickness, and weight. Findings revealed that 100% cotton t-shirts shrank significantly after washing for chest width, front length, sleeve length, sleeve seam, and sleeve opening. Differences were not significant for neck opening. Blended t-shirts shrank significantly higher for all six locations after washing.

    Chowdhary and Adnan (2017) uncovered that knits shrank in wales and grew in courses. Fiber content impacted dimensional stability and appearance retention. Appearance retention was the highest for poly/spandex. Bamboo/spandex shrank the most in wales direction and grew in courses direction for interlock knits. For interlock knits, poly/spandex had the best appearance retention. Chowdhary and Vijaykumar (2017) compared three brands of weft knits and found that they did not differ for abrasion resistance and stretch and recovery. However, they differed for fabric count, thickness, weight, and pilling.

Uttam, D., & Sethi (2016) examined the impact of physical factors on dimensional stability of cotton after repeated laundering. Researchers found that repeated laundering cycles increased shrinkage as well as fabric weight, thickness, and cover factor. They also noted most change until the fourth laundering. Telli and Ozdil (2015) asserted that adding cotton to polyester increased dimensional instability of the fabric in both directions. However, it was higher in widthwise than lengthwise direction.

Rahman, Biswas, Mitra, and Rakesh (2014) examined dimensional stability, and pilling resistance of jersey with Lycra, plain single jersey, 1x1 rib, single Lacoste, double Lacoste, and interlock knit for grey fabric, with and without enzyme. Enzyme treatment challenged the stability of all types of weft knits and increased their shrinkage except for single Lacoste and interlock. Yesmin et al (2014) found that single jersey shrank 12,5% in width and double pique shrank only 3.75%. Single Lacoste had lowest shrinkage of three fabrics. Decrease in stitch length reduced shrinkage in jersey but higher in double pique knit. Lengthwise dimensional stability was better than the widthwise stability.

Das and Thakur (2013) found that change in the number of picks impacted shrinkage in the warp direction and number of ends in the weft direction for woven fabrics. Collectively, number of ends, number of picks, warp tension, back rest position, and pick insertion rate per minute explained 99.02% in warp and 82.81% of the variance in the filling direction. Agarwal, Koehl, and Perwuelz (2011). Found that fabric softener impacted the drape of the knitted fabrics from viscose and polyester the most of 20 washes. Doty and Easer (2009) uncovered that workwear did not shrink more than 1% after 20 wash and dry cycles. However, activewear showed a shrinkage of >4% for some garments. Singh, Roy, Varshney, and Goyal (2011) examined problems with cotton knits for dimensional change. The findings of their study revealed that loop length, fabric count, gauge of machine and twist factor impacted dimensional stability. Stitch length was singled out as the most dominating factor. Thiry (2009) stressed that laundering loosens up the swimwear. Therefore, it is important that quality of the elastane fiber is critically examined before making the final decision.

Chiwese and Crews (2000) reported that wet softeners caused more pilling than the dry ones. Additionally, they decreased the breaking strength also. The scholars recommended that liquid softeners should not be used for shirts, pajamas and sleepwear made from flannel. The *Consumer Reports* (2000) article reported that liquid softeners increased the flammability. However, dry sheets did not change the flammability. Cellulase enzymes were effective in reducing pilling from cotton fabrics. Schwartze and McKinnon (2000). Recommended that reducing drying time by three minutes and keeping temperature under 140^0C can control the color change.

Baumert and Crews (2000) found that the liquid fabric softeners improved the wrinkle recovery of polyester/cotton blends. Dryer sheets enhance the wrinkle resistance of broadcloth. Recovery angle was higher for warp than wet for all fabrics except the poly/cotton blend. Anand, Bishop, and Mackay (1996) examined the shrinkage behavior of cotton, wool, and acrylic to laundering. In their study laundering impacted the stitch length and loop shape. Calcium Phosphate deposits mase knits stiffer and heavier than before laundering. Wool shrank some and linear density of cotton increased. Acrylics stretched after tumble drying.

As evident from the preceding information that laundering impacts dimensional stability of woven and knitted fabrics. Pre and post laundering impact on several structural (count skew, thickness, and weight) and performance attributes abrasion resistance, breaking strength, and pilling resistance) is obvious. For understanding the concept fully, it is critical to pay attention to the minute details that may impact the performance of the fabric.

Care aspect is very important for consumer in today's fast paced society. The daily tasks are diversified, and consumer has less and less time to respond to the multiple tasks. Providing colorfast and stain repellant clothing, easy laundering ability, less damage, and enhanced ability to retain its original appearance with less difficulty should be considered by the industry.

COMFORT

Absorbency, water repellence, water vapor resistance, and wicking behavior of textiles are associated with comfort in apparel. This section explains the details to allow for the pass/fail interpretation of the results.

Moisture Transfer/Absorbency (AATCC TM79, 2010e2, 2018e) is also known as the absorbency test. The test is based on the time taken by a water drop to disappear. Originally, it was developed to test the absorbency of the bleached material. However, later its use was extended to measure water repellency and resistance also. It measures fabrics ability to absorb and retain moisture. It requires use of 2-5 specimens of 8" x 8" or 200 x 200 mm dimensions. Just like all other tests, it is important to bring specimens to the moisture equilibrium by conditioning them for fiber content appropriate duration explained in a previous chapter.

Place your specimen on the embroidery hoop. Apply one drop of water from one inch distance either with burette or medicine dropper. Make sure that the hooped fabric is wrinkle-free. Start the stopwatch and record the times when the water drop disappears. You just watch the drop for 60 seconds. If it takes longer than that, just record 60+ sec. For reporting, use means and standard deviation. To pass the fabric, it should take five seconds or less (≤ 5) seconds. Of course, opposite of absorbency is repellency, look at the data and make appropriate judgment for the water repellence or repellency attributes. Use means for the interpretation. Address variability based on the standard deviation. Moisture transfer for all three weaves (plain, twill, and satin) was higher for washed than the unwashed form (Chowdhary & Islam, 2019).

Water Repellency

Water Spray Method (AATCC 1TM22, 2017e) tests the wetting of the textile materials. It can be used for both finished and unfinished fabrics. It is designed on the premise that a water pattern is formed when a set amount of water is dropped on a wrinkle free and taut material from a certain height. Three 7" x 7" specimens are used for this test. 250 ml of distilled water is used through a funnel. It should take 25-30 seconds for water to go through. Immediately after tapping the funnel to make sure that every drop is transferred to the fabric, compare the water pattern to the "Standard Spray Test RATINGS" (p.

93). Record the ratings for all three specimens and report them individually. The six possible ratings are 100, 90, 80, 70, 50 and 0. You need a minimum of 70 rating to pass the textile for water repellency. It could vary for different end uses. For example, the umbrella fabric requires the original rating of ≥90, and after laundering at ≥70. Same is true for the rain wear in smooth texture. However, for the rough texture, original should be ≥80 and after laundering ≥70.

Jonas et al. (2020) reported that water repellency can be increased by making fibers textured through nano technology individually or packed form as well as by adding different finishes. Ratings were different for water repellency in post wash form for plain and satin weave (Chowdhary and Islam, 2019). However, it did not change for twill weave for washed and unwashed forms). All fabrics passed except the bleached plain weave in the unwashed form. However, in washed farm, all failed except the twill weave. Unal, Kartal, and Yilonu (2019) tested polyester, acrylic and viscose for six different chenille yarns (Flatter than the regular yarn) to be used for upholstery. The fabric used two different pile heights and finished it with 60% and 80% fluorocarbon finish. Findings revealed that the Finish enhanced the water repellency of the fabric and abrasion resistance reduced it.

Tumble Jar Method (AATCC TM70, 2015e2, 2020) is founded on the weight change (%) principle. Specimens are soaked in water are tumbled for twenty minutes. Dynamic tumble tester is used for this method. For this test two specimens of 20 x 20 cm dimensions are cut on bias and sealed on all four edges by latex cement for each sample (You will have a total of ten pieces). The latex cement is applied to prevent raveling. Take 5 specimens and weigh them to the nearest of 0.1% for both sets of five specimens. Place both sets in a jar and run for 20 minutes in a tumbler filled with water. Remove one set of specimens (5 stacked together) and pass it through ringer and between two blotting papers to dry until it is down to twice the dry weight. Place the specimens in a plastic container. Repeat the process with the second set. Specimens are then weighed. Calculate the percentage using formula below. Report the average % of two specimens.

$$WA = 100 \frac{(W-C)}{C}$$

WA % of absorbed water
W   Wet specimen
C   Conditioned specimen

Water Resistance: Rain (AATCC TM35, 2018e) backs the fabric with blotter and is sprayed with water for five minutes under controlled conditions. The blotter is weighed before and after the treatment to determine the amount of water that leaked through the fabric. The specimen size of 20 x 20 cm and it is backed by a blotting paper of 15.2 x 15.2 dimensions. Water penetration is shown by the gain in the weight of the blotting paper. If it is more than 5 grams, then you denote as 5+. Based on ASTM D7017-2014 (*2019 Annual Book of ASTM Standards 7.02*, p. 783), the weight should not increase by more than 1gram.

Water Resistance: Impact Penetration (AATCC TM42, 2018e) uses process like AATCC 35. However, the water is penetrated through higher height. 500 cc distilled water is sprayed via funnel from 2-3 feet height. The blotting paper backing the specimen is pre-weighed and recorded. On completion of the penetration, specimen is removed from the blotter and the wet blotter is reweighed. Results are reported as 5 or 5+ grams. Based on ASTM D7017-2014 (*2019 Annual Book of ASTM Standards 7.02*, p. 783), the weight should not increase by more than 1gram.

Water Vapor Resistance

Water vapor resistance measures breathability of fabric for thermal comfort (Shim, 2016) and important for the intimate apparel. The scholars used hot plate testing to examine the transfer of vapors Their focus was to observe the thermoregulatory processes during laundering. (Reljic, Stepanovic, Lazic, Cercovic, and Cerovic, 2016). It is represented in g/100 in^2/24 hours in US standard units and g/m^2/24 hours in metric (or SI) units. Melba Wildfire (undated), an Australian company used <10m^2 PA/W as the specification based on the ISO 11092 standard. They reported the range of eight Nomex fabrics of 3.5 to 6.24 for firefighters' apparel. The Nomex fabrics were noted to be more light weight, durable, and comfortable than the traditional FR cotton options.

Coruh (2015) examined four blends (cotton/viscose, cotton/polyester (40/60, and 30/70), and cotton/poly as single jersey knit. Results revealed that increase in the loop length decreased the tightness, as well as fabric thickness. Increase in loop length increased the air permeability and wearer's comfort. Increase in thickness reduced the air permeability. Increase in loop length increased the water vapor permeability. However, tightness reduced water vapor permeability.

Das, Das, Kothari, Fanguiero, and Araujo (2007). Reported that in water vapor transference, liquid water as well as water vapor along with fabric are considered to determine the rate. Water vapor diffusion is impacted by the porosity of the fabrics and utilizes the convection process of transferring the sweat from the skin to the atmosphere. The water vapor resistance uses the combined effect of wicking and evaporation processes.

Wicking Behavior

Wicking behavior is related to comfort via moisture management. **Wicking** refers to the spread of moisture through capillary action in the material.

Liquid Moisture Management Properties (AATCC TM195 – 2011e2, 2017 e3) test uses a sophisticated equipment called Moisture Management Tester (MMT}It has specimen size of 8 mm x 8 mm. It measures wicking in mm/second for both top and bottom of the fabric.

Vertical Wicking (AATCC TM197 – 2011e2, 2018e) also measures wicking rate as mm/second. The specimen size is 165 ±3 x 25 x ±3 mm. The formula used is as follows.

W = d/t

W = Wicking rate

D = wicking distance in mm

t = wicking time in seconds.

For time, this test has two options. Option A requires five minutes or 300 seconds. Option B uses time taken to wick 2 mm height.

Summary of statistics is provided for both option A and option B. For option A, it gives values for four methods and jersey, interlock, polyester woven, cotton woven, and poly/cotton woven in both length and width directions. For option B, they are provided for cotton pique, polyester jersey, polyester mesh, and polyester/spandex in both directions. Eyeballing the data provided reveals that very minor directional differences poly/cotton blend in option A. However, the differences are higher for jersey, interlock, polyester woven and cotton woven. For option B, differences exist between long term and short-term tests, different fiber contents and various fiber contents.

Horizontal Wicking (AATCC TM198 – 2011e3, 2020) utilizes both length and width as opposed to the unidirectional wicking for vertical wicking rate. The specimen size is 8" x 8" or 200 mm x 200 mm. Horizontal wicking rate formula is provided below.

$W = \pi (1/4) (d_1) (d_2)/t$

W = Wicking rate in mm²/second

Π = 22/7 03 3.14

¼ = 0.25

d_1 = wicking distance in length

d_2 = wicking distance in width

t = 5 minutes or 300 seconds (Option1)

Option 2 = Time taken in seconds to hit the periphery of a 4" diameter circle. Horizontal wicking for 100% woven cotton was given as 78 mm²/sec, for 100% Cotton jersey as 53mm²/sec, and 23 mm²/sec for 100% cotton interlock (*AATCC Manual of International Test Methods,* 2021, p. 411).

A horizontal wicking study of the relationship between wicking area and wicking time found it to be linear (Morent, Geyter, Leys, Vansteenkiste, & Phillips, 2006). The relationship had a with R^2 of .9987. Their method yielded a wicking rate of 80 mm²/s. For nonwoven plasma treated polyester, the wicking rate was 129 mm²/s and its R^2 was 0.9941. The authors noted that oxygen rate increases with plasma treatment. Therefore, wettability of the fabric also increases. Importance of determining wicking rate of woven and nonwoven fabrics was emphasized. The wicking rate of natural cotton was found to be 80 mm2/sec.

Fangueiro, Filgueiras, Soutinho, & Meidi (2010) examined fabrics polyester and released® and viscose Outlast® as back fabrics for both sets. Researchers tested wicking and drying behavior of the selected fabrics. Viscose had the best wicking and drying ability. Coolmax® had good wicking and best drying ability. Elastane had poorer wicking and drying ability than ®, PBT Dry-released®. Overall, polyester performed better than polypropylene for the face side of the fabric. A research study compared cotton, bamboo, viscose, and plaited fabric (nylon and spandex) for its wicking behavior (Duru & Candan, 2012). Authors reported that fiber type and stitch length impacted wicking properties. Repeated laundering revealed varied impact on different fiber contents. Repeated laundering enhanced wicking ability of bamboo the most followed by cotton and viscose.

A team of scholars compared three methods of measuring wicking behavior for 12 fabrics (Raja, Ramakrishnan, Babu, Senthikumar, & Sampath, 2012). Three methods were found to have a correlation of 0.9. This value suggests that any of the three methods will work well. The three methods used were: manual water spreading, MATLAB software (EIAS), and commercial image analysis with Photoshop. Correlation between Photoshop and EIAS was higher than the one between, manual and EIAS method. Another study examined 27 knit types and nine knit structures using combed spun yarns with 30/1Ne (Oner & Okur, 2014). The study tested the effect of various knit structures on liquid absorption, transportation, and permeability. The findings revealed that tight of structure impacted air permeability adversely. Fabrics with float structures had better wicking ability and moisture management than those without floats.

"Trans-planar" wicking was higher for combed rather than carded yarns. Consequently, it took them longer to dry (Jhanji, Gupta, & Kothari, 2015). Results of the study revealed that for warp, liquid moved from longitudinal yarns to hydrophilic weft yarns but not through hydrophobic weft yarns (Zhu & Takatera, 2015). In weft direction, migration was seen for cotton weft yarns. There was no migration when weft had polyvinyldene fluoride.

Another research study compared three brands of 100% cotton t-shirts for horizontal wicking within the context of frequency of washing with commercial detergent (Chowdhary, 2017). Findings revealed that wicking increased significantly for all three brands of t-shirts between 5th and 25th wash. However, change was dramatically different for one of the three brands. Marsha and Chowdhary (2018) found that horizontal wicking was higher for both fiber contents in washed than unwashed forms. It was 22.834 mm^2/second for 100% cotton and 24.622 mm^2/second for the blend in washed form; and was .848 mm^2/second for 100% cotton and .754 mm^2/second for the blend in the unwashed form. Kundu and Chowdhary (2018) found that three fabrics (cotton/spandex, rayon/spandex, and polyester/spandex) differed significantly for wicking. Polyester/spandex and rayon/spandex had zero wicking rate and cotton had 0.80 mm^2/second. Findings also showed that fabric thickness impacted recovery and air permeability but not stretch and wicking.

Plied yarns had lower wicking than the spun yarns. Post-wash wicking was higher than the pre-wash wicking for interlock, jersey, and pique knits (Chowdhary, Adnan, & Cheng, 2019). Differences were observed for different fiber contents and knit structures. Fabric weight, thickness, and count affected horizontal wicking of the knitted fabrics differentially. The plain weave had higher horizontal wicking than the twill and satin weaves (Chowdhary & Islam, 2019). Additionally, wicking was higher for bleached than unbleached form for both horizontal and vertical method.

Clothing comfort refers to the pain or irritation free use of clothing for the tasks at hand. Moisture transfer contributes toward absorbing the excessive sweat for providing solace. Additionally, having it in towels assists with drying the skin effectively and giving contentment to the user. Water repellent clothing comforts in the rainy weather from getting wet. Water vapor resistance can be used advantageously for situations and occasion where excessive sweating takes place on the human body. Optimum wicking in the clothing helps with discomfort from clamminess. Wrinkle resistant clothing provides comfort in the social settings.

Summary and Conclusions

Wet performance tests are of critical importance in determining the quality of the textile products. These attributes help consumer with making better selections and taking better care of the apparel products than in the absence of this knowledge. They also help the textile and apparel manufacturers with production of quality textiles and apparel. Additionally, the apparel manufacturers can use these standards for determining compatibility between different layers used in the garment. Finally, the apparel retailers can use the information foe selling the product.

REFERENCES

Agarwal, G., Koehl, L., & Perwuelz, A. (2011). "Interaction of wash-ageing and use of fabric softener for drapeability of knitted fabrics". *Textile Research Journal, 81*(11), 1100-1112.

Anand, S. Bishop, D. and Mackay, C. (1996). Effects of laundering on the sensory and mechanical properties of 1x1 rib knitwear fabrics. *Textile Research Journal, 66*(3), 131-149.

Annual book of ASTM standards. (2020). *7.01,* West Conshohoken, PA: ASTM International.

Annual book of ASTM standards. (2019). *7.02,* West Conshohoken, PA: ASTM International.

Bao, L., & Yun-Jun, L. (2018). Silicone softener for stain repellent stain release and wrinkle resistance fabric finishing. *Journal of Engineered Fibers and Fabrics 13* (3), 1-5.

Baumert, K. J., & Crews, P. (2000). Influence of household fabric softeners on properties of selected woven fabrics. *Textile Chemist and Colorist, 32(9), 41-47.*

Bueno, L., Laso, C., Amador, C., & Bakalis, S. (2019). Modelling the kinetics of stain removal from knitted cotton fabrics in a commercial Front Loader Washing Machine (FLWM). *Chemical Engineering Science, 200,* 176-185.

Chiwese, A., & Crews (2000). Influence of household fabric softeners and laundry enzymes on pilling and breaking strength. *Textile Chemist and Colorist and Dye Stuff Reporter, 32*(9), 41-47.

Chowdhary, U. (2007). *Textile analysis: An annotated bibliography.* Deer Park, NY: LINUS. Chowdhary, U. (2009). *Textile analysis, quality control and innovative uses.* Deer Park, NY: LINUS.

Chowdhary, U. (2017). Comparing three brands of cotton t-shirts. AATCC Journal of Research, 4(3), 22-33. DOI: 10.14504/ajr.4.3.

Chowdhary, U., & Adnan, M. M. (2019). Knit structure and its relationship to dimensional stability, appearance retention, industrial stretch, pilling resistance, and colorfastness to crocking. *International Journal of Polymer and Textile Engineering, 6* (2), 1-8.

Chowdhary, U. & Adnan, M. M. (2017). Dimensional stability and appearance retention by knit type and fiber contents. Paper presented at the AATCC's international conference.

Chowdhary, U., Adnan, M. M., & Cheng, C. (2019). Pre-post washing comparison for horizontal wicking behavior of three types of knits in different fiber contents. *Journal of Textile Science and Fashion Technology,* 2(5), 1-9. DOI: 10.33552/JTSFT.2019.02.000548.

Chowdhary, U., & Islam, M. R. (2019). Pre-post wash wicking behavior, moisture transfer, and water repellency of plain, twill and satin weaves. *Journal of Textile Science and Fashion Technology, 2*(3), 1-13.

Chowdhary, U. & Vijaykumar, K. (2016). Past laundering evaluation of three brands of t-shirts. Paper presented at the AATCC's international conference.

Clothing flammability test. Fabric softeners and flammability. (2000, August). *Consumer Reports, 65*(8), 44.

Coruh, E. (2015). Optimization of comfort properties of single jersey knit fabrics. Fibres and Textiles in Eastern Europe, 23, 4 (112), 66-72. DOI: 10.5604/12303666.1152728.

Das, D. & Thakur, R. (2013). Taguchi analysis of fabric shrinkage. *Fibers and Polymers, 14*(3), 482-487.

Das, B., Das, A., Kothari, V. K., Fanguiero, R., & Araujo, M. D. (2007). Moisture transmission through textiles Part I: Processes involved in moisture transmission and the factors at play. *AUTEX Research journal, 7* (2), 100-110.

Devanand, G., & Parthiban, M. (2019). Sea water for reactive dyeing of cotton fabrics. *Indian Journal of Fibre and Textile Research, 44*, 122-124.

Doty, K. C., & easter, E. (2009, May). An analysis of the care and maintenance of performance textiles and effects of care on performance. *AATCC Review, 37-42*.

Duru, S. C., & Candan, C. (2012). Effect of repeated laundering on wicking and drying properties of fabrics of seamless fabrics. *Textile Research Journal, 83*(6), 591-605.

Eladwi, M.T.M., Shaker, R. N., & Abdelrahman, S. H. (2017). Creating sustainable fashion Designs treated with soil release finishing via used household textiles, 8th International conferences of Textile Research Division 25-27 September 2017. 1-12.

Fangueiro, R., Filgueiras, A. Soutinho, F., & Meidi, X. (2010). Wicking behavior and drying capability of functional knitted fabrics. *Textile Research Journal, 80(15), 1522-1530. DOI: 10.1177/0040517510361796.*

Ferreira, I. L. S, Medeiros, I., Steffens, F., & Oliveira, F. R. (2019). Cotton fabric bleached with seawater: Mechanical and coloristic properties. *Materials Research, 22* http://orcid.org/0000-0002-5711-3482

Hassan, M. M., & Leighs, S. J. (2017). Effect of surface treatments on physico-mechanical, stain-resist, and UV protection properties of wool fabrics. *Applied Surface Science, 419,* 348-356.

Hassan, M. M. (2018). Wool fabrics coated with an anionic bunte salt-terminated polyether: Physico-mechanical properties, stain resistance, and dyeability. *ACS Omega, 3,* 17656-17667.

Hati. S. & Das, B. R. (2011). Seam Pucker in Apparels: A Critical Review of Evaluation Methods. *Asian Journal of Textile, 1*, 60-73. DOI: 10.3923/ajt.2011.60.73

Hofer, D. (2006[a]). Antimicrobial textiles, skin borne diseases, and odor. In Burg, G. Hipler, U. C., & Eisner, P. (Eds. *Biofunctional textiles and the skin. Current problems in dermatology. 33,* 67-77. New York, NY: Karger.

Hofer, D. (2006[b]). Silver in healthcare: Antimicrobial effects and safety in use. In Burg, G. Hipler, U. C., & Eisner, P. (Eds. *Biofunctional textiles and the skin. Current problems in dermatology. 33,* 42-50. New York, NY: Karger.

Innovations in advanced textiles (2021, March). *Specialty Fabrics Review,* 15.

Jhanji, Y., Gupta, D. & Kothari, V.K. Thermo-physiological properties of polyester–cotton plated fabrics in relation to fibre linear density and yarn type *Fashion and Textiles (2015) 2:* 16. https://doi.org/10.1186/s40691-015-0041-x

Jhatial, A. K., Khatri, A., Ali, S., Babar, A. A. (2019). Sol–gel finishing of bamboo fabric with nanoparticles for water repellency, soil release and UV resistant characteristics. *Cellulose, 26,* 6365-6378.

Jonas, M., Cai, R., Vermeyen, R., Nysten, B. Vanneste, M., Smet, D., Glinel, K. (2020). How roughness controls the water repellency of woven fabrics. *Materials and Design, 187.* https://doi.org/10.1016/j.matdes.2019.108389Get rights and content

Kabbari, M., Liouane, N., Fayala, F., Ghith, A. G. (2017). Predicting stain repellency characteristics of knitted fabrics using fuzzy modeling and surface response methodology. *The Journal of Textile Institute, 108:*5, 683-691.

Ketema, A., & Worku, A. (2020). Antibacterial finishing of cotton fabric using stinging nettle (Urtica Dioica L.) plant leaf. Journal of Chemistry. ID 4049273 |https://doi.org/10.1155/2020/4049273

Kundu, S. K. and Chowdhary, U. (2018). Effect of Fiber Content on Comfort Properties of Cotton/Spandex, Rayon/Spandex, and Polyester/Spandex Single Jersey Knitted Fabrics. *SSRG International Journal of Polymer and Textile Engineering, 5*(3), 33-39.

Kut, D., Orhan, M., Gunesoglu, C., & Ozakin, C. (2005, March). *AATCC Review, 25-28.*

Kuzuhara, A., & Hori, T. (2002). Reducing wrinkle formation in wool with 2-Iminotheorane hydrochloride. *Textile Research Journal, 72*(11), 949-953.

Manual of international test methods and procedures (2021). Research Triangle Park, NC: American Association of Textile Chemists and Colorists.

Marsha, S. S. & Chowdhary, U. (2018). Comparison of selected structural and performance attributes of cotton and C/P blend of t-shirts. International Journal of Polymer and Textile Engineering (SSRG - IJPTE), 5(3), 40-49.

Menezes, E., & Choudhari (2007). Special finishes and effects. *AATCC Review, 7*(3), 29-32.

Miranda, T.M.R., Santos, J., & Soares, G. M. B. (2017). Soil-release behaviour of polyester fabrics after chemical modification with polyethylene glycol. *Materials Science and Engineering, 254,* 1-6.

Moiz, A., Padhye, R., and Wang, X. (2018). Durable superomniphobic surface on cotton fabrics via coating of silicone rubber and fluoropolymers, *Coatings, 8-104,* 1-17.

Morent, R., Geyter, N. D., Leys, C., Vansteenkiste, E, Bock, J. D., & Phillps, W. (2006). Measuring the wicking behavior of textiles by combination of a horizontal wicking experiment and image processing. *Review of Scientific Instruments, 77,* 093502. Doi: 10.1063/1.2349297.

Murphy, D. R. (2015) Fabric softener technology: A review. *Journal of Surfactants and Detergents, 19*, 199-204.

Oner, E., & Okur, B. A. (2014). The effect of different knitted fabrics' structures on the moisture transport properties. *The Journal of Textile Institute, 104*(11), 1164-1177.

Pan, R., Gao, W., Li, W. Xu, B. (2017). Image analysis for seam-puckering evaluation. *Textile Research Journal, 87*(20), https://doi.org/10.1177/0040517516673330.

Rahman, H., Biswas, P. K., Mitra, B. K., Rakesh, M.S.R. (2014). Effect of enzyme wash (cellulase enzyme) on properties of different weft knitted fabrics. *International Journal of Current Engineering and Technology, 4*(4), 4242-4248.

Raja, D., Ramakrishnan, G., Babu, V. R., Senthikumar, M., & Sampath, MB (2012). Comparison of different methods to measure the transverse wicking behavior of fabrics. *Journal of Industrial Textiles, 43*(3), 366-382. DOI: 10.1177/1528083712456054.

Reljic. M., Stepanovic, L., Lazic, B. Circovic, N., & Cerovic, D. (2016). The change of water vapor resistance of materials used for the clothing production during exploitation. *Advanced Technologies, 5*(2), 73-78.

Sarkar, J., & Khallil, E. (2014). Effect of industrial bleach wash and softening on the physical, mechanical and color properties of denim garments. *IOSR Journal of Polymer and Textile Engineering (IOSR-JPTE), 1*(3), 46-49.

Schwartze, J. P., & McKinnon, J. (2000). Wool color changes in superheated steam. *Textile Research Journal, 70*(3), 205-209.

Shalini, G. and Anitha, D. (2016). A review: Antimicrobial properties of textiles. *International Journal of Science and Research (IJSR)*, 5*(10)*, 766-768.

Shim. H. S. (2016). The evaluation of water vapor transport and waterproofing properties of waterproofs and breathable fabrics. *The Korean Journal of Community Living Science,* 27(2), 295-304. DOI: 10.7856/kjcls.2016.27.2.295

Singh, G., Roy, K., Varshney, R., & Goyal, A. (2011). Dimensional parameters of single jersey cotton knitted fabrics. *Indian Journal of Fibre and Textile Research, 36*(2), 111-116.

Suna, Y., Zhaoa, X., Liua, R., Chena, G., & Zhoua, X. (2018). Synthesis and characterization of fluorinated polyacrylate as water and oil repellent and soil release finishing agent for polyester fabric. *Progress in Organic Coating, 123,* 306-313.

Telli, A. & Ozdil, N. (2015). Effect of recycled PET fibers on the performance properties of knitted fabrics. Journal of Engineered Fibers and Fabrics, *10*(2), 47-60.

Thiry, M. (2009, July). In the swim. *AATCC Review,* 28-33.

Unal B. Z., Kartal, B., & Yilonu, S. (2019). The effect of water repellency finishing on selected performance properties of upholstery produced from chenille yarn. *The Journal of Textile Institute, 111* (9), 1260-1268. https://doi.org/10.1080/00405000.2019.1694352

Uttam, D., & Sethi, R. (2016). Impact of repeated washing on dimensional stability and physical factors of cotton woven fabric. *International Journal of Research in Engineering and Applied Sciences.* 6(2), 126-135.

Yesmin, S., Hasan, M., Mia, M.S., Momotaz, F., Idris, M.A., & Hasan, M.R. (2014). Effect of Stitch Length and Fabric Constructions on dimensional and mechanical properties of knitted fabrics. *World Applied Sciences Journal,* 32(9), 1991-1995.

Wang, L. Liu, J., Pan, R., Gao, W. (2014). Dynamic measurement of fabric recovery angle by video sequence processing. *Textile Research Journal, 84*(7), https://doi.org/10.1177/0040517513507363

Yatagai, M., & Takahashi, Y. (2005, January). Effect of citric acid DP finishing with particulate soil of cotton fabric. *AATCC Review, 5,* 17-21.

Zerin, I., Foisal, A. B. M., Datta, & Rana, M.S. (2017). Dyeing of cotton with groundwater and seawater. *Journal of Polymer and Textile Engineering, 4* (5), 32-35. DOI: 10.9790/019X-04053235

Zhong, Q., Lu, M., Nieuwenhuis, S., Wu, B., Wu, G., Xu, Z., Muller-Buschbaum, P. (2019). Enhanced stain removal and comfort control achieved by cross-linking light and thermo dual-responsive copolymer onto cotton fabrics. *Applied Materials and Interfaces, 11,* 5414-5426.

PRACTICE ACTIVITIES

1. What do you understand by the performance attributes related to aesthetics, care, and comfort? Provide specific examples.

2. Why natural fibers are likely to be impacted by the micro-organisms the most? What does their attack do to the textile materials?

3. List four indicators of microbial attack.

4. Based on the literature in the text, how many washes should the antimicrobial finish withstand?

5. In everyday wear, where do you see the microbial attack the most?

6. Which microbe attacks textiles?

7. Identify six methods of applying the antibacterial finishes.

8. How relevant are crease retention and the electrostatic charge tests today? What are the reasons for change if any?

9. How important are frosting, mildew and rot resistance? Can they be prevented?

10. On which fiber contents should the oil repellency be tested and why?

11. What is the importance of the wrinkle recovery angle method of measuring wrinkle recovery? How do you convert angle to the five-point scale ratings? Provide one example.

12. Why is colorfastness to crocking important? How does it help with the quality of fabric? What are the passing ratings for dry and wet crocking?

13. Why is it important to test colorfastness of different types of water? Why does testing the ground water alone is not sufficient?

14. What do you understand by the dimensional stability? Which fiber contents are more likely to shrink?
15. What causes growth in the knitted fabrics? How can it be controlled?
16. What is the role of stains in the care process of garments?
17. What is the unit of measurement for colorfastness tests?
18. What is the unit of analysis for electrostatic charge?
19. What is the unit of measurement for dimensional stability?
20. What is the unit of measurement for appearance retention?
21. What is the unit of measurement for stain removal?
22. What is the unit of measurement for moisture transfer?
23. What is the unit of measurement for water repellency using the spray method?
24. What is the unit of measurement for wrinkle recovery?
25. What is the unit of measurement for vertical wicking?
26. What is the unit of measurement for horizontal wicking?
27. What is the unit of measurement for water vapor resistance?
28. What is the unit of measurement for water resistance?
29. If you had to produce a line of dry cleanable coats, what will be the minimum acceptable rating for appearance retention?
30. You plan to design a swimwear for teenage girls. What criteria will you use to pass/fail the fabric based on the colorfastness to chlorine and seawater?
31. What is the difference between the accelerated laundering and household laundering?
32. If the passing grade for moisture transfer is <5 seconds for the disappearance of the water drop, which of the two towels will you pass and why?

# of Observation	Towel A	# of Observation	Towel B
1	2	1	4
2	3	2	5
3	4	3	6
4	4	4	6
5	5	5	8

33. Where would you use water repellence and water resistance tests? What do these tests measure? What are the similarities and differences between two tests?

34. For which type of end use, you should use the colorfastness tests and why? Provide a convincing rationale.

35. Is color transference same for all fiber contents? If you washed your polyester clothes with a cotton garment that bleeds while laundering. Will your polyester garments be stained with the color of the cotton garment? Provide rationale for your choice.

36. Which garments must have water repellency with the passing grade? What is the minimum rating necessary for passing the garment?

37. Use data below to determine if it will pass or fail the dimensional stability test?

Pre-Wash Length	Post Wash Length	Pre-Wash Width	Post Wash Width
10	9.2	10	10.6
10	9.2	10	10.6
10	9.2	10	10.6
10	9.3	10	10.5
10	9.3	10	10.5
10	9.3	10	10.5
10	9.5	10	10.4
10	9.5	10	10.4
10	9.5	10	10.4

TEXTILE CARE AND UPKEEP

7
CHAPTER

Consumers intend to retain the original appearance of the apparel after refurbishing. Different textiles require different treatments for the best results. The needs are based on their physical as well as chemical attributes. ASTM guide to care symbols (ASTM D5489-2018) provides several parameters to consider for washing, bleaching, dry, ironing, and professional textile care. Care labels are based on these guidelines both in words and figures. Every ready-to- wear garment has care labels to help consumer avoid safe practice due to ignorance. Consumers can take care of the clothing by hand, machine, or dry cleaning. Care instruction refers to the processes recommended for taking care of the textile products without harming.

Occasionally, apparel manufacturers offer labels in multiple languages to reach diverse consumer segments. A brief account of symbols for various stages, and their interpretation is provided below to set-up the foundation. Except for dry cleaning or special care, labels should have information on the safest washing, bleaching, drying, and ironing. However, the label should be brief. Symbols could be supplemented by words in English and/or national language for enhanced communication. ASTM D5489-2018 (*Annual book of ASTM Standards*, 2019). *7.02)* test also provides the standard and common usage terms established by the Federal Trade Commission (FTC).

Wash symbol is shown by a tub that has one line below it for the permanent cycle and two lines for delicate/gentle. Tub with hand signifies hand wash. The guidelines also give water temperatures for various washes ranging from in six categories of temperatures in Fahrenheit and Celsius. They are also denoted by 1 to 6 dots. One dot means the coldest temperature (30^0C or 85^0F) and 6 denotes the warmest temperature (95^0C or 200^0F). Do not wash is represented by crossing out the tub. **Bleach** symbol is shown with a triangle that is kept blank for any bleach.

For the non-chlorine bleach, it shows three diagonal lines inside the bleach. For no bleach, the triangle is shown with an X.

Dry symbol is a square. For tumble dry, it shows a circle within the square. Simple square with a circle means a normal cycle. When one horizontal line is added below, it signifies permanent press cycle. Two lines below the symbol represent a delicate/gentle cycle. Heat settings are represented by a black circle means no heat/air, white circle indicates any heat, one dot implies low heat, two dots denote medium heat, and three dots imply high heat. Symbols are also provided for the line drying, drip drying and flat drying. Additional symbols are given for do not wring, do not tumble dry, and dry in the shade. For **ironing**. Iron is shown with low, medium, high, and no steam settings.

Professional Textile Care is signified by a circle. It includes both dry cleaning as well as wet cleaning options. For a normal cycle, the circle has either letter F or P. F refers to using tetrachloroethane or petroleum only, and P means Petroleum solvent only. For a mild cycle, one horizontal line is added below the circles with P and F. For wet clean, the symbols have W in the circle and horizontal lines. One line is labeled mild and two as very mild. Clear circle is shown with X for no dry cleaning and Black circle with X for no wet cleaning.

Effective cleaning process involves knowledge of different types of soils, soaps, detergents, bleaches, fabric softeners, washing machines, dryers, irons, and ironing accessories. **Soils** refer to unwanted mechanical or chemical elements that cling to the textile materials. Some soils just stick to the fabric and others are wet. Wet soils can be water or oil borne and get infused in the textile through the absorption process.

Soaps or detergents can be used for laundering. **Soaps** are derivatives of fatty acids and are used to clean soil from the textile materials. They may come in bar or flake form. **Detergents** are cleaning agents that have surfactants with chemicals that enable the removal of stains. They come in powder, liquid, and pods forms. Stained clothing requires pre-treatment for their removal. One can use household products or commercial stain removers depending on the availability or accessibility. Stains can be classified to understand their chemistry for neutralizing their impact. Several previous scholars have provided tables to clean the stains (Cohen & Johnson, 2010; Chowdhary, 2009; Collier, Bide, & Tortora, 2009; Kadolph & Langford, 2002). Chowdhary (2009) classified them in six categories: Acid-base, alkaline, oil-based, protein-based, combination, and other (Table 21).

Most of the previous scholars as well as the commercial products indicated that stains come off easily when they are fresh. Old stains become stubborn and are hard to remove. They may need additional treatments to soften them before treating. Stain removal finishes are also another solution. The finishes could be applied through resin applications or via nanotechnology. These finishes offer a self-cleaning process because of their ability to repel water. For a long time, fluorocarbons or silicone gels have been used to develop stain-repellent finishes. They mostly removed water and oil stains. With GreenShield less is more. (2021) has come up with Fluorine zero finish that uses nanotechnology particles to remove waterborne and oily stains from cotton, nylon, polyester, rayon, and blends. Some companies in today's market make detergents multifunctional and add stain removal ingredients in it, others use it in the solvent before spinning, and other sell stain removers exclusively. **Always read instructions carefully for exclusions.**

Textile Care and Upkeep

Table 21: Stain categories with examples, and household and commercial removers.

Category	Examples	Household Removers	Commercial Removers*
Acid-Base Stains	Fruits, Juices, Tea, Coffee Alcoholic beverages Perspiration	Baking Soda Dishwashing liquid	Shout Spray N' Wash Ammonia OxiClean
Alkaline Stains	Food Stains	Lemon juice Vinegar	Acetic acid Citric Acid Shout Spray N' Wash OxiClean
Oil-Based Stains	Cosmetics, curry, grease, mustard, oil paint, peanut butter, shoe polish	Blotting Paper Dishwashing liquid Talcum Powder	Glycerine Shout Spray N' Wash
Protein-Based Stains	Blood, eggs, meats, milk, and milk products	Cold water and air dry Heat coagulates stains and make them hard to set on the fabrics.	Shout Spray N' Wash OxiClean
Combination	Contain both water and grease Curries, gravy, ice-cream	Dishwashing liquid	Shout Spray N' Wash OxiClean
Other	Adhesive tape and Chewing gum Candle Wax Grass Ink Mildew Mud Nail Polish Perfume Permanent marker Turmeric	Ice and scraping with knife White vinegar Hair Spray Vinegar or bleach Vinegar X Hair Spray Dry in sunlight	OxiClean Acetone or Nail Polish Remover Rubbing alcohol might work

*Read labels carefully for warnings. All removers can not be used for all fabrics.

Oil specimen size requirement for AATCC 130 stain removal procedure is 15" x 15". However, Chowdhary (2009) and Chowdhary and Mock (2009) used 4" x 4" specimens to approximate the size used in the replica provided by AATCC 130. Chowdhary and Mock used a set number of Q-tips rubs 300 times and rinsed with 50 rubs. Following stain removal, the specimens were washed and dried. Total Tide detergent was used for the laundering procedure. Rating of 3 indicated the partial removal of the stain and ≥4 was used for passing the stain. Table 22 shows the revised table to provide a basis for furthering the research in future for other stains and stain removers.

Interpretations from table 22 reveal many interesting but useful findings. They are not consistent with Rabideau's (2021) findings who rated Oxy Wash as the most effective commercial remover. Ball point pen stain was best removed by the Ammonia, dish washing liquid, hair spray, and Spray N' Wash spray. Even though Goo Gone and hairspray were not effective as stain removers, laundering helped with fully removing the stain. Coffee stain was fully removed after laundering for all cleaners, even though hair spray as such was not effective in removing this stain. Coke was removed by all thirteen stain removers. Cranberry juice was also removed for all satin removers except the weak performance of hairspray and vinegar. Goo Gone, OxiWash, and Vinegar were not effective on all stains for the cranberry juice. However, laundering removed them all. Ammonia and Comet with bleach were not as effective on formula stains as the rest of the stain removers.

For grass stains, the best stain removers were Clorox, comet with bleach, dish washing liquid, Shout with brush as well as gel, and Spray N' Wash stick as well as gel. Ketchup was removed for all stain removers after laundering. However, Goo gone, and hair spray were not effective, and acetone, comet with bleach, and OxiWash were less effective than the remainder of them. Most effective removers for lipstick stain were Comet with bleach, dish washing liquid, gel and stick of Spray N' Wash, and brush as well as gel of Shout. Clorox removed the mustard stain the best. None of the used chemicals removed the nail polish stain except Acetone. Better outcome was expected than achieved in this study for the nail polish remover.

Table 22: Cleaning efficiency of 13 stain removers for 12 stains.

Stain Remover	Post Stain Removal	Post Laundering	Final Decision	Effectiveness
Ballpoint Pen/AC	2-2.99	2-2.99	Fail	No
Ballpoint Pen/AM	2-2.99	2-2.99	Fail	No
Ballpoint Pen/CB	2-2.99	3-3.99	Pass	Yes
Ballpoint Pen/CLO	3-3.99	3-3.99	Maybe	No
Ballpoint Pen/DWL	4-4.99	4-4.99	Pass	Yes
Ballpoint Pen/GG	2-2.99	2-2.99	Fail	No
Ballpoint Pen/HS	4-4.99	4-4.99	Pass	Yes
Ballpoint Pen/OW	2-2.99	2-2.99	Fail	No
Ballpoint Pen/SB	3-3.99	3-3.99	Maybe	No
Ballpoint Pen/SG	3-3.99	3-3.99	Maybe	No
Ballpoint Pen/SNWG	2-2.99	2-2.99	Fail	No
Ballpoint Pen/SNWS	3-3.99	4-4.99	Pass	Yes
Ballpoint Pen/VIN	2-2.99	2-2.99	Fail	No

Textile Care and Upkeep

Stain Remover	Post Stain Removal	Post Laundering	Final Decision	Effectiveness
Blood/AC	4-4.99	4-4.99	Pass	Yes
Blood/AM	4-4.99	4-4.99	Pass	Yes
Blood/CB	3-3.99	4-4.99	Pass	Yes
Blood/CLO	4-4.99	4-4.99	Pass	Yes
Blood/DWL	4-4.99	4-4.99	Pass	Yes
Blood/GG	2-2.99	4-4.99	Pass	Yes
Blood/HS	2-2.99	4-4.99	Pass	Yes
Blood/OW	4-4.99	4-4.99	Pass	Yes
Blood/SB	4-4.99	4-4.99	Pass	Yes
Blood/SG	4-4.99	4-4.99	Pass	Yes
Blood/SNWG	3-3.99	4-4.99	Pass	Yes
Blood/SNWS	4-4.99	4-4.99	Yes	Yes
Blood/VIN	3-3.99	4-4.99	Pass	Yes
Coffee/AC	4-4.99	4-4.99	Pass	Yes
Coffee/AM	4-4.99	4-4.99	Pass	Yes
Coffee/CB	3-3.99	4-4.99	Pass	Yes
Coffee/CLO	4-4.99	4-4.99	Pass	Yes
Coffee/DWL	4-4.99	4-4.99	Pass	Yes
Coffee/GG	4-4.99	4-4.99	Pass	Yes
Coffee/HS	2-2.99	4-4.99	Pass	Yes
Coffee/OW	4-4.99	4-4.99	Pass	Yes
Coffee/SB	4-4.99	4-4.99	Pass	Yes
Coffee/SG	4-4.99	4-4.99	Pass	Yes
Coffee/SNWG	4-4.99	4-4.99	Pass	Yes
Coffee/SNWS	4-4.99	4-4.99	Pass	Yes
Coffee/VIN	3-3.99	4-4.99	Pass	Yes
Coke/AC	4-4.99	4-4.99	Pass	Yes
Coke/AM	4-4.99	4-4.99	Pass	Yes
Coke/CB	4-4.99	4-4.99	Pass	Yes
Coke/CLO	4-4.99	4-4.99	Pass	Yes
Coke/DWL	4-4.99	4-4.99	Pass	Yes
Coke/GG	4-4.99	4-4.99	Pass	Yes
Coke/HS	4-4.99	4-4.99	Pass	Yes
Coke/OW	4-4.99	4-4.99	Pass	Yes

Stain Remover	Post Stain Removal	Post Laundering	Final Decision	Effectiveness
Coke/SB	4-4.99	4-4.99	Pass	Yes
Coke/SG	4-4.99	4-4.99	Pass	Yes
Coke/SNWG	4-4.99	4-4.99	Pass	Yes
Coke/SNWS	4-4.99	4-4.99	Pass	Yes
Coke/VIN	4-4.99	4-4.99	Pass	Yes
			Pass	
Cranberry Juice/AC	4-4.99	4-4.99	Pass	Yes
Cranberry Juice/AM	4-4.99	4-4.99	Pass	Yes
Cranberry Juice/CB	4-4.99	4-4.99	Pass	Yes
Cranberry Juice/CLO	4-4.99	4-4.99	Pass	Yes
Cranberry Juice/DWL	4-4.99	4-4.99	Pass	Yes
Cranberry Juice/GG	4-4.99	4-4.99	Pass	Yes
Cranberry Juice/HS	3-3.99	4-4.99	Pass	Yes
Cranberry Juice/OW	4-4.99	4-4.99	Pass	Yes
Cranberry Juice/SB	4-4.99	4-4.99	Pass	Yes
Cranberry Juice/SG	4-4.99	4-4.99	Pass	Yes
Cranberry Juice/SNWG	4-4.99	4-4.99	Pass	Yes
Cranberry Juice/SNWS	4-4.99	4-4.99	Pass	Yes
Cranberry Juice/VIN	3-3.99	4-4.99	Pass	Yes
Crayon Black/AC	4-4.99	4-4.99	Pass	Yes
Crayon Black/AM	4-4.99	4-4.99	Pass	Yes
Crayon Black/CB	4-4.99	4-4.99	Pass	Yes
Crayon Black/CLO	4-4.99	4-4.99	Pass	Yes
Crayon Black/DWL	4-4.99	4-4.99	Pass	Yes
Crayon Black/GG	2-2.99	2-2.99	Fail	No

Textile Care and Upkeep

Stain Remover	Post Stain Removal	Post Laundering	Final Decision	Effectiveness
Crayon Black/HS	4-4.99	4-4.99	Pass	Yes
Crayon Black/OW	3-3.99	4-4.99	Pass	Yes
Crayon Black/SB	4-4.99	4-4.99	Pass	Yes
Crayon Black/SG	4-4.99	4-4.99	Pass	Yes
Crayon Black/SNWG	4-4.99	4-4.99	Pass	Yes
Crayon Black/SNWS	4-4.99	4-4.99	Pass	Yes
Crayon Black/VIN	2-2.99	2-2.99	Fail	No
Formula/AC	4-4.99	4-4.99	Pass	Yes
Formula/AM	3-3.99	4-4.99	Pass	Yes
Formula/CB	4-4.99	4-4.99	Pass	Yes
Formula/CLO	4-4.99	4-4.99	Pass	Yes
Formula/DWL	4-4.99	4-4.99	Pass	Yes
Formula/GG	4-4.99	4-4.99	Pass	Yes
Formula/HS	4-4.99	4-4.99	Pass	Yes
Formula/OW	3-3.99	4-4.99	Pass	Yes
Formula/SB	4-4.99	4-4.99	Pass	Yes
Formula/SG	4-4.99	4-4.99	Pass	Yes
Formula/SNWG	4-4.99	4-4.99	Pass	Yes
Formula/SNWS	4-4.99	4-4.99	Pass	Yes
Formula/VIN	4-4.99	4-4.99	Pass	Yes
Grass/AC	2-2.99	3-3.99	May be	No
Grass/AM	3-3.99	4-4.99	Pass	Yes
Grass/CB	4-4.99	4-4.99	Pass	Yes
Grass/CLO	4-4.99	4-4.99	Pass	Yes
Grass/DWL	4-4.99	4-4.99	Pass	Yes
Grass/GG	2-2.99	4-4.99	Pass	Yes
Grass/HS	2-2.99	2-2.99	Fail	No
Grass/OW	3-3.99	3-3.99	Maybe	No
Grass/SB	4-4.99	4-4.99	Pass	Yes
Grass/SG	4-4.99	4-4.99	Pass	Yes
Grass/SNWG	4-4.99	4-4.99	Pass	Yes
Grass/SNWS	4-4.99	4-4.99	Pass	Yes
Grass/VIN	2-2.99	2-2.99	Fail	No

Chapter 7

Stain Remover	Post Stain Removal	Post Laundering	Final Decision	Effectiveness
Ketchup/AC	3-3.99	4-4.99	Pass	Yes
Ketchup/AM	4-4.99	4-4.99	Pass	Yes
Ketchup/CB	3-3.99	4-4.99	Pass	Yes
Ketchup/CLO	4-4.99	4-4.99	Pass	Yes
Ketchup/DWL	4-4.99	4-4.99	Pass	Yes
Ketchup/GG	2-2.99	4-4.99	Pass	Yes
Ketchup/HS	2-2.99	4-4.99	Pass	Yes
Ketchup/OW	3-3.99	4-4.99	Pass	Yes
Ketchup/SB	4-4.99	4-4.99	Pass	Yes
Ketchup/SG	4-4.99	4-4.99	Pass	Yes
Ketchup/SNWG	4-4.99	4-4.99	Pass	Yes
Ketchup/SNWS	4-4.99	4-4.99	Pass	Yes
Ketchup/VIN	4-4.99	4-4.99	Pass	Yes
Lipstick/AC	2-2.99	2-2.99	Fail	No
Lipstick/AM	2-2.99	2-2.99	Fail	No
Lipstick/CB	4-4.99	4-4.99	Pass	Yes
Lipstick/CLO	3-3.99	4-4.99	Pass	Yes
Lipstick/DWL	4-4.99	4-4.99	Pass	Yes
Lipstick/GG	2-2.99	2-2.99	Fail	No
Lipstick/HS	2-2.99	2-2.99	Fail	No
Lipstick/OW	2-2.99	2-2.99	Fail	No
Lipstick/SB	4-4.99	4-4.99	Pass	Yes
Lipstick/SG	3-3.99	4-4.99	Pass	Yes
Lipstick/SNWG	4-4.99	4-4.99	Pass	Yes
Lipstick/SNWS	4-4.99	4-4.99	Pass	Yes
Lipstick/VIN	2-2.99	2-2.99	Fail	No
Mustard/AC	2-2.99	3-3.99	Maybe	No
Mustard/AM	2-2.99	2-2.99	Fail	No
Mustard/CB	2-2.99	2-2.99	Fail	No
Mustard/CLO	4-4.99	4-4.99	Pass	Yes
Mustard/DWL	3-3.99	4-4.99	Pass	Yes
Mustard/GG	2-2.99	4-4.99	Pass	Yes
Mustard/HS	2-2.99	2-2.99	Fail	No
Mustard/OW	2-2.99	2-2.99	Fail	No
Mustard/SB	3-3.99	4-4.99	Pass	Yes

Textile Care and Upkeep

Stain Remover	Post Stain Removal	Post Laundering	Final Decision	Effectiveness
Mustard/SG	2-2.99	3-3.99	Maybe	No
Mustard/SNWG	2-2.99	3-3.99	Maybe	No
Mustard/SNWS	3-3.99	4-4.99	Pass	Yes
Mustard/VIN	2-2.99	2-2.99	Fail	No
Nail Polish/AC	3-3.99	3-3.99	Maybe	Yes Made exception
Nail Polish/AM	2-2.99	2-2.99	Fail	No
Nail Polish/CB	2-2.99	2-2.99	Fail	No
Nail Polish/CLO	2-2.99	2-2.99	Fail	No
Nail Polish/DWL	2-2.99	2-2.99	Fail	No
Nail Polish/GG	2-2.99	2-2.99	Fail	No
Nail Polish/HS	2-2.99	2-2.99	Fail	No
Nail Polish/OW	2-2.99	2-2.99	Fail	No
Nail Polish/SB	2-2.99	2-2.99	Fail	No
Nail Polish/SG	2-2.99	2-2.99	Fail	No
Nail Polish/SSWG	2-2.99	2-2.99	Fail	No
Nail Polish/SSWS	2-2.99	2-2.99	Fail	No
Nail Polish/VIN	2-2.99	2-2.99	Fail	No

AC = Acetone
AM = Ammonia
CB = Comet with Bleach
CLO = Clorox
DWL = Dishwashing Liquid
GG = Goo Gone
HS = Hair Spray
OW = OxiWash
SB = Shout with Brush
SG = Shout Gel
SNWG = Spray N' Wash Gel
SNWS = Spray N' Stick
VIN = Vinegar

Remember that all commercial removers can not be used on all fiber contents. Read labels carefully. Each container provides both claims and warnings with tips. Stain removal is a pre-treatment. The garment should be laundered after this pre-treatment. Laundry detergent also has cleaning efficiency and can supersede the failure of the individual stain removers.

Sequence of Laundering

There are no standards for sequence of laundering. However, there are effective steps that can be used in household routing of laundering for best results. It is always best to wash clothes when they are lightly soiled. However, if soiled heavily or washed less frequently, they should be soaked to loosen up the soil settled on it. Several washers give this option also. Again, one should not soak it for too long because soil can then settle back on the fabric. It is more critical for hand washing than machine washing because machines have time set for it. For the best results, follow the following six steps.

Step 1 Sorting

Sort by the color and fiber content of the garment. It is important step because all fiber contents do not have the same requirements. Do not mix white and colored. It will help you maintain the integrity of your textile materials. For example, if you are planning to use Clorox bleach for whitening the clothes, do not include colored garments that can lose their color and you can ruin your garment. See figure 24 as an example.

Figure 24: An example of damage in fabric from bleach.

Step 2 Spot Cleaning

Spot clean unwanted stains using household or commercial stain removers. This practice gives better finished laundry. Collars of men's collars and cuff edges collect more soil than the rest of the shirt because of the pivoting neck and moving wrists. They need to be spot cleaned prior to laundering for best results.

Step 3 Soaking, if necessary

It is good to use the soaking option for very dirty clothes. If someone comes from a mud slide or is dealing with the old stains that are stubborn are good examples of situations that lend themselves to this option. Washing machines also have this pre-soak option,

Step 4 Washing with or without softeners and bleach

Set your machine at correct settings based on the size of the load, type of fiber content, and personal needs. If you plan to use the liquid softener, it is applied in the rinse cycle. Some machines have a space for it, and you can fill along with the detergent in the beginning. So is true for the bleach. Read instructions on your machine and operate as directed.

Step 5 Drying

Use a load appropriate setting for best results. Some consumers prefer to use dry sheets rather that liquid fabric softeners. You can use them in the drying cycle. Fabric softeners add fragrance, softness, and freshness to the synthetic garments along with the anti-cling property.

Step 6 Ironing:

Iron at the fiber-content appropriate setting to prevent adverse effects. It is more critical to pay attention when you are ironing the lined garments with different fiber content. If your fashion fabric is made of cotton, linen, or rayon but the lining is made from polyester; hot temperature used for the fashion fabric material can melt down the lining material at that temperature. Figures 25 -29 show examples of impact of laundering on the garment appearance after refurbishing. The examples include double stitched seams, hole formation, impact of ironing, snagging of woven material, and pilling of suede.and

Figure 25: Double stitched seam appearance of a washed garment.

Figure 26: Hole formation from laundry.

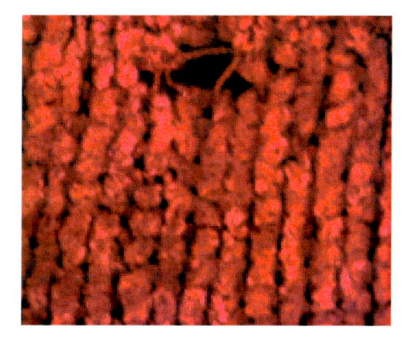

Figure 27: Appearance of ironed (a) and un-ironed (b) specimens.

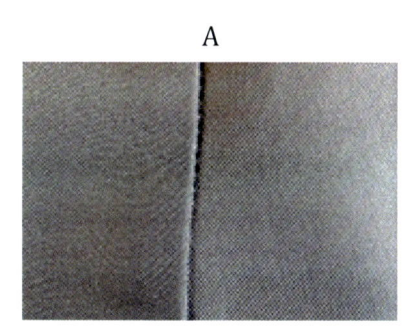

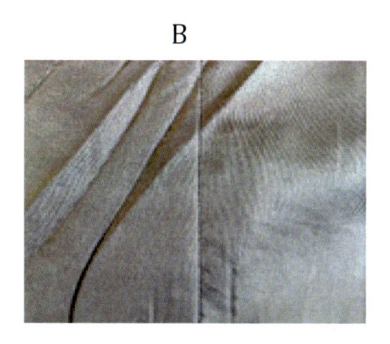

A   B

Figure 28: An Example of Snagging.

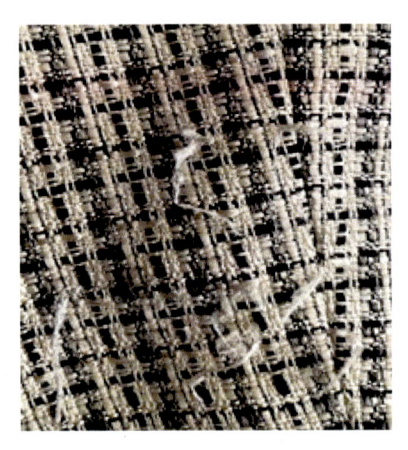

Figure 29: An example of refurbished suede – pills.

The following section provides literature on laundering procedures, washer and dryers, stain removal and storage of textiles.

Laundering Procedures

Bockmuhl, Schaqes, and Rehberg, (2019) noted the need of removing microbial contamination via laundering in the medical field. Recent changing in the laundering of reducing the washing temperature for energy conservation can impact the efficiency of cleaning. The researchers noted that the Center for Disease Control and Prevention (CDC) recommends the temperature of laundering as 71°C. The team of researchers noted that a minimum of 60°C is required to maintain the elimination of microbial contamination.

Gocek, Sahin, Erdem, Namal, and Acikgoz (2013) examined linen to reduce the wrinkling problem of this premium comfort fabric after laundering. Previously, scholars tried a delicate cycle to reduce wrinkling to laundering in the linen fabric. The laundering parameters set for the study were temperature between 30-40°C, high water level with 16 liters water, rotational speed of 52 rpm, and adding four steaming steps before the second spinning, before the softening cycle, and before the last two spin cycles. The temperature of the steaming process was 50⁰C. The seventy-six minutes laundry cycle included cold washing, heating, 1st spinning, rinsing, 2nd spinning, softening, and last spinning. Even though the revised process improved the smoothness from 1.3-2.0 by the third washing, it still did not reach the passing grade of 3.5.

Chen-Yu, Guo and Gatterson (2009) reported that using rinse cycle softener increased the flammability of both 100% cotton and 100% polyester fabrics. However, the dryer-sheet did not show any significant change. Consumers do not read labels. *AATCC Review* (2009, September) reported that 97% of the consumers launder their own clothes. However, the percentage of those who read labels is dropping continually. It was 77% in 2003 and 64% in 2007 and reached 54% in 2009. Consumers' faulty laundering habits could affect garments' performance regarding fading and shrinking. The study also asserted that those under 35 years of age are less likely to read labels then the older consumers. Doty and Easter (2009) reported that differences were not significant between activewear and workwear.

Easter (2004) examined the performance of the Fluorocarbon treated pants for 20 launderings. Results revealed that the ironing process improved smoothness from 3.3-3.7 without affecting the edge abrasion and color. Washing inside out improved the color retention and edge abrasion. Use of fabric softener improved color retention. The powder detergent performed better than the liquid detergent. Stain repellency was better with warm water and absence of fabric softener. For this part, liquid detergent performed better than the powder detergent. Fluorocarbon treated pants released stains like chocolate sauce, grapes, orange juice, and spaghetti irrespective of the conditions. However, bacon, grease, and dirt were improved better with liquid versus powder detergents, warm water, and no softener. The care label recommended warm wash, liquid detergent, no fabric softener, and ironing after five cycles. Finally, use of fabric softener reduced performance for stain repellence but enhanced the colorfastness.

The findings also identified some additional facts as follows. Stain repellency was maintained up to 30 launderings. Water repellency rating was maintained until 20 washes. Oil Repellency was maintained for 20 washes. Unlike previous finishes, it was not detectable by touch and did not make the fabric stiff either. The cleanability improved. Finally, it met the consumer demand for comfortable feel, easy care, and maintenance, freshness, great appeal, and nice smell.

Washers and Dryers

The minimum energy factor for the top loaders will be 1.57 and the maximum will be 6.57. It will be 1.84 for the minimum of the front loaders and 4.7 as the maximum (Appliance Standards Awareness Project, ASAP, 2021). Lower energy factor is better than the higher energy factor. The standard factors were published in 2012. Mauer (2017) informed that energy efficient washers and dryers will hit the market in 2018. They are bigger, cheaper, and have higher efficiency than 2015. Top loaders will have 26% saving in energy and 16% in water efficiency. Front loaders will have 43% in energy and 52% in water efficiency.

Kirchhoff (undated) asserted that the dryer filter must be cleaned on a regular basis for enhanced effectiveness of the dryer. Mitchell (undated) quoted, "An accumulation of lint in your dryer doesn't just make the machine less efficient, it also creates a fire hazard. Clothes dryers cause about 15,600 fires each year, according to a 2007 report by the United States Fire Administration, and regular cleaning could prevent up to 43 percent of them."

A group of scholars made presentations on the laundering process at the international Congress of International Federation of Home Economics held from July 16-21, 2012. **Gocho** from Japan Used washing temperatures at 35ºC and 60ºC. The washing cycle was 20 minutes long and the rinsing cycle lasted for10 minutes. She used Tury O Meter because it had 35% more efficiency than the laundreometer. **Emir Lasic** from Germany described the four-step washing process as a function of temperature, chemistry, time, and mechanics. He emphasized that water consumption was the highest for an eight Kilogram load. The energy consumption was the best for the five Kilogram load. **Hester Styn** compared front and top load washers. He asserted that water heaters utilize 90% of the energy. Top loaders were found to use more water and detergent and caused more wear and tear. Front loaders used more water but had less wear and tear. He also claimed that temperature increases cleaning efficiency. Hester further stressed that the temperature between 70-100ºC, removes soil, kills germs, and results in color loss. If temperature is kept between 40-60ºC, it neither kills germs, nor results in color loss. Moisture retention was less for the front loader than the top loader. Soil removal was higher in the front load than top load washer. Top loader was also noted to be deeper than the front loader. **Vanzyl** from South Africa used catholyte (5% salt added in water) to change the molecular structure of water in his investigation. He limited the Phosphate level to 0.4%. Vanzyl stressed that a detergent is a combination of surfactant (lowers surface tension) and builders. His findings revealed that the efficiency increased by 20-30% with addition of the catholyte.

Beatty (2008) reported that the amount of energy used reduced over the years. Water usage reduced from 20-65%. Front loading washers were introduced as energy efficient washers that use 20-65% less water. They also acknowledged that top loading washers cost around $350 whereas the energy efficient washers were anywhere from $1000-1200.

Kirchhoff (undated) asserted that the dryer filter must be cleaned on a regular basis for enhanced effectiveness of the dryer. Mitchell (undated) quoted, "An accumulation of lint in your dryer doesn't just make the machine less efficient, it also creates a fire hazard. Clothes dryers cause about 15,600 fires each year, according to a 2007 report by the United States Fire Administration, and regular cleaning could prevent up to 43 percent of them."

Stain Removal

The Market Analysis Report (2021) informed that based on the 2018 data, the US market was 20. 55 billion in 2019 and 21.48 billion in 2020. It is predicted to be 27.15 billion in 2025 (4,7% gain from 2019-2025). The global market on stain removal products was noted to be 19.7 billion US dollars. The report covered the stain removers in the bar, liquid, powder, spray forms, and other. Other category would include foams, gels, packets, sticks, tablets, and wipes (Transparency Market Research, https://www.transparencymarketresearch.com/stain-remover-products-market.html. Globally, it covered U.S, U.K, Germany, France, China, India, Brazil, Middle East, and Africa. The report mentioned that the increasing awareness of health and hygiene and attention to clothing has given this boost to the industry.

Some specifics are chosen to be discussed about the stain removers that can be of interest to the consumer. One wash miracle from Tide of Proctor and Gamble is claimed to remove stubborn stains from sweaty athletic wear, smelly pet items, regular clothing, and musty towels. Tide-to-go instant stain remover (bleach free) pens are noted to be effective and were listed to cost $7. The website lists that it is effective on wool, polyester and cotton for wine, tea, coffee, spaghetti sauce, grape juice etc. (Rabideau, 2021)

Rabideau (2021) provided a list of 6 effective stain removers with their prices ranging from $ 5-162. The author proclaimed "OxiClean MaxForce" to be the best overall and cost $5 for 12ounces. The other removers were "Tide to Go", "Zout Triple Enzyme Formula", "OxiClean Versatile Stain Remover Powder", "OxiClean White Revive Laundry Whitener + Stain Remover", Shout gel, "Shout Wipe & Go", and the non-toxic "Biokleen Bac-Out Enzyme Stain Remover". The author provides links for further links on the selected items.

Power pods of Tide are the best seller at the Amazon followed by the shout color catcher dryer sheets (https://www.amazon.com/Best-Sellers-Health-Personal-Care-Laundry-Stain-Removers/zgbs/hpc/15356211). Manning-Schaffel (2019) reported information from several experts. Use of baking soda and vinegar, heavy duty detergent, and rubbing alcohol stood out the most for clothing.

Storage of Textiles

At museums and in academic historic collections, neither visitors nor organizers are allowed to directly touch the textile. One is required to wear gloves to prevent damaging of the material. Caring for textiles (2021, http://www.ala.org/alcts/preservationweek/howto/textiles) is important for museums also. Avoid damp places to prevent the microbial attack. Fold as less as possible. Use acid free boxes and tissues to store. Keep dyed fabrics away from light. Hang clothing on padded hangers. Ritzenthaler (2016, 2020) identified five essentials of storage as storage, handling, cleaning and mending, housing and displaying. For storing, use cool and dry place to avoid damage. Do not use basements. For handling use both hands. If the product is heavy, use boxes or board for support while moving. Cleaning and mending should be avoided if the textile is weak to prevent additional damage including color loss. For housing, stuff hats, purses, and shoes. For display, store in dark and use as little light as possible.

Summary and Conclusion

Refurbishing is an important factor to retain the original look of the garment and be able to use it for an extended period. It is important the consumers follow the care instructions on labels for best results. This chapter highlights textile care and upkeep. It emphasizes the importance of stain removal before laundering. and includes information on laundering, fabric damages, stain removal and storage of textiles. Understanding the nature of the stains before treating them is important. Most of the commercial products are designed to clean a variety of stains. Knowing the nature of the stain helps with selecting the correct cleaners that can neutralize the effect and lift the stain when possible. For example, treating the acid stains with alkaline solutions and vice versa. For best results, understanding both equipment and processes are important from consumer, commercial, industry, marketing, and museum perspectives. *AAICC Manual of International Methods and Procedures* 2021) has one standard on oil repellency. In real life, there are more stains than oil that soil clothing of consumers. Alternate method is proposed for future use. The information provides practical implications of The discussed categories that can be used by manufacturers, retailers, and consumers alike.

REFERENCES

Annual book of ASTM Standards (2019). *7.02*, West Conshohoken, PA: ASTM International.

Appliances: The history and advancements of the washer and dryer. https://www.easyapplianceparts.com/resources/History-and-Advancements-of-the-Washer-and-Dryer.aspx

Beatty, A. E. (2008, October 10,). Cycles change with washer/dryer. *Chicago Tribune.* Retrieved 3/13/2021. https://www.chicagotribune.com/real-estate/chi-washers-choices_chomes_1010oct10-story.html

Bockmuhl, D. P., Schaqes, J., & Rehberg, L. (2019). Laundry and textile hygiene in healthcare and beyond. *Microbial Cell, 6*(7), 299-306. doi:10.15698/mic2019.07.682

Caring for textiles. (3/14/2021). Retrieved on 3/14/2021. http://www.ala.org/alcts/preservationweek/howto/textiles

Chen-Yu, J. H., Guo, J., & Gatterson, B. K. (2009, March). Effect of household fabric softeners on flammability of cotton and polyester fabrics. *AATCC Review, 9,* 43-47.

Chowdhary, U. (2009). *Textile analysis, quality control, and innovative uses.* Deer Park, NY: LINUS.

Clothes Washers. (2021). Appliance Awareness Standards Project. *ASAP.* https://appliance-standards.org/product/clothes-washers.

Cohen, A. C., & Johnson, I. (2010). *Fabric science.* New York, NY: Fairchild.

Collier, B. J., Bide, M., & Tortora, P. G. (2009). *Understanding textiles.* Upper Saddle River, NJ: Prentice Hall.

Consumers don't read care label (2009, September). *AATCC Review, 9,* 20.

Easter, E. P. (2004). Care practices for Fluorocarbon treated garments: A case study. *AATCC Review, 4*(3), 12-16.

Gocek, I., Sahin, U. K., Erdem, I, Namal, O., & Acikgoz, H. (2013). A study on easy-care laundering of linen fabrics. *Textile Research Journal, 83*(18), 1961-1973. https://doi.org/10.1177/0040517513485624

Kirchhoff, H. (undated). Dryer filter cleaning. Retrieved 3/14/2021. https://homeguides.sfgate.com/dryer-filter-cleaning-68153.htm

Laundering team session: Gocho, Lasic, Hester Styn and Vanzyl. (2012). held at the International Congress of the International Federation of Home Economics from July 16-21, 2012.

Mauer, J. (2017, December). A new spin on clothes washer efficiency coming in January 2018. Appliance Awareness Standards Project. *ASAP.*

Mitchell, S. (Undated). How to keep dryer lint out of the house. Retrieved 3/14/2021. https://homeguides.sfgate.com/keep-dryer-lint-out-house-23884.html

Rabideau, C. (2021, February 18). The best 8 laundry stain removers of 2021. Retrieved on 3/15/2021. https://www.thespruce.com/top-stain-removers-for-laundry-1900909

Ritzenthaler, M. L. (2016, 2020). Preserving textiles. *Prologue Magazine, 48 (2). No page #s.*

Stain remover products market size, share and trends analysis report by product (powder, spray), by distribution channel (offline, online), by region, and segment forecasts 2019-2025. *Market Analysis Report.* Retrieved 3/15/2021. https://www.grandviewresearch.com/industry-analysis/stain-remover-products-market

With GreenShield less is more. (2021). Retrieved 3/13/2021. https://greenshieldfinish.com/applications/

PRACTICE ACTIVITIES

1. Make groups and discuss different methods of refurbishing textiles. Compile a list of methods presented by different groups.

2. Purchase organic and inorganic detergents for laundering. Compare them for their cleaning efficiency with focus on appearance retention, dimensional stability, fabric hand, and stain removal.

3. What is the role of fabric softeners in the cleaning process?

4. Identify the most found stains clothing in everyday life. Which of them are hard for you to remove?

5. Compare the impact of different stain removers on a variety of stains.

6. Compare the use of dry and liquid fabric softeners in the laundering process.

7. Examine the cleaning efficiency of different detergents. It could mean powdered and liquid, or across or within brands.

8. How does knowing the nature of stains help with their removal?

9. What is the role of bleaches in the refurbishing process? How do the Clorox and color safe bleaches work? Read the labels to determine if they list the distinctions.

10. What is the difference between top and front-loading washers? Which ones are recognized as the high efficiency washers and why?

11. What is the role of wearing well ironed clothes? Examine as a group the ironing practices used by you. Interview your parents or grandparents to understand the changing patterns of refurbishing your clothes.

COLOR, THEORY, EVALUATION, MEASUREMENT AND USE

CHAPTER 8

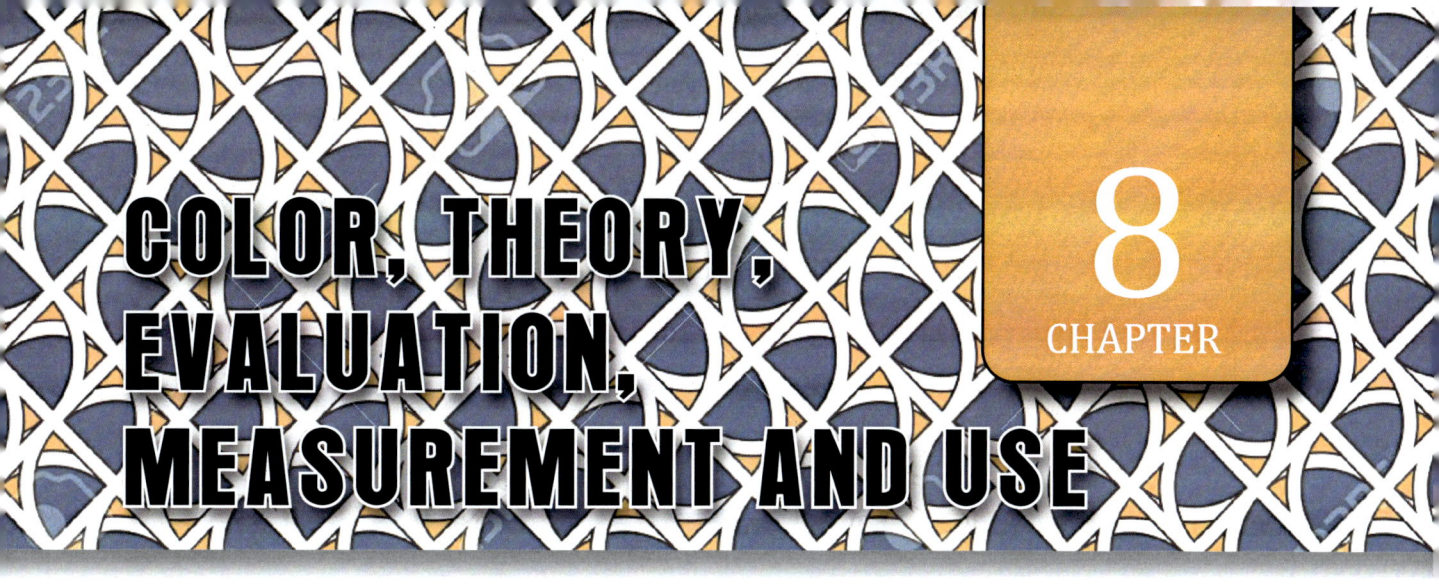

Color is the first thing that a consumer sees when he/she enters the retail store. Psychologically, color brings several emotions for human beings. Scientifically, it is very strategically grouped together to bring a rainbow of nature in a person's nearest environment. Color is an intriguing concept that is used and appreciated by artists and scientists alike. They integrate art, physics, chemistry, environment, fashion, mathematics, philosophy, psychology, sociology, and theatre amazingly well. The ability of individuals to see color differently adds a unique dimension and fascination in viewing the world around oneself. A rainbow's seven colors can be seen in nature, on embellishments of apparel, costumes of actors in theatre, and a human desire for harmony all around us.

This chapter will discuss color both at a micro as well as macro levels. At micro level even a child gets aesthetic pleasure when he/she sees a rainbow in the sky. That pleasant sensations always delights individuals even into adulthood. Scientifically, it is measured by wavelengths that are measured in nanometers. The rainbow colors range between 400-700 nanometers (Figure 30). The sequence of colors is represented by Violet, Indigo, Blue, Green, Yellow, Orange, and Red. If we pass through a beam of white light, we see seven colors in the presence of sunlight. Rainbow range is also known as the visible light. Figure 30 shows color and approximate wavelength for each color of the rainbow. The ultraviolet light, x-rays, gamma rays, and cosmic rays have shorter wavelengths than the visible light (<400 nanometers) and the infrared, microwave, radar, television, radio, and ultrasonic have longer wavelengths (≥700 nanometers). The wavelength of the ultraviolet rays is between, 315 to 400 nanometers (Long, 2013, p. 97). The colors that fade in both ultraviolet and visible lights are called the **fugitive colors. X-rays** have wavelength between, 0.1 and 10 nanometers. **Gamma rays** have wavelength of less than .01 nanometers. They are used in the medical field. **Infrared** rays have the wavelengths between 780 nanometers to 1mm. The wavelengths of the microwaves is between 30cm-.1 mm, **radar** is from 0.8-10 cm, **television** uses 2.25 to 4.5 meters, **radio** 1 mm- 100 kilometer, and the ultrasonic rays is less than 1.9 cm.

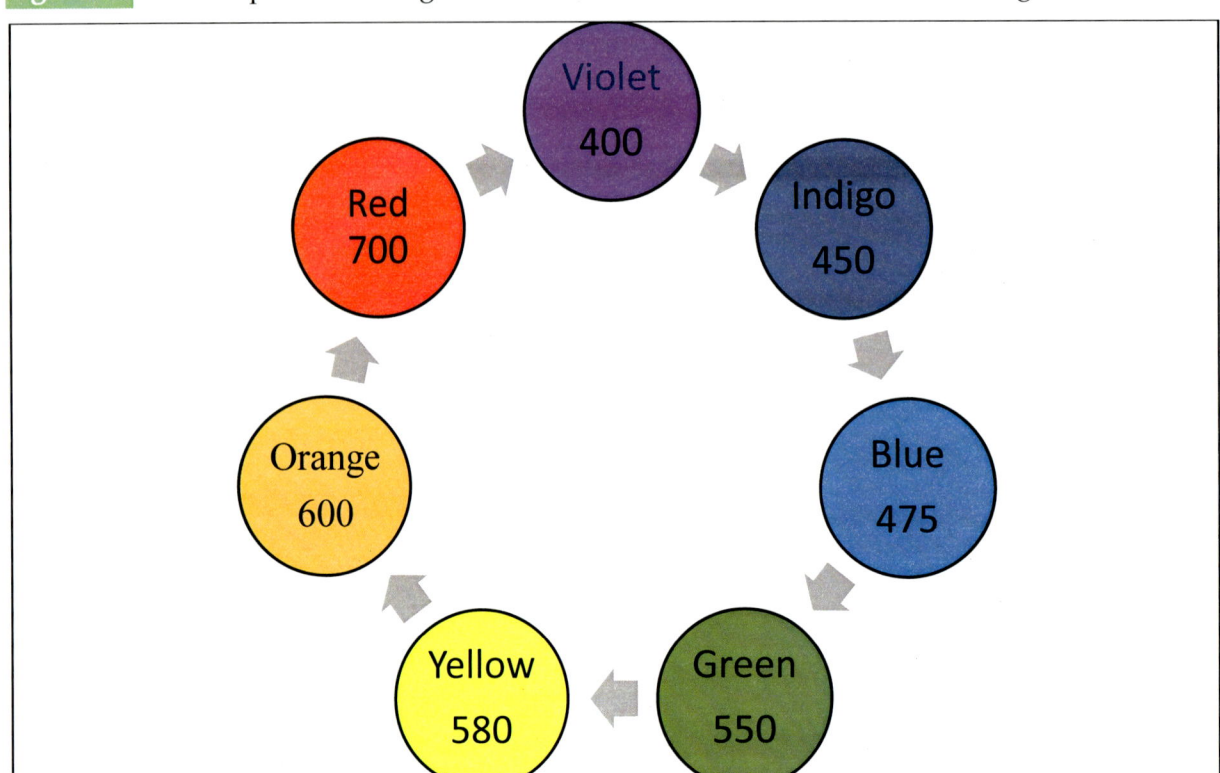

Figure 30: Visible Spectrum of Light. Numbers indicate nanometers for wavelength.

[Figure 30: Circular diagram showing the visible spectrum of light with colors and their wavelengths in nanometers: Violet 400, Indigo 450, Blue 475, Green 550, Yellow 580, Orange 600, Red 700.]

Hue, value and chroma or intensity are the three elements of color that are critical in understanding their use in design. **Hue** refers to the name of the color such as red, yellow, blue, etc. **Value** refers to the lightness and darkness of the color. Adding white to the color is called **tint** and adding black to the color is labeled as a **shade**. For example, adding white to red makes pink. Pink is tint of red. Adding black to red makes maroon. Maroon is a shade of red. **Intensity** refers to the saturation of color and influences the brightness and dullness of colors.

Color Theories and Their Uses

There are several theories of color that have been identified in the literature on color. Light, Prang or Brewster, Munsell, and Psychological (Ostwald). Brief description of each theory is provided below.

Light Theory

This theory is based on the RGB (Red, Green, and Blue) concept. In this case, these three colors are considered the primary colors. Yellow, magenta, and cyan are considered the secondary colors. Besides using in the fashion industry, this theory is also used in the computer television technology, and Pantone color schemes used in the industry. This theory is based on the reflection of light. It has two dimensions: Additive and subtractive. **The additive theory** is based on the use of primary colors that start on the black background and reflection of the light. When RGB hues are added, it becomes white (Figure 31). Adding primary colors provide the secondary colors. **The subtractive theory** refers to absorption of the wavelength from the reflected light. Absorption takes away from the original. Therefore, it is called the subtractive theory. It is initiated with white background and becomes black as red, green, and blue are subtracted from it (Figure 32). Source of the pictures (both figure 31 and figure 32) is https://physics.stackexchange.com/questions/23830/why-is-there-a-difference-between-additive-and-subtractive-trichromatic-color.

Figure 31: Additive theory of color (Red, Green and Blue) as the primary colors.

Figure 32: Subtractive theory of color (Yellow, Magenta and Cyan) as the primary colors.

Prang's Pigment Theory

This theory has been used extensively in academe for fashion design to understand fashion fundamentals and their ability to create optical illusions that camouflage defects but accentuate the body strengths. It uses a twelve-part wheel that strategically uses primary, secondary, and tertiary colors. This wheel provides visual analysis more than the three color dimensions: hue, intensity, and value (Figure 33) downloaded from https://www.google.com/search?q=Shutterstock.com.+Prang%27s+Color+Wheel&sxsrf=ALeKk0082RsasDB9eBrKCJK9jdzO6mdiww:1615902278463&tbm=isch&source=iu&ictx=1&fir=N7vwivn68ZDOWM%252Clrh1m86tsIecCM%252C_&vet=1&usg=AI4_-kSGUAPyqOaqx_L0f28Ql_RDVfqU0w&sa=X&ved=2ahUKEwj-orKK-bTvAhUaHs0KHflEAXEQ9QF6BAgIEAE#imgrc=p7EawDUo6tpjgM on 3/16/2021. Davis (1996, p. 173)) offered several color schemes by using this wheel. They were monochromatic (one hue), analogous (uses hues next to each other on the wheel), single-split complementary, double complementary (two adjacent hues, and their complements), double split complementary (colors on each side of both complements), triad (Every fourth color), and tetrad (every third color). They are good guides for new designers. The wheel provides to easily establish the color schemes for its users to organize the designs based on colors.

Figure 33: Prang's color wheel with twelve hues.

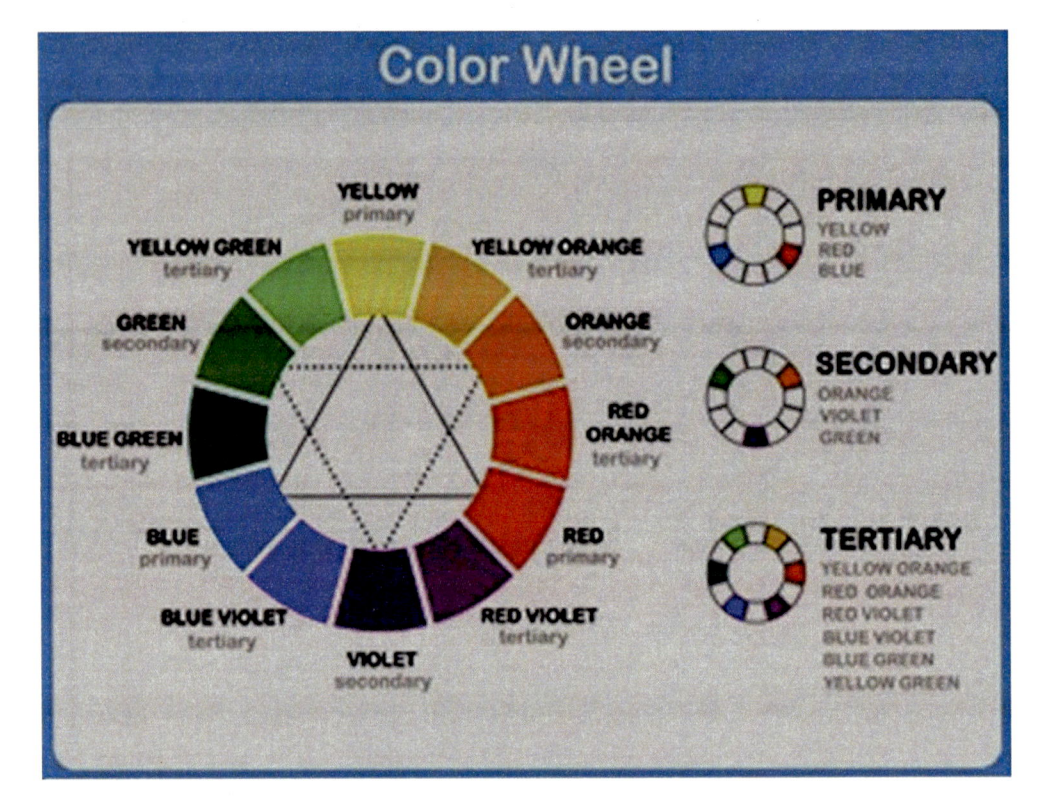

Munsell hue circle is based on ten rather than twelve colors of the Prang or Brewster's wheel. It is made of five principal and five intermediate colors (figure 34). The five principal colors are red, yellow, green, blue and purple. The five intermediate colors are yellow-red, green-yellow, blue-green, purple-blue, and red purple. When color is abyss, it is called neutral. Black, grey, and white are three such examples. On the Munsell hue circle, it is denoted by N in the center of the circle. These colors are further divided to ten. Munsell's colors have a total of 100 colors. Its poster also talks about two organizations of RGB (Red, Green, and Blue) and CMYK (Cyan, Magenta, Yellow, and Key or Black). It is used in printing. Pantone colors are based on the CMYK system. This system is extended to color matching, color measurement systems, as well as color perception tools that are used by industry to test employees ability to discriminate colors with precision. Fashion designers use it for finalizing their apparel design details and promotions. With introduction of computers, they are used in decision making for products also.

Figure 34: Munsell wheel of hue circle.

Munsell System of Color Space (Figure 35) projects the concept of lightness and darkness in the central column from black to white and 1-9 numbers. Lightness increases with ascendance of numbers, and darkness increases as numbers lower. 1 refers to black and 9 to white. They are shown with neutrals. Circle around the column projects both principal and intermediate colors. Chroma is shown as a radius from column to the periphery ranging from 2-10. 2 means less intensity or saturation and 10 means the highest intensity and saturation. This color space system fully integrates hue, chroma, and value.

Figure 35: Munsell System of Color Space (Periyaswamy in Chowdhary, 2009)

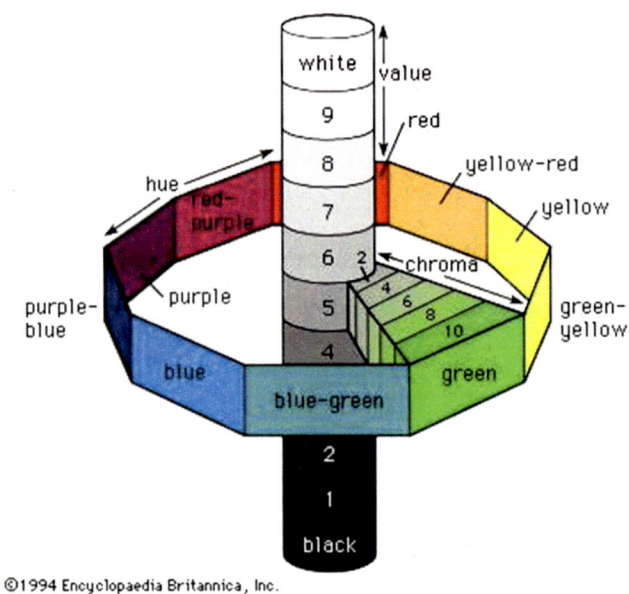

International Commission of Illumination (CIE) was founded in 1931. It is related to the color measurement systems. It focuses on the standard combination of the source of light, an object, and an observer. They derived numbers under standard light and observer. CIE method uses L*a*b* system. L* refers to the lightness and darkness of the color. a* implies the redness and greenness of the color. Finally, b* denotes blueness or yellowness of the color. This methodology is used in spectrophotometers.

Figure 36 is designed on the basis that L*'s lightness and a* and b* are the "chromatic coordinates". It shows positive and negative values to allow for informed interpretation of the values. Firstly, a* shows red to green directions. +value shows the red direction and -value shows the green direction. Secondly, b* yellow to blue directions. Positive value shows the yellow direction, and negative value shows the blue color. Total range for all directions and both colors ranges from ±10-±60. Daylight is denoted by D65. Figure 36 is used for yellow to blue direction and red to green directions only. It does not provide values for L*. If your value on the b* scale is 40.80, it will have yellow undertone. If it is -40.80, then it will be on the blue side. Likewise, a value of + 45 refers to the red direction and -45 to the green direction.

L*a*b* values are used to calculate ΔE value that denotes color difference (Mokrzycki, and Tatol (2011). Chowdhary and Wroblewski (2016) reported that the value of ≥2 is visible to the human eye. Several websites report that the values of 3-6 are generally acceptable for reproduction purposes when people do color matching. However, when it relates to colorfastness to laundering, light, perspiration, or water, different parameters may be set.

Phillips (2015) provided an image to understand the tristimulus values and color measurement. The concept is used to enhance communication between manufacturers and customers on color preferences. Spectrophotometer uses the "human eye technology" for objectively quantifying the color measurement values. These measurements offer constancy for all stakeholders alike. Human eye

Color, Theory, Evaluation, Measurement and Use

Figure 36: L*a*b* color space chromaticity diagram (Hue and Saturation) in *Precise color communication: Color control from perception to instrumentation* (2007-2013, p. 16)

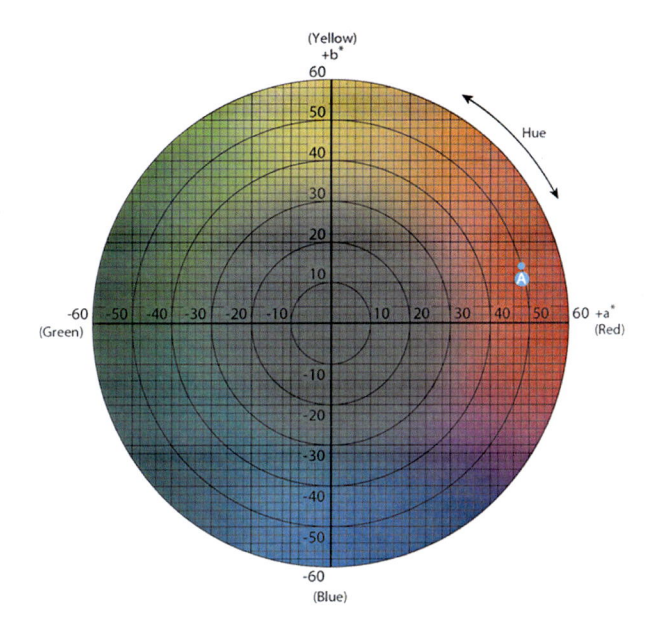

measures color based on the cone cells. Based these cone cells, eye sees in terms of short, medium, and long wavelengths. Within the visible spectrum terms, the short wavelength is blue, medium is green, and long is red. This is the foundation of RGB, and is denoted by XYZ as shown in figure 37. Using this universal color language by CIE provides precision in communication of color with consistency.

Figure 37: Quantification of three primary color receptors of the human eye with X, Y, and Z values. Source: Wikimedia Common user Sakurambo.

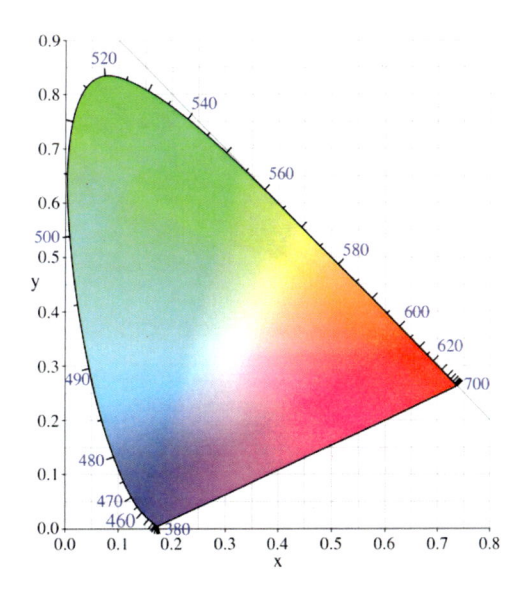

Islam (2020) found that CIE L*a*b* values differed significantly based on the fabric structure, placement of dress form, light sources, and exposure time. Key findings of the research indicated that CIE L*a*b* values differed significantly based on the (a) fabric structures, (b) placement in three-dimensional dress form, (c) light sources, and (d) exposure time. The findings may have implications to understand the physical representation of textile materials scientifically for visual merchandising.

Islam and Chowdhary (2019) examined the color exhaustion of three knits: single jersey, rib, and fleece. Reactive dyes in three basic colors (rad, yellow, and blue) were used in the dyeing process simultaneously. Results revealed that three knits differed for the color based on the CIELAB values. The dye values were adjusted to optimize the process so that uniform color is achieved for all three knits because single jersey and rib knit may be used in the same garment.

Adnan (2018) found that both red and green colors differed for two- and three-dimensional forms. They also differed for three different lights (daylight, Fluorescent, and incandescent). Three weaves (plain, twill and satin) do not differ from each other. Differences were the highest for the underarm area and side seams for two- and three-dimensional forms. Green differed significantly for all body parts. Green differed the most for two- and three- dimensional forms. Chowdhary (2017) reported that the color of three brands of red cotton t-shirts received a ΔE of 3.30, 4.23, and 2.25, respectively. All three brands became lighter, less red, and less yellow.

Farnsworth Munsell's 100 Hue Test

This kit takes about 15 minutes to complete. It measures the color vision of individuals to determine color acuity for 4 tray sets that were started with 100 hues. However, after testing, it was found out that 15 of them were too close to call. Therefore, they were eliminated from the set. The four test trays with case and software cost $750.

Participants are asked to jumble up the color tiles for each tray set with color side up and then compare to the original numbering for determining the ability to color discrimination. The participants are classified as superior, average, and low. In industry, they are used by inspectors for color matching,

Figure 38: Example of images with rating scale.

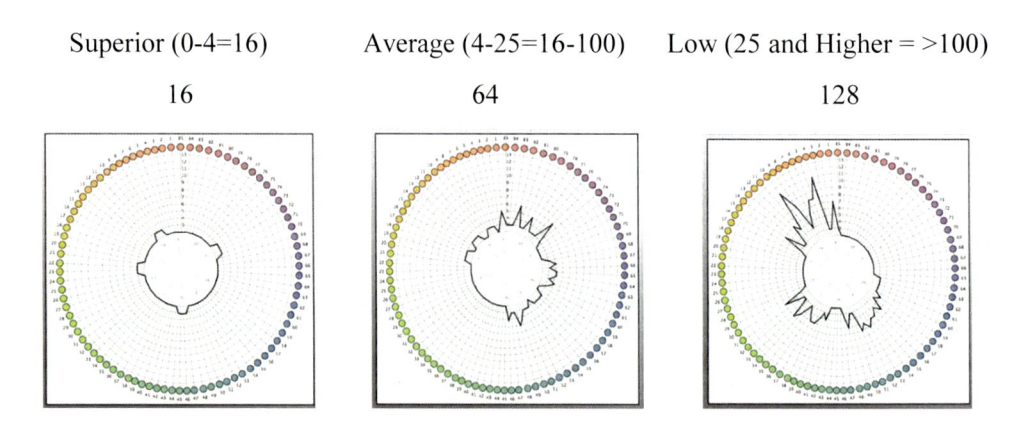

Superior (0-4=16)   Average (4-25=16-100)   Low (25 and Higher = >100)
16   64   128

https://munsell.com/wp-content/uploads/2017/03/farnsworth-munsell-100-hue-test-scores-meaning.jpg

Color, Theory, Evaluation, Measurement and Use

by selectors of vocational jobs to make choices of the jobs, to test an individual's type and degree of color deficiency, verify the effect of medical treatments. The knowledge from this measure helps individuals to perform their job well. This test can be downloaded free online also to know one's score. Figure 38 shows the rating range for superior, average, and low scores along with one example for each type provided by the company. The software does show other than this form also to present the information. It is worth noting that the same score can show different patterns.

    Figure 39 shows examples of average and superior score patterns. As noted in figure 38, the superior rating ranges between 0-16 and a maximum of four deviations. Each deviation is worth 4 points. Deviations of 5-25 and score of 20-100 is rated as an average rating. Finally, Score of >100 is rated as the low classification. Examples below show several patterns, as well as two examples of 28 and 32 scores that look different from each other. These numbers and classifications can be used for employees and trainees in the field of color matching and evaluation. This kit is used both in the design and retailing industry to allow accurate interpretation and superior decision making.

Figure 39: Examples of different patterns in general and for the same scores.

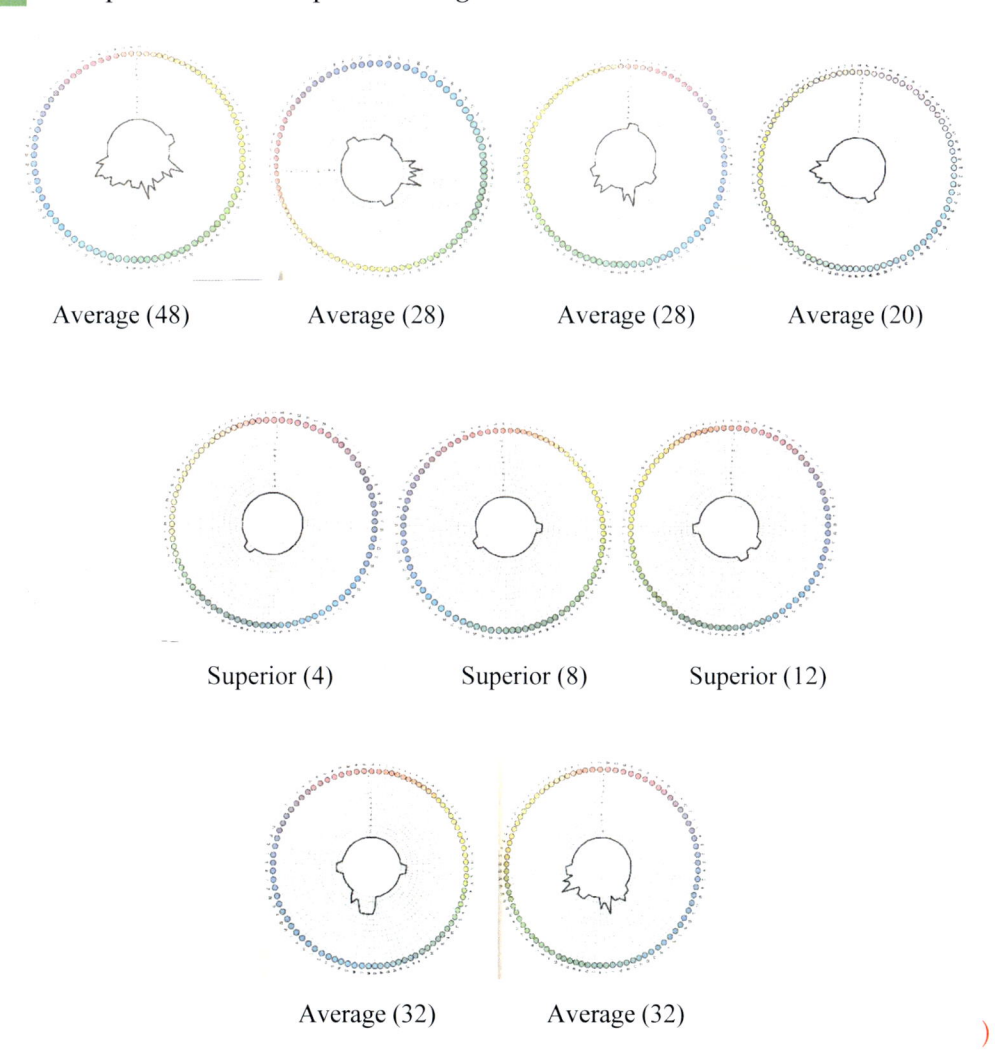

Average (48)　　Average (28)　　Average (28)　　Average (20)

Superior (4)　　Superior (8)　　Superior (12)

Average (32)　　Average (32)

)

Coloring Process

In textiles, color can be obtained by dyeing, printing, or painting. Of these three, dyeing and printing are used the most universally. During can be done at fiber/solution, yarn fabric, and garment stages. Printing that is done via pigments is done in fabric or garment stages only. Dyes and pigments have one common element that they add color to the textile. However, there are several differences between the two.

Table 23: Distinctions between dyes and pigments.

Category	Dyes	Pigments
Application	Needs fiber-content specific Dye.	One machine and same pigment can be used on different types of fabric
Binder	Not used	Binder is required to fix pigment to the fabric.
Chemical Nature	Mostly, organic	Mostly, inorganic
Combustible Properties	Combustible	Non-combustible
Imparting Nature	Imparts color by absorption.	Imparts color by scattering of light or selective absorption.
Lightfastness	Less than pigments	More than dyes.
Longevity	Less than the pigments	Last longer than dyes.
Size	Smaller than pigments	Larger than dyes
Solubility	Dyes are soluble in water.	Pigments may or may not be soluble in water.

COLARIS PIGMENT pamphlet (2018) by Zimmer reported that 97% of the conventional printing used 45% pigment printing in 2017. Only 3% was digital printing. Only 1% was represented by the pigment. One billion square meter was produced via digital printing and 333 billion square meters by conventional printing. The document highlighted six benefits of using pigment printing. First, Pigments work on all types of fabrics using one machine. Second, It is an easy process and much know-how is not needed. Third, there is no water wastage and uses less energy. Fourth, investment is low. Fifth, 406 base colors are used. Sixth, printing coss are low. The company proposed that digital printing could replace the traditional printing processes because they are cost effective in comparison with reactive and disperse printing. The resource also suggested that using pre and top coating sharpens the print, provides a clear image, stiffens the fabric, and enhances the rub fastness. The document provided examples of digital printing applications for home textiles, outdoor fabrics, workwear, and uniforms, as well panels.

Classification of Colorants

The colorants are classified in many ways by different groups. The American Association of Textile Chemists and Colorists (AATCC) and the Society of Dyers and Colourists (SDC) collectively developed the Colour Index™. It includes two systems: CIGN for the generic names, and CICN for the constitution number. CIGN focuses on the application method, and CICN on the chemical structure. The colour index has two sections. Part I focuses on "pigments and solvent dyes" used in the industry. Part II concentrates on the dyes used in several types of industry. The dye classes listed on the website are "acid, basic, direct, disperse, food, fluorescent brightener, mordant, reactive, sulphur and vat, plus several other classes of minor or historical importance.

Acid dyes are anionic dyes that have one of the sulfonic or other acidic groups. He used Acid Yellow 35 as one of the examples (Mawla 2021). This dye is used for wool and silk. Acid works better on them because they are damaged by alkali.

Basic dyes are cationic and the first synthetic dye that was used on all types of fiber contents. Tannic acid was used as a mordant for cotton and rayon. Mawla (2021) gave an example of Basic Brown 1 that is dyed with 2-5 pH solution. Basic dyes work the best for acrylic fibers.

Direct dyes can be applied to the fabric without any mordant and can be used on natural fibers and nylon. Mawla used Direct Orange 26 as its example.

Disperse dyes were first developed for the regenerated fiber acetate. Today, they are found to be most effective on polyester, nylon, and acetate. Mawla (2021) identified Disperse yellow 3, Disperse Red 4, and Disperse Blue 27 as good examples of disperse dyes.

Fluorescent brightener is used for whitening and brightening the fabrics while laundering. They change the UV rays to enhance blue and minimize yellow Peltier, 2019). They replace traditionally used bluing to whiten the white fabric. They reflect more than 100% of light and make the surface lighter and brighter.

Mordant dyes require a binding agent and do not dye the fabric by themselves (Mawla, 2021). They are used on cotton, wool, silk, etc.

Reactive dyes make covalent bonds with the cellulosic fibers and provide colorfast dyeing. These are commonly used dyes.

Sulphur dyes are used for deep shades on cotton, linen, and rayon. It makes fabric tender when dyeing with black color.

Vat dyes are colorfast dyes that were originally used for the indigo dyes and are the "insoluble complex polycyclic molecules based on the quinone structure (ketoforms)" (Mawla, 2021). They are used on cotton, linen, nylon, rayon, silk, and wool. Its example based on the colour index is Vat Blue 4 (Indanthrene).

Dye classification is used to select fabric appropriate dyes for the vest results. Different dyes offer varying degrees of colorfastness. Chowdhary (2008) used different types of dye for various fiber contents. The images are provided below. Polyester picked up color only with the disperse dyes. In general, acid dyes are best for wool and silk. Disperse dyes are great for acetate, acrylic, nylon, and polyester. Basic and direct dyes are good for the cellulosic fibers. Basic dyes also work well on acrylic.

Chapter 8

Color Matching Systems

Color matching is an important factor in color usage for streamlining coordination between and among various stakeholders from different organizations. Several Color matching systems exist in the industry.

Pantone® Color Matching System was founded in 1962. It uses spot colours via CMYK procedure that is based on the subtractive theory of color. It uses the same process as used in computers today. It is housed in the United Kingdom but is globally recognized by industry and academe alike. In recent years, the governments of Canada, Scotland and South Korea are using the system to match the colors of their flags. AATCC launches design and merchandising competitions for students based on the Pantone® colors. Ideally, it is used in the product development process to match colors when creators and users are thousands of miles apart. Besides, color matching via color coding, the pantone colors also include color symbolism. Table 24 shows color symbolism from 1990.

Leatrice Eiseman, Creative Director of the Pantone Color Institute (2021, March 22) quoted, "The union of an enduring Ultimate Gray with the vibrant illuminating yellow expresses a message of positivity supported by fortitude. Practical and rock solid but at the same time warming and optimistic. This is a color combination that gives us resilience and hope. We need to feel encouraged and uplifted; this is essential to the human spirit." Evidently, Ultimate Gray and Illuminating Yellow are the colors of 2021 (https://visme.co/blog/pantone-color-of-the-year/, 3/22/2021). Pantone introduces one or two colors for every year. A table of the 1990s is provided below for five colors with their symbolism. The website noted that "graffiti, grunge, and zen" and "dark shades of pops of color" existed. https://christinaweisensel.wordpress.com/2015/12/03/pantone-colour-of-the-year-1960s-1990s/.

It is evident and both gray and yellow existed in the 1990s also but their descriptors for meaning and labels were different. It is worth noting that the color symbolism is used for both personal and professional uses. Symbolism may change from one time to another to reflect the changing environment of the societies.

Table 24: Pantone colors of the 1990s and their symbolism.

Pantone Color	Symbolism
14-0105 Overcast	Balance, calm
17-1118 Lead Gray	Stability, reliability, comfort
16-0540 Oasis	Peaceful, growth, health
14-0754 Super Lemon	Optimism, clarity, warmth
16-1452	Friendly, cheerful, confident
16-4725 Scuba Blue	Trust, dependability, strength

Testfabrics, Inc. (Undated) provided images of swatches from original, wash I and Wash II. The swatches show fading of color from laundering and have ramification for the consumer. If a company wants to check colorfastness to laundering, this process of color matching can used to offer real life situations to draw conclusions and make decisions to continue or change the material for future productions.

Figure 39: Source: Mach 5: Multi-area color-measurement hardware. For more information, contact Testfabrics, Inc. .

Original **Washed A** **Washed B**

The Russell Corporation from Alexander City, Alabama prepared color cards with actual fabric samples of the jersey (Figure 40) and fleece fabrics (Figure 40) for their "JERZEES BUILT TO LAST". Those days, technology was not as developed and accessible to the manufacturer and consumer alike as today. Textile was perceived to be touchy feely material. Fabric hand was an important attribute that was used in the decision-making process. Today's high-tech industry makes the most decisions are based on what is visible on the computers and/or the scientific parameters using L*a*b* values. That progression will be shown in the promotional materials from the Cotton Incorporated in figures 41-43.

Figure 40: Color Card from late 1980s with Jersey and Fleece Fabric C

Jersey Fabric **Fleece Fabric**

Cotton incorporated publishes its color stories on a regular basis and upgrades materials periodically through themes, colors, and their interpretations. The materials are shared with budding and established professionals through websites and various professional conferences. The author compared their changing techniques of presenting colors of the year for 1996, 2008, and 2015. The 1996 materials were received at the Bobbing Show, and 20028 and 2015 were collected at the AATCC conference.

In 1996, the company made packets with spiral binding, design prints and framed yarns with descriptors. For example, Figure 41 that is from 1996 shows real yarns for twelve colors with "Blazing, Passionate and Hearty" for the top six and "Tropical Exotic, and Magical" for the lower six colors. Page to the left shows colored prints and the following page shows description of energy for the top six and wisdom for the bottom six. Two additional sets are provided in the package titled as the "Time of Endurance." The second set is of "Health" and "Nature". The third set is "Endurance". The third set is of "Pleasure" and Peace". Additionally, it provides examples of "Established, Flexible, Interactive, Elementa and Expressive." With fabrics and samples. The packaging is aesthetically pleasing and very artistic. The well put together packet was tied with a ribbon.

Figure 41: Cotton Incorporated's Promotional style in 1996. Taken from a large package.

Color, Theory, Evaluation, Measurement and Use

The Home Color 2008 is much more concise than the 1996 version (Figure 42). It is made on a glossy paper with six themes, sets of six colors of yarns, sub-adjectives to describe the mood, and images that are not restricted to the textiles alone. The six themes were **"Wonder"**, **"Chameleon"**, **"Perspective", "Stability", "Borrowed", and "Pure".**

Wonder is represented by innocence, agelessness, creativity, and innocence. **Chameleon** was signified by frequently changing personalities depicted by the moody colors. **Perspective** indicated challenging the norm and pushing the boundaries. **Stability** was shown by the echoes of the architectural qualities and intellectual palette. **Borrowed** was shown by the expressive and symbolic tones. **Pure** was expressed with carved ricks, delicate snow, and cloud formation. Boundaries in the picture were blurred. Name of the colors also reflected the emotions corresponding to the environment.

Figure 42: Cotton Incorporated's Promotional style in 2008. Taken from a large package.

The promotional material from 2015 shows the transformation of theme themes and photographic images that reflects the updated technology. However, they continued to use the concept of themes, interpretation, and imagery. The 2015's folding pamphlet had five themes of "Quintessence", "Everyday Radical", "Disguised", "Tectonic", and" Tres Gentille." Corresponding examples as well as descriptions were provided. Quintessence is associated with versatility and luxury. Everyday Radical suggests that people look for meaning in the process. Disguised addressed using a bold color story to counter reveal with conceal. Tres Gentille indicates beauty, civility, kindness, and simplicity that is calming and comforting. Finally, Tectonic represents the blurring lines with a layered approach. Promotional materials represent color with a similar thought process that is adjusted to the spirit of new times with modern products and processes.

Chapter 8

Figure 43: Cotton Incorporated's Promotional style in 2015. Taken from a large package.

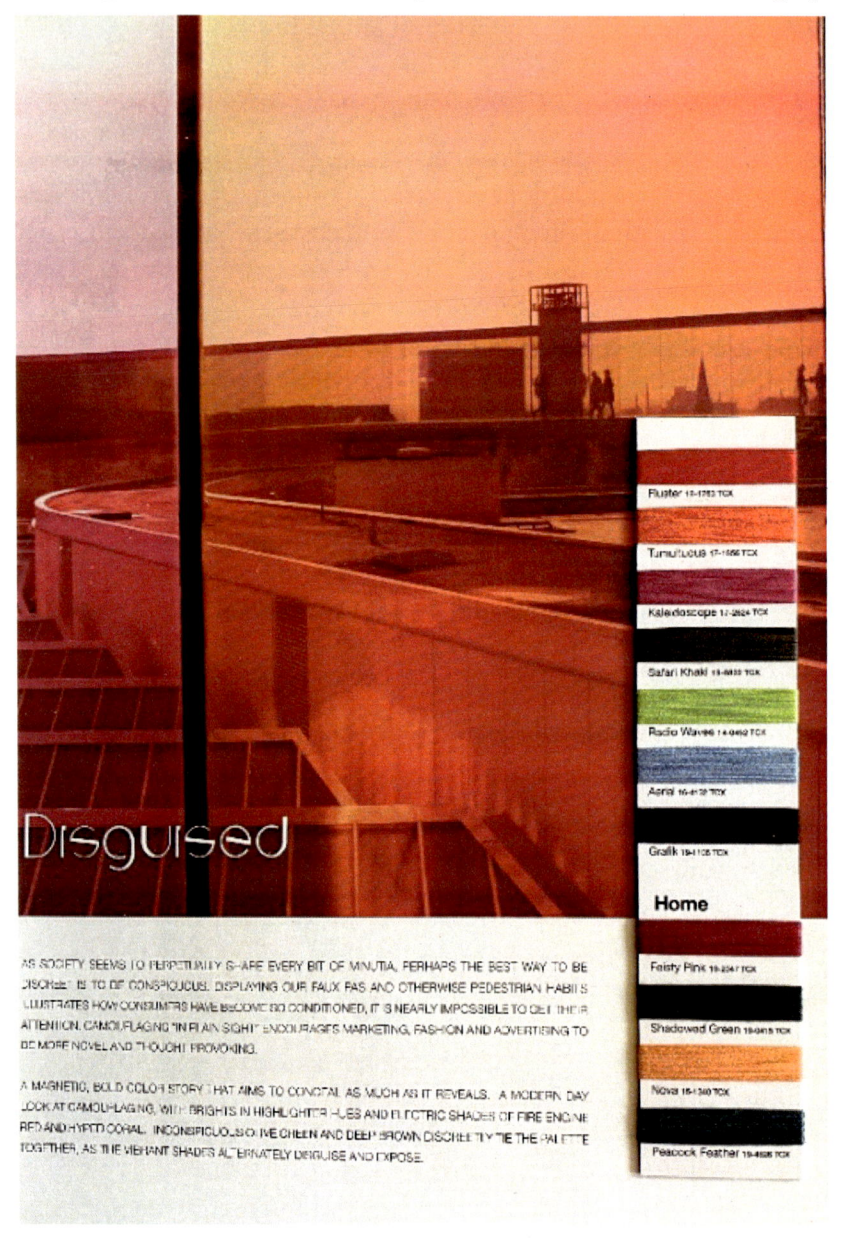

DyStar® shows the role of color in the Apparel Product Development Process for "Sustainable Fashion" and 360⁰ Color View (Figure 44). Figure 45 highlights the first step of design illustrates inspiration, color wall and design tools for the color selection process. Standardizing includes quality control to ensure the color matching and distribution process. DyStar® supports it via econfidence® branding. The promotional piece also mentions about the use of textile science in reducing the lead time enhancing compliance. In addition to giving importance to color the promotional piece also.

Color, Theory, Evaluation, Measurement and Use

Figure 44: Promotional pamphlet from DyStar® color use in product development.

Figure 45: Color integration in the apparel product development process.

Psychological Dimension of Color: Optical Illusion

The preceding information focused on the theoretical, scientific, creative, analytical, and aesthetic dimensions of color. This section will focus on the psychological dimensions where color is used to create optical illusions. It will discuss the concepts of advancing and receding colors and neutrals, shade and tint, the fluorescent colors plus emotional significance.

Between neutrals, white has an advancing effect because it reflects 1005 light. Black is receding color because it absorbs 100% light. Same wearer will look larger in white and smaller in black. That is why it is called the optical illusion. Figure 46 reflects the opposing effects of black and white.

Color, Theory, Evaluation, Measurement and Use 175

Figure 46: Advancing and Receding Neutrals

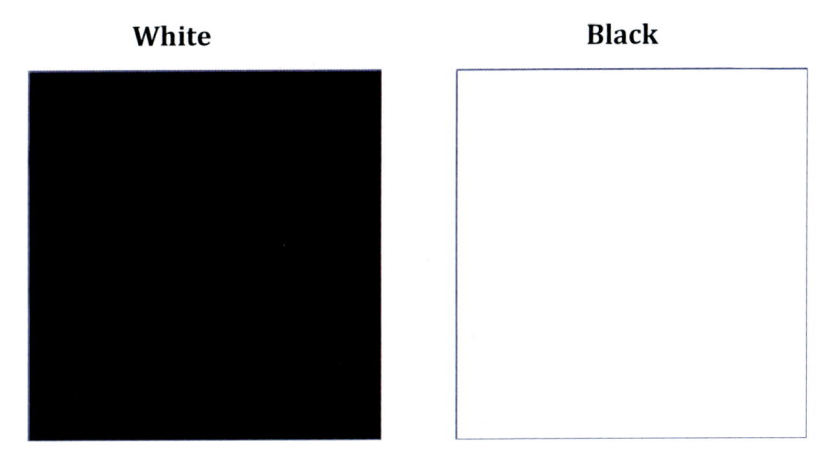

White

Black

Figure 47 shows two advancing and two receding colors. Red and yellow come from the fire and sun and extend both warmth and advancing effect. In contrast, blue and green provide cooling effects. Green comes from nature and blue from the sea and sky. Human eye sees red and yellow before it sees blue and green for that reason.

Figure 47: Advancing and Receding Colors

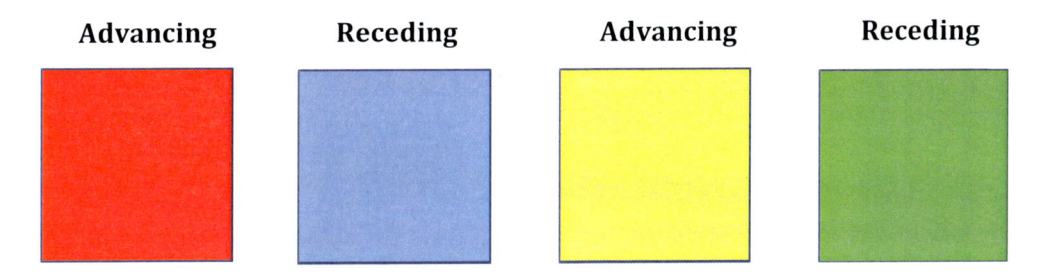

Advancing **Receding** **Advancing** **Receding**

Adding black to the hue creates a shade and addition of white creates a tint (Figure 48). Due to the inherent nature of the neutral, shade creates receding effect and tint creates the advancing effect. Adding black makes it reflect less light than its original status and the reverse is true with the addition of white to the pure hue.

Figure 48: Shade and Tint

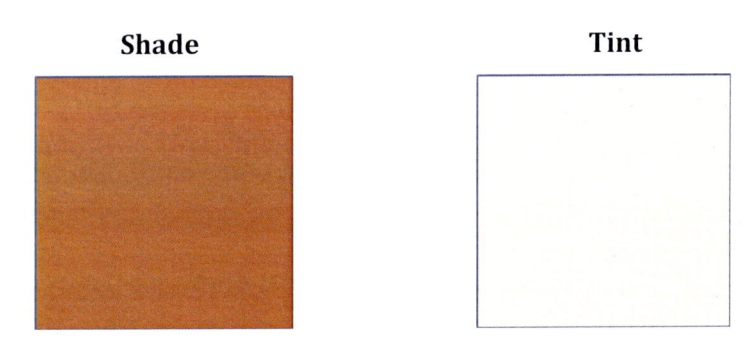

Shade **Tint**

Fluorescent colors reflect more than 100% light (Figure 49). Consequently, it glows in the dark. Therefore, it is used for nighttime running and biking. Generally, it is placed on the moving body parts such as knees and elbows, and on feet through shoes. This way an auto driver can see a moving person even in the dark. Long (2011) reported that fluorescence process absorbs ultraviolet radiation and then reflects the color with longer wavelength with illumination. Besides using these colors in shows, running apparel, bike riders gear, they are also used in the Air Marshaller's jacket and ships of marines also. Air Marshallers lead airplanes in the dark and ships sail in the dark and fluorescent colors are helpful. Historically, they have been used on the ceilings of the bathrooms at homes for children in pace of night lights as well as on the roads for driving safety purposes.

Figure 49: Fluorescent Colors (Source: Google, pintrest.com; 5/17/2021)

Generally, it is well understood that the vertical lines create slenderizing effect and represent dignity and sophistication. In contrast, the horizontal lines create widening effect and are calm and gentle. However, space and thickness of line add another dimension and change the perception of the same direction Figure 50). For example, chalk stripes create less slandering effect than the pi stripes. Awn stripes give more widening effect than the Bengal, candy, and pencil stripes. So is true for checks when both horizontal and vertical lines are combined. They create different perception based on thickness and spacing. Figure 50 pictures labelled tartan, plaid, Madras, and Windowpane create more widening effect than the houndstooth. Whereas houndstooth creates more enlarging effect than the 'nailshead' and tattersall. Additionally, the impact of gingham and shepherd's checks are not identical with each other. Shepherd's check comes across as more slenderizing than the gingham. If we look at the floral print, paisleys, and the sharkskin, the former two create more widening effect than the third one.

The preceding information confirms that line, thickness, and space do impact the optical illusion exclusively. However, they have varying effects inclusively also. Attention to detail can simplify the interpretation of this complex phenomenon. One should use this understanding creatively in both design and merchandising of apparel fashion. However, avoid overgeneralizing for precision and efficacy of interpretation. The impact of intensity and value has already been discussed in this chapter.

Metamerism is a special phenomenon which suggests that the same color does not look the same under different lights such as daylight, fluorescent light, and incandescent light. Several light boxes are available to measure so. The wavelength of the same color varies with different types of lights. Figure 51 reflects those variations because the same fabric was shot under the daylight, fluorescent, incandescent lights. Figure on the left (L) was taken under the daylight setting of the lightbox. The middle figure (M) was shot under the fluorescent light. The right figure ® was taken under the incandescent light. This effect prevails in consumer purchases when they experience color difference in store purchases made in store lights and viewed under home lights. The Fluorescent light created the blue undertones, and the incandescent light showed the yellow underlines.

Color, Theory, Evaluation, Measurement and Use | 177

Figure 50: Lines and Prints. Source: https://ivyandpearlboutique.com/wp-content/uploads/2018/08/fabric-and-textile-pattern-bible-illustrated-examples-of-fabric-patterns.jpg, 3/22/2021.

Chalk stripes	Pinstripes	Houndstooth	Harringbone	Plaid
Paisley	Barleycorn	Floral	Windowpane	Sharkskin
Glen check	Nailshead	Gingham	Polka dot	Twill
Tartan	Shepherd's check	Graph Check	Tattersall	Madras
Birdseye	Awning Stripe	Bengal Stripe	Candy Stripes	Pencil Stripe

Figure 51: Same red looks different under three different light sources

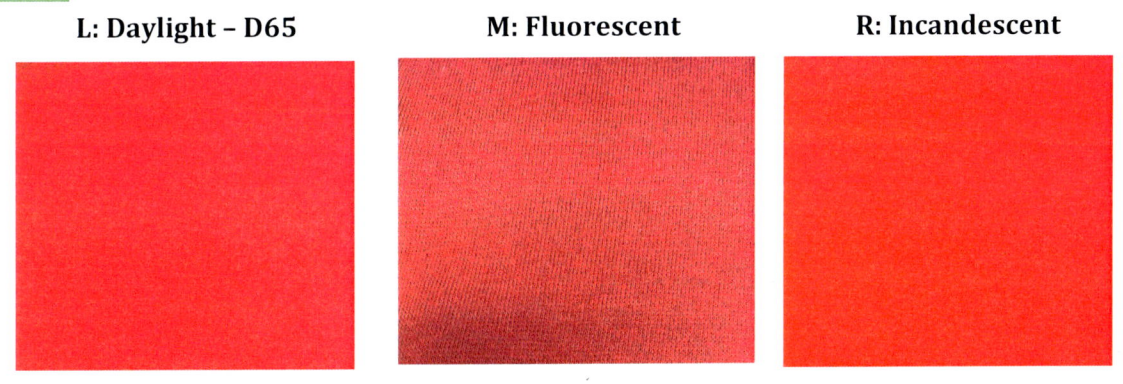

L: Daylight – D65 **M: Fluorescent** **R: Incandescent**

Chapter 8

Dyeing and the Chemical Structure of the Fabrics

Dyeing is impacted using certain types of dye solutions based on the fiber content of the fabric. All yarns and fabrics were put in the same dye bath for the same duration. Results of the experiment revealed that disperse dyes worked the best for Acetate followed by the basic dyes (Figure 52). Acid and reactive dyes were ineffective. So was true for the Acrylic yarns Figure 53). It was interesting that disperse dyes worked the best for cotton also (Figure 54). Disperse and acid dyes worked the best for Nylon (Figure 55). For polyester, disperse dyes was the only one that showed some promise (Figure 56). Acid dye worked the best for the woolen specimen. The preceding discussion illustrates that all dyes do not work with the same level of effectiveness for all fiber contents.

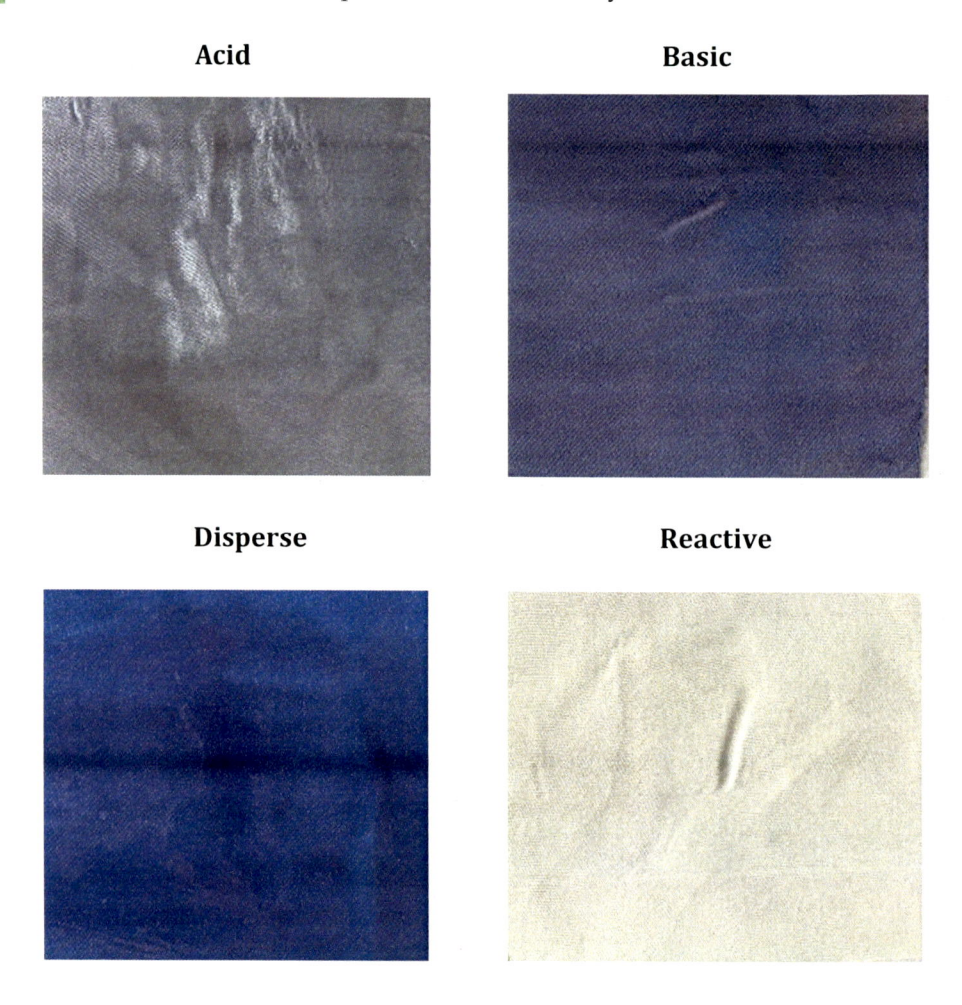

Figure 52: Acetate in Acid, Basic, Disperse and Reactive Dyes

Color, Theory, Evaluation, Measurement and Use

Figure 53: Acrylic in Acid, Basic, Disperse and Reactive Dyes

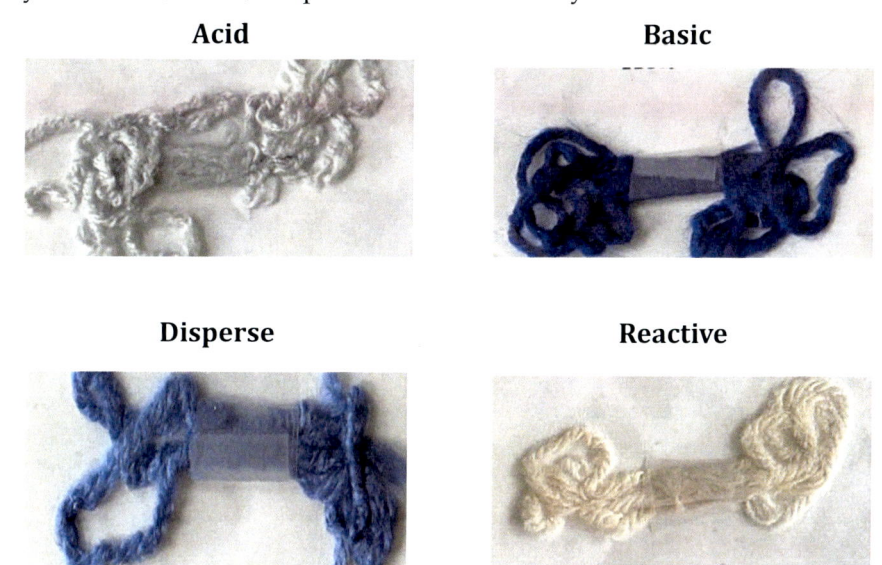

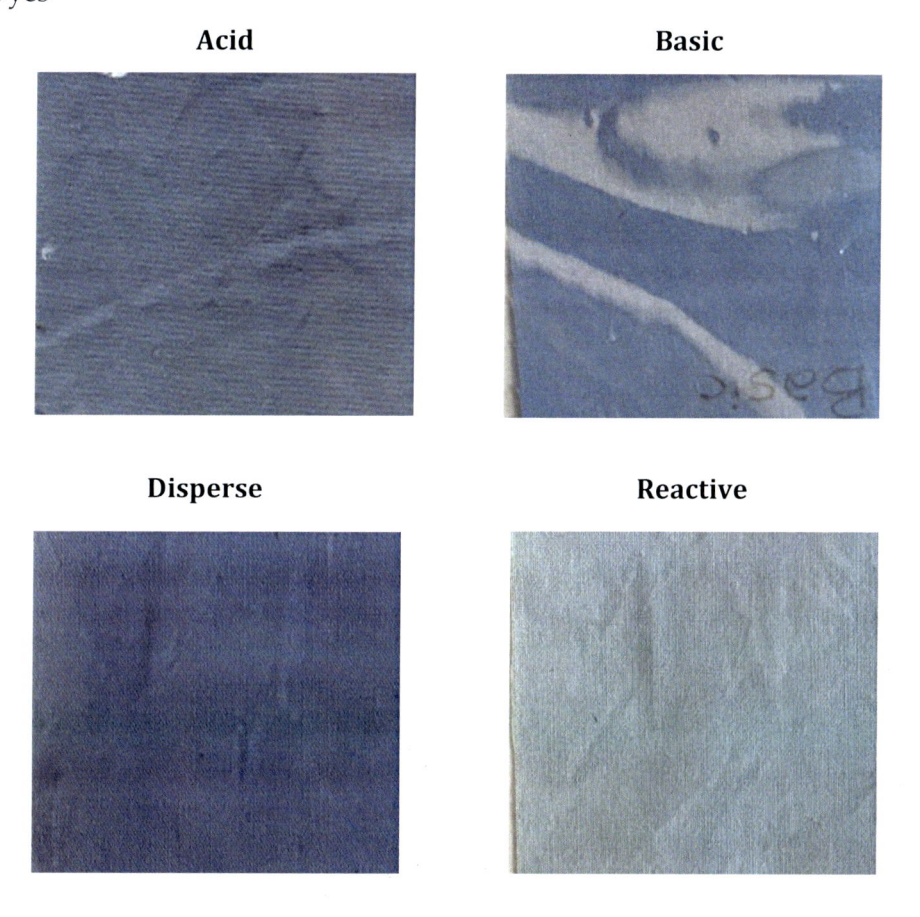

Acid

Basic

Disperse

Reactive

Figure 54: Cotton in Acid, Basic, Disperse and Reactive Dyes in Acid, Basic, Disperse and Reactive Dyes

Acid

Basic

Disperse

Reactive

Figure 55: Nylon in Acid, Basic, Disperse and Reactive Dyes

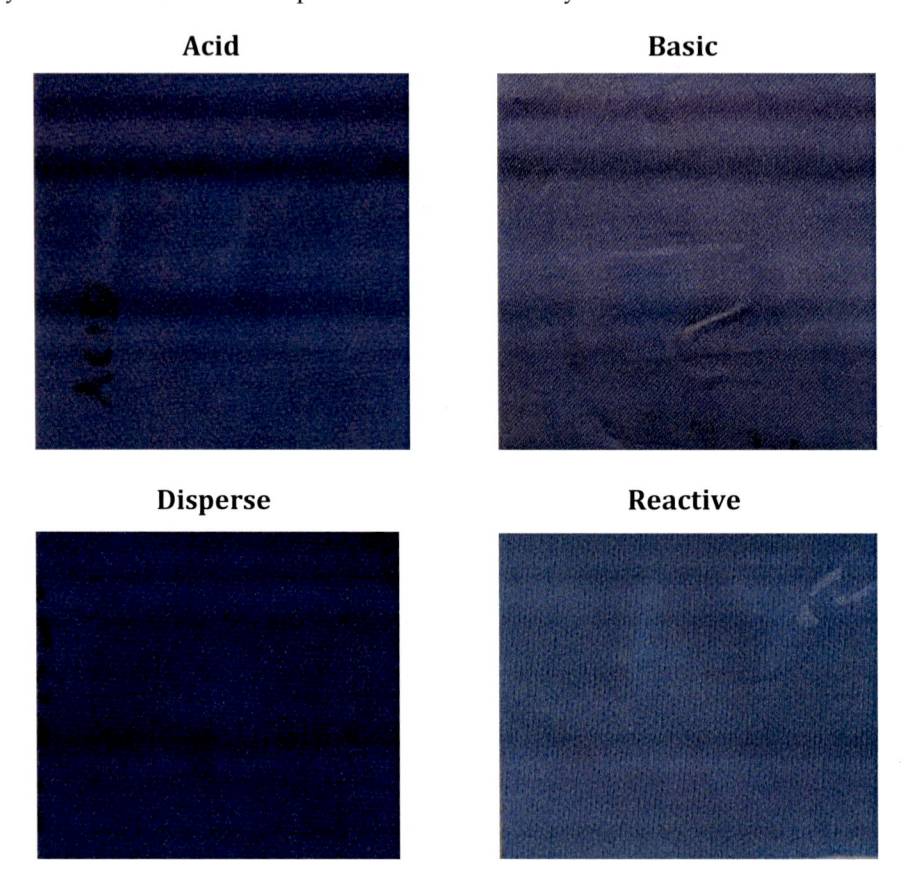

Acid

Basic

Disperse

Reactive

Figure 56: Polyester in Acid, Basic, Disperse and Reactive Dyes

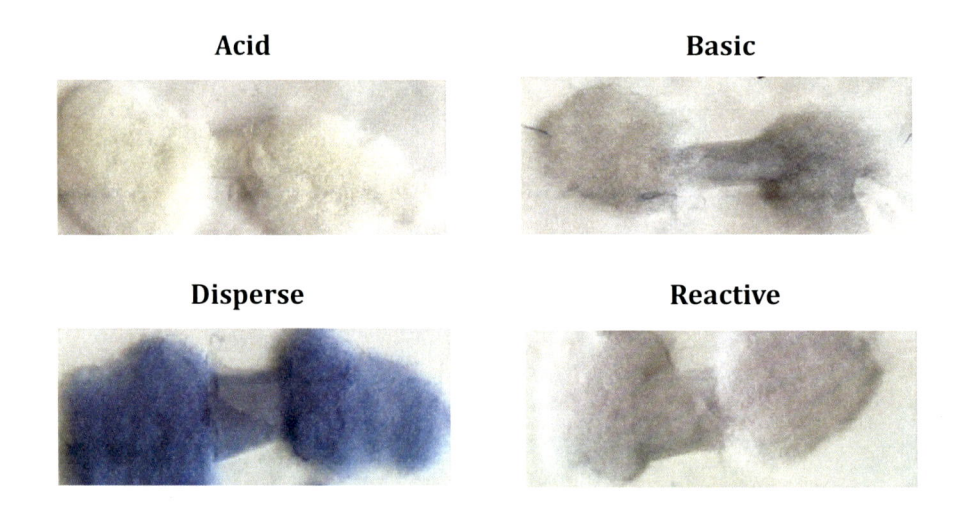

Acid

Basic

Disperse

Reactive

Figure 57: Wool in Acid, Basic, Disperse and Reactive Dyes

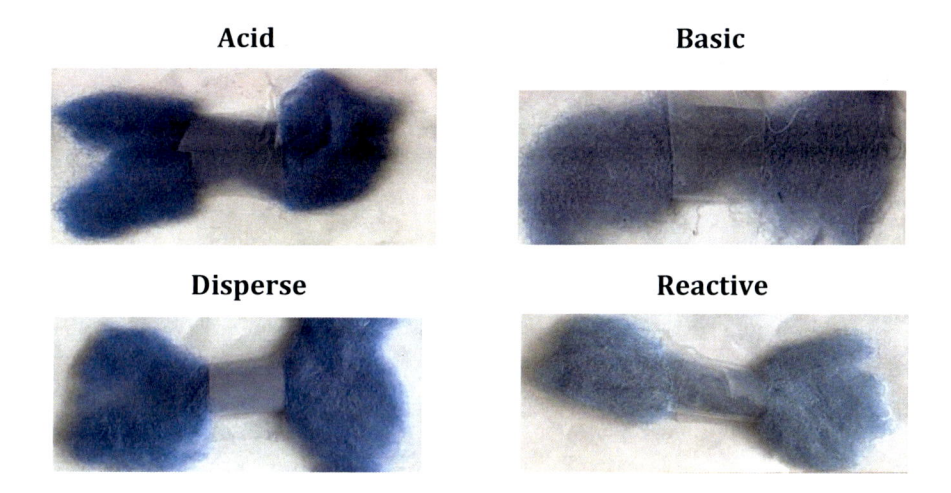

Acid

Basic

Disperse

Reactive

Summary and Conclusions

Color continues to be an integral part of the apparel product development process. It provides foundation as inspiration is developed and evaluated scientifically, used creatively and aesthetically in fashion designing and merchandising, and enchants consumers in the decision-making process. It is incorporated by dyeing, printing, embroidery, applique, tackle twill, and other such means. The first two have the lion's share. Use of colors is all pervasive in everyday life. Colors are developed scientifically, integrated in apparel creatively, used in merchandising visually, and evoke emotions in consumers psychologically. They add interest in life and are symbolic in several different areas in a multitude way. It is a complex concept but prevails in simplistic ways of everyday existence.

REFERENCES

Adnan, M. M. (2018). Color Measurement and Colorfastness of Different Weaves, and Dimensional Forms, unpublished master's thesis, Central Michigan University.

Chowdhary, U. (2009). *Textile analysis, quality control and innovative uses*. Deer Park, NY: LINUS.

COLARIS PIGMENT: Inkjet printing for all fibers. (2018, March 12). Retrieved on 3/19/2021.

Zimmer, Austria, 1-8. Kufstein, Austria: Zimmer Machinebau GmbH. www.zimmer.austria.com

Colour Index™ explained. Retrieved on 3/19/2021. https://colour-index.com/ci-explained

Davis, M. L. (1996). *Visual design in dress*. Upper Saddle River, NJ: Prentice Hall.

Differences between dyes and pigments in flooring. (2021, March 19). *Duraamen*. https://www.duraamen.com/blog/differences-between-dyes-and-pigments/

Islam, MdRashedul (2020). Color assessment of three knitted structures in three-dimensional body form under different lights and three different lengths of exposure. Unpublished master's thesis. Central Michigan University.

Islam, M. R., & Chowdhary, U. (2019). Relative color pickup of three different knits and predictive dyeing recipe formulation. *International Journal of Polymer and Textile Engineering (SSRG - IJPTE),* 6(3), 1-16.

Long, J. T. (2001). *Color.* New York, NY: Fairchild.

Mawla, Golam (2021, January 10). Different types of pf dyes with chemical structure. Retrieved on 3/19/2021. https://textilelearner.net/different-types-of-dyes-with-chemical-structure/

Mokrzycki, W., and Tatol, M. (2011). Color difference delta E-a survey. *Machine Graphics and Vision, 20,* 383-411.

Pantone® Colour Matching System (2021). Retrieved on 3/19/2021 https://www.designface.co.uk/pantone-articles/pantone-history/

Peltier, K. (2019). Why optical brightening chemicals are not needed in laundry detergents. Retrieved on 3.19.2021 https://www.thespruce.com/optical-brighteners-chemicals-not-needed-1707025

Phillips, K. (2015). Understanding tristimulus values and the CIE color system. https://blog.hunterlab.com/blog/color-measurement/understanding-tristimulus-values-taking-guesswork-color-measurement-instrumentation/

Precise color communication: Color control from perception to instrumentation (2007-2013). Japan: Konica Minolta.

The electromagnetic spectrum (2013). Retrieved on 3/16/2021. https://imagine.gsfc.nasa.gov/science/toolbox/emspectrum1.html

The fundamentals: Dyes and pigments. Retrieved on 3/19/2021. https://www.chemworldintl.com/fundamentals-dyes-pigments.html

What Is the Pantone Color of the Year and Why Is It Important? (2021, March 22). https://visme.co/blog/pantone-color-of-the-year/

Color, Theory, Evaluation, Measurement and Use

PRACTICE ACTIVITIES

1. Why should one study color? What is its role in the textile industry?

2. What do you understand by the visible spectrum of light?

3. What is the significance of understanding hue, value, and intensity? How are they used in Munsell's Hue Cycle?

4. What is the difference between the Prang's color wheel, and Munsell's Hue Cycle?

5. What are the additive and subtractive theories? Which theory is used for creating the Pantone's Color Matching System?

6. What does the L*a*b* color space chromaticity diagram in figure 36 explain? Describe with an example.

7. What does figure 37 represent? Describe.

8. What is the role of the **Farnsworth Munsell's 100 Hue Test?** Who uses it in the textile and apparel industry and why? How are the numbers of the instrument interpreted?

9. What do you understand by the coloring process? What should one consider regarding the compatibility between the colorant and the fiber content?

10. What type of colorants are used in the textile industry?

11. What is metamerism? How can you use it for personal and professional situations?

12. What is the role of the color matching systems? How many systems do you know? What else would you like to know?

13. What is the role of color in the apparel product development process? Provide specific examples to make your point.

14. What is optical illusion? How does it impact human perception?

15. Which element of design impacts color effect? Provide examples.

16. Can color add to the comfort dimension for the users. Is, why? If not, why not?

17. John compared a test fabric for colorfastness to light. The ΔE for the fabric turned out to be 3.2. Should he pass this fabric for a high-quality garment?

18. If the ΔE of a swimwear for colorfastness to sunlight was 1.5. Will you pass/fail the fabric for its end-use. Justify your response.

184 Chapter 8

COMFORT AND TEXTILES

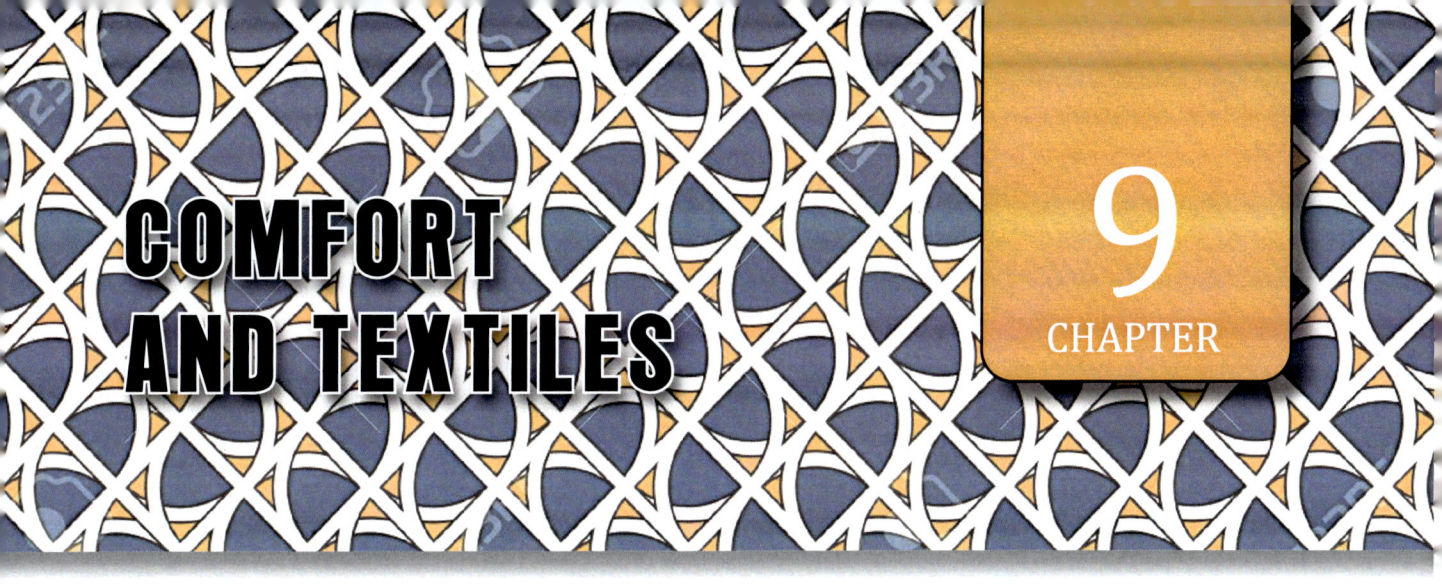

9 CHAPTER

Comfort is an important consideration in selection and use of textiles. Comfort makes people feel good about themselves. Comfort is of two types: Body comfort and clothing comfort. **Body comfort** is the result of interaction between the environmental conditions and four principles of heat exchange. Hot temperatures call for conduction and cold weathers for insulation. Under hot temperatures, the overheated body wants to cool down for satisfaction. In contrast, under cold conditions, the body wants to generate more heat by exercise and/or the layered clothing. Clothing choices can impact the body's comfort both positively and negatively. **Clothing comfort** is a cohesive outcome from integration between and among clothing, cultural, environmental, physical, social, and thermal attributes.

Branson and Sweeney (1991) recognized comfort as a function of several textile attributes. *Merriam's Webster's Collegiate Dictionary* (2003, p. 248) defines comfort as "a feeling of relief or encouragement, contented well-being, and a satisfying or enjoyable experience." Chowdhary (2009) reported it as the pain-free state of the body and mind. One can measure comfort both subjectively and objectively. Same situation can yield varying results with different people.

Subjectively, people could be asked how they feel under the same environmental conditions. Objectively, a thermal camera can be used to observe changing effects of the environment and the body. The thermal images use the rainbow colors of the visible lights to check the micro-environment or interface between the body and the environment. Red represents the hottest part and violet the coldest parts. The whole scale ranges from white to black. White and pink precede red and black follows the violet color. Using thermography enhances objectivity of measurement. However, interpretation and subjectivity inherent in comfort cannot be denied. Similar conditions could be experienced at different levels of comfort depending on the age, environment, gender, health conditions, physiological factors, psychological mindset, sociological expectations and much more.

Price and Cohen (1982) reported that clo value of 1 under standard conditions offers adequate body comfort for the human body. Cohen and Johnson (2010, p. 223) defined clo "as the insulation required to keep the person at rest comfortable in a normal indoor environment (i.e., about 70^0F or 20^0C, with little air movement)". Clo is a unit of thermal resistance that is like the R value used in the selection or evaluation of insulation in the housing materials. Ogulata (2007) identified thermal comfort as a function of climate, clothing, and physical activity. Clothing reduces the heat losses that occur from skin through clothing. With increase in metabolism, heat loss through radiation and convection decreases, but through evaporation increases. Ogulata (2007, p. 68) provided clo values for both men's and women's garments to enhance understanding of this concept (Table 25).

The clo values provided in the table can be used to create a garment that has a collective clo value close to 1. One should recognize that clo value on 1 is recommended for the standard conditions. If the weather is hot, clo value of less than one could be sufficient. If the weather is cold, one will need more than one clo value to feel comfortable. One may wear cool socks, briefs, t-shirt, undershirt, cool trousers (shorts, .15), and shoes. The clo value will range between .47-.57 and a man may feel comfortable. In contrast, in cold weather, he may wear warm socks, briefs, undershirt, long sleeved shirt, warm trousers, warm Jacket, and shoes. All these items will add up to 1.32.

Figure 25: Clo-Values for selected men's and women's garments.

Men's Garments	Clo-Value	Women's Garments	Clo-Value
Cool Socks	.03	Bras and Panties	.05
Warm Socks	.04	Pantyhose	.01
Briefs	.05	Girdle	.04
T-Shirt	.09	Half-Slip	.13
Undershirt	.06	Full Slip	.19
Woven Shirt (Short Sleeved)	.19	Cool Dress	.17
Woven Long Sleeved Shirt	.29	Warm Dress	.63
Cool Short Sleeves Knit Shirt	.22	Warm Long Sleeves Blouse	.29
Warm Short Sleeves Knit Shirt	.25	Warm Skirt	.22
Cool Long Sleeves Knit Shirt	.14	Cool Long Sleeves Blouse	.20
Warm Long Sleeves Sweater	.37	Cool Slacks	.26
Warm Jacket	.49	Warm Slacks	.44
Cool Trousers	.26	Cool Sleeveless Sweater	.17
Warm Trousers	.32	Warm Long Sleeve Sweater	.37
Shoes	.04	Cool Short Sleeve Sweater	.17

Comfort and Textiles

Role of Textiles

Textile plays a critical role in making the human body feel comfortable. Use of absorbent textile in summer and insulated materials in winter are just two examples from everyday life. Air permeability, elongation, drape, drape, hand, moisture management, pilling resistance, recovery, strength, stretch, and wicking ability influence human comfort. Therefore, it is necessary to understand their role in diverse settings to understand the importance of choosing the right fabrics for diverse contexts. Table 26 describes it for ten different sports.

Table 26: Sportswear and function of textiles.

Sport	Garment	Textile Features
Basketball	Accessories	Sweat bands of absorbent and stretch fabrics
	Shirt	Mesh material with breathability and ventilation
	Shoes	Soft and lightweight materials
	Shorts	Matching with shirt material, soft and absorbent for comfort, and lined for cover.
	Socks	Cotton and blends with nylon, acrylic and Spandex in knitted construction.
Bicycle Wear	Accessories	Stretchy material from fleece or leather for cold weather and of knitted materials for the warm weather.
	Gloves	Fingerless padded gloves should be used to prevent sores from long-distance biking. If hands sweat a lot, provide good ventilation or use absorbent materials with good wicking.
	Helmet	Use a hard shell with shock absorbent liner and adjustable chin straps. Knitted soft and absorbent materials.
	Jersey	Soft and absorbent material for comfort.
	Shorts	

Sport	Garment	Textile Features
Cricket	Gloves	Abrasion resistance and stretch
	Helmets	Cushioning with strong materials for preventing fractures
	Padding	Absorbent materials Cotton gabardine
	Pants	Cotton or stretch
	Shirt	Leather with padding
	Wicket Keepers Pads	
Figure Skating	Accessories	Padded skating gloves with rhinestones
	Boots	Tongue is lined with sponge rubber. Pad of silicone gel for tension relief Lipetz & Kruse, 2000)
	Bodysuits	Stretch nylons and bodysuits for warmth and flexibility.
	Shirts & Trousers for men	For men, soft and flexible materials
Football	Accessories	Nylon/Lycra five pocket girdle for stretch and strength
	Gloves Helmets	Lycra/Spandex Shell plastic is fitted with sponge pads and cushioning materials.
	Pants and Shirt	Football pants and shirt is made from polyester and spandex. Logos are made of polyurethane because it bonds well. Polyester is used for strength and Lycra for stretch. (https://tvfinc.com/Polyester-Spandex-Football-Pant.item)

Comfort and Textiles

Sport	Garment	Textile Features
	Shoes	Nike shoes have synthetic upper for durability, mesh tongue for ventilation, non-stretch mid-foot spat strap for a superior fit, and molded rubber cup sole for better traction in trenches.
		Use plastic with padding and covers shoulder and chest areas.
	Socks	Padding at heels, toes, and ankle.
	Shoulder pads	Shoulder pads are used for protection.
Runners and Joggers	Jackets	Nylon jackets good for wet weather
	Shoes	Lightweight materials
	Shorts	Soft and absorbent textiles
	Swift Suit	Absorbent and comfortable
		Olympic suit with dark colors to absorb heat and keep muscles warm.
	T-Shirts	100% Cotton
	Thermal Clothing	Special thermal clothing from polypropylene that keeps the body dry and irritation free for the elderly.
	Visibility Enhancers	Use of fluorescent materials as trims for nighttime visibility. The visibility enhancers allow to be seen from 500 feet.

Sport	Garment	Textile Features
Soccer	Cleats	Synthetic fibers, rubber, or plastic studs and sole for comfort and function. Socks are added to enhance comfort
		https://www.shoesforsoccer.com/what-are-soccer-shoes-made-of/
	Shin Guards	Made from fiber glass, foam, and rubber. Occasionally from plastic and metal https://en.wikipedia.org/wiki/Shin_guard
	Shorts and Shirts	Made of polyester for strength, Swoosh shorts from 100% nylon and 100% cotton for tees. Poly-cotton blends for jersey; nylon with drawstring or elastic waist of boxer shorts with undershorts.
Sports Bra	Textiles	Soft cotton or spandex blend and knit fabrics, high modulus thick and thermally insulative fabrics were disliked. Lawson and Lorentzen, 1990.
		Today, nylon/polyester with spandex for light weight. Cotton is believed to be heavy weight.
Swimwear	Fiber content	Nylon/Spandex blend is used the most. Nylon is good for smoothness and quick drying ability. Spandex has good stretch and recovery. In Davies (1996), polyester/Lycra blend's popularity was highlighted.
		For care and maintenance, rinse them in cold water. Dry flat away from sunlight. Read labels for proper care. Do not leave them rolled in a towel for long times.
Tennis wear	Shirt	Mercerized cotton, poly/cotton blend, and jersey knit for the top or shirt.
	Shoes	Polyester, rubber, and EVA foam.
	Short/Skirt	Microfiber and poly cotton blend for shorts and polyester for skirt (Dolbow, 1995).
	Sweat bands, & Wrist Bands	Mostly made of terry cloth, polyester, and nylon.

Role of Clothing and Accessories

Appropriate clothing can enhance the body comfort in everyday life as well as the workplace. Some examples could be aesthetics, design, fashionability, functionality, fit, style and texture. To optimize the

Comfort and Textiles 191

body comfort, attention should be paid to the integration of both textile and clothing system details. For example, runners and joggers should select absorbent, soft, and stretchy fabrics for comfort and fluorescent trims for the nighttime visibility. For clothing design, freedom of movement, good fit and ventilation in design, adequate stretch, and high nighttime visibility will be good features.

Table 27: Sportswear and function of clothing.

Sport	Garment	Garment Features
Basketball	Accessories	Circular design. One size fit all. Logos help with boosting of self-esteem. Little tightness for compression therapy
	Shirt	Well-fitted and light weigh, good ventilation.
	Shoes	Foot should land on the forefoot to prevent injuries. Cushioning necessary for agility and allowing the foot to adjust constantly with the movement necessary to perform this sport.
	Shorts	Drawstring waist for frequent adjustment in this hyperactive sport.
	Socks	Sweat absorption, comfort from cushioning to avoid adverse effects from abrasion and friction.
Bicycle Wear	Arm warmers, wrist, and headbands	Arm warmers are good for the colder climate, and wrist and headbands for the warmer weather. Use fluorescent trims for nighttime visibility.
	Gloves	Fingerless padded gloves should be used to prevent sores from long-distance biking. If hands sweat a lot,
		Provide good ventilation or use absorbent materials with good wicking.
		Use a hard shell with shock absorbent liner and adjustable chin straps.
	Helmet	Closefitting to prevent flapping, well fitted to cover the long back to cover shorts, and 7-10 inches below the waist.
	Jersey	Well-fitted with soft liner for comfort, fewer seams, and longer back and shorter front to add comfort in the bent and seated postures.
	Shorts	

Sport	Garment	Garment Features
Cricket	Gloves	Adequate padding for blister-free grip during batting.
	Padding	**In gloves for hands, helmet for head, and for legs. Padding helps with protection.**
	Shin Guards	To protect delicate parts.
	Wicket Keepers Pads	To protect leg injuries.
Figure Skating	Boots	Have room for toes to wiggle. Lacing should be 1.5-2". Men's shoes should be 9" from the floor. Women's shoes should be 8' from the floor. Have separate shoes and skates for high efficiency. Mean wear black shoes and women wear white or fawn.
	Dress	Women wear one piece suit over a body tights. Men wear pants and shirts
	Shirts	Men's shirt should have embellishment if tight sleeves or fullness so that they puff up when on the move for aesthetic grace.
	Trousers	Trouser should be well - fitted with some stretch built-in to allow for various jumps.
Football	Accessories	Black paint under the eyes of the football players is used to prevent glare while playing.
		Football towels are used by the quarterback to keep the hands dry.
	Gloves	Palm of the gloves are treated with chemicals to enhance tackiness. Receiver's gloves have enhanced palm grip, light padding on the back hand, and lightweight. Lineman's glove should have back and palm padding, heavier and durable materials, and rigid frames.
	Helmets	Has four parts for protection. Shell protects the face, jaws, skull, and temples. Foam padding for impact absorption, facemask to protect face, and chinstraps to keep it in place.
	Pants	Sewn with seven pads in the areas of hit.

Sport	Garment	Garment Features
Football (continue)	Shirt	Polyester and polyurethane give both protection and flexibility.
	Shoes	Cleats
	Socks	Antimicrobial finish, stretch, reinforced heels and toes, compression for arch, and padding on ankle for protection. Designed for shock absorption and protection by padding.
	Shoulder pads	Padding to protect from injuries.
Runners and Joggers (Chowdhary, 2009)	Jackets	Layering and zipper in polyester with good moisture management.
	Shoes	Maximum shock absorption! Touch of the fluorescent trims for running and jogging in the dark.
	Shorts	Drawstring or elasticized waist
	Swift Suit	Fabric coating and surface roughness impacted the aerodynamics of the athlete's apparel and thereby the performance (Oggiaro et al., 2013).
	T-Shirts	Well-fitted to prevent drag and entanglement from the loose clothing and chafing and irritation from the tight clothing. Using Raglan sleeves can also enhance the body comfort.
	Thermal Clothing	Lightweight with an extra layer for warmth. Water repellency further improves it in the wet weather.
	Visibility Enhancers	Fluorescent trims at the moving parts of the body (ankles, elbows, and knees) for the nighttime visibility.

Sport	Garment	Garment Features
Soccer	Ankle braces	For ankle protection
	Cleats	For anti-slip measure
	Gloves	Goal keepers wear.
	Shin Guards	All players wear for safety.
	Shirt	Well-fitted with comfort and support, side vents for kinesthetics and performance.
	Shorts	Wearing two pairs of shorts with 3.5 to 4.5" inseam.
	Socks	Knee length in absorbent material to cover the shin guards.
Sports Bra	Details	No fasteners, and Y shaped back strap to prevent slippage during exercising. Design features should include maximum coverage, wide shoulder straps, bands, and panels than the regular bra, minimum fasteners, ventilating features, flat seams, back support, easy care, and maintenance, and keeping close to the body.
Swimwear	Fiber content	Sold by bra/dress size for women and waist measurement for men.
		Line the light colored and white swimsuits to impart additional cover.
Tennis wear	Shirt	100% cotton or blends with short sleeves. Never wear sleeveless t-shirts.
	Shoes	Should have classic looks, color and looks, comfort, cushioning and stability, easy lacing, good fit, improved ventilation, light weight, shock absorption, proper support, toe boxes and toe drag protection.
	Short	Inseam length should be 9" or less, pocket depth should be enough to hold tennis balls without falling out. Add mobility through vents and stretch, use mesh material with lining. Adidas was chosen as the best brand for men and Nike for women. (https://www.thetennistribe.com/best-tennis-shorts/)
	Sweat bands	Stretch cotton terry cloth is used for both headbands and wrist bands.

Ergonomics: Body and Clothing Comfort

Relationship between worker and his environment is called **ergonomics** (Chowdhary, 2009). Armstrong (1986) asserted that ergonomics enhances efficiency, health, quality, and safety of the worker in his/her workplace. He emphasized that several factors could result in body discomfort for the worker at the workplace. Some examples include work activities with vibrations, unfamiliar tasks, repetitiveness, posture, mechanical stress, temperatures, and forcefulness. The resulting condition could be carpal Tunnel Syndrome (CTS) or "Tenosynovitis". Some of the remedial tools were changing the angle of the tools used in the industry to match the worker's body for reducing the disorder possibilities. It was suggested to allow 25^0C temperature to prevent the loss of dexterity. It was recommended to wear gloves for enhancing the dexterity of the fingers. Using additional garments by the worker was recommended to maintain body temperature for enhanced efficiency of the worker.

Chowdhary (2017) reported that computer stands, CTS splints, collapsible crutches, ergonomic footrests, ergonomic keyboards, gel mats, large screens, revolving chair, and wrist support, as ergonomic tools for occupational safety in the office settings.

Tilted tables, within 14-16 inches and at the elbow level enhances people's comfort level.

Kelly et al. (1992) examined ergonomic related problems, identified low-cost interventions, explored high technology solutions, and developed a self-study ergonomics course for the supervisors in apparel manufacturing. Musculo-skeletal discomfort, posture issues, workstation, and repetitive manipulations were some of the key issues that were identified. They found that a change of 8.3 degrees angle reduced the musculoskeletal discomfort by 56%. Ergonomic chairs reduced the discomfort by 90%. Several large plants began to institute automatic operations, ergonomic workstations, and modular manufacturing.

Braunstein (1990) presented anatomy of various bones, ligaments, nerves, and tendons that cause CTS. Kunkel (1990, p.1) quoted, "CTS refers to an inflammation of any of the nine ligaments that extends from the wrist into the palm area of the hand. The swollen tendons cause the median nerve to press against transverse carpal ligament." Dr Saroj Shah In her lecture for "Clothing for Special Needs" class in 1990 reported that CTS is caused by the awkward posture, high rates of repetition, infection, lack of adequate rest, occupational trauma, tumor, and excessive force." Its six symptoms provided by the Carpal Tunnel Syndrome (1990) were numbness and tingling; itching; prickling in the wrist or the first three fingers and the thumb; clumsiness, pain, and weakness; swelling; and heaviness. Chowdhary, (2009, p. 140) provided anatomy of the hand to understand the cause of the Carpal Tunnel Syndrome better than possible with simple conceptualization (Figure 58).

Compression therapy helps with reduction of pain from the Carpal Tunnel Syndrome. The compression can be created by tight knits, lacing, and use of Velcro. Figure 59 shows an example of a splint with lacing and figure 60 shows one with use of the Velcro (Chowdhary, 2009, p. 141). Today, several pharmacies, online sites and discount stores carry these splints in the market that have easy access for the consumer.

Chapter 9

Figure 58: Anatomy of the Hand.

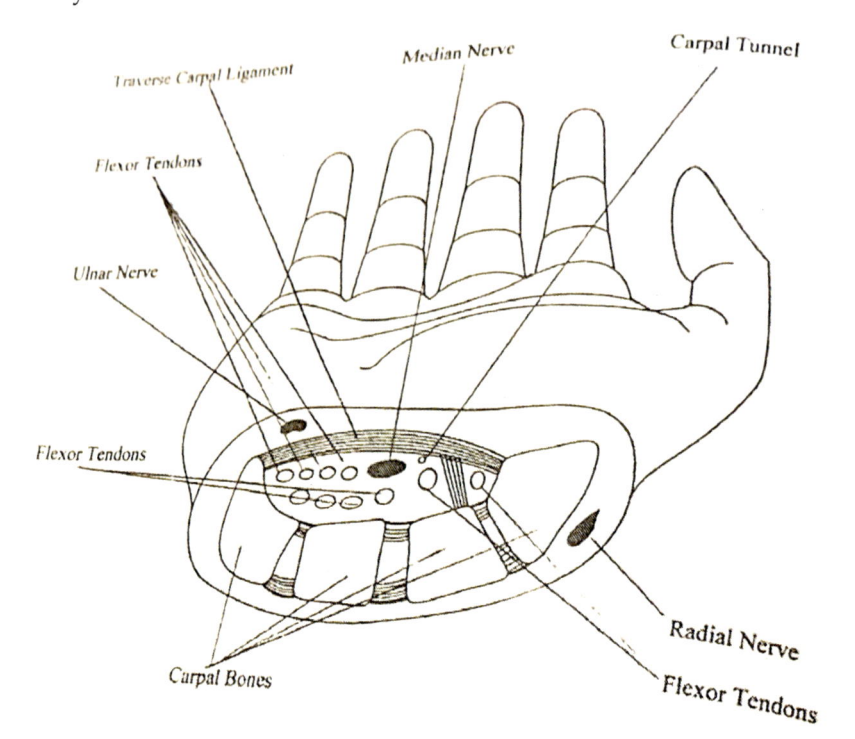

Figure 59: Splint with Lacing

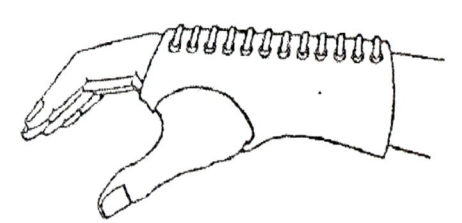

Figure 60: Splint with Velcro

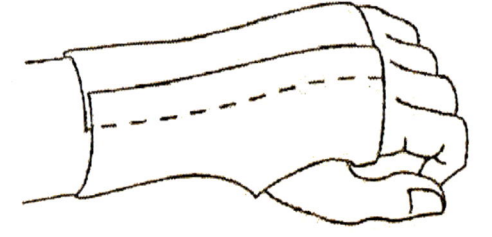

CTS is only one of the issues that is directly related to body comfort with or without the use of textiles. The other area that could be included in the comfort section is special needs clothing. Table 28 lists those categories with the relevance of textiles. The categories listed as examples are arthritis, children, incontinence, Mastectomy, preschoolers, older people, visual impairment, and wheelchair users.

Table 28: Role of textiles in special needs clothing.

#	Category	Design Need	Textile Choice
1	Arthritis	Limited motion	Velcro/zipper with pull, stretch fabrics
2	Children	Comfort and durability	Absorbent, durable, flexible, flame resistant for sleepwear, soft without hairiness
3	Incontinence	Improved absorbance, water repellence, and odor control	Inner liner should be from absorbent woven/nonwoven materials to keep the wearer dry. The fiber should have excellent moisture management. Outer liner should be made from a water repellent material to keep the outer layer dry. Fluorocarbon treatment for water repellency should be tested. Antimicrobial finish for odor control. Hydropur®, Cyclofresh®, and Cyclofresh® plus develop antimicrobial effect and impart fragrance to counter the bad odor. They have been tested for sweat and should be tested for incontinence also.

#	Category	Design Need	Textile Choice
4	Mastectomy	Lymph edema, lost breast, prosthesis cover Figure 61: With Gauntlet Figure 62: Without gauntlet Figure 63: Bosom Buddy Design I	Lymphedema sleeve helps with reduction of swelling via compression therapy. It is made from the tightly knitted material. It can be made with or without the gauntlet. Figure 61 shows the one with gauntlet and figure 62, shows it without the gauntlet. Bosom buddies are made from absorbent materials. They can be added at the seam of the yoke if the design of the dress has one. Otherwise, it can be attached with a Velcro. Figure 63 shows two designs of the bosom buddies that were initially introduced by Norma Deyo Pitts of the Ohio State University in an extension project. Prosthesis cover is made from knitted material for protecting the prosthesis that is filled with silicone gel. Figure 64: Bosom Buddy Design II
5	Preschoolers	Comfort, growth, safety, self-help	Absorbent fabrics, poly/cotton blends, soft knits, soft textures, and stretch fabrics.
6	Older People	Feeling cold, dry, and wrinkled skin	Use textile for warmth by layering, use soft and absorbent fabrics, avoid plain fabrics to avoid accentuating wrinkles, avoid contrasting colors.
7	Visual Impairment	Identification	Use different textures and colors for easy identification.
8	Wheelchair Users	Durability	Use strong, flexible, and breathable fabrics.

Textile and Comfort

Several previous researchers have focused on body, clothing and thermal comforts. Findings from the selected scholars are provided to offer deeper understanding on the subject for the readers of textile and comfort.

Adnan and Moses (2020) found that fabrics with higher value of silk had better thermal resistance than the Lyocell or Lyocell enhanced fabrics. Blends with higher % of Lyocell had superior absorbency, water vapor permeability and wicking ability as compared to silk fabrics. Additionally, Lyocell and its blends had higher "drape, bending length, and crease recovery" than 100silk material. Teyeme, Malengier, Tesfaye, Vasile, and Langenhove (2020) found that the fabric polyamide/elastane (58/42 PA6.6/EL) with good air permeability, thermal conductivity, moisture management properties, and short drying time was optimally suited for the summer cycling clothing. Dalbasi and Kayseri (2019) reported that all finishes enhanced summer use related attributes of the linen fabrics. Due to shrinkage of the fabric, air permeability was decreased.

Cimilli, Nargis, and Candan (2009) that coarse yarns increased the wicking ability. However, using finer fibers increased the drying time of the fibers. For the slacks made from the finer yarns had higher water vapor transmission as well as wicking than the tight fabrics. Haventh (2009) emphasized the need to focus on the areas of the body that sweats the most. Those body parts were identified as back, chest, upper arm and legs. Martines, Gonzales, Ross, and Alcantara (2009) tested two shirts for eight subjects and six phases and measured the fluid loss for the high and low resistance shirts by weighing before and after the treatment. Findings revealed that running in higher temperatures affected the comfort level.

The six factors (2009) listed four environmental factors as air temperature (around the body), radiant temperature (heat generated from the hot object like sub), , air velocity (air movement), and air humidity (water vapors in the air). Of these six factors, four air pressures were reported as the most used factors that influenced the thermal comfort. The other two were clothing (affects heat loss from the body) and work or metabolic heat (used for thermal risk assessment). Besides, the four identified factors, additional factors (age, sex, and weight of individual) also influenced the body comfort.

Gao, Weidong, and Pan (2007) examined the morphological structure and physical properties of the down feathers as they relate to the thermal resistance. The angle of the branching ranged from 30-90 degrees. Chemically, down is a protein fiberwith amino acid and polypeptide changes. Down feathers had a moisture regain of 8.1% as opposed to 9.9% of cotton and 17.1% for wool. Overall, the down fiber was noted to have highest bulkiness and recovery. Findings on thermal conductivity revealed that down possessed lowest thermal conductivity and the highest thermal insulation.

Lee and Obendorf (2007) found porosity to be of critical importance for water vapor transmission. For the typical workwear, nonwovens showed higher permeability than the woven materials. Cao, Branson, Peksoz, Nam and Farr (2006) examined 18 fabrics and reported that 80/20 polyester/spandex blend was rated as the best of all fabrics for a liquid cooling garment because it had a knitted structure, better wicking ability, moisture transfer, and stretch. They further found that the metallic fibers did not have any wicking ability than other woven structures. Cotton Variety May Affect Comfort (2006) reported that adding to Kevlar will enhance comfort because it would improve moisture vapor permeability.

Azoulay (2005) asserted that stretch has changed the comfort and sexiness of jeans. It has also influenced consumer expectations, fit, and style of jeans. Walzur (2004) focused on the use of spandex for added comfort and stretch next to skin for activewear, hosiery, and swimwear. Chen, Fan, and Zhang (2003) found that thermal insulation reduced by 208% during perspiration. Lau, Fen, Siu, and Siu (2002) tested the comfort level of three 100% cotton polo shirts. The results revealed that moisture absorption was lower for the treated versus untreated shirts. However, differences regrading comfort level were not significant. The three negative experiences for the subjects were non-absorbency, clinginess, and dampness.

Thermography and Thermal Comfort

Comfort is a multidimensional aspect. Both clothing and environment can impact thermal comfort. Even though adding or removing layers in clothing influences thermal comfort and so do the textile attributes. An infrared camera can be used to examine the impact of clothing on surface temperature using spectral colors of the rainbow. Physicists divide the electromagnetic spectrum is divided into bands based on the wavelength regions. The six regions include X-Ray, UltraViolet, Visible, Infrared, Microwaves, and Radiowaves.

> "Thermography makes use of the infrared spectral band. At the short wavelength end the boundary lies at the limit of visual perception, in the deep red. At the long wavelength end it merges with the microwave radio wavelengths in the millimeter range. ----------- The infra red band is further subdivided into four smaller bands, the boundaries of which are also arbitrarily chosen. They include the near infrared (0.74- the middle infrared (3-6μm), far Infrared (6-15 μm), and the extreme infrared from 15-100 μm). 3μmAlthough the wavelengths are given in μm (micrometers), other units are still used to measure wavelengths in this special region, e.g. nanometer (nm) and AngstrOm (A). The relationship between the different wavelength measurements is: 10,000 A = 1000 nm = 1μ = μm," (ThermoVision™A20M, 2004, pp 177-178).

Chowdhary and Harder (2008) worked on a project where ThermoVision™ Camera was used to examine the impact of clothing on the body's warmth using spectral colors. The impact of color goes from white (as the hottest) to pink , red, orange, yellow, green, blue, violet, and black as the coolest surface temperature (Figure 64).

Figure 64: The hottest to the coolest depiction. There is white band over pink that is not clearly visible.

The picture on the left was taken soon after coming in from a snowy weather to normal conindoor condition (Figure 65, Left). With coat, sweater and t-shirt combination for the upper torso. Pink and white at the neck area and inner pits of the elbow show the warmest atrea. The rest of the area shows yellow and green that are the mid-range colors of the rainbow. After fifteen minutes, another picture was taken (Figure 65, Right). It showed the same effect for the neck and the elbows. However, yellow has increased and green area decreased because the wearer was in a warmer temperature than the outdoor temperature.

Figure 65: An individual with a woolen coat, acrylic sweater, and cotton t-shirt at two-time intervals. Photographs taken by Dana Harder and cropped by the author.

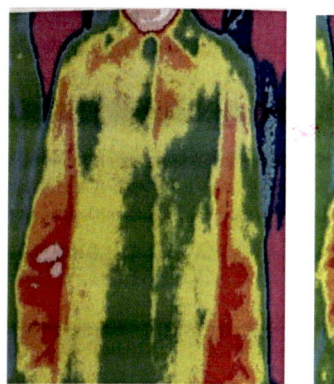

Time 1   Time 2

In figure 66, coat was removed and the wearer only has the acrylic sweater and cotton t-shirt. Pictures were taken every 15 minutes to assess the impact of removing coat and change over time on the outer surface. Pictures on the far left shows that the front torso looks cooler after the removal of the coat. In other two pictures (middle and right), red and yellow increased to show the increasing warmth and thereby the comfort level for the wearer. Elbow area continue to be warmer due to the cavitiy created at the inside of the elbow.

Figure 66: An individual with an acrylic sweater and cotton t-shirt at three time intervals. Photographs taken by Dana Harder and cropped by the author.

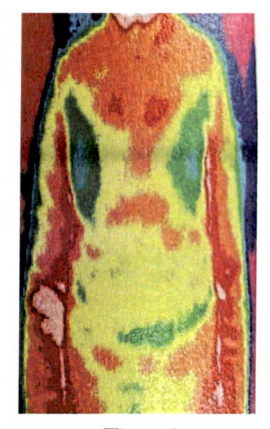

Time 1   Time 2   Time 3

Figure 67 shows the similar trend as we saw after removal of the woolen coat in figure 66. The left picture shows the cooling effect and the one on the right shows warming up. The finding shows the impact of layers in the layered clothing measured by the thermal camera with color effects.

Figure 67: An individual with a cotton t-shirt at two different times. Photographs taken by Dana Harder and cropped by the author.

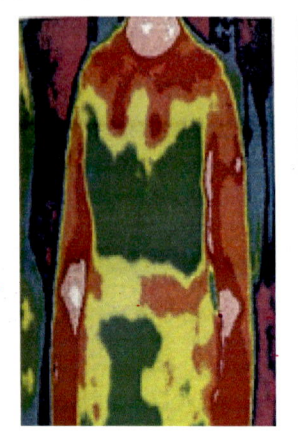

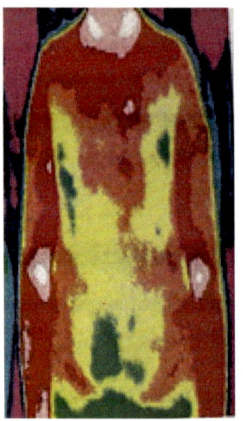

Time 1   Time 2

Summary and Conclusions

Comfort is an important aspect in textiles. Consumers want the textile that is comfortable to touch, non allergenic, and has adequate air permeability, cover, moisture management, porosity and thermal insulation. Several scholars have studied it from different perspectives. Textile and clothing could be activity and need specific. Comfort represents seven different types of comfort: body, clothing, physical, physiological, psychological, social, and thermal. Ergonomics that is otherwise seen as the relationship between the worker and his/her environment, is also associated with physical and psychological comforts finishes.

REFERENCES

Armstrong, T. (1986). Ergonomics and cumulative disorders. *Health Clinics,* 2(3), 553-565.

Adnan, M., & Moses, J. (2020). A study on the thermophysiological and tactile comfort *properties of silk/lyocell blended fabrics.* Matéria (Rio de Janeiro), 25(3), https://doi.org/10.1590/s1517-707620200003.1096

Azoulay, J. F. (2005, January). It's the stretch. *AATCC Review, 5,* 9-12.

Branson, D. H., & Sweeney, M. (1991). Conceptualization and measurement of clothing comfort: Toward a metatheory. In S. B. Kaiser and Mary Lynn Damhorst (Eds.), *Critical Linkages in Textiles and Clothing Subject Matter: Theory, Method, and Practice* (pp116-124). Monument, CO: International Textile and Apparel Association.

Braunstein, J. (1990). *Cumulative trauma disorders: Definitions and diagnosis.* A paper presented at the conference, "Ergonomics Consideration in the Apparel Workplace" on May 16, 1990 in Atlanta, Georgia.

Cao, H., Branson, D. H. Peksoz, S. Nam, J., and Farr, C. (2006), Fabric selection for a cooling garment. *Textile Research Journal, 776,* 587-595.

Chen, Y. S., Fen, J. & Zhang, W. (2003). Clothing thermal insulation during sweating. *Textile Research Journal, 73(2), 152-157.*

Chowdhary, U. (2017). Ergonomics in the Apparel Industry and Cross-Application. Presented at for Golden Jubilee International Conference on Gender Issues and Socio-Economic Perspectives for Sustainable Rural Development, held at Haryana Agricultural University in Hisar, India from October 23-25, 2017.

Chowdhary, U. (2009). *Textile analysis, quality control, and innovative uses.* Deer Park, NY: LINUS.

Chowdhary, U., & Harder, D. (2009). *Thermography and layering. Unpublished project.* Mount Pleasant, MI: Central Michigan University.

Cimilli, M. G. Nergis, U. B. and Candan, C. (2009). An experimental study of some comfort-related properties of cotton—Acrylic knitted fabrics. *Textile Research Journal, 70*(10), 917-923. https://doi.org/10.1177/0040517508099919

Cohen, A.C., & Johnson, I. (2010). *Fabric Science.* New York, NY: Fairchild.

Cotton variety may affect comfort (2006). *AATCC Review, 6I(3),* 5.

Dalbasi, E. S., & Kayseri, G. O. (2019). A research on the comfort properties of linen fabrics subjected to various finishing treatments. *Journal of Natural Fibers,* https://doi.org/10.1080/15440478.2019.1675210

Davies, E. (1996). Engineering swimwear. *The Journal of Textile Institute, 88, Part 3, I32-36.*

Dolbow, S. (1995, October). Tenniswear: It's tough, it's athletic, it's you. *Tennis,* 66-72.

Freddie (2021, March 24). Our choice for the best football socks. https://bestfootballgloves.net/best-football-socks-reviews/

Gao, J., Weidong, Y. and Pan, N. (2007). Structures and properties of the goose down as a material for thermal insulation. *Textile Research Journal, 77*(8), 617-626.

Haventh, G. (2009). Clothing protection against the natural environment: The relevance of local sweating and local ventilation for thermal comfort. Retrieved on 2/17/2009 from http://www.lboro.ac/uk/departments/hu/groups/htel/Sweating_ventilation_comfort.htm.

Kelly, M. J., Oritz, D. J., Courtney, T. K., Folds, D. J., Davis, N. D., Gerth, J. M., & Rose, S. (1992). *Ergonomic Challenges in conventional and advanced apparel manufacturing.* Georgia Tech Project A-8311. Georgia Institute of Technology.

Kunkel, K. (1990). Posture plays role in wrist, head injuries. *Upholstering: The Manufacturing Magazine of the Upholstery Industry,* 10(16), 1, 3.

Lau, L., Fan, J., Siu, T., & Siu, L. Y. C. (2002). Comfort sensations of polo shirts with and without wrinkle-free treatment. *Textile Research Journal, 72*(11), 949-953.

Lawson, L. & Lorentzen, D. (1990). Selected sport bras: Comparison of comfort and support. *Clothing and Textiles Research Journal, 8,* 55-60.

Lee, S., & Obendorf, S. K. (2007). Barrier effectiveness and thermal comfort of protective clothing materials. *The Journal of Textile Institute, 98,* 87-97.

Liddane, L. (2000, September 27). Suits may improve performance. *Wisconsin State Journal,* 5F.

Lipetz, J., & Kruse, R. J. (2000). Injuries and special concerns of female figure skaters. *Clinic in Sports Medicine, 19*(2), 369-380.

Martinez, N., Gonzales, J. C., Rosa, D., & Alcantara, E. (2009). A methodology of selecting a suitable garment for sports use. *International Journal of Clothing, Science, and Technology, 21*(2/3), 146-153.

Oggiaro, L, Brownlie, L., Troynikovc, O., Bardal, L. M., Sætera, C., and Sætrana, L. (2013). A review on skin suits and sport60*, 91-98* garment aerodynamics: guidelines and state of the art. *Procedia Engineering, 60,* 91-98.

Ogulata, R. T. (2007*). The effect of thermal insulation of clothing on human body comfort. Fibers and Textiles in Eastern Society, 15*(2), 67-72.

Teyeme, Y., Malengier, B., Tesfaye, T., Vasile, S., & Langenhove, L. V. (2020). Comparative analysis of thermophysiological comfort related properties of elastic knitted fabrics for cycling sportswear. *Materials, 13*(18), 4024. doi:10.3390/ma13184024

The chemistry of a football shirt (2014, August 14). https://www.compoundchem.com/2014/08/14/the-chemistry-of-a-football-shirt/

The nine best tennis shorts: Reviews and buyer's guide (https://www.thetennistribe.com/best-tennis-shorts/.

The six basic factor. (2009). Retrieved on 2/17/2009 from http://www/hse.gov.uk/temperature/thermal/factors.htm.

Understanding clo values (2021, March 24). A blog retrieved on 3/24/21 from https://roastsurvey.com/blog-post/understanding-clo-values/

Walzur, E. (2004, January). Focus on function, freshness. Apparel, 23-26.

What are soccer shoes made of? (August 14, 2019). https://www.shoesforsoccer.com/what-are-soccer-shoes-made-of/

What are the differences between lineman and receivers' gloves? (March 24, 2021). https://www.sportsunlimitedinc.com/how-to-buy-football-gloves.html

What makes a football helmet? (March 24, 2021). https://www.hibbett.com/expert-advice/what-makesafootballhelmet.html#:~:text=Look%20for%20a%20more%20rounded,padding%2C%20face%20and%20chin%20strap.

Wilson, J. (2012). Best football shoulder pads. https://www.latimes.com/bestcovery/best-football-shoulder-pads

PRACTICE ACTIVITIES

1. What is the role of textiles in feeling comfortable in cold and warm climates?
2. What is the role of heat transfer in creating body or clothing comfort? In what ways can textiles help it? Provide appropriate examples.
3. What is the difference between moisture management and thermal insulation?
4. Which textile attribute enhances moisture management?
5. List the textile attributes that enhance thermal insulation.
6. What is the role of air movement in creating body comfort?
7. How is ergonomics related to body comfort?
8. What is the role of textiles in enhancing comfort for various age groups?
9. Identify the body aching experiences you have felt in your lifetime. Did you use any clothing or textile related items to comfort yourself? If so, what were they?
10. How can you interpret the thermographic images based on the rainbow colors?
11. How will you justify the presence of pink and white colors in the elbow and neck areas?
12. Would you prefer woven or knitted materials for children's activewear?
13. What will help the post-mastectomy survivor to create comfort from the lymphedema?
14. Who can use Velcro to advantage? What are its disadvantages?
15. What gets blocked when one gets Carpal Tunnel Syndrome (CTS)?
16. What is swimwear sold by?
17. What do cleats do?
18. Use the table below to identify aching areas and times.

#	Body Part	Morning	Afternoon	Evening	Night
1	Head				
2	Neck				
3	Left Shoulder				
4	Right Shoulder				
5	Upper Back				
6	Left Arm				
7	Right Arm				
8	Middle Back				

#	Body Part	Morning	Afternoon	Evening	Night
9	Lower Back				
10	Buttocks				
11	Left Hand				
12	Right Hand				
13	Left Leg				
14	Right Leg				
15	Left Foot				
16	Right Foot				

INNOVATIVE TREATMENT AND USES

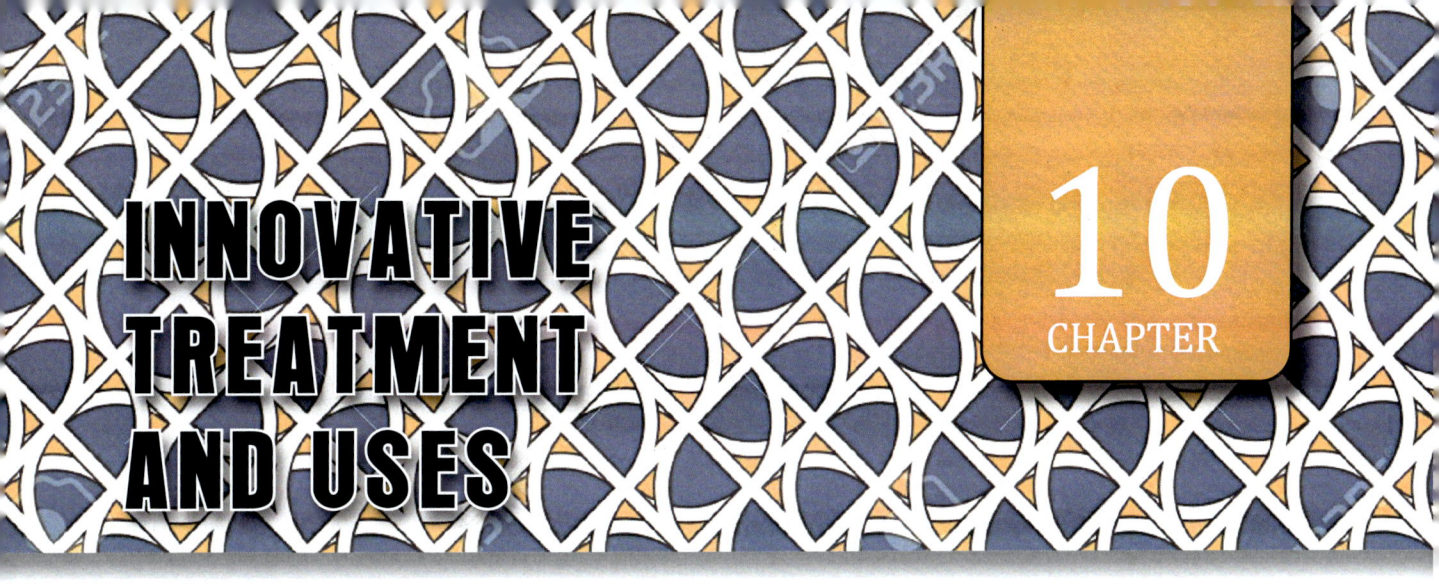

CHAPTER 10

Innovative treatments are given to textiles for making them better for the end-use. The treatment makes them better than their intrinsic ability to perform. For example, cotton can be made flame resistant, and modacrylic can be made absorbent. The purpose of these innovations is to enhance aesthetics and/or function of textile and apparel. Traditionally, finishes also performed a similar function to enhance efficiency in production, distribution, and consumption of textile. This chapter focuses on finishes and other innovative uses.

Finishes

Finishes are used in textiles to improve appearance, function, or hand of the textiles to make it appropriately serviceable. Finishes can be added any time during the manufacturing of textiles at solution, fiber, yarn, fabric, and/or garment stages. Some examples follow. **Bleaching** can be used at the fiber, yarn, fabric, as well as garment stage to whiten the greige goods, or to remove colors if so needed. Bleaching finishes is also applied to make the fabrics better prepared for subsequent dyeing or other procedures. Yarns may be treated with starch or chemicals that allow them to withstand the wear and tear during the weaving process. The process is also termed as **slashing**. The sizing added in the yarn stages is removed after the fabric stage to allow for better penetration of dyes and finishes. **Singeing** is done on a fabric to get rid of the short hairy structures during the weaving process. **Bio-polishing** performs a similar function except the treatment includes the use of enzymes. **Cleaning and scouring** helps with removal of unwanted dirt or grease to better prepare the fabric. Likewise, the **mercerization** treatment can be given at the yarn or the fabric stages. This alkali treatment of sodium hydroxide given to cotton reduces its twist, gives longer staple length to the staple fiber, and makes it smoother and more absorbent than possible without the treatment. Like bleach, optical brighteners can be used to whiten the cottons in the fabric stage, and for synthetics in the solution stage before extrusion. **Calendering** is a taken for granted treatment that smoothens the fabric for attaining effective dye and finishing treatments as well as offering smoother fabric that appeals the consumer more than the wrinkled look.

Finishes are categorized as aesthetic and functional types. **Aesthetic** finishes are used to improve appearance, drape, hand, and texture. **Functional** finishes are used to enhance functionality that may or may not improve appearance. Some examples of the **aesthetic finishes** are glazed, moire, or schreiner calendering, and embossing for **appearance and luster.** Parchmentization and starching are examples of **drape**; using enzymes, sandblasting, sueding, or stonewashing for **hand**; and brushing, flocking, pleating, puckering, and tufting for **texture** (Chowdhary, 2009).

Functional finishes are used to improve performance of the textile for the specialized need. **Relaxation shrinkage control** can be induced by overfeeding in between two rollers for knitted materials. For woven materials, one can roll moistened fabric around a blanket made from felt (Kadolph and Langford, 2002). **Felting Shrinkage** for wool is an example of **Progressive Shrinkage** which can be prevented by the treatment to reduce the locking power of the scales or damage them. This can be accomplished by coating or by using chlorine through Halogenation.

For thermoplastic fibers, **Progressive Shrinkage** can be controlled through the heat setting process. Aldehyde resins work the best (Kadolph and Langford, 2002). **Wrinkle Recovery and Durable Press** finishes are two examples of shape retention finishes that are applied in the resin form. Soil and stain release finishes are fluorocarbons that make the fabric stain repellent. Fluorocarbons are used for water repellency also. **Resins** are also used for abrasion resistant finishes. Blending natural fibers with synthetic fibers can also enhance the abrasion resistance. Silicone is the most frequently used product for water repellency. Fabric softeners, phase change, static control, and water absorbency were all noted to impact the comfort factor of the textiles.

NanoSphere offers visible protection through nanostructure for wool and silk. This technique offers self-cleaning processes to remove stains such as ketchup and honey due to its ability to repel water (NanoSphere to the rescue of wool and silk from stains, 2009). However, the report did not address the ability of the nanostructure to repel oils. **Antimicrobial finishes** are used to reduce microbial growth, enhance odor control, freshness, and cleanliness amongst fabrics. This can be accomplished through encapsulating or by use of chemicals. **Flame retardant finishes** are used for safety from fire and are mandatory for children's sleepwear. These finishes should withstand at least fifty launderings. The finishes are achieved through resins or ammonium care.

Entropy Solutions (2016) has developed shape-stabilized versions of two of its Pure-Temp bio-based Phase Change Materials (PCM). These PCM materials are gel like and retain the shape in both solid and liquid forms and release and store energy as needed. This material does not leak, is moldable, soft in the liquid stage, stiff in the solid stage, and has minimized leakage when punctured. It has a purity level of 99%. It uses the capsulation procedure that uses latent heat for energy. Rahman, Biswas, Mitra, and Rakesh (2014) examined dimensional stability, and pilling resistance of jersey with Lycra, plain single jersey, 1x1 rib, single Lacoste, double Lacoste, and interlock knit for grey fabric, with and without enzyme. Enzyme treatment challenged the stability of all types of weft knits and increased their shrinkage except for single Lacoste and interlock.

The preceding material reveals that functional finishes are either obtained through some coating or resin applications. Finishes make textiles appropriate for the special end-uses. Antistatic capability can be enhanced by using additives in the spinning solutions prior to extrusion of the filaments through the spinneret. Similar process could be used for the liquid barrier finishes. Selected research findings are reported to understand the recent developments of the textile finishing industry with innovative ideas.

Antibacterial Finishes

They have become popular in many fields, such as auto marines, and medicine. **Japanese apparel brand Goldwin Inc** has come up with a knitted sweater made from microbially fermented brewed protein that is soft and comfortable (*Innovations in advanced textiles* (February 2021). It has come to the US and is made to emulate the traditional ski sweater. MICROBAN® is the brand of Microban International that has partnered with Sinomax that has recently launched an antimicrobial foam mattress pad with mattress for hospitals.

Doty and Easter (2009) claimed that the bacterial growth after 20 wash and dry cycles reduced for all garments of activewear and workwear. Specifically, the finish provided 99% reduction against K. Pneumonia, and 96% for S. Aureus. Parikh, Edward, and Condon (2008) asserted that silver has long been used for the antimicrobial treatment as silver nitrate because it is effective on more than one type of bacteria including the S. Aureus which is known to damage the textiles. The treated material was used for dressing, and healing wounds more effectively than the untreated materials. Desmarteau (2007) reported that cotton with copper provide antimicrobial effects. Initially, they were introduced by the marines. Kusterback (2007) introduced antimicrobial hats. The line included smart silver technology that uses 200 weight polyester fleeces for hats and neck warmers.

INNOVATIONS IN PROGRESS

Apparel

Tuff -N-Lite offers socks that are cut, slash and abrasion resistant. They also produce aprons, gloves, jackets, and pull-overs. (https://tuffnlite.com/product-category/socks/, 3/28/2021). Nomex continues to be the protective fabric. DriTan™ keeps the shoes dry. (FabricLink, 2018). Polartec® introduced a cycling kit (Champion: cycling in style, 2018, p.10) that consisted of "jerseys, a tank, bib shorts, arm warmers, vests, a jacket, gloves, a cap, and a neck warmer." The fabrics used were Polartec® Power Wool® for "comfort and moisture management". The Polartec Power Stretch® was used for aerodynamics, comfort, compression, and supporting the muscles. Delta™® offers cooling relief and Alpha gives "breathable insulation."

Preuss (2017) identified six sustainable fibers as hemp fibers that are antibacterial, durable, and resilient; nettle fibers that are versatile; coffee ground fibers; pineapple fabrics; banana fibers, and lotus fibers. Petit Pli (2017), a children's line developed outerwear that has pleats which expand both ways for growth. They are made from synthetic materials that are both rainproof and windproof. Mills-Senn (2017) quoted Dr. MacGillivray of Central Michigan University who stressed the use of stretchy fabrics with antimicrobial properties, light weight, and ability to change with the weather. Phase Change Materials were sourced from the aerospace industry. She stressed that the PCM tighten the fabric when the temperature drops that results in less porous material. When hot, the fabric melts and creates more pores than before. The article also mentioned Kottinu® that is a polyester with sense of comfort and an exceptional moisture management ability. Iceskin™ was developed to lower the surface temperature by blending polyester and nylon using microfiber technology. Coldskin™ and Warmskin™ are two other smart fabrics that change with change in the temperature. Key Markets in 2017 are tabulated below.

Table 29: Key Markets in Apparel

Category	Market Size Global	Market Size U.S.	Drop/Rise % from the previous year
Military	$1.7 trillion	$ 598.5 billion	Global – Drop 5.6% US – Drop 2%
Advanced Textile Products	Not available	$5.6 billion	Stable
Narrow Fabrics	Not available	Not available	2.5 – 3% growth in US and Canada
Geosynthetics	Not Available	$2.6 billion	Up 3.5% - 4%
Tarpaulins and Truck Covers	Not Available	Not Available	Growth 4.5-5%
Equipment	Not Available	$565 million	Growth 5%

Textile, heal thyself (2017) reported that a polymer coating can be used by positively and negatively charged polymers through layering and it changes the treatment from liquid to solid. Enzymes are added to the coating. Polymer self-heal itself. The coating depth is less than on micron. Davies (2017) reported on the transformation of Jogbra to Smart bra. The sports bra had the heart rate technology added to it. OMbra has a double cup design that also has adjustable straps and hooks and eyes. On the left, it had OMbox with an accelerometer to count steps. Besides sports bras, smart shorts are also designed with sensors. Preus (2016) reported that adding sensors for making clothing comfortable and durable have gained popularity. Preus (2015) asserted that innovation is the thriving force in the textile industry.

Breezeway®(undated) is a Nomex® and Lenzing FR® blend used for the safety of the electrical worker. The fabric weights ranged between 4.75 oz/yd^2 to 8.0 oz/yd^2. Nomex® was noted to have lowest life cycle cost and is sold as the Flamer resistant fabric. Lenzing® keeps the body cool and dry and protects from both heat stress and stroke. It is heat resistant and does not drip or melt. It insulates the wearer and is durable to the extent that it lasts for 125 launderings. It has higher tear and tensile strength than the treated cotton. It lasts longer and retains its original appearance. It has permanent wicking behavior with WikQik®. High visibility orange color meets the "Bright Background" requirements. The pamphlet provides both structural and performance attributes of three weights. It is available in Chambray, Heather, Navy, Orange, Royal, and Tan 525 colors.

Denim trend collection (2014/2015) by Stoll reported that created knitwear with traditional woven denim effects with addition of faded looks through knitted fabric construction. They have branches and agencies in China, France, Hong Kong, India, Italy, Japan, Taiwan, Thailand, United States, and Vietnam. Figure 68 shows some examples.

Figure 68: Knit machine created denim. (Winter Denim Trend Selection, Stoll, 2014/15, p. 35 & 46)

In the 7th "Safety Products Student Design Challenge in 2011, Central Michigan University Students received the first place for Aircraft Marshaller's Safety Jacket. This two-layer jacket used the LED lights in sleeves and "LilyPad Arduino technology" that allowed switching on and off lights. The second place was awarded to the Institute of Technology in Ireland. This award was for the mountain bike armour that needs comfort, protection, and support. The winners used the breathable materials. The Active Protection System was borrowed from Dow Corning and "ThermoCool" from Advansa.

Ballistic Protection

Cobb (2021) stated that demand of ballistic protection apparel is growing globally in both developing and developed nations. It is projected that between 2020-2030, $12.4 billion will be spent on body armor. 28.2% of it will be sold globally. The latest version of shirts and pelvic protector will have 20% less weight than the existing ones. Lessened weight will enhance mobility. The article provided a picture of the Warwick Mills' TurtleSkin Metal Flex Armor (MFA). It was introduced in 2008.

"Discreet Body Armor" that is also known as the "Innocent Armor" (p. 34) is designed to look like the streetwear. They will offer comfortable styles with extra UV protection and water resistance.

Care Labeling

Care labeling is the guide for refurbishing the clothes for retaining the original appearance (Le. 2018). In Canada and Europe, the care labels are not mandatory. China and Korea have different sets of symbols than the United States. The care labeling concept is very complex and needs harmonizing. Timeliness in creating the standards is a challenge that needs to be streamlined better than now. Wet cleaning and banning of chemicals in California such as perchloroethylene used for traditional dry cleaning are additional challenges that must be faced.

Color

GTI (Undated) provided five key elements for accurate color matching and inspection. They are Color quality, evenness, geometry, light intensity, and surround. Daylight was represented by a D65 light simulation that has a color temperature of 6500K. Inspection should be done in the neutral surroundings for accurate interpretation. Make sure to use the same angles while evaluating. Variance in angles can change the color perception. Light sources can cause metamerism. Daylight can be D50, D65, and D75. Other types of lights are store, home, ultraviolet, and LED.

Digital Printing

Davies (2020) provided innovations in machine and ink for 3D and 4D printing for healthcare and fit. A professor at Harvard university is working on the silicone-based gel. This hydrogel can be used for changing the appearance and shape. Sherburne (2019) reported that interpretation of ΔE is different for the graphic arts and textile and apparel. For graphic art 1.0 is acceptable but it is not so for textile and apparel. Digital printing is gaining popularity because Textile printing operates based on the subtractive theory. CMYK development uses Cyan, Magenta, Yellow, and Black colors. CMYK originated from the RGB additive theory but is very popular in color and printing. King emphasized that customers are forgiving but seek for consistency. Her company still uses the RGB system. Industry is trying to streamline the product development and sampling process. Ken Butts of data color eluded that for the final approval still needs the physical sample. Some steps are handled virtually and not all of them. The experts believe that the digital and actual samples appear to be different by 0.5 ΔE.

Knapp used an example of a ski jacket to demonstrate that its shell, jacket, and thread are made of nylon, and buttons and zippers from metal or plastic. Therefore, color matching becomes a challenge when they come from different sources. Calibrating computers can eliminate the problem. Anchroma's official iterated that to overcome the matching problem, most companies start with virtual processes and move toward the physical samples before making the final assessment. Future direction is to focus on developing sophisticated processes that will allow for making the final decisions virtually.

Dyes

Le (2018) Asserted that under the umbrella of sustainability, natural dyes are becoming popular. Forward thinking brands are considering the impact of the process on performance. Colorfastness needs work for the enhanced consumer appeal. Archroma has a patented method for creating dyes from nature. They create "high performance dyes from leaves and non-edible shells of nuts." (*AATCC Review, 16*(2), 7).

Flame Resistant and Retardant Fabrics.

Totolin, Sarmadi, Manolache, and Denes (2009) claimed the successful use of the low-pressure plasma technique to create flame retardant cotton by cross-linking the pre-deposited silicate layers. California State Fire Marshal developed FR Comshade™ in leadfree form for safety (*Specialty Fabrics Review, 2018,* 48). For durability in waterline, a quality fabric was advertised for scratch resistance and stain resistance (*Specialty Fabrics Review, 2018,* 61). They were STRATAGLASS® and RIVIERA®.

Health Care

AATCC M14-2020 (Face Covering Guidance Approved, 2020) developed a standard monograph that has eight considerations: Regulatory, fit and sizing, material and construction, particle filtration, breathing resistance, laundering and service, tie and ear loop, and product labeling and marking. **Sure-Chek® Fusion** (*Specialty Fabrics Review*, 2016, April) was reported as an ergonomic fabric that is used for cushions, mattresses, pillows, and other support fabrics. It uses antimicrobial, antistatic, and flame-retardant finishes.

Lighting

Sherburne (2018) stressed the role of Leonard da Vinci's seminal work on the impact of lighting on color. The International Commission of Illumination (CIE) was inspired by him. Color is evaluated for color difference, metamerism, and illuminant conditions in various settings. LEDs (light emitting diodes) are semiconductors and last longer than the incandescent and fluorescent lights. For home, 800 lumens are needed, and for work, 1000-1600 lumens work. They do not use the original unit of watts that was used for the incandescent bulbs.

Lycra

The author compared cotton and cotton/spandex blend for physical and mechanical attributes of single jersey materials. Findings revealed that increase in spandex percentage decreased fabric recovery and bursting strength. However, the extension and fabric hand increased with increase in the loop length for cotton. The blend showed an increase in density, thickness and recovery but decrease in extension, porosity and width of fabric. Lycra addition increases the fabric weight.

Marine Fabrics

Tornquist (2016) reported that comfort, durability, performance, and style are important for the textiles used in marine. Colorfastness, mildew resistance, strength, and water repellency are critical considerations for marine fabrics. WeatherMAX® was identified as one such fabric.

Military Wear

Globally, military expenditure was $1.7 trillion. It dropped 5.6% from 2014. In the United States, it was 598.5 billion dollars in 2015 and was 2% less than 2014. Nanowire networks for uniform excellence. (2017) re-examined the clothing of the soldiers stationed in the arctic regions. Currently, they use, protective clothing is bulky that gets overheated and sweaty fast. They have now designed a uniform in the lightweight material with polyester and cotton/nylon blends with 3 volts through 1" x 1" swatches that reach 100^0F in one minute. Dial is attached to adjust the temperature depending on the weather. They also added a layer of hydrogel that absorbs sweat and controls dampness. The hydrogels are made of polyethylene glycol or poly(N-isopropylacrylamide). The researchers are investigating to ensure that the nanowires and hydrogels are compatible and safe to launder.

Seeking innovation (2017) reported that the U.S. Army's Natick Soldier Research, Development and Engineering Center is seeking for "stronger, lighter weight uniforms, equipment, shelters and parachutes" in addition to the antimicrobial and flame-resistant attributes. Comfort in hot weather is an important factor in the military uniform (Military-grade comfort, 2016). Advanced Combat Fabric (ACF)that was made from GORE® is a "no melt/no drip" fabric with high air permeability. It is woven with cotton and nylon combination and is a quick drying material. It is strong and resists tears and breaks. Blouse considers breathability, durability and stretch. To withstand abrasion and "terrain", the fabric is double layered at the elbows, forearms, and knees. Knit stretch is used for dynamic movement at the wrists, underarms and yoke in blouse, and crotch and back yoke of the pants.

Moisture Management

Wojciechowska (2018) asserted that gym and hiking clothes are worn more for function than fashion. It is important to have standardized tests for uniform interpretation.

Outdoor

Outdoor yarns (2019, p. 60-61) To add brilliance, durability, and performance for yarns of the awnings help with resistance to chemicals, salty water, and abrasion. Sunbrella® fabrics have introduced the zipper that resists fading, microbes, and bleach. Cut-Tex® has come up with slash resistant fabrics for those in law enforcement. Bermuda shorts by brrr® use the cooling technology called "triple chill effect" (*Specialty Fabrics Review,* 2019, p.12). It is designed to draw heat away from the body and moisture via active wicking process. It reduces temperature by 3^0F in just 20 minutes and is quick drying. It was designed to provide comfort for the wearer. Timeless shade (2018, April). Claimed that the RAIN KLEEN finish® has excellent dimension stability, fungus and mildew resistance, and flame resistance it also provides five years warranty and has a large selection. selection.

Mills-Senn (2017) reported that Polartec fabrics are used for the outdoors. They are recommended for cycling, golf, and running. Outdoor brand bags balloon fabric (2015) reports use of textiles that is antimicrobial, waterproof and wind resistant. They use nylon 6 which is a very strong material.

Smart Textiles

Innovations in advanced textiles (February 2021) unfolded on several innovations that are provided below. **Strung** is a robotically designed shoe to match the athlete's specifications by a German sportswear company adidas®. This new shoe with lightweight and seamless upper is designed for fast and short distance running. It uses red thread for extra support at "the heels, midfoot, toe box." Outer sole is made of rubber for a strong grip. **Japanese scientist** developed an ultra-thin membranous sensor that promotes the sensitivity and allows people to perform exacting tasks. Examples being surgeons and artisans. **BMW** created a wingsuit that is attached to the pilot's suit. It weighs 26 pounds. It uses a 50 V lithium battery. Three Austrians tried jumping from 3000 meters height and landed successfully with parachutes. **The Samsonite® has come up with a backpack** with **Jacquard™** technology that allows to take calls, hear text messages and play music.

Columbia Sportswear has introduced its "Omni Heat" Black Dot technology (January, 2021). It is an external shield to protect from cold. It uses lots of multilayered black dots that use solar heat and trap warmth. It is the first of its kind. For additional information, go to www.columbia. Com. Mills-

Senn (2021) claimed that the Minnesota lab is working on bringing out a compression vest with a sensor that will use memory to change shape. Sensoria INC has come up with a sock made from 96% Coolmax® and 4% spandex. It measures how far, fast, and well, the wearer runs. It also shows the contact time, loading technique and pace of running. Sensoria® knee-brace monitors range of motion and reports feedback to the coach.

Ralph Lauren (2018) introduced self-heating jackets were made from the carbon electronic and silver conductors for the Olympics. Batteries were used for charging. The wearer only feels the warm comfort. He also designed the bomber jackets for the closing ceremony. Additionally, both jackets were water repellent. The is an example of designers' interest in using wearable technology. Sportswear is using sublimation technology. (Eamon (2017) reported the use of plastic for more than 11 million pairs of shoes by the end of 2017 by Adidas. Additionally, debris and fishnet were chosen for the swimwear line. They were reported to be like nylon.

October 2016 issue of the *Specialty Fabrics Review* talked about the wearable muscle shirt the was designed use data that transforms what a person feels. Increase in the heartbeat tightens the t-shirt knit on the torso gradually. What t-shirts may come... (2016, February, p. 13) created "Reality Dreams Hydrophobic t-shirts" that repel liquids but do not lose their breathability and comfort. Teamwork: Matching thread, needle and tension (2016).

Hu, Meng, Li, and Ibekwe 2012) on multiple uses of smart textiles. It includes but is not limited to changing aesthetics, color and responding to environmental changes. Table 1 of the article mentions its use for shape memory fibers, fabrics, finishes, and foams; "breathable fabrics", and "phase change materials" (p. 3). They can make cotton fabrics wrinkle free. in fiber form they change the molecular orientation and improve conduction of fibers. Temperature changes result in increase or decrease in molecular structure and result in enhanced "water vapor permeability". Shape memory foams can be used for foot soles of shoes. Thermo-chromatic materials are used in microcapsules to create color changes at varying temperatures. The article also talked about the "moisture-responsive shape memory polymers" that can cause cooling for the overheated body.

Wright (2018) emphasized the use of interactive textiles with sensing monitors for the physiological functions. E-textile can enhance voice or data transfer in the medical, military, and safety fields. Compression is increased to improve the circulatory problems. Seshadri (2018) asserted when textiles perform functionally, they are called smart. From sustainability standpoint, he talked about the use of lotus leaf for developing super hydrophobic textiles. He identified it as an example of bioengineering and molecular biology. Using spider for silk was another example of smart textile. Davies (2018) reported that researchers from the Ohio State University have used the conductive threads for carpets and curtains to enhance their functionality. They plan to further understand the walking pattern of the elderly to provide safety. SDL Atlas provided examples for confidence, conformity, and consistency.

Space Clothing

Forrest (2019) stated that space textile should be lightweight, strong, and tolerant to the extremes of cold, heat and ultraviolet radiations. Straps are used to use them for parachuting, diapers to replace underwear, and flag of nylon. Same textile does not respond the same in space due to low gravity.

Swat stays, clothes are worn for longer time than on earth, they must exercise more. Fabrics should have enhanced wicking ability. Form fitting skin suits are worn for increasing the gravity. Low gravity made the moon dust to cling strongly. Today's space suits are made more lightweight and flexible.

Davies (2019) asserted that the three-layered fabric is called ACES. The first layer is made of Gore-Tex. The second layer is made of the "Linknet", and the third layer is made of high visibility Nomex in orange color. The third layer offers abrasion resistance, fire protection, and high visibility. Sleek styling for space (2017) reported on suits with 20 pounds weight that were 40% lighter than the previous versions. Safety, mobility, and functionality were the key factors considered in designing. It was layered and used noncommercial Gore-Tex® for its air resistance, coolness, good shape retention and a lightweight Nomex® that is abrasion resistant and flame-resistant. Instead of bubble helmet, it had a soft attached helmet cap with communication with the ground with a visor made from polycarbonate. Light weight leather gloves and breathable leg pockets completed the ensemble.

Orndoff (2016) informed that the spacesuits have constantly been redesigned to make them appropriate for the intra-vehicular and extra-vehicular activities. Celanese Corporation developed flame-retardant polyester to replace cotton for the crew for both clothing and sleeping bags. Monsanto Co. developed flame retardant materials via halogenation and heat for the aramid fibers in 1969. Research is ongoing to get fibers that are comfortable in space with minimal need for laundering.

Special Needs

Dr. Gozde Goncu Berk, an assistant professor at UC-Davis has developed a glove that stimulates nerves through skin via "the embroidered e-textile electrodes and transmission lines created through integration of conductive threads on textiles." Smart glove designed to treat rheumatoid arthritis. *(Specialty Fabrics Review*, January 2021). They are used for treating "swan neck deformity of fingers and ulnar deviation of the hand., compression thermoplastic membranes are laminated on finger joint areas of the glove, and a support structure for the wrist is integrated into the glove as a splint.

Socks with sense (2018) reported that Siren from San Francisco developed a **Neurofabric™**, with sensors on the fabric that can help with resulting numbness of the diabetic feet. The sensors help with monitoring the temperature of the feet in six locations. Help for Stroke Patients (2017, p. 12) developed an "exosuit" that is flexible and lightweight for stroke patients in their road to recovery. Space blankets (2017, p. 19) keep the satellite contamination free and provide "sound absorption, vibration reduction, and static bleed-off with carbon Teflon™."

Sustainability

Bide (2000) provided a historical perspective with focus on the underlying trends. Energy and water consumption, textile manufacturing processes, Awareness of circularity and growth were noted as the continuing issues. Corp (2000) presented in formation on ten issues of sustainability ranging from **animal welfare** to water consumption. New Zealand banned anesthetics, but Australia introduced them in the wool production. Concerns for soft feathers of down tht are used for insulation. For **biodegradability,** the author used the example of cotton and nylon products that take six months to 40 years for degradation. Moisture management technology was reported to combine staple and filament yarns to enhance degradability by July 2020. Lenzing company is wanting to become the first company to accomplish **carbon neutrality** and contribute toward a clean environment. ZDIC (Zero Discharge of Hazardous Chemicals) is working on alleviating the risk of chemicals. **Circular Economy** is considering have materials either durable or recyclable even though they can be made biodegradable.

Fiber particulate is dangerous for fish and breathability in general. Industry is working on reducing the risk. Polartec is taking the lead. This relates to shedding of the microfibers in wear and tear process. Several companies are using **recycled** products. Re-commerce and the **secondhand / vintage clothing** have gained popularity in the last few years. Industry is also working on created **transparency** between and among several sectors. Finally, the **water consumption** is another area of concern. Cotton is believed to consume 2500 liters in growing, 20 liters in production, and another seventy liters in laundering. The degree of consumption varies for different textiles.

Forrest (2019) delineated several steps of the circular economy that was introduced to overcome the flaws of the linear approach used in the past. The four main steps of this economy were: To phase out the harmful substances, focus on durability and increase the use, enhance the recycling, as well as ability to recycle, and make better use of resources. Wrangler has introduced the use of foam overwater for dyeing of denim. They intend to maximize the potential by 2025. McKeegan (2019) informed the existence of circular design, quest for sustainability, use of recycling technology, and biodegrading were the key steps.

Cattermole (2018) promoted the circular economy and defined it as "extract, make, use, and dispose" model (p. 37). The author talked about renewal and reuse of products via leasing, recycling, Both the industry and consumers are trying to come up with innovative strategies to recreate the renewable energy.

The Textile Testing

Mahony (2016, 33) quoted, "-------- Textile testing, inspection and certification expected to reach more than 7 billion by 2020 ---------." She identified testing as an integral part of standardization. Application of the nonwoven materials was listed for backing upholstery, filtration, insulating, reinforcing tires, and silencing home loudspeakers. INDA (Association of the nonwoven fabrics and America), and the European Disposables and Nonwovens Association (EDANA) asserted that using standards harmonized the industry by using the common language. It helps with building the reputation. W. L. gore and associates Inc. was used as an example. It noted that if they wanted to guarantee the consumer of staying dry. They had to be sure and testing allowed them to do so. Therefore, they performed 100 tests that ranged from comfort to the rain-test.

Summary

It is evident from the preceding information that ongoing research and development has resulted in many innovations to promote aesthetics, durability, and performance of the textile industry. Everyday new products are created, improved, and marketed to retailers and consumers. Technological advances have accelerated the process. Textiles are omnipresent and have made valuable contributions in several areas of life. Such as apparel, automobiles, marines, medical, military smart textiles and special needs.

The goal of all innovations is to enhance the quality of life of consumers through appropriateness of choices that are both aesthetically pleasing and functional for the end-uses, as well as offer improved efficiency of processes of the creators of the products.

REFERENCES

As the child grows – so do the clothes (2017, December). *Specialty Fabrics Review*, p.10.

Breezeway by DIFCO (Undated) difco@pginw.com

Carp, B. (2020, September/October). A more sustainable textile supply chain. *AATCC Review, 20*(5), 34-40.

Cattermole, A. (2018, March/April). How the circular economy is changing fashion. *AATCC Review, 18*(2), 36-42.

Champion: Cycling in style (2018, March). *Specialty Fabrics Review*, p.10.

Chowdhary, U. (2009). *Textile analysis, quality control, and innovative uses*. Deer Park, NY: LINUS.

Clothing that keeps cool. (2019, June). *Specialty Fabrics Review*, 12.

Cobb, D. (January 2021). A new age in ballistics protection. (January 2021). *Specialty Fabrics Review*, 30-36.

Columbia introduces 'heat magnet' textile to the outdoors market. (January 2021). *Specialty Fabrics Review*, 12.

Davies, N. (2020, September/October). Digital printing: Machine and ink innovations. *AATCC Review, 20*(5), 26-33.

Davies, N. (2019, March/April). Taking textiles to space. *AATCC Review, 19*(2), 42-47.

Davies, N. (2017, September/October). Smart fabrics for women's sports apparel. *AATCC Review, 17*(5), 46-49.

Denim trend collection (2014/2015). New York, NY: Stoll America Knitting Machinery, Inc.

Desmarteau, K. (2007, February). Copper brings copper technology. *U.S. Apparel*, 40.

DIFCO (undated). *difco@pginw.com* .

Doty, K. C., and Easter, E. (2009, May). An analysis of the care and maintenance of performance textiles and effects of care on performance. *AATCC Review*, 37- 42.

Eamon, H. (2017, June). Infinite possibilities. *Specialty Fabrics Review*, 52-57.

Entropy Solutions develops shape-stabilized versions of2 Pure-Temp PCMs (August 2016). https://www.puretemp.com/stories/entropy-solutions-develops-shape-stabilized-versions-of-2-puretemp-pcms.

Fabric Link Networks' Top 10 textile innovation awards (2018) *FabricLink Guides* Retrieved on 3/28/2021. https://www.fabriclink.com/consumer/TopTen-2018.cfm.

Face covering guidance approved (2020, September/October). *AATCC Review, 20*(5), 10-11.

Forrest, F. (2019, November/December). Sustainability, slow fashion, and the circular economy – is it the next great opportunity? *AATCC Review, 19*(6), 22-29.

Forrest (2019). Bringing space textiles down to earth. *AATCC Review,19*(2), 34-41.

GTI (Undated). Newburgh, NY: GTI Graphic Technology Inc.

Hu, J., Meng, H., Li, G., & Ibekwe, S. (2012). A review of stimuli-responsive polymers for smart textile applications. *Smart Materials and Structures, 21,* 053001 (23 pp.)

Innovations in advanced textiles (February 2021). Specialty Fabrics Review, 14-15.

Kadolph, S. J. & Langford, A. L. (2002). *Textile.* Upper Saddle River, NJ: Merrill.

Key Markets (2017, March). Key Markets. *Specialty Fabrics Review,* 49-54.

Kusterback, S. (2007, June). Turtle fur goes antimicrobial. *Apparel*, 41-42.

Le, K. (2018, November/December). Care labeling: Challenges in Harmonization. *AATCC Review, 18*(6), 22-27.

Le, K. (2018, July/August). Natural dyes - Return of the classics. *AATCC Review, 18*(4), 42-48.

McKeegan, D. (2019, November/December). Going fort and coming home: Hospitality and home fabrics tackle sustainability. *AATCC Review, 19*(6), 30-35.

MICROBAN® (2020, September/October). *AATCC Review, 20*(5), 8.

Mills-Senn, P. (February 2021). Getting smarter about wearables. *Specialty Fabrics Review,* 30-36.

Mills-Senn, P. (2017, March). Game on. *Specialty Fabrics Review,* 38-46.

Military-grade comfort (2016, May). *Specialty Fabrics Review,* 15

NanoSphere to the rescue of wool and silk from stains (2009, July 15). Retrieved on 10/1/2009 From www.fibre2fashion.com/news/textile-news/switzerland/newsdetai...

Nanowire networks for uniform excellence. (2017, December). *Specialty Fabrics Review,* p.10.

O'Mahony, M. (2016, April). The testing issue. *Specialty Fabrics Review,* 32-39.

Orndoff, E. (2016, February). Textile in space. *Specialty Fabrics Review,* 28-35.

Outdoor brand bags balloon fabric (2015, October). *Specialty Fabrics Review,* 14-15.

Parikh, D. V., Edwards, J. V., & Condon, B.D. (2008, August). Silver-carboxylate ion-paired alginate and carboxymethylated cotton with antimicrobial activity. *AATCC Review,* 38- 43.

Preus, J. (2016, April). Smarter every day. *Specialty Fabrics Review,* 62-63.

Preus, J. (2015, October). Thriving on Innovation. *Specialty Fabrics Review*, 49-5.

Preuss, S. (2017). 6 sustainable textile innovations that will change the fashion industry. https://fashionunited.com/news/business/6-sustainable-textile-innovations-that-will-change-the-fashion-industry/2017100917734

Rahman, H., Biswas, P. K., Mitra, B. K., Rakesh, M.S.R. (2014). Effect of enzyme wash (cellulase enzyme) on properties of different weft knitted fabrics. *International Journal of Current Engineering and Technology, 4*(4), 4242-4248.

Robotic glove for hand paralysis (July 2020). *Specialty Fabrics Review*, 12.

Seeking innovation (2017, December).

Seeking innovation (2017, December). *Specialty Fabrics Review*, 10.

Self-heating jackets, for the gold. (2018, April). *Specialty Fabrics Review*, 10.

Seshadri, R. (2018, July). Active and smart. *Specialty Fabrics Review*, 54-57.

Sherburne, C. (2019, July/August). The new digital world: Color management challenges. *AATCC Review, 19*(4), 34-43.

Sleek styling for space (2017, April). *Specialty Fabrics Review*, 8-9.

Socks with sense (2018, July). *Specialty Fabrics Review*, 14.

Space blankets (2017, December). *Specialty Fabrics Review*, 10.

Teamwork: Matching thread, needle and tension. (2016, January). *Specialty Fabrics Review*, 47-49.

Timeless shade (2018, April). *Specialty Fabrics Review*, 2.

Tornquist, S. (2016, April). Innovation on the water. *Specialty Fabrics Review*, 40-45.

True performance: Wearable intuition (2016, October). *Specialty Fabrics Review*, 14.

What t-shirts may come… (2016, February). *Specialty Fabrics Review*, 13.

Wojciechowska, I. (2018). Challenges in moisture management testing. *AATCC Review, 18*(2), 30-35.

Wright, B. N. (2018, July) Our bodies, our structures. *Specialty Fabrics Review*, 46-53.

PRACTICE ACTIVITIES

1. Explore various possibilities of using textiles beyond apparel and accessories.
2. What do you see as the future of integrating textile technology and apparel design?
3. Select one existing apparel and explore to make it more functional and aesthetically pleasing by changing the use of textiles.
4. What is the role of cross-application in the textile world?
5. What is the role of nonwoven in the world of woven and knitted textiles?
6. Review latest textile publications to identify innovative textiles for multiple end-uses.
7. What is the role of antimicrobial finishes in today's lifestyle?
8. Which finishes are used for enhancing the aesthetic appeal of the textile?
9. Where do you use the phase changing materials in everyday life? Provide concrete examples.
10. What should be changed in athletic apparel to enhance comfort and effectiveness for competitive sports?
11. What is the role of moisture barrier clothing in everyday life for different age groups?
12. How has the use of nonwovens influenced the apparel industry?
13. What can the textile industry do to improve the function for outdoor apparel?
14. What role has NASA played to enhance comfort and convenience for the common consumer?
15. What do moisture management and wicking of textiles do for the consumer?
16. List some examples of using textiles in the forensic testing.
17. Explore sources and process of stain removal.
18. How has use and measurement of color changed in the last five years?
19. Write three changes in textiles brought by the finishes in the textiles.
20. What role does textiles play in the life of marines?
21. What changes have been brought in the textiles of military uniforms in the past five years?
22. Provide five examples of smart textiles.
23. What role does textile play in space travel? Provide a couple examples.
24. Provide one example each for the use of textile on earth, in water, and in space? Identify some similarities and differences.

25. Is the fabric below woven, nonwoven, or knitted? Provide rationale for your choice.

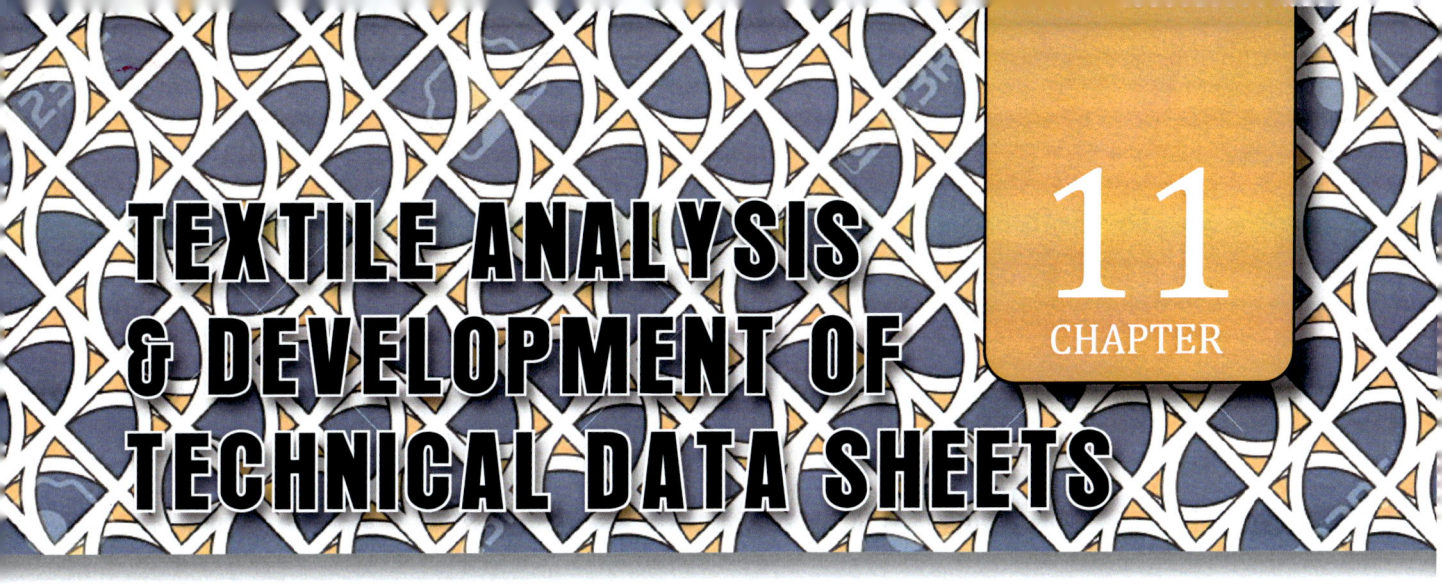

TEXTILE ANALYSIS & DEVELOPMENT OF TECHNICAL DATA SHEETS

11 CHAPTER

This chapter focuses on the formatting of providing succinct information about the tested textile materials for the company's decision-makers. The first section will provide worksheets of examples for necessary tests for different end-uses. The second section will provide examples of data sheets with various end-uses. Textile analysis generates data for making educational guesses for selected end uses and offers quality assurance through standardized indicators. Textile Data Sheet (TDS) gives abstracted information on structural and performance attributes of the textile material (Chowdhary, 2009). The idea of developing the Technical Data Sheet came from the author's visit to Southern Mills that provided educational materials to the visiting delegates for their product. TDS serves as an efficiency tool for decision-making by the higher-level executives of the company who may not be familiar with the academic lingo and processes of textile testing and quality control.

Textile projects can be designed for testing fabrics to determine appropriateness for their possible end-uses. Or one can buy ready-to-wear (RTW) apparel and test them for appropriate performance attributes using the performance criteria provided by the *Annual Book of Standards* (2019, and 2020). Chowdhary and Mathews (2018) Two examples of designing such projects are provided following the worksheets. Project sequence and details are provided in table 30. Table 31 offers the writing format.

Table 30: Fabric Analysis Sequence[a].

#	Description
1	Identify the end-use.
2	Select five structural and five performance tests relevant for the selected end-use and/or availability of the equipment for those tests.
2	Purchase the fabric to be used for the chosen end-use based on the structural and performance tests to be performed.
3	Perform the standardized tests using AATCC/ASTM/ISO manuals.

#	Description
4	Make sure that you cut at least 2.5" from the selvage from both sides of the fabric. It will reduce the fabric width by 5". Selvage is excluded to fairly represent the fabric because the selvage is made from more closely woven fabric than the rest of the material.
5	Use the permanent marker for marking the specimens for all selected tests. You must mark lengthwise grainline on each specimen before cutting it. It is good to develop a fabric layout for all tests for enhanced efficiency.
6	Cut the marked specimens and place them in the environment chamber for conditioning as per ASTM D1776.
7	Complete tests and record data using the standardized procedures.
8	Compare your results against the ASTM Manual standards to pass or fail the fabric.
9	Pass or fail the fabric for each performance test and classify for the structural test.
10	Write a report using categories provided in Table 31.

[a] Repeat the process for each fabric of the garment. As an example, for a lined garment complete the process for lining and interfacing/interlining also.

Table 31: Format for the written fabric analysis project. [b]

#	Description
1	Introduction: Purpose and significance
2	Literature Review
3	Selection of tests and Rationale
4	Methodology: Test Descriptions; Fabric layout for the chosen tests
5	Results and Discussion: Comparison charts for lined garments, Technical Data Sheet (TDS), and Comparison of results with literature review
6	Summary and Conclusions
7	Future Recommendations: Possibilities of extension
8	References: Appropriate depth and format on the list; and documentation in the text.
9	Grammatical Structure: Correct grammar; clear and concise expression.
10	Include tested specimens in the Appendix and refer to them in the text.

[b] Use comparison charts when testing for the lined garments and provide the compatibility statement and final decision.

Oral presentation rubric includes six sections: Motivation, presentation, content, audiovisual sources, responsiveness, and overall, impression. Make sure that you cover all the six categories optimally for full credit. Table 32 shows the requirements of the oral presentation with additional details for each category. It is critical that you are clear about the test numbers to be used for different tests, number of specimens and their dimensions. It assists the tester with making decisions about the purchase of the fabric as well as ensure that all tests are covered. Table 33 provides dimensions of different tests that were selected for testing the Jeans fabric. Figure 69 provides the fabric layout for the five structural and 5 performance tests.

Table 32: Presentation Format

#	Description
1	Motivation: Interest generated and reflected in the topic.
2	Presentation: Audibility, clarity, confidence, eye-contact, and logical order.
3	Content: Well focused, researched, and organized. Added to the information presented by the instructor.
4	Audiovisual Use: Sources well selected, prepared and executed; reflective of thinking and time; and supplemented the content.
5	Responsiveness: Motivated to ask questions; and responded accurately, confidently, and intelligently.
6	Overall Impression of content and method.

The fabric layout ensures that a number of specimens are clearly shown along with the lengthwise grainline marked on each of them. The bias-cut direction is shown by the diagonal lines. Fabric layout can be made at 1/5, 1/5, or ¼ scale. This exercise will help you with determining the material required for testing purposes. Invariably, fabric stores do not cut fabric on the straight of the grain. It is advised to add extra length to accommodate for the fabric loss from this practice.

Table 33: Specimens' details for the selected structural (S) and Performance (P) tests. tests.

#	Name	Test #	# of Specimens	Specimen Dimensions
1	Fabric Count (S)	ASTM D3775 – 2017	5 in warp and 5 in weft directions	1" x 1"
2	Fabric Weight (S)	D776/3776M -2020	5	5" x 5"
3	Weave Identification (S)			
4	Yarn Size (S)	ASTM 6612-2016	5 or 10	One meter in warp and text (Multiply x 1000 for Tex and 9000 for Denier)

#	Name	Test #	# of Specimens	Specimen Dimensions
5	Bow and Skew (S)	ASTM D-3990-12 (Reapproved in 2020).	1	Whole width and length without selvages
6.	Abrasion Resistance	ASTM 3884-09 (Reapproved 2017)	5 Face-up 5 Face down	6" x 6"
7.	Appearance Retention (P)	AATCC TM 124-2018t	3	15" x 15" (Woven)
8.	Breaking strength (P)	ASTM D5034 – 2017	Warp 2, 5, 10 Weft 2, 5, 10	6"x4" 4"x6"
9.	Colorfastness to crocking (P)	AATCC- TM8 -2016e	2 bias-cut	2" x 5.1"
10	Dimensional stability (P)	AATCC TM135-2018 t	3	15" x 15" (Woven)

Sources:
2020 *Annual Book of Standards* (2020). *7.01*. West Conshohocken, PA: ASTM International.
2019 *Annual Book of Standards* (2020). *7.02*. West Conshohocken, PA: ASTM International.

If the fabric width of both fashion fabric and lining is similar, the same layout can be used. One of the goals of having the layout is to create a blueprint that takes care of all the testing specimens and make best use of the fabric dimensions. For example, if you will replace dimensional stability and appearance retention with pilling resistance and wrinkle recovery, you will require much less length of the fabrics. Likewise, if fabrics width will be more than 45", you will require less length. You may need to reorganize the specimen's layout though. You may need more length if the fabric will be 36".

Chowdhary and Matthews (2018) found that structurally, cotton and acetate were not compatible with each other. One was a staple fiber and the other one was filament and regenerated fiber even though both were cellulosic in origin. For performance, lining failed appearance retention, dimensional stability, and tear strength tests but fashion fabric passed them. The first two could be managed via dry cleaning and ironing. However, tear resistance could not be managed. Despite the perceived similarity based on the structural performances, two fabrics were not compatible to be used together.

Table 34 shows an example of a Technical Data Sheet with five structural and five performance attributes. Data in table 34 suggest that the chosen fabric is a poly/cotton blend with plain weave, light weight, and high fabric count structurally. Regarding performance attributes, it passes for appearance retention, colorfastness to crocking, dimensional stability, pilling resistance, and tensile/breaking strength. Overall, the decision is to pass the fabric for its intended end-us. It is worth noting when warp and weft strengths were above and below the standard, one should take the mean for decision-making.

Textile Analysis & Development of Technical Data Sheets

Figure 69: Fabric layout for jeans' textile testing.

Scale: 1/10   Length = 45" + ¼ yard   Width = 40"

Structural Attributes

1. Bow and Skew: Entire length and width
2. Fabric Count: (5) 1"x1"
3. Fabric Weight: (5) 5"x5"
4. Weave identification: (1) 1" x1"
5. Yarn Size: (10) 1 meter in warp

Performance Attributes

6. Abrasion Resistance: 6"x6" (5)
7. Appearance Retention: 15"x15" (3)
8. Breaking Strength: 6" x 4" (5 in warp)
   4" x 6" (5 in weft)
9. Colorfastness to Crocking: 2"x5" on bias as well as weft (2)
10. Dimensional Stability: Use from Appearance Retention – (15"x15")

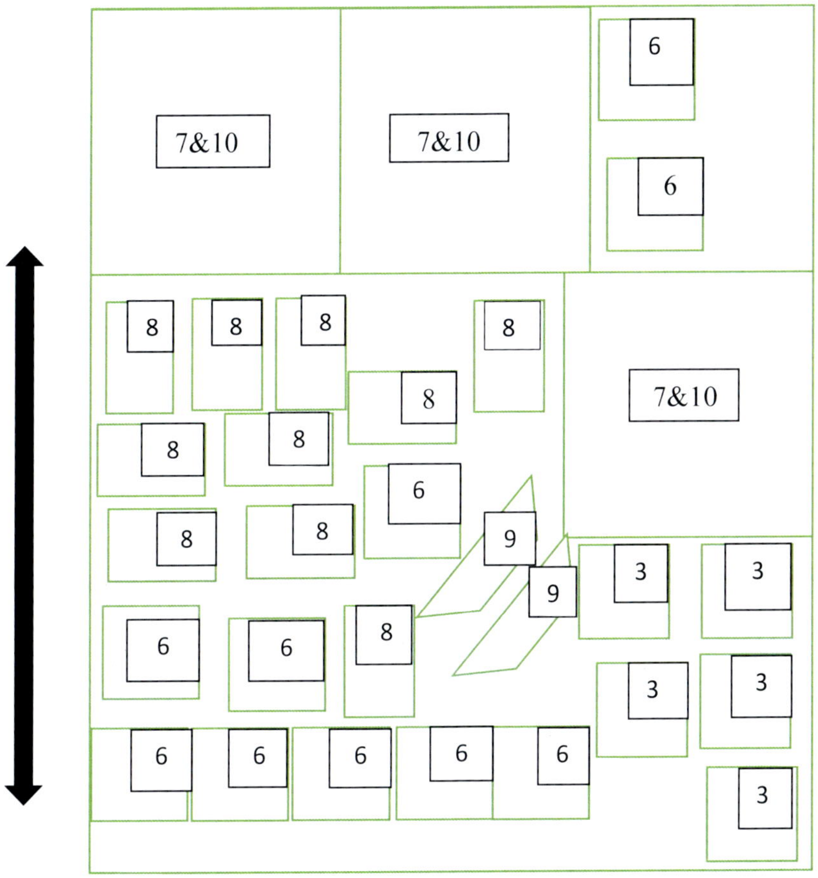

Table 34: An example of TDS for unlined dress.

UC Industries
Technical Data Sheet
Fashion Fabric
Structural Attributes

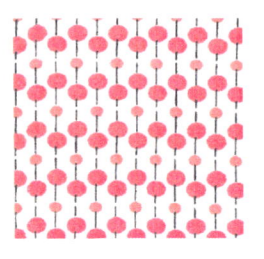

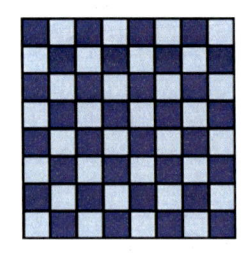

| Fabric Specimen | Plain Weave: 1x1 Weave |

Skew: 2% (Passes); Standard: 2.5% maximum

Fabric Weight: 2.98 oz./yd^2, Light

Fabric Count: 116x86=202, High

Fiber Content: 65% polyester, 35% cotton

Performance Attributes

Attribute	Standard	Performance	Decision
Dimensional Stability	3%	0.83%	Passes
Appearance Retention	≥3.5	4	Passes
Tensile Strength	50 lb./inch^2	Dry Warp 76.055	Passes
		Wet Warp 82.74	Passes
		Dry Weft 42.654	Approaches
		Wet Weft 47.864	Approaches
Pilling Resistance	≥4	5	Passes
Colorfastness to			
Crocking: Staining	≥4	4	Passes
Shade Change	≥4	5	Passes

Overall Decision: Passes

Table 35: TDS for lined dress.

G & H Labs
Technical Data Sheet
Lined Skirt: $4.00/Yard
Structural Attributes

Attribute	Fashion Fabric	Standard/ Classification	Decision	Lining	Classification	Decision
Bow	2.47%	2% maximum	Fails Compatible	2.57%	2% maximum	Fails Compatible
Fabric Count	87x63= 150	High	Compatible	107x81=188	High	Compatible
Fiber Content	100% Polyester	Strong	Compatible	100% Polyester	Strong	Compatible
Weave	Plain	1x1	Compatible	Plain	1x1	Compatible
Yarn Size	Warp Weft	Fine Medium	Compatible	Warp Fine Weft Fine	Optimum	Compatible

Performance Attributes

Attribute	Fashion Fabric	Standard	Decision	Lining	Standard	Decision
Colorfastness to Crocking	Staining 5 Shade 5	4 4	Passes Compatible	Staining 5 Shade 5	4 4	Passes Compatible
Dimensional Stability	0%	3% maximum	Passes Compatible	0%	3% maximum	Passes Compatible
Fabric Hand Smoothness Softness Warmth	5.6 5.9 5.5	9-Point Scale Little over neutral	Passes	8.0 7.2 5.1	9-Point Scale Smoother and softer than the fashion fabric	Passes and Compatible
Solubility	Acetone Bleach	Unaffected	Passes Compatible	Acetone Bleach	Unaffected	Passes Compatible
Wrinkle Recovery	5	3.5 Minimum	Passes	2	3.5 Minimum	Fails Needs Ironing

Final Decision: Pass and Compatible (Lining needs ironing)

Included with permission from Armine Ghalachyan as an example of a completed project.

Table 35 provides TDS for a lined skirt from 100% polyester for both fashion fabric and the lining. Data reveal that both fashion fabric and lining are compatible for the structural attributes. For performance attributes, the two fabrics are compatible for all the selected attributes except for the wrinkle recovery. Lining will need to be ironed for becoming compatible with the fashion fabric even though both fabrics are polyester.

Figure 36 shows an example of lined suit made from line fashion fabric and polyester lining. Structurally, they are compatible for all the selected attributes. Performance wise, fashion fabric fails for the dimensional stability and lining for wet staining. They are compatible for breaking strength, elongation, and appearance retention. Using dry cleaning for care over laundering will resolve the problem of shrinkage as well as wet staining. Overall, the decision could be to go for dry cleaning or preshrinking the fashion fabric and use colorfast colors for the lining.

Tables 37-47 provide worksheets for eleven different end-uses. You can test the performance of those for better understanding than without this exercise. Those end-uses are woven swimwear fabrics (Table 37), woven sportswear for women (Table 38), woven dry cleanable coats for women and girls (Table 39), as well as for men's and boys' (Table 40), umbrella fabrics (Table 41), seamless knitted fabrics (Table 42), rainwear (Table 43), knitted swimwear fabrics (Table 44), knitted career vocational apparel (Table 45), knitted career dress apparel (Table 46) and lining (Table 47).

Textile Analysis & Development of Technical Data Sheets

Table 36: TDS for lined woolen suit with polyester lining

SU Fashions
Technical Data Sheet
Lined Suit: $50/Yard (Fashion Fabric) & Lining ($ 9.99/yard)
Structural Attributes

Attribute	Fashion Fabric	Standard/ Classification	Decision	Lining	Classification	Decision
Yarn Size	16 Tex	Medium	Compatible	9 Tex	Fine	Compatible
Fabric Count	100 x60=160	High	Compatible	130x100=230	High	Compatible
Fiber Content	100% Linen	Strong	Compatible	100% Polyester	Strong	Compatible
Weave	Plain	1x1	Compatible	Plain	1x1	Compatible
Bow/skew	1.5% skew	2.5% Maximum	Passes Compatible	0.5% Bow	2% Maximum	Passes Compatible

Performance Attributes

Attribute	Fashion Fabric	Standard	Decision	Lining	Standard	Decision
Colorfastness to Crocking	Wet-Staining 3 Shade 5	3 4	Passes, Not Compatible	Wet Staining 2 Shade 5	3 4	Fails for wet staining Passes, Not Compatible
Dimensional Stability	6%	3% maximum	Fails Not Compatible	0.5%	3% maximum	Passes Compatible
Breaking Strength	57.34 psi	≥50 psi	Passes and Compatible	70.35 psi	≥25psi	Passes and Compatible
Elongation	5%	≥5%	Passes Compatible	5%	≥5%	Passes Compatible
Appearance Retention	4	3.5 Minimum	Passes and Compatible	4	3.5 Minimum	Passes and Compatible

Final Decision: Pass and Compatible (If Dry cleaned)

Table 37: Worksheet for woven swimwear fabrics.

Worksheet for Woven Swimwear Fabrics
(ASTM D3994 - 2014)

Enter Price:
Structural Attributes
Fabric Weight:
Fabric Thickness
Fabric Count:
Fiber Content

Fabric Construction   Fabric Specimen

Attribute	Standard	Fabric Value	Decision
Dimensional Change			
Laundering	3% Maximum		
Dry Cleaning	2% Maximum		
Bursting/Breaking Strength	≥ 30psi (Non-stretch)		
	≥ 20psi (Stretch)		
Tear Strength	≥ 1.5 psi		
Colorfastness			
Dry	≥4		
Wet	≥3		
Staining	≥3		
Lighting	≥4		

Overall Conclusion:

Table 38: Worksheet for women's sportswear fabrics.

Worksheet for Women's Sportswear Fabrics
(ASTM D4155-14)

Enter Price:
Structural Attributes
Fabric Weight:
Fabric Thickness
Fabric Count:
Fiber Content

Fabric Construction   Fabric Specimen

Attribute	Standard	Fabric Value	Decision
Dimensional Change			
Laundering	3% Maximum		
Dry Cleaning	2% Maximum		
Tensile Strength	Warp Worsted 35 psi min.		
	Weft worsted 30 psi min.		
	Woolen 20 psi min.		
Tear Strength	≥ 2 psi		
Colorfastness			
Dry	≥ 4		
Wet	≥ 4 for most		
Wet Laundering	≥ 3		
Lighting	≥ 4		
Fabric Smoothness	≥ 3.5		

Overall Conclusion:

Table 39: Worksheet for woven dry cleanable coat fabric for women's and girls'

Worksheet for Dry Cleanable Coat fabric
(ASTM D3562-14)

Enter Price:
Structural Attributes
Fabric Weight:
Fabric Thickness
Fabric Count:
Fiber Content

Fabric Construction   Fabric Specimen

Attribute	Standard	Fabric Value	Decision
Dimensional Change			
Dry Cleaning	2% Maximum shrinkage, 0% growth		
Breaking Strength	$\geq$ 30psi		
Colorfastness			
Shade Change	≥ 4		
Staining	≥ 3		
Lighting	≥ 4		
Fabric Appearance	≥ 4		

Overall Conclusion:

Table 40: Worksheet for woven dry cleanable coat fabric for men's and boys'

Worksheet for Woven Dry Cleanable Coat Fabric
for Men's & Boys'
(ASTM D3562-14)

Enter Price:
Structural Attributes
Fabric Weight:
Fabric Thickness
Fabric Count:
Fiber Content

Fabric Construction   Fabric Specimen

Attribute	Standard	Fabric Value	Decision
Dimensional Change			
Dry Cleaning	2% Maximum Shrinkage and 0% Growth		
Breaking Strength	$\geq$ 30psi		
Colorfastness			
Dry	≥ 4		
Wet	≥ 3.5		
Lighting	≥ 4		
Fabric Appearance	≥ 4		

Overall Conclusion:

Table 41: Worksheet for umbrella fabrics.

Worksheet for Umbrella
(ASTM D4112- 02)

Enter Price:
Structural Attributes
Fabric Weight:
Fabric Thickness
Fabric Count:
Fiber Content

Fabric Construction   Fabric Specimen

Attribute	Standard	Fabric Value	Decision
Dimensional Change			
Laundering (5 washes)	5% Maximum		
Dry Cleaning	2% Maximum		
Bursting Strength	≥ 50psi		
Colorfastness			
Dry	≥4		
Wet	≥4		
Lighting	≥4		
Water Resistance	2' 30 second shower		
	2' two-minute rain		
	3' three min. storm		
Water Repellency	Original Smooth (90 min.)		
	Original Rough (80 min.)		
	After Laundering (70 for both)		
Fabric Smoothness	≥ 3.5		

Overall Conclusion:

Table 42: Worksheet for seamless knitted fabrics.

Worksheet for Seamless Knitted Fabrics
(ASTM D7268 - 2014)

Enter Price:
Structural Attributes
Fabric Weight:
Fabric Thickness
Fabric Count:
Fiber Content

Fabric Construction   Fabric Specimen

Attribute	Standard	Fabric Value	Decision
Dimensional Change			
Laundering	5% Maximum		
Dry Cleaning	3% Maximum		
Bursting Strength	$\geq$ 30psi		
Colorfastness			
Dry	≥ 4		
Wet	≥ 3		
Staining	≥ 3		
Lighting	≥ 4		

Overall Conclusion:

Table 43: Worksheet for rainwear.

Worksheet for Rainwear
(ASTM D7017-14)

Enter Price:
Structural Attributes
Fabric Weight:
Fabric Thickness
Fabric Count:
Fiber Content

Fabric Construction   Fabric Specimen

Attribute	Standard	Fabric Value	Decision
Dimensional Change			
Laundering (5 washes)	5% Maximum		
Dry Cleaning	2% Maximum		
Bursting Strength	$\geq$ 50psi		
Colorfastness			
Dry	$\geq$4		
Wet	$\geq$4		
Lighting	$\geq$4		
Water Resistance	2' 30 second shower		
	2' two-minute rain		
	3' three min. storm		
Water Repellency	Original Smooth (90 min.)		
	Original Rough (80 min.)		
	After Laundering (70 for both)		

Overall Conclusion:

Table 44: Worksheet for knitted swimwear fabrics.

Worksheet for Knitted Swimwear Fabrics
(ASTM D3996 - 2014)
Enter Price:
Structural Attributes

Fabric Weight:
Fabric Thickness
Fabric Count:
Fiber Content

Fabric Construction   Fabric Specimen

Attribute	Standard	Fabric Value	Decision
Dimensional Change			
Laundering (5 washes)			
Non stretch	5% Maximum		
Stretch	7.5% Maximum		
Wet Growth	10% Maximum		
Dry Growth	7% Maximum		
Bursting Strength	$\geq$ 30psi		
Colorfastness			
Dry	≥ 4		
Wet	≥ 3		
Lighting	≥ 4		

Overall Conclusion:

Table 45: Worksheet for knitted career dress apparel.

Worksheet for Knitted Career Vocational Apparel
(ASTM D3995 - 2014)
Enter Price:
Structural Attributes

Fabric Weight:
Fabric Thickness
Fabric Count:
Fiber Content

Fabric Construction　　　　　　　　　　　　　Fabric Specimen

Attribute	Standard	Fabric Value	Decision
Dimensional Change			
Laundering (5 washes)	3% maximum		
Dry Cleaning (3)	3% maximum		
Bursting Strength	≥ 60psi		
Colorfastness			
Dry	≥4		
Wet	≥3		
Lighting	≥4		
Fabric Appearance	≥3		

Overall Conclusion:

Table 46: Worksheet for knitted career dress apparel.

Worksheet for Knitted Career Dress Apparel
(ASTM D3995 - 2014)
Enter Price:
Structural Attributes

Fabric Weight:
Fabric Thickness
Fabric Count:
Fiber Content

Fabric Construction   Fabric Specimen

Attribute	Standard	Fabric Value	Decision
Dimensional Change			
Laundering (5 washes)	3% maximum		
Dry Cleaning (3)	3% maximum		
Bursting Strength	≥ 60psi		
Colorfastness			
Dry	≥4		
Wet	≥3		
Lighting	≥4		
Fabric Appearance	≥4		

Overall Conclusion:

Table 47: Worksheet for lining.

Worksheet for Lining
(ASTM D4114-14)
Enter Price:
Structural Attributes

Fabric Weight:
Fabric Thickness
Fabric Count:
Fiber Content

Fabric Weave		Fabric Specimen	
☐		☐	

Attribute	Standard	Fabric Value	Decision
Dimensional Change			
Laundering	3% maximum		
Dry Cleaning	2% maximum		
Tensile/Breaking Strength	≥25 psi		
Tear Strength	≥1.5 psi		
Colorfastness			
Dry	≥4		
Wet	≥3		
Lighting	≥4		
Fabric Appearance	≥3.5		

Overall Conclusion:

Summary

Use of TDS helps with getting the information organized in a succinct manner. It also allows the developers and users to focus on the most important fabric attributes for the end-uses for appropriateness and compatibility. TDS also allows for the leaders to cut the unnecessary jargon and make quick decisions based on the selected structural and performance attributes. For students, it allows them to rethink the criteria used to make decisions for different intended uses in the product development process. It is worth noting that the textile materials that look structurally alike, may not perform similarly for performance attributes for various reasons.

REFERENCES

Annual book of ASTM Standards (2020). *7.01*, West Conshohoken, PA: ASTM International.

Annual book of ASTM Standards (2019). *7.02*, West Conshohoken, PA: ASTM International.

Chowdhary, U. (2009). *Textile analysis, quality control, and innovative uses.* Deer Park, NY: LINUS.

Chowdhary, U., & Mathews, S. (2018). Textile analysis and interpretation for decision making. *Trends in Textile Engineering and Fashion Technology, 4*(1), 1-3.

Chapter 11

PRACTICE ACTIVITIES

1. *Compare the standards with readings and make the final decision to accept or reject the fabric for the t-shirts.*

Test	Standard	Your Reading	Decision
Bursting Strength	≥25 psi	22 psi	
Dimensional Stability	<5%	6%	
Appearance Retention	≥3.5	4	
Colorfastness to Laundering Shade Change Staining	≥4 ≥4	4 3	
Colorfastness to Crocking Dry Wet	≥4 ≥3	4 3	

Overall Decision and Rationale

2. *Compare the standards with readings and make the final decision to accept or reject the fabric for the sweatshirts.*

Test	Standard	Your Reading	Decision
Bursting Strength	≥25 psi	22 psi	
Dimensional Stability	<5%	6%	
Appearance Retention	≥3.5	4	
Colorfastness to Laundering Shade Change Staining	≥4 ≥4	4 3	
Colorfastness to Crocking Dry Wet	≥4 ≥3	4 3	

Overall Decision and Rationale

Textile Analysis & Development of Technical Data Sheets

3. *Compare the standards with readings and make the final decision to accept or reject the fabric for the knitted overcoats and jackets.*

Test	Standard	Your Reading	Decision
Bursting Strength	≥70 psi	58 psi	
Dimensional Stability	<3%	4%	
Colorfastness to Laundering Shade Change Staining	 ≥4 ≥4	 4 3	
Colorfastness to Crocking Dry Wet	 ≥4 ≥3	 4 3	

Overall Decision and Rationale

4. *Compare the standards with readings and make the final decision to accept or reject the fabric for rainwear.*

Dimensional Stability	<3%	2%	
Breaking Strength	≥40 psi	45 psi	
Appearance Retention	≥3.5	4	
Water Repellency Water Resistance	Original (Rough) 80 Original (Smooth) 90 After Laundering 70 2' 30 seconds Shower 2' 2 minutes Rain 3" 5 minutes Storm	100 80 70 27 seconds 2 minutes 3 minutes	
Colorfastness to Crocking	Dry ≥4 Wet ≥4		

Overall Decision and Rationale

Chapter 11

5. Compare the standards with readings and make the final decision to accept or reject the fabric for lining.

Test	Standard		Your Reading	Decision
Breaking Strength	≥25 psi		21 psi	
Dimensional Stability	<3%		2%	
Fabric Appearance	≥3.5		4	
Colorfastness to Perspiration	Dry Wet	≥4 ≥4	≥4 ≥3	
Tear Strength	≥1.5 psi		1.2 psi	
Colorfastness to Crocking	Dry Wet	≥4 ≥4	4 2	

Overall Decision and Rationale

6. Compare the standards with readings and make the final decision to accept or reject the fabric for the bathrobes.

Test	Standard	Your Reading	Decision
Breaking Strength	≥20 psi	22 psi	
Dimensional Stability	<3%	3.5%	
Appearance Retention	≥3.5	4	
Tear Strength	≥1.5 psi	2 psi	
Colorfastness to Crocking & Perspiration Dry Wet	 ≥4 ≥3	 4 3	

Overall Decision and Rationale

Textile Analysis & Development of Technical Data Sheets   247

7. *Compare the standards with readings and make the final decision to accept or reject the fabric for the woven neckties and scarfs.*

Test	Standard	Your Reading	Decision
Breaking Strength	≥20 psi	22 psi	
Dimensional Stability	<3%	3.5%	
Appearance Retention	≥3.5	4	
Tear Strength	≥1.5 psi	2 psi	
Colorfastness to Crocking & Perspiration	Dry ≥4 Wet >3	4 3	
Dimensional Stability to Dry Cleaning	≥2% No growth	1.5 0	

Overall Decision and Rationale

8. *Compare the standards with readings and make the final decision to accept or reject the fabric for the woven dry cleanable coat fabrics.*

Test	Standard	Your Reading	Decision
Breaking Strength	≥70 psi	68 psi	
Dimensional Stability Dry Cleaning	<2% in each Direction	1.5%	
Fabric Appearance	≥3.5	4	
Colorfastness to Laundering Shade Change Staining	 ≥4 ≥4	 4 3	
Colorfastness to Crocking Dry Wet	 ≥4 ≥3	 4 3	

Overall Decision and Rationale

9. Compare the standards with readings and make the final decision to accept or reject the fabric for the children's sleepwear.

Test	Standard	Your Reading	Decision
Breaking Strength	≥40 psi	40 psi	
Dimensional Stability	<3%	2.75%	
Appearance Retention	≥3.5	4	
Flammability	Char Length ≤ 7"	b.e.l.	
Colorfastness to Crocking Dry Wet	 ≥4 ≥3	 4 3	

Overall Decision and Rationale

10. Compare the standards with readings and make the final decision to accept or reject the fabric for the sweatshirts.

Test	Standard	Your Reading	Decision
Bursting Strength	≥25 psi	22 psi	
Dimensional Stability	<5%	6%	
Appearance Retention	≥3.5	4	
Colorfastness to Laundering Shade Change Staining	 ≥4 ≥4	 4 3	
Colorfastness to Crocking Dry Wet	 ≥4 ≥3	 4 3	

Overall Decision and Rationale

TEXTILE ANALYSIS: A SUMMATIVE RESERVOIR

CHAPTER 12

This chapter focuses on the question answer approach to allow for a summative reservoir for comprehensive review of the course. The intent was to develop questions that may be helpful with understanding the content and be able to apply in solving everyday problems. The questions are organized for fibers, yarns, fabrics, and special treatments.

A. FIBERS

Technical fiber is the basic unit of textiles with longer length than width that can range from centimeters/inches to kilometers and miles. Shorter fibers that are measured in inches or centimeters are called **staple** fibers. Most of the natural fibers except for silk are examples of staple fibers. The longer fibers that are measured in miles or kilometers are called **filaments**. Silk as well as all manmade fibers (regenerated as well as synthetic) are examples of this category. To take the advantage of the positive attributes, filaments are cut into staples.

Q1   What are five common examples of commonly used natural fibers by the consumer?

A   Bamboo, cotton, flax, silk, wool

Q2   Which of the five natural fibers listed above is a filament?

A   Silk

Q3   What is bamboo fiber known for the most?

A   Sustainable nature, and moisture management.

Q4   Where does cotton come from?

A   Seed

Q5   Which of the natural fibers come from stem?

A   Flax

Q6   What does an amorphous region do?

A.   Increases moisture absorption

Q7   What does crystallinity do?

A.   Increases strength

Q8   Does wool have higher crystallinity than polyester?

A   No

Q9   Which natural fiber has the highest level of crystallinity?

A.   Silk

Q10. Which of the natural fibers is likely to have the best insulation and why?

A   Wool because of its scales and medulla that hold still air.

Q11 Does cotton have higher wet strength than the dry one?

A   Yes!

Q12 Does wool have higher wet than dry strength?

A   No!

Q13 How can you use the knowledge of low wool strength in everyday wear?

A   Either dry flat or get it dry cleaned

Q14 Are natural fibers more biodegradable than the synthetic fibers?

A   Yes

Q15 Which silk is the smoothest: Raw or cultivated?

A   Cultivated

Q16 Is the hair removal process from sheep for wool painful for the animal?

A   No! Hair is made of dead cells. The removal does not hurt the animal if done properly.

Q17 What are three regenerated fibers?

A   Rayon, Acetate, and Lyocell.

Q18 Which of the three regenerated fibers is like cotton and why?

A   Rayon! It has good absorbency and poor wrinkling tendency like cotton and flax. It burns like other cellulosic fibers too.

Q19 Which of the three regenerated fibers is like synthetics and why?

An   Acetate. It melts at high temperatures.

Q20 Where is Lyocell used?

A   It is used for apparel and window treatments. It is cheaper than rayon, and blends well with wool and cotton.

Q21 What are the most common uses of Acetate?

A   Dresses and lining

Q22 Why has acetate been used for linings for the longest time?

A   The slipperiness provided by acetate makes the donning and doffing of lined garments easier than its absence.

Q23 What are the names of four most used synthetics?

A   Acrylic, nylon, olefin, and polyester.

Q24 Which fiber content was used for the space suit of Apollo 11 astronauts?

A   Fiber glass and Teflon.

Q25 Which of the natural fiber has the best flame resistance?

A   Wool

Q26 Which of the natural fibers has the best absorbency?

A   Cotton and Linen

Q27 Which of the natural fiber has the best wrinkle resistance due to its resiliency?

A   Wool

Q28 Which of the manufactured fibers have strong abrasion resistance?

A   Nylon, olefin, and polyester

Q29 Which of the manufactured fibers have strong sun resistance?

A   Acrylic and Modacrylic

Q30 Which of the manufactured fibers have strong sun resistance?

A   Nylon and Spandex

Q31 Which of the manufactured fibers have an excellent flame resistance?

A   Aramid and Modacrylic

Q32 Which of the manufactured fibers have an excellent absorbency?

A Rayon and Lyocell

Q33 What does crimp do in a fiber?

A impacts the contour

Q34 Which chemical damages acetate the most?

A Acetone

Q35 Which chemical damages wool the most?

A Alkali like bleach

Q36 Which chemical damages silk the most?

A Alkali like bleach

Q37 What is the term used for the silk made from two cocoons?

A Dupioni

Q38 Name two wild silks.

A Taser and Tussah

Q39 Which process improves the drape of silk?

A Weighting to restore the weight lost during the degumming process of wool.

Q40 Is weighting used for the raw silks?

A No

Q41 Which of the fibers are wet spun?

A Acetate, rayon, spandex

Q42 Which of the fibers are dry spun?

A Acetate, acrylic, modacrylic, spandex

Q43 Which of the fibers are melt spun?

A Nylon, olefin, polyester, saran

Q44 Which of the fibers is solvent spun?

A Lyocell

Q45 Which special-use fiber stretches the most?

A   Elastomeric

Q46 Which category of fibers does Lycra belong to?

A   Spandex

Q47 What is the most popular use of Kevlar?

A   Bullet Proof Vests

Q48 What is the most popular use of Nomex?

A   Firefighter's clothing

Q49 What does the use of carbon do in polyester?

A   Enhances absorbency

Q50 How can you strengthen the weak fibers?

A   By blending them with strong fibers

Q51 At what stage can you add color, optical brighteners, and other additives for the best results in synthetic fibers?

A   Solution Stage

Q52 Which stage of dyeing provides the most even distribution of color for the natural fibers?

A   Fiber Stage

Q53 Which stage of dyeing is most expensive for the natural fibers?

A   Fiber Stage

Q54 Which of the cross-sectional shapes of fibers reflects poor structure?

A   Serrated

Q55 Which of the cross-sectional shapes of fibers reflects poor structure?

A   Trilobal

Q56 Which of the cross-sectional shapes of fibers reflects fair structure?

A   Circular

Q57 What are the fibers with affinity for water called?

A.   Hydrophilic or hygroscopic

Q58 What are the fibers that do not absorb water called?

A Hydrophobic

Q59 What are the fibers that melt on application of heat called?

A Thermoplastic

Q60 Which other attributes are influenced by the absorbent fabrics?

A Body comfort, electrostatics charge, dimensional stability, stain removal, water repellency, and wrinkle recovery

Q61 Which fibers pill the most?

A Hydrophobic and staple lengths

Q62 Which fiber attribute impacts drape the most?

A Flexibility

Q63 What is a micro-fiber?

A When 9000 meters of length weighs less than one gram.

Q64 What does hollowness of the fibers impart to yarn or fabric?

A Better absorbency, bulk, and insulation as well as lighter weight

Q65 What are the fibers with affinity for oil called?

A Oleophilic

Q66 What is a micron?

A Just like macro is 10^6, micron is 10^{-6}

Q67 Where do we use micron?

A To measure diameter of fiber and infra-red rays

Q68 How do you express a Denier in the metric system?

A Weight in grams of 9 kilometers (km) of fiber or yarn, or g/9km

Q69 How do you express a Tex in the metric system?

A Weight in grams of 1 kilometer of fiber or yarn, or g/1km

Q70 How do you express a Decitex in the metric system?

A Weight in grams of 10 kilometers of fiber or yarn, or g/10km

Q71 How will you calculate denier per filament (dpf) for a 75deniers yarn with 15 filaments?

A   Divide the denier value with the number of filaments. In this case, it will be 5.

Q72 What is a polymer?

A   A long chain of monomers is called a polymer. It is created by the polymerization process.

Q73 What is felting?

A   Matting the fibers through exposure to higher temperature in the presence of moisture is called felting.

Q74 Which of the fiber properties affect the microbial resistance or activation the most?

A   Absorbency

Q75 What does the wicking in fibers help with the most?

A   Moisture management

Q76 What is the difference between elasticity and resilience?

A   Elastic fibers come back to their original form soon after the release of the stretch. However, the resilient fibers do so over time. Resiliency is also known as delayed elasticity.

Q77 Which of the natural fibers burn with a strong smell due to the presence of sulfur in its chemical structure?

A   Wool

Q78 Which natural fiber(s) is(are) damaged by the hydrochloric acid?

A   All cellulosic fibers and silk

Q79 Which synthetic fiber is damaged by the hydrochloric acid?

A   Nylon

Q80 Which fiber content is appropriate for lining?

A   Acetate, nylon, olefin, polyester

Q81 Which fiber content is used the most in RTW for lining?

A   Polyester and acetate

Q 82 What is sericulture?

A   Cultivating silkworm to produce silk

Chapter 12

Q83 What is the botanical name of cotton?

A Gossypium (Koe, 2007)

Q 84 What are some examples of the bast fibers?

A Flax, hemp, jute, and Ramie

Q85 What is retting?

A Separating fiber from the unusable parts of the stem.

Q86 What is the botanical name of silk?

A Linum usitatissimum (Koe, 2007)

Q87 Which two synthetic fibers have poor sensitivity to light?

A Acetate and Nylon

Q88 Which synthetic fibers are known for good sun and weather resistance?

A Acrylic, olefin, and polyester

Q89 What do you understand by the term moisture content?

A A ratio of difference between the oven dried and conditioned specimen to the conditioned weight represented in percentage.

Q90 What do you understand by the term moisture regain?

A A ratio of difference between the oven dried and conditioned specimen to the oven dried weight represented in percentage.

Q 91 Which of the moisture content and moisture regain is likely to have higher value and why?

A Moisture regain because the numerator will be the same for both, but denominator will be lower for the moisture regain.

Q92 How will you describe the 70/30 poly/cotton blend?

A 70% polyester and 30% cotton

Q93 How will you describe the 70/30 cotton/poly blend?

A 70% cotton and 30% polyester

Q94 How will you describe the 55/40/5 Rayon/Acetate/Spandex blend?

A 55% Rayon, 40% Acetate, and 5% Spandex.

Q95 What does addition of 5% spandex to denim do for the jeans?

A Adds to stretch and comfort

B. YARNS

Q96 What is a yarn?

A Yarn is created from twisting/crimping/combining more than one fiber or filaments.

Q97 What is a twist?

A Spiraling of natural fibers to create yarns

Q98 What is a S twist?

A Twisting of fibers for S configuration

Q99 What is a Z twist?

A Twisting of fibers for Z configuration

Q100 How would you determine the twist direction of a yarn?

A Through untwisting the yarn.

Q101 What is a single or spun yarn?

A Single or spun yarn is the result of the first twisting operation where two or more fibers are held together by some mechanism. Untwisting breaks the yarn and one can see fibrous structures at the broken edges.

Q103 What is a ply yarn?

A Ply yarn is the result of the second twisting operation where two single yarns are twisted together to create a yarn. Untwisting results in separation of single yarns. For example, a four-ply yarn shows four singles on untwisting.

Q104 How can you distinguish between a Z and S twist?

A If yarns separate when you untwist in the left direction (anticlockwise), it is Z twist. If they separate when untwisting in the right direction (clockwise), it is S twist.

Q105 What is the spinning process?

A It refers to the straightening and twisting of yarns.

Q106 What is a carded yarn?

A Carded yarn is a roughly twisted yarn.

Q107 What is carding?

A It is a process of aligning fibers into somewhat parallel form for the ease in spinning for creating a sliver.

Q108 What is combing?

A   It is a process to create high quality smooth staple yarn that removes all loose and short fibers from the carded yarns. Combed yarns create smoother and finer fabric than the carded yarns. Worsted yarns used for the men's suits are an example of combed yarns.

Q109 What is the difference between woolen and worsted yarns?

A   Woolen yarn is made of carded yarn, and the worsted yarn is made from the combed yarn.

Q110 What are filament yarns?

A   They are made from manufactured fibers and are much longer than the natural fibers with the exception of silk.

Q111 What are bulk Yarns?

A   They are produced to enhance cover, loftiness, and warmth.

Q112 What are the pinning processes used by the textile industry?

A   jet spinning, ring spinning, and rotor spinning

Q113 Which of the three listed in Q112, the most expensive?

A   Ring spinning

Q114 What is a blended yarn?

A   When two or more fiber contents are mixed in the spinning solution before extrusion to diffuse the original identity of each fiber content, it is called a blend.

Q115 What is a mixture?

A   When the original identity of each fiber content is retained. For example, the warp is polyester, and the weft is cotton.

Q116 What is the role of twist in determining the fabric quality?

A   It strengthens the textiles. To create a crepe effect, high and low twist yarns are used.

Q117 Which fabrics create power stretch?

A   Spandex used in active wear

Q118 What is the role of novelty yarns?

A   To provide decorative effect.

Q119 What is constant in the direct method of yarn numbering?

A   Length is constant, and weight varies.

Q120 What is constant in the indirect method of yarn numbering?

A   Weight is constant, and length varies.

Q121 What does increase in number represent in the direct system of yarn numbering?

A   Heavier or thicker yarn

Q122 What does decrease in number represent in the direct system of yarn numbering?

A   Finer and lighter yarn

Q123 What does increase in number represent in the indirect system of yarn numbering?

A   Finer and lighter yarn

Q124 What does decrease in number represent in the indirect system of yarn numbering?

A   Heavier and thicker yarn

Q125 What do you understand by the constant length in the Direct system?

A   1,000 meters for Tex, 9,000 meters for Denier, and 10,000 for Deci-Tex

Q126 What are the ranges in Deniers for fine, medium, and coarse yarns?

A   Fine (50-100), Medium (150-400), and coarse (500-2000)

Q127 Can one find conversions to different yarn size systems?

A   Yes! Refer to ASTM D#2260-03 (2013)

Q128 What is a sewing thread?

A   Sewing thread is the yarn that is created for stitching by hand and/or machine.

Q129 Do sewing threads have special finish to be effective?

A   Yes! They are made flame and heat resistant to prevent melting during high-speed industrial sewing.

Q130 Should one use different thread sizes for different end uses?

A   Yes! It should be 18-29 Tex for general apparel: 30-59 Tex for athletic wear, jeans and outerwear; 60-104 for overcoats, workwear, and footwear; and 105+ for luggage and golf bags (adapted from Cohen and Johnson, 2010).

Q131 What is a cord yarn?

A   It is created by twisting two or more ply yarns.

Q132 Where is the cord yarn used?

A Tie backs for drapes, sewing thread, and ropes in general

Q133 Where do we see a use of tweed yarn?

A Apparel, drapes, and upholstery

Q134 Where are the novelty yarns used the most?

A Apparel and furnishings.

Q135 What is the major strength of spun yarns?

A Warmth and absorbency

Q136 What is the major strength of smooth filament yarns?

A Coolness and strength

Q137 What do the bulk yarns offer?

A Strength and warmth

Q138 What is the major weakness of spun yarns?

A Soils easily

Q139 What is the major weakness of smooth filament yarns?

A May snag easily

Q140 What is the major weakness of bulk yarns?

A Likely to snag and soil easily

C. FABRICS

Q141 What is a fabric?

A It is produced by interlacing of yarns for woven fabrics, and inter-looping of yarns for the knitted fabrics. Nonwoven fabrics are made by bonding mechanically, felting, melting, or fusing of fibers as fusible and non-fusible fabrics,

Q142 What is weaving?

A It is a process of interlacing warp and weft yarns at right angles to create a fabric.

Q143 What is warp?

A The lengthwise yarns in a fabric are called the warp yarns. They run parallel to the selvage and are generally stronger than the weft yarns.

Q144 What is weft?

A The crosswise yarns in the fabric are called weft yarns. They run at right angle to the selvage and are generally weaker than the warp yarns.

Q145 What is a selvage?

A A selvage refers to the closely woven edges used to anchor the fabric during the weaving process. Selvage runs parallel to the lengthwise yarns of the fabric.

Q146 What are the three basic weaves?

A Plain, twill, and satin

Q147 Which of the three basic weaves has the highest tear strength?

A Satin weave

Q148 Which of the three basic weaves has the highest breaking strength?

A Twill weaves

Q149 Which of the three basic weaves is most likely to snag?

A Satin weave

Q150 Which of the three basic weaves is most likely to ravel easily?

A Satin (warp floats), Sateen (Weft floats)

Q151 Which of the three basic weaves is most likely to be the most lustrous one?

A Satin or Sateen

Q152 What are the units of fabric thickness?

A Millimeters or inches

Q153 What is the name of the instrument used for measuring fabric thickness?

A Anvil

Q154 How much pressure is applied on the fabric while measuring fabric thickness?

A One pound

Q155 What is fabric count?

A Yarns per inch

Q156 What is the relationship of fabric count to fabric quality?

A Higher the count, better the quality

Chapter 12

Q157 How is the fabric count measured?

A   It is measured with a linen tester, fabric counter or teasing out warp and weft yarns for one square inch in both warp and weft directions. For example, 90 x 60 = 150

Q158 What is the convention of reporting fabric count?

A   # od warp yarns x # of weft yarns = # od warp yarns + # of weft yarns: 100 x 60 = 160.

In this example, 100 represents the warp yarns that are listed first and 60 represents the weft yarns.

Q159 In which direction does the woven fabric stretch the most?

A   Bias cut (Warp and wet make an angle of 45 degrees).

Q160 What is the definition of a knitted fabric?

A   Fabric created by the inter-looping of yarns is called the knitted fabric.

Q161 In which direction does the weft knit stretch the most?

A   Crosswise except for the purl knit.

Q162 In which direction does the warp knit stretch the most?

A   Diagonal

Q163 What is the warp knit used for?

A   Baby blankets, lingerie, and slips

Q164 What is the main characteristic of a double-knit fabric?

A   It looks alike on both sides.

Q165 List some examples of double knits.

A   Interlock knit, rib knit, and purl knit

Q166 What is an interlock knit?

A   It looks the same on the back and front and is used for sportswear including t-shirts.

Q167 What is a pique knit?

A   It is a textured knit used for polo shirts. It is thicker than the jersey knit.

Q168 What is a wale?

A   A column of the knit stitches is called a wale.

Q169 What is a course?

A   A row of the knit stitches is called a course.

Q170 What is torque?

A   A bow or skew in the knitted fabrics is called a torque.

Q171 What is a bow?

A   It is a fabric defect and is reflected through a convex or concave structure created across the width of the fabric. It is more likely to happen in the synthetic than the natural fibers. It should be 2% maximum for the woven fabrics and 5% maximum for the knitted fabrics without any adverse effects.

Q172 What is a skew?

A   It is also a form of fabric defect. It occurs when warp and weft do not make an angle of 90 degrees. It is more likely to be seen in the natural fibers than the synthetic fibers. It can be corrected by pulling the fabric diagonally. It should be 2.5 or less for woven fabrics and 5% or less for the knitted fabrics to meet the ASTM standards.

Q173 Where can you find the standard terminology of the fabric defects?

A   ASTM D3990-12 (Reapproved in 2020)

Q174 What are some other examples of fabric defects other than the bow and skew?

A   Tear, stain, snag, slub, seam mark, run, broken filament etc.

Q175 What is the acceptable number of the penalty points for the first class woven fabrics with ≤50" width?

A   ≤ 41/100 yards

Q176 What is the acceptable number of the penalty points for the first class woven fabrics with ≥50" width?

A   ≤45/100 yards

Q177 What is the maximum bow percentage acceptable for the woven fabrics?

A   2% maximum

Q178 What is the maximum bow percentage acceptable for the knitted fabrics?

A   5% maximum

Q179 What is the maximum skew percentage acceptable for the woven fabrics?

A   2.5% maximum

Q180 What is the maximum skew percentage acceptable for the knitted fabrics?

A   5%

Q181 Which test # is used for the fabric count of the knitted fabrics?

A   ASTM D8007 – 15 (2019) Previously used 3887 was withdrawn in 2017.

Q182 Which test # is used for the fabric count of the woven fabrics?

A   ASTM D3775-2017

Q183 What is the test number or fabric thickness

A   ASTM D-1777 – 1996 (Reapproved 2019)

Q184 Which test # is used for the fabric weight?

A   ASTM D3776/3776M-2020

Q185 Which dyes are the best choice for the synthetic fibers?

A   Disperse

Q186 Which dyes are Which dyes are the best choice for the protein fibers?

A   Acid

Q187 Which dyes are the best choice for the cellulosic fibers?

A   Basic, direct, and reactive

Q188 What is the passing grade for colorfastness to dry crocking?

A ≥ 4

Q189 What is the passing grade for colorfastness to wet crocking?

A ≥ 3

Q190 What is the test # for colorfastness to crocking?

A   AATCC TM8 (2016e)

Q191 What is the test # for colorfastness to bleach?

A   AATCC 172-2007

Q192 What is the test # for colorfastness to the burnt gas fumes?

A   AATCC TM23-- 2015e, 2020

Q193 What is the test # for colorfastness to sea water?

A   AATCC TM106– 2009e, 2013e3

Q194 What is the test # for colorfastness to the chlorinated water?

A   AATCC 188-2010e3(2017) e

Q195 What is the passing grade for water repellency test based on the AATCC 1TM22, 2017e?

A   70 minimum

Q196 What is the commonly allowed dimensional stability to five launderings for most end uses?

A   3% maximum

Q197 What is the commonly allowed dimensional stability to three dry cleanings for most end uses?

A   2% maximum

Q198 What is the passing grade of moisture transfer based on AATCC TM79, 2010e2, 2018e?

A ≤ 5 seconds

Q199 What is the unit of measurement for the vertical wicking?

A   mm/second

Q200 What is the unit of measurement for the horizontal wicking?

A mm^2/second

Q201 What height is used for the water resistance test AATCC TM42, 2018e is used for

A   2-3 feet

Q202 Which test is used for colorfastness to light?

A   AATCC TM16.1, 2013e

Q203 Adding carbon in the uniforms of the hospitality workers decreases the development of the electrostatic charge.

A   True

Q204 Passing grade for appearance retention on the 5-point scale is _____.

A   3.5 or higher

Q205 What is the passing grade of tear strength for lining?

A   1.5 psi

Q206 What is the unit of tear strength?

A   pounds per square inch

Q207 What is the passing grade of breaking strength for lining?

A   25 psi

Q208 What is the unit of tear strength?

A   pounds per square inch

Q209 What is the unit of seam efficiency?

A   %

Q210 What is seam efficiency?

A   A ratio between the seam strength and fabric strength represented in percentage.

Q211 What is the passing grade of tear strength for fashion fabric?

A   2.5 psi minimum

Q212 What is the passing grade of breaking strength for fashion fabric?

A ≥ 50 psi

Q213 What is the passing grade of abrasion resistance for trousers by Taber methods?

A ≥ 750 cycles

Q214 What is the unit of abrasion resistance for trousers by Taber methods?

A   Cycles

Q215 What is weight or strength loss by the accelerotor method represented by?

A   %

Q216 What is the test standard for piling resistance that uses the random tumble pilling tester?

A   ASTM D3512/3512M – 2016

Q217 What is the passing grade for the pilling tests?

A ≥ 4

Q218 What is the unit of analysis for pilling resistance?

A   None

Q219 What is the rating scale of pilling resistance?

A   1-5

Q220 What is the unit of measurement for air permeability?

A   In inch-pound units as $ft^3/min/ft^2$ and SI units as $cm^3/s/cm^2$.

Q221 What did Ogulata (2006) find in his study?

A   Increase in fabric count decreased the air permeability.

Q222 What were the findings from Wroblewski (2017) for air permeability?

A   Findings revealed that three quilting structures did not differ for air permeability. Additionally, air permeability was not found to be related to fabric thickness and weight either.

Q223 What were the findings from Kundu and Chowdhary (2018) for air permeability?

A   Kundu and Chowdhary (2018) found that air permeability was highest for polyester followed by rayon and cotton. Spandex was common fiber content in all blends.

Q224 Will piles of towels enhance or lower the air permeability?

A   Lowered air permeability due to increased cover

Q225 What is the minimum percentage recommended by Chowdhary (2007, 2009) for elongation?

A   5% minimum

Q226 Do serged or unserged seams elongate more?

A   serged seams

Q227 Based on Chowdhary and Wentela's (2018) research, ___ fiber had the lowest elongation.

A   Linen

Q228 Based on Chowdhary and Wentela's (2018) research, acetate had higher elongation than polyester. Is it true or false?

A   False

Q229 Zaman, Mondal, & Saha (2017) reported that stretch of weft knit is influenced by fabric count, thickness, and weight. Is it true or false?

A   True

Q230 Based on Kundu and Chowdhary's (2018) study, fabric thickness was not related to stretch but fabric count was. Is it true or false?

A   True

Q231 Based on Kundu and Chowdhary's (2018) study, what was the % of recovery for rayon/spandex, polyester/spandex, and cotton/spandex?

A   Around 90%

Q232 Kavitha & Gokarneshan (2019) reported that engineered clothing can help with enhancing comfort for human beings in changing environments. Is it true or false?

A   True

Q233 Atasagun, Okur and Psikuta (2019) asserted that the raw material of the undershirt had higher impact on the chest and fit influenced back the most. Is it true or false?

A True

Q234 Based on the AATCC 93 standard, specimen size increases with decrease in the fabric weight. Is it true or false?

A True

Q235 Which tests standards are used for breaking strength?

A ASTM D5034 (2017) and ASTM D5035 (2017)

Q236 Picture below shows the set up for the breaking strength.

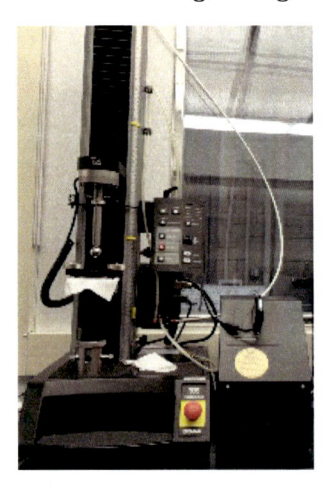

False

Q237 Based on the ASTM recommendation, what should be the minimum bursting strength of the knitted career and vocational dress?

A 60 psi

Q238 Based on the ASTM recommendation, what should be the minimum bursting strength of knitted swimwear?

A 30 psi

Q239 Based on the ASTM recommendation, what should be the minimum bursting strength of beachwear for boys?

A 25 psi

Q240 Based on the ASTM recommendation, what should be the minimum bursting strength of the seamless knitwear?

A 30 psi

Q241 Based on the ASTM recommendation, what should be the minimum bursting strength of the knitted overcoat and jackets?

A   70 psi

Q242 Based on the ASTM recommendation, what should be the minimum bursting strength of the knitted gloves?

A   50 psi

Q243 Increase of polyester content increased the bursting strength. Is it true or false?

A   True

Q244 Increase in stitch length, increased the bursting strength. Is it true or false?

A   False

Q245 Chowdhary, Adnan, and Cheng (2018) found that bursting strength was higher for the polyester/Spandex than the rayon/Lycra for interlock knits.

A   True

Q246 Chowdhary, Adnan, and Cheng (2018) found that bursting strength was the highest for the 60/40 cotton /polyester blend and the lowest for the Rayon/Lycra in jersey knits.

A   True

Q247 For Pique knits, cotton had higher bursting strength than polyester (Chowdhary, Adnan, and Cheng, 2018). Is it true or false?

A   False

Q248 What is the standard used for seam strength?

A   ASTM D1683/D1683M-17(2018)

Q249 What is the unit of seam strength?

A   psi

Q250 What is the unit for seam efficiency?

A   %

Q251 What is seam efficiency?

A   It is the ratio between seam strength and fabric strength represented in %.

Q252 Chowdhary and Poynor found that seam strength was the highest foe the stitch density of 10-12 and the lowest for 6-8 stitches per inch. Is it true or false?

A   True

Q253 Chowdhary (2009) found that stitch density impacted the seam strength.

A   True

Q254 Which three treatments of jeans did Chowdhary (2002) tested for seam strength?

A   Antique, sandblasted, and stonewashed

Q255 How many warp and weft yarns were used by Chowdhary in the 2009 study for 95% level of confidence?

A   Warp 34 and Weft 54

Q256 What concept is supported by the number of warp and weft yarns listed in question # 255?

A   You need less number in warp direction because they are stronger than the weft yarns.

Q257 Which structural attribute should you use to determine the number of warp and weft yarns needed for different confidence levels?

A   Fabric Count, Fabric Weight, and Yarn Size

Q258 What is the difference between the findings of Chowdhary (2009, Chowdhary and Wentela, 2018, and Chowdhary (2019) regarding the impact of interfacings on the strength of the fabric?

A   It showed impact in the 2009 study. However, it did not either have an impact or resulted in mixed results.

Q259 Does lining increase the strength of the fabric?

A   Based on Chowdhary (2009), Chowdhary and Wentela (2018), and Chowdhary 2019) lining did strengthen the strength of the fabric.

Q260 Based on Kang and Kim's (2001) study, Silicone treatment given to the woolen fabric, enhanced its tear strength. Is it true or false?

A   True

Q261 Eryuruk and Kalaoglu, 2018 reported that the tearing strength was higher for ribbed fabrics than plain fabrics. Is it false or true?

A   True

Q262 Eryuruk and Kalaoglu, 2018 reported that the fabrics with filament yarns had higher tearing strength than those with the textured yarns. Is it false or true?

A   True

Q263 How many launderings should the flame-resistant finishes last?

A   At least 50

Q264 Chang, Condon, and Nam (2020) found that casein coated flame-resistant fabrics can be used effectively for commercial and industrial use of textile materials.

A   True

Q265 Measuring smoothness/roughness of fabrics is an example of ____ ___.

A   Fabric Hand

Q266 What is dyeing?

A   It is the process of applying soluble color on textile materials.

Q267 At which stage of fabric construction the color should be added?

A   Solution, fiber, yarn, fabric, sewn garment

Q268 Even though the color could be added in several stages, which one gives the best results?

A   Solution for synthetic fibers and fiber stage for the natural fibers.

Q269 What is a resist dye?

A   When certain areas of the fiber, yarn, or fabric are blocked from receiving the color from the dye bath.

Q270 In how many ways can one create the resist dyeing?

A   Batik (Use wax for resist), and Tie-dye (using threads, stones, lentils, objects like paper clips and t-pins, as well as mashed potatoes and mud).

Q271 What is printing?

A   Application of color paste in certain localized areas or the entire fabric.

Q272 What are some examples of printing methods?

A   Block, discharge, heat transfer, inkjet, resist, roller, screen (flat + rotary) printing, and stencil

Q273 How do you differentiate dyed and printed fabrics?

A   Dyed fabric shows penetration of color on both front and back of the fabric. Printed fabric shows color darker on the face of the fabric than the back except for the duplex printing.

Q274 What are some color related problems in textile materials?

A   Bleeding, crocking, fume fading, light fading, and lack of colorfastness to crocking, laundering, perspiration, regular water, and sea water

Q275 What could be the cause for bleeding of color?

A   Incompatible choice of dye

Q276 What causes frosting and tendering?

A   Abrasion during wear and tear as well as care

Q277 What is out of register printing?

A   Poor alignment of screens results in non-matching of edges of the fabric.

Q278 What is off-grain printing?

A   When printing is not done on the straight of the grain. Lengthwise and/or crosswise lines of the yarn are not parallel to the lengthwise and/or crosswise lines of the print.

Q279 Do dyeing and printing processes impact the environment adversely?

A   Yes!

Q280 How can the adverse effects of dyeing/printing be mitigated?

A   Using natural gas, reusing dyeing water, use smaller amounts of chemicals, or using natural dyes. Using carbon dioxide for better fixation of dyes (Kadolph and Langford, 2002).

Q281 Which instrument is used to measure color?

A   Spectrophotometer

Q282 What is the range of colors in the rainbow in terms of nanometers?

A   40-700 nanometers

Q283 Which of the colors of rainbow has the shortest wavelength?

A   Violet

Q284 Which of the colors of rainbow has the longest wavelength?

A   Red

Q285 What are the primary colors based on the additive theory?

A   Red, Green, and Blue

Q286 What are the primary colors based on the subtractive theory?

A   Cyan, magenta, and Yellow

Q287 Which theory of color does television use?

A   Additive

Q288 Which theory of color is used by the Pantone?

A   Subtractive

Q289 How many hues does the Prang/Brewster system have?

A   12

Q290 How many hues does the Munsell system have?

A   10

Q291 Which values are used to calculate the ΔE values to determine color differences?

A   L*a*b*

Q292 What did the Islam and Chowdhary's (2019) study revealed for three different knits.

A   Adjustment had to be made for getting uniform color.

Q293 What did Islam (2020) found in his master's thesis?

A   Islam (2020) found that CIE L*a*b* values differed significantly based on the fabric structure, placement of dress form, light sources, and exposure time.

Q294 Colors red and green are complementary colors. Red is a warm color and green is _____ color.

A   Cool

Use the wheel below for questions 295-298.

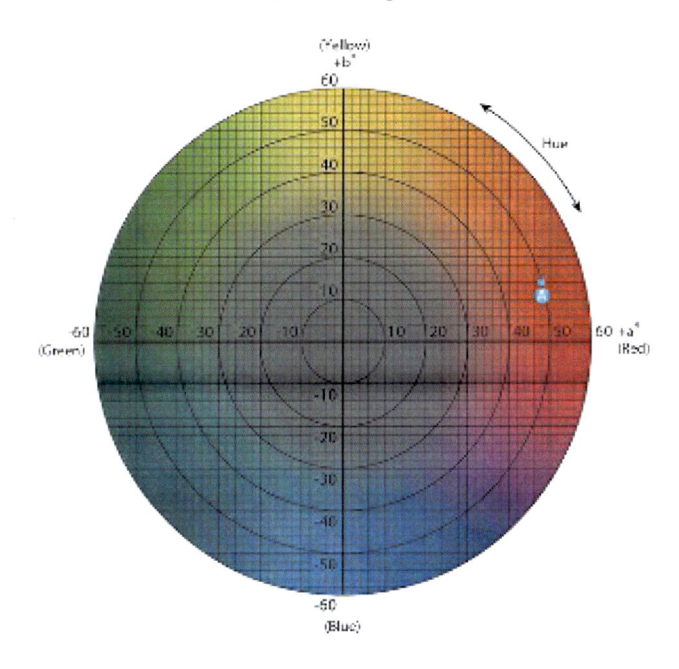

Q295 Based on the color wheel above the value of -30 on the yellow to blue continuum is more likely to be _____.

A   Bluish

Q296 Based on the color wheel above the value of +30 on the yellow to blue continuum is more likely to be _____.

A   Yellowish

Q297 Based on the color wheel above the value of +25 on green to e continuum is more likely to be _____.

A   Reddish

Q298 Based on the color wheel above the value of +25 on green to e continuum is more likely to be _____.

A   Greenish

Q299 What was the outcome of Adnan's (2018) study on color?

A   Green differed the most for two and three-dimensional forms for various body parts.

Q300 What did Chowdhary (2017) find about three red shirts?

A   All three brands of red t-shirts became lighter, less red, and less yellow based on the ΔE values.

Q301 What is metamerism?

A   Same color does not look the same under different lights.

Q302 What is typical about the fluorescent colors?

A   They reflect > 100% light.

Q303 Where can the fluorescent colors be used in apparel?

A   Where night-time visibility is of critical importance.

Q304 What is a light booth or box?

A   It is a small box with the ability to produce incandescent, fluorescent, and daylight.

Q305 What is cross dyeing?

A   Using one dye bath for two different fiber contents. Two fiber contents pick up different colors and create a shaded effect.

Q306 What is union dyeing?

A   A method of dyeing that uses the same color for two different fiber contents.

Q307 What is nanotechnology?

A   A process that changes the molecular structure of fibers to make them appropriate for a specific end use. Examples could be water repellent and stain repellent.

Q308 What are dry prints?

A   Heat-set prints that do not use any liquids.

Q309 What are wet prints?

A   Prints created from liquid dyes are called wet prints.

D. FINISHES/SPECIAL TREATMENTS

Q310 What is a finish?

A   A treatment given to the textile for enhancing its appearance, hand, and/or performance.

Q311 Which finishes are used to give soft hand to the fabrics?

A   Brushing, napping, and sueding

Q312 Which finish is used to give fabric a smooth wrinkle-free appearance?

A   Calendering

Q313 Which finish gives a watery appearance on the textile?

A   Moiré

Q314 Which finish creates a raise effect like the notary public's seal

A   Embossing

Q315 What do the optical brighteners do?

A   Enhance whiteness

Q316 Which finish is given to cotton for making it stronger and lustrous?

A   Mercerization

Q317 What is the name of the chemical used for mercerization?

A   Sodium Hydroxide

Q318 Which finishes are used to impact the drape of the fabric?

A   Parchmentization (Acid finish) and weighting of silk

Q319 Why is an enzyme treatment used on denim?

A   To create a worn-out look.

Q320 What methods are used to create a worn-out look?

A   stonewashed, sand-blasted, enzymes, and bleached

Q321 What is the difference between the progressive and relaxation shrinkage?

A   Progressive shrinkage represents the changes in dimensions in several successive launderings. Relaxation shrinkage results when the fabric is removed from the Tentering frames.

Q322 How can one control for the progressive shrinkage in synthetic fibers?

A   Heat setting

Q323 Which fiber content has the most progressive shrinkage?

A   Wool

Q324 How can progressive shrinkage be controlled in wool?

A   Treatment with polyamide film or chlorination

Q325 How can progressive shrinkage be controlled in rayon?

A   Treating the fabric with resins to reduce water absorption

Q326 How can cotton be made wrinkle-resistant?

A   By resin treatment

Q327 What is the most used method of making textiles stain and soil repellent, wash and wear and anti-slip?

A   Resin finishes

Q328 Are resin finishes durable?

A   Not always

Q329 Which treatment is used to make textiles stain and water-repellent?

A   Fluorocarbon (Poly Tetra Fluoro Ethylene)

Q330 Which metal has been used the most historically for the antimicrobial finish?

A   Silver

Q331 Why is cotton better than most synthetics for moisture management?

A   fabric thickness, and the ability to keep the wearer dry because of its ability to hold water.

Q332 Can synthetic fibers have higher wicking ability?

Yes! Microfibers are one such example.

A   Yes! Microfibers are one such example.

Textile Analysis: A Summative Reservoir

Q333 Which finish does MICROBAN represent?

A   Antimicrobial

Q334 What were the key findings of Easter (2004)?

A   Ironing enhanced smoothness, washing inside out as well as fabric softener improved the color retention and edge abrasion, and cold wash enhanced the color retention. She also found that the powder detergent performed better than the liquid detergent. Additionally, the pants with the fluorocarbon finish released most stains effectively. However, fabric softeners reduced stain repellency but enhanced the colorfastness.

Q335 How many launderings did the stain repellency treatment last in the Easter's study?

A   30

Q336 What was the water repellency rating after 20 washes in Easter's study?

A   80

Q337 How many washes did the oil repellency finish last in Easter's study?

A   20

Q338 What consumer demand did the fluorocarbon finish meet in Easter's study?

A   Comfortable feel, easy care, freshness, great appeal, and pleasant scent

Q339 What does Delcron® Hydrotec Fiber polyester staple fiber do?

A   It offers moisture management and comfort.

Q340 Which of the following are used to infuse the fabrics with essential oils for aromatherapy (West & Annett-Hitchcock, 2014)?

A   Microencapsulation, fragrance method, traditional pad method, and mixed habits.

Q341 Microencapsulation has been used to change color of textiles with change in temperature as well as aromatherapy infusion in textile materials. What is the main problem with this method?

A   Capsules do not rejuvenate after bursting and must be supplemented by alternate methods.

Q342 Shrimali and Dedhia (2015) talked about using encapsulation as what stage in textiles?

A   Finishing

Q343 What does the market for smart textiles amount for in 2021?

A $1.8 Billion

Q344 What are smart and interactive textiles?

A   Textiles that can sense the environmental stimuli and react by adapting.

Q345 Which of the following are the uses of nano-sensors as of January 2021?

A   Covid 19 infections, infection in wounds, preventing ulcers, recognizes hand gestures based on the electrical signals.

Q346 Who has come up with a soft and comfortable knitted sweater made from microbially fermented brewed protein?

A   Japanese apparel brand Goldwin Inc

Q347 What is special about the Tuff-N-Lite socks?

A   They are slash and abrasion resistant.

Q348 What is care labelling?

A   Care labeling is the guide for refurbishing the clothes for retaining the original appearance (Le. 2018).

Q349 Who stated that demand for ballistic protection apparel is growing globally in both developing and developed nations?

A   Cobb (2021)

Q350 What is Strung?

A   It is a robotically designed shoe to match the athlete's specifications by a German sportswear company adidas®.

Summary

This chapter is designed with Questions and Answers (Q & A) based on the assumption that this technique of learning allows filtering the acquired information through critical thinking for both scholars and learners. Q & A approach forces the users to think outside the box and compel to upgrade what does not make sense. Additionally, this methodology contributes towards sharpening the information retention and enhancing the spontaneity of information processing for learners and scholars.

REFERENCES

Adnan, M. M. (2018). Color Measurement and Colorfastness of Different Weaves, and Dimensional Forms, unpublished master's thesis, Central Michigan University.

Annual book of ASTM standards. (2020). *7.01,* West Conshohoken, PA: ASTM International.

Annual book of ASTM standards. (2019). *7.02,* West Conshohoken, PA: ASTM International.

Atasagun, H. G., Okur, A., & Psikuta, A. (2019). The effect of garment combination on thermal comfort of office clothing. *Textile Research Journal,* https://doi.org/10.1177/0040517519834609 First Published March 11, 2019 Research Article

Atasagun, H. G., Okur, A., & Psikuta, A. (2019). The effect of garment combinations on thermal comfort of office clothing. *Textile Research Journal*, 89 (21-22), 4425-4437.

Chang, Condon, & Nam, (2020). Development of flame-resistant cotton fabrics with casein using pad-dry-cure and supercritical fluid methods. *International Journal of Materials Science Applications., 19*(4), 53-61.

Chang, S., Condon, B. Nam S. (2020). Development of flame-resistant cotton fabrics with Casein using pad-dry-cure and supercritical fluid methods. Journal of Material Science and Applications, 9(4), 53-61.

Chowdhary, U. (2019). Impact of interfacings and lining on breaking strength, breaking strength, elongation and duration of the knitted wool. International Journal of Textile Science and Engineering, 3(1), 1-6.

Chowdhary, U. (2017). Comparing three brands of cotton t-shirts. *AATCC Journal of Research 4*(3), 22-35. DOI: 10.14504/ajr.4.3.3

Chowdhary, U. (2009). *Textile analysis, quality control and innovative uses.* Deer Park, NY: LINUS.

Chowdhary, U. (2007). *Textile analysis laboratory manual.* Deer Park, NY: LINUS.

Chowdhary, U. (2002). Does price reflect emotional, structural, or performance quality? *International Journal of Consumer Studies, 26,* 128-133.

Chowdhary, U., Adnan, M. M., & Cheng, C. (2018). Bursting strength and extension for jersey, interlock and pique knit. Trends in Textile Engineering and Fashion Technology, 1(2), 1-9.

Chowdhary, U., & Poynor, D. (2006). Impact of stitch density on seam strength, seam elongation and seam efficiency. International Journal of Consumer Studies, 30 (6), 561-568.

Chowdhary, U. & Wentela, C. (2018). Impact of support fabrics on breaking strength, elongation, and time taken for the test for woven fabrics in different fiber contents. SSRG International Journal of Polymer and Textile Engineering, 5 (5), 1-6.

Cobb, D. (2021, January). A new age of ballistic protection. *Specialty Fabrics Review, 30-36.*

Cohen, A.C., & Johnson, I. (2010). *Fabric Science.* New York, NY: Fairchild.

Delcron® Hydrotec Fiber. Retrieved on 4/16/2021. https://www.dakamericas.com/us-en/products/fibers_delcron_hydrotec.php

Easter, E. P. (2004). Care practices for Fluorocarbon treated garments: A case study. *AATCC Review, 4*(3), 12-16.

Eryuruk, S. H. & Kalaoglu, F. (2018). The effect of weave construction on tear strength of woven fabrics. AUTEX Research Journal, 15(3), 207-213.

Islam, M. R. (2020). Color assessment of three knitted structures in three-dimensional body form under different lights and three different lengths of exposure. Unpublished master's thesis. Central Michigan University.

Islam, M. R., & Chowdhary, U. (2019). Relative color pickup of three different knits and predictive dyeing recipe formulation. *International Journal of Polymer and Textile Engineering (SSRG - IJPTE),* 6(3), 1-16.

Kadolph, S. J., & Langford, A. L. (2002). *Textiles.* Upper Saddle River, NJ: Prentice Hall.

Kang, T. J., & Kim, M. S. (2001). Effects of silicone treatments one the dimensional properties of wool fabric. Textile Research Journal, 71(4), 295-300.

Kavitha S, & Gokarneshan N. (2019). A Review of Some Significant Research Trends in Thermophysiological Comfort of Fabrics to Suit Varied Areas of Applications and Weather Conditions. *Current Trends in Fashion Technology and Engineering,* 5(5): 555673. DOI: 10.19080/CTFTTE.2019.05.5673.

Koe, F. T. (2007). *Fabric for the designed interior.* New York, NY: Fairchild.

Kundu, S. K. and Chowdhary, U. (2018). Effect of Fiber Content on Comfort Properties of Cotton/Spandex, Rayon/Spandex, and Polyester/Spandex Single Jersey Knitted Fabrics. *SSRG International Journal of Polymer and Textile Engineering,* 5(3), 33-39.

Le, K. (2018, July/August). Natural dyes - Return of the classics. *AATCC Review,* 18(4), 42-48.

Manual of international test methods and procedures (2021). Research Triangle Park, NC: American Association of Textile Chemists and Colorists.

Shrimali, K, & Dedhia, E, (2015). Microencapsulation for textile finishing. R *Journal of Polymer and Textile Engineering (IOSR-JPTE),* 2(2), 1-4. www.iosrjournals.org DOI: 10.9790/019X-0220104 www.iosrjournals.org 1

West, J. A. & Annett-Hitchcock, K. E. (2014). A critical review of aroma therapeutic application for textiles. *Journal of Textile and Apparel Technology and Management, 9* (1), 1-13

Wroblewski, S. M. (2017). Quilting structure: Impact of air permeability and thermal properties of a non-woven, a two-fold study. Unpublished research project, Central Michigan University.

Zaman, M.S., Mondal, B. V., & Saha, P.K. (2017). Investigation of stretch and recovery property of weft knitted regular rib fabric. Researchgate.com

PRACTICE ACTIVITIES

I The questions can be organized as a jeopardy show. It can be used for both individual and group settings. One simple example is provided below. It can be adapted to meet the specific needs by the instructor for additional topics.

#	Fiber	Yarn	Fabric	Dyes/Print	Finishes/Special Treatments
1	1	1	1	1	1
2	2	2	2	2	2
3	3	3	3	3	3
4	4	4	4	4	4
5	5	5	5	5	5
6	6	6	6	6	6
7	7	7	7	7	7
8	8	8	8	8	8
9	9	9	9	9	9
10	10	10	10	10	10

Ten Statements on Fibers: Answers are in the parenthesis.

1. I am the only filament among natural fibers. **(Silk)**
2. This natural fiber self-extinguishes. **(Wool)**
3. This synthetic fiber is flame-resistant. **(Modacrylic and Aramid)**
4. This synthetic fiber replaces wool for sweaters to get brighter colors. **(Acrylic)**
5. This fiber is absorbent and good for summer use. **(Cotton/Linen)**
6. This fiber has been used traditionally for the lining of coats and jackets. **(Acetate)**
7. This fiber is used for firefighters' clothing. **(Nomex)**
8. This fiber is used for the bullet-proof vest. **(Kevlar)**
9. This fiber gets the best results with acid dyes. **(Wool and silk)**
10. This fiber is used for parachutes. **(Nylon)**

Ten Statements on Yarns: Answers are in the parenthesis.

1. The type of yarn that snags easily.
2. This yarn is most lustrous.

3. This yarn is used as a tie-back of drapes. **(Cord)**
4. This type of yarn is most used for knitting. **(Ply)**
5. This yarn is the result of the single twisting operation. **(Single)**
6. This type of yarn is used for men's high-quality suits. **(Worsted)**
7. This attribute of yarn is measured in Tex or denier. **(Yarn Size)**
8. This type of yarn is used for making fabrics more distinctive and decorative. **(Novelty yarns)**
9. Finish given to sewing threads for industrial sewing. **(Made flame and heat resistant)**
10.. This operation makes the yarn stronger than without it. **(Twist)**

Ten Statements on Fabrics: Answers are in the parenthesis.

1. They are created by interlacing the warp and weft yarns at right angles to each other. **(Woven Fabrics)**
2. They are created by interloping of yarns. **(Knitted Fabrics).**
3. Woven fabrics have maximum stretch in this direction. **(Bias-Cut)**
4. This type of weave shows diagonal lines. **(Twill)**
5. This fabric attribute is used to determine the quality of fabric. **(Fabric Count)**
6. This weave has the highest tear strength. **(Satin)**
7. This weave is most likely to snag. **(Satin/Sateen)**
8. This weave is used for Oxford shirts. **(Half-basket)**
9. This is an example of double knit. **(Interlock, Purl Knit, Rib Knit)**
10. A type of knit that is used for lingerie. **(Warp knit)**

Ten Statements on Dyes/Print: Answers are in the parenthesis.

1. This stage of dyeing is best for stripes/plaids. **(Yarn)**
2. This process of coloring shows evenly on the front and back of the fabric. **(Dyeing)**
3. This type of coloring of textile looks darker on the face of the fabric and lighter on the back of the fabrics. **(Printing)**
4. This is another name of tie dye technique. **(Resist or Ikat)**
5. Name of fabric when warp and weft have different fiber contents. **(Iridescent)**
6. What type of dye does the best on synthetic fibers? **(Disperse)**

7. ΔE of two or more represents ____ _____ ____ __ __ ____ __ **(difference visible to the human eye).**

8. When printing does not align with the lengthwise and crosswise grain, it is called _____. **(Off-Grain)**

9. Poor alignment of screens results in non-matching of edges of the fabric. **(Out of Register Print)**

10. Removing solid color with chemicals is called _____ Printing. **(Discharge Printing)**

Ten Statements on Finishes/Special Treatments: Answers are in the parenthesis.

1. I make cotton stronger and lustrous. **(Mercerization)**
2. I proved mildew resistance to the fabric. **(Antimicrobial)**
3. I prevent wool from progressive shrinkage. **(Chlorination)**
4. I look like the seal of the notary public. **(Embossing)**
5. I am instrumental in stain repellency. **(Nanotechnology)**
6. I can be created by sandblasting and stonewashing. **(Faded Look)**
7. I give smooth appearance to the finished look. **(Calendering)**
8. They are slash and abrasion resistant. **(Tuff-N-Lite Socks)**
9. Treatment used to make textiles stain and water-repellent uses _____. **(Fluorocarbon - Poly Tetra Fluoro Ethylene)**
10. Finishes that impact the drape of the fabric. **(Parchmentization (Acid finish) and weighting of silk)**

II Debates can be organized to discuss various aspects of textiles. Some topics to choose from are provided below.

*Natural fibers are a better choice than synthetic fibers for apparel.

*Use of care labels is irrelevant.

*Synthetic fibers are the best choice for apparel.

*People should always wear lined garments for insulation.

*Polyester linings work best with cotton and wool.

*Textile testing is not needed in the industry.

*Color is important for consumers.

*Technical Data Sheets are must for decision-making in Linum usitatissimum the textile industry.

Chapter 12

*Textile innovations are a waste of money.

*Textile analysis is important for designers.

*Textile analysis is important for fashion designers.

*Compatibility between fabrics is important for everyday wear.

*Printing is more environment -friendly than dyeing.

*Knowledge of structural attributes is more important than performance attributes.

* Knowledge of performance attributes is more important than structural attributes.

*Filaments are stronger than the staple fibers.

*Quality assurance is important for confidence building among various stakeholders.

*Globalization impacts the quality control for the textile industry.

*All innovations revolutionize the textile choices for consumers.

*Woven fabrics are better than knitted textiles.

*Knitted textile is perfect for casual apparel.

CHAPTER 13
QUALITY ASSURANCE, QUALITY CONTROL, AND SPECIAL APPLICATIONS

Total Quality Satisfaction (TQS) is a function of quality assurance, quality control, and special applications. **Quality Assurance** refers to the guarantee given by the apparel manufacturers to back their product. **Quality control** implies the use of checkpoints at various stages of production to ensure that the final product meets the standards adequately or exceptionally for the intended use. **Special Applications** refer to the use of textiles for niche markets, new treatments, and new intended end-uses. This chapter will discuss the three-dimensional concept in a problem-solving format and establish the relationship between globalization and quality control.

Quality Assurance

The word quality means different things to different people. Some equate with comfort and others with comfort. Durability and easy care are some other considerations of importance. There are several ways to communicate quality to various stakeholders. To maintain cost effectiveness and beat competition, standards can be relaxed but still be adequately appropriate for the intended end use. Doing so is called **quality assurance** where the manufacturer backs the product, uses technical standards, considers compatibility with the end-use (Figure 70). For example, if the design has several means of fullness and the dimensional change of the used fabrics is 4% against the standard of 3% maximum, fabric could be pre-shrunk, and the problem could be resolved. Or, manufacturer can back the product, and offer reduced price or accept returns in case of customers' dissatisfaction. Quality assurance allows for flexibility that quality control does not. In other words, tolerances are higher in case of quality assurance than the quality control concept.

Problem: Quality Assurance for the Camping Equipment

Solution: Use standards such as abrasion resistance, breathability, breaking strength, mildew resistance, and water repellency. Consider end-use camping and selected standards. If you must discard one of the tests, consider thoughtfully and discard the least important test. Supplement your decision with support for your customer if the product does not sell well to maintain a good relationship.

Figure 70: Quality Assurance as function of standards, compatibility with end-uses, and manufacturer's backing of the product.

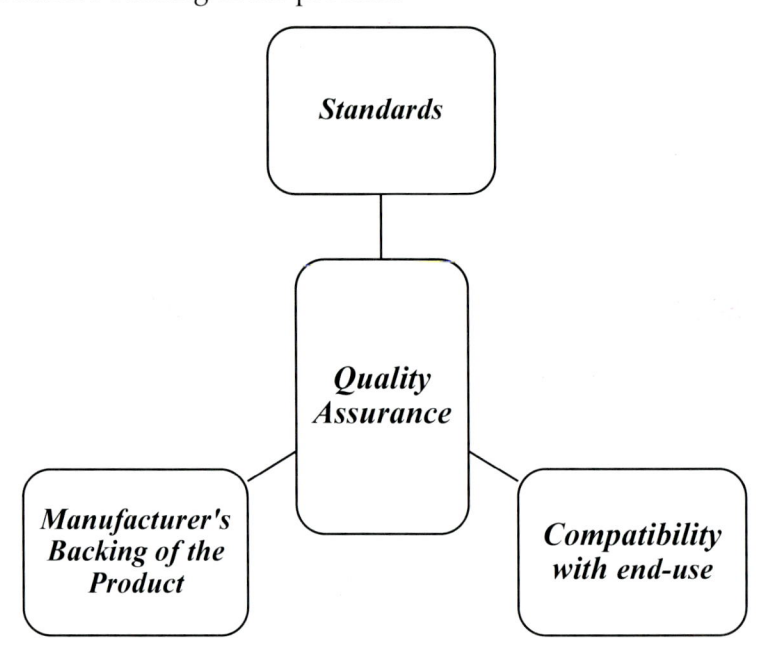

Quality Control

Quality control is function of testing the product during its development, use, and care at various stages to insure that it is appropriate for its intended use. Figure 71 shows it as conglommerate of standardization, use and care, and product development. Most manufacturers and retailers of apparel do not select and interpret standards in the same manner. Therefore, it s important for the buyers of the products to use technical standards based on AATCC, ASTM, and ISO as indicators of quality that meet or exceed the standards. The recommended standards Manufacturers should do the same for selling their merchandise.

Problem: If a customer needs outdoor camping equipment, what rationale would you provide as an evidence to justify the quality of the product?

Solution: The customer will be told about the standardized tests conducted to test abrasion resistance, breathability, mildew resistance, and tensile strength with the resulting values and outcomes. Meeting or exceeding the standards guarantees quality, establishes consumer's trust, and develops confidence in the product.

Problem: Convincing buyers for the quality of lined garments.

Solution: Determining compatibility will be the key factor. Dimensional stability will be the most important factor. If two fabrics are not compatible based on the laundering, recommend ddry cleaning. Fabric weight is also of critical importance. Lining is a support fabric and should negate the impact of the fashion fabric. It should weigh less than the fashion fabric unless the fashion fabric is made of lace material. Consider these factors carefully. Also remember that Vinyl should not be dry cleaned. The dry cleaning solvent creates a bubbly effect. So is true for acrylic buttons. That is why drycleaners cover the buttons with aluminum foil to protect them from damages from the dry cleaning solvents.

Figure 71: Quality control as function of standardization, use and care, and product development

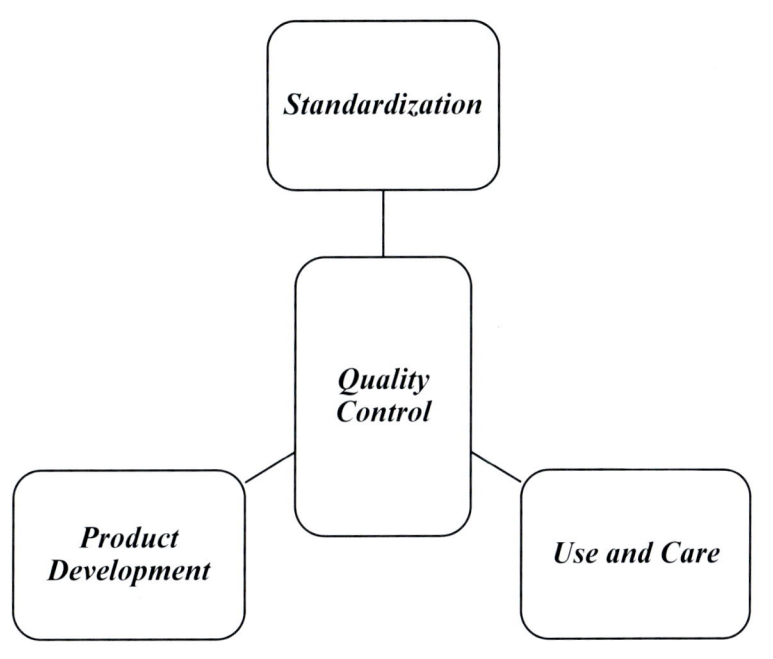

Special Applications

Special Applications also requires standardization, use and care, as well as product development. Figure 72 provides the graphic presentation. For special treatments, it is important to consider quality control via new treatments, new end uses and niche markets for providing confidence and trust between the buyer and the seller.

Problem: **Quality Rainwear**

Solution: Water repellency is the main criteria. The fabric must pass it. Sometimes, it lower after laundering. One must ensure that it is not less than 70 after laundering.

Problem: **Bullet Proof Vest**

Solution: Flame resistance is the key factor. One can accomplish so by the use of Kevlar that is a form of Aramid.

Problem: **Firefighters or Race Car Drivers' uniform**

Solution: Flameresistance is of critical importance. Nomex is generally used for these end-uses. One can use it for a Chef's coat also.

Outdoor Clothing

Problem: What materials are available in the market to meet the needs identified in Problem listed for quality assurance?

Solution: WeatherMAX 80 collection is available for $ 13.81 per yard. It is a breathable polyester with mildew and mold resistance and is used for the marine covers and outdoor coverings (https://canvastraining.com/product/weathermax-80-collection/). WeatherMAX has a distinctive ability to offer breathability, and resist UV, and water. Without any coating. It has patents from both Canada and the United States (https://weathermax.com/innovations/).

Figure 72: Special applications as function of new treatments, new end-uses, and niche markets

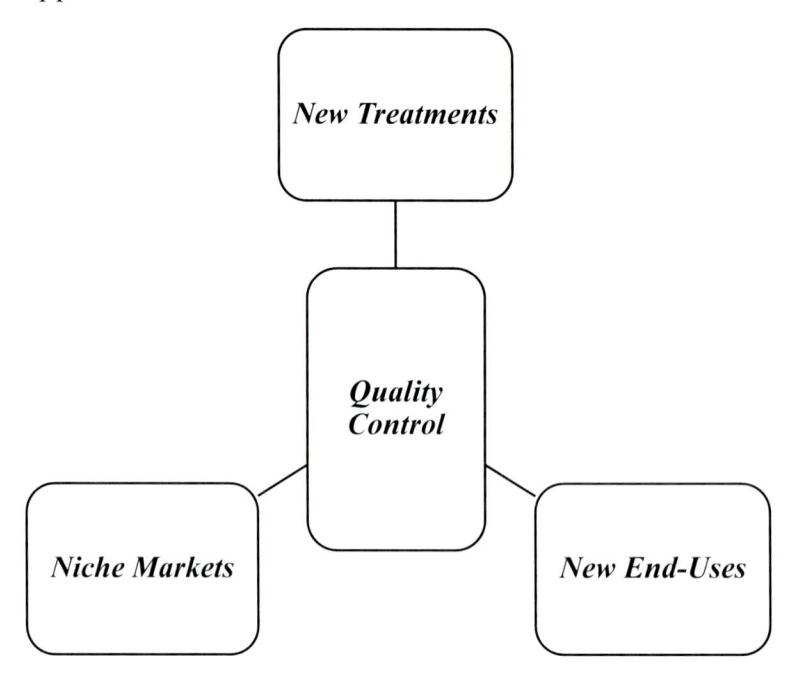

Coatings impact breathability adversely. Additionally, coatings call clamminess despite very little moisture vapor transmission the coatings also decrease the recyclability of the fabric. In contrast WeatherMAX is perfectly (100%) recyclable. WeatherMAX 3D use special construction for offering durability, elasticity, and resistance to UV and color for eliminating fade resistance (https://weathermax.com/innovations/). Additionally, it stretches 20% under tension and comes back to its original position when released.

Globalization and Quality Control

Globalization of the recent years has forced users to incorporate standards for testing textile materials for appropriateness of materials and compatibility of different fiber-contents to create the fabric. With the increased outsourcing effects, standardization has become more important to normalize the differences amongst the cultural and economic forces. Figure 73 shows the relationship between globalization and quality control through a three-prong model.

Figure 73: Globalization and quality control as function of advanced technology; accuracy, reliability, and validity; and importance of textile standards

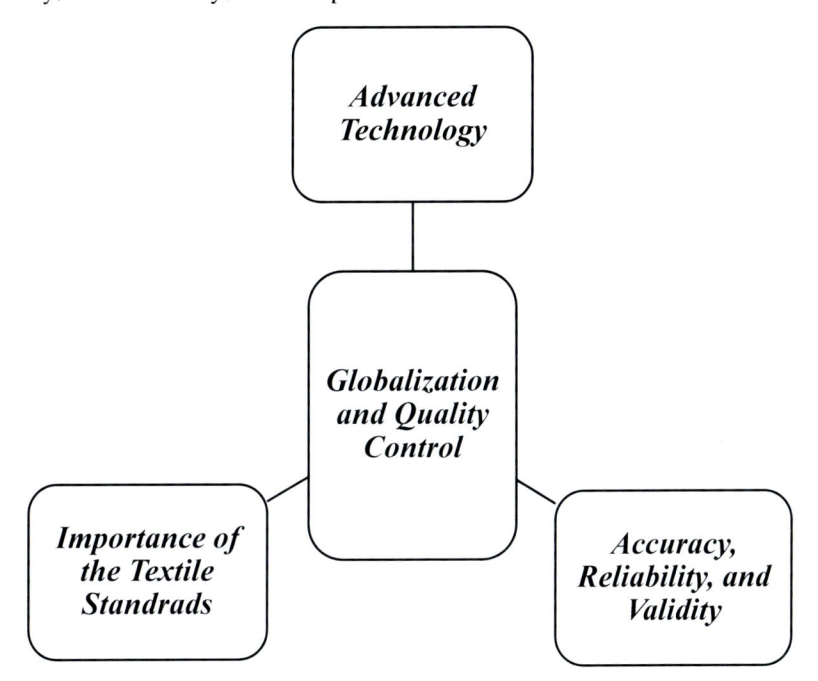

```
              ┌──────────────┐
              │   Advanced   │
              │  Technology  │
              └──────┬───────┘
                     │
              ┌──────┴───────┐
              │ Globalization│
              │ and Quality  │
              │   Control    │
              └──┬────────┬──┘
                 │        │
   ┌─────────────┘        └─────────────┐
   │ Importance of │      │ Accuracy,   │
   │ the Textile  │      │ Reliability,│
   │  Standrads   │      │ and Validity│
   └──────────────┘      └─────────────┘
```

Three national and international organizations of standardization (AATCC, ASTM, and ISO) offer consumer trust and confidence for the merchandise. Performance is shown by meeting or exceeding the minimum standards. Accomplishing this milestone inspires the repeated purchase by the consumer. Establishing quality control at every step of the product development process perpetuates a long-term relationship between the negotiating parties which helps with sustaining products and processes. Doing so results in good quality without question. Precise execution of reliable tests enhances cost effectiveness and ease in establishing outsourcing mechanisms. It also ensures that the manufacturers will provide quality products for their consumers. Consequently, globalization becomes a means to maximize and optimize the production of quality goods. These considerations also help with having successful joint ventures.

Advanced technology has shortened the distances, and enhanced the accessibility to information within, between, and among various countries. Using appropriate technology and standards allows mutual trust without giving away competing secrets to the competitors. Globalization requires external validity which forces people to offer better quality and competitive prices. Of course, one must pay attention to the elasticity of this concept. Overstretching the concepts can spread the process thin and make it a complicated operation.

Antoshak (2016) reported several factors that impact the textile and apparel industry with China being the largest player. He concluded by quoting, "The cost of garment has always played a central role in sourcing decisions. Even so, the reasons behind that – margins, customer preferences and efficiencies – may change if the consumer market textiles and apparel migrate into something new. Many consumer markets remain filled with shirts, jeans, and dresses. What happens if Americans opt to clean out their closets and change their habits? After all, a new generation of consumers is ascendant. What are their preferences? Are cheap clothes enough to satisfy these consumers or do they demand something else? To be blunt: Is fast fashion a permanent fixture for the business or will consumers increasingly demand alternatives?" Viswaprakash & Senthamilselvan (2012) reported that trade barriers have been reduced because of globalization.

Globalization changes the face of textile, clothing, and footwear industries (1996) reported that globalization resulted in an increase of employment in the developing and reduction in jobs of the informal workers in the developed countries. China has the most workers that amounted to **5.3 million**. "In the twenty years from 1970-1990, the number of TCF workers increased by 597 percent in Malaysia; 416 percent in Bangladesh; 385 percent in Sri Lanka; 334 percent in Indonesia; 271 percent in the Philippines; and 137 percent in Korea." In 1990, Germany produced 12% of the world textiles followed by 8.6% in Italy. Hong Kong was third (7.4%), China was fourth (6.5%), Belgium and Taiwan (5.7%) fifth and sixth, Korea seventh (5.6%), France (5.5%) eighth, Japan (5.3%) ninth, and the United States (4.5%) tenth.

Even though globalization offers more variety and lower prices for consumers technical and communication issues must be resolved at an ongoing basis due to the changing technology. It forces companies to be flexible and willing to take risks for expanding their scope. Color matching requires the use of sophisticated equipment and management systems. Timely transportation can become an issue in the pandemic times due to increased border restrictions and within country lockdowns.

Globalization and Examples of Quality Control

This section provides examples to further establish the relationship between globalization and quality control. The content includes antimicrobial technologies for fabrics and textiles and odor eating technologies, Flammability, Moisture management, stain removal, UV protection, and foreign influences.

1. **Antimicrobial and Odor Eating Technologies**

    Bamboo is naturally antimicrobial because it has several characteristics like wood. Organic cotton has moderate levels of antibacterial properties (Google, 4/20/21) Microban® partnerships provide enhanced product performance (2021) partners with 300 companies world-wide to create a better product that removes bacteria, stink, and stains. It was established in 1984 and became global in 1994. It went green in 2009 and participated actively in the sustainability campaign. In 2011, it was acquired by Barr Brands International. In 2020, Procter and Gamble joined hands and produced antibacterial home sanitizing products.

    SARPU uses nano-silver for antimicrobial end products in South Korea (2021, https://product.statnano.com/product/6810/sarpu-(antimicrobial-nano-silver). Bio-San laboratories do the antibacterial testing.

    Antimicrobial protection for fabrics and Textiles (2021) informed that antimicrobial finishes are used for pleasant odor and stain-free existence of textiles. Microban® antimicrobial fabric additives That are applied to fabrics such as cotton, polyester, and rayon as finish to make it antimicrobial. Microban uses sustainable technologies and is popular worldwide. Biostatic: Stay fresh technology (2021) uses silver salt and reduces odor for lifetime, cuts down the growth of bacteria and fungi, enhances hygiene, and makes the textile smell fresh. It also saves water due to reduced need for frequent laundering.

Pleasant smell of fabrics to enhance freshness is valued worldwide (Thiry, 2008). Researchers and scientists are trying to create products that makes it possible to accomplish the goal of making fabrics odor and stain free. Cognis, a leading company of Germany is committed to Green Engineering and sustainability. **Cyclofresh™** is a product of Cognis that can release deodorants in fabric that delete the unpleasant odors. It is designed to meet the needs of leisure wear, outdoors, and sportswear. It uses cyclodextrins that are obtained from maize and introduced in the manufacturing process. Fragrances are released when sweat molecules burst on the skin. Laundering does not impede the ability to remove odor and release fragrance. Another article from 2009 stated that Cyclofresh® Plus prevents odor for longer time because it is created by a dual mechanism of cyclodextrins with silver ions. The finish lasts for at least 50 launderings. Stahl and Schamp (2007) introduced antimicrobial technology.

2. **Moisture Management**

   HydroPur® provides unrivaled security and comfort with an excellent moisture management property (https://www.dakamericas.com/us-en/products/fibers_hydropur_fiber.php, 4/20/2021). Stay Cool in the Heat with Advanced Moisture Management (2020) provided rationale for the advance moisture management process for comfort, quick drying, and regulating the body temperature. It has three levels: absorbent (within fabric), wicking (Inner to outer layer movement), and repellent (warding off the moisture). It is important for activewear, automotive, furniture, intimate apparel, medical field, and military. The Apex Mill offers DryRUN+, DryRUNX, and DryRUN a.m. for advanced moisture management. Stahl and Schamp (2007) introduced Skintex® Supercool for cooling feelings. They used "Menthol, Myritol, emollients, and synthetic coolants in the microcapsules that are released from friction and body heat.

3. **Mosquito Protection**

   Stahl and Schamp (2007) introduced "Skintex Mosquito Protection" called Mosquito Repellent in the United States to protect from the mosquito bites that were approved by EPA. Garments used the encapsulation technique and application was good for 25 washes. Garments treated with Skintex microcapsules containing Mosquito Protection make sure that all areas of the body covered by the fabric are well protected. Unlike creams, consumers do not have to worry about the effect wearing off during the day. The repellence remains effective for 25 washes. Sanitized® was used in Switzerland. Termovel® was first used for leisure clothing. Later, it was used as thermal clothing in Czechoslovakia for the army, mountaineers, policemen, rescue workers and sportsmen. Delcron® Hydropur from DAK America provides both moisture management and antibacterial functions.

   Partnership between different companies from different parts of the world is an example of globalization. Additionally, recognition of the importance of antibacterial function of textiles by using the antibacterial and odor eating technology in the United States, Switzerland, South Korea, Germany, and Czechoslovakia justify the importance of globalization. Using appropriate technology and standards allow mutual trust without giving away competing secrets to the competitors. Globalization offers external validity which also forces people to offer good quality and competitive prices simultaneously.

4. **Electronic Textiles**

Hayward (2021) reported that e-textiles will reach 1.4 billion dollars by 2030. An electronic textile is a fabric with electronic elements that can sense heating and lighting in addition to transmitting data. Sensors are the interface between the electronic system and the user. Six benefits of the electronic textiles are that it is flexible for comfort, provide accurate data, do not snag, invisibly cover the large area of sensing, has affordable manufacturing, is strong and permeable, and offers electrical and thermal resistance (https://www.google.com/search?q=Electronic+TExtiles&sxsrf=ALeKk00680legb1yCbHioSCjUANmnS9sTw%3A1618948642084&source=hp&ei=IjJ_YOLWM_-p0PEP78K3-Ao&iflsig=AINFCbYAAAAAYH9AMtrjAKzCW2jSewe-4KPZlOT-kDxa&oq=Electronic+TExtiles&gs_lcp=Cgdnd3Mtd2l6EAMyBwgAEIcCEBQyAggAMgI-IADICCAAyAggAMgcIABDJAxAKMgIIADIGCAAQFhAeMgYIABAWEB4yBggAEBYQHjoHCCMQ6gIQJzoECCMQJzoFCAAQkQI6CAgAELEDEIMBOgUIABCxAzoECAAQQzoKCC4QxwEQrwEQQzoEC-C4QQzoLCAAQsQMQgwEQyQM6BQgAEJIDOgUIABDJAzoLCC4QsQMQxwEQowJQ4RVYuUJgy-ERoAXAAeACAAf4DiAGOF5IBCDAuMTguNS0xmAEAoAEBqgEHZ3dzLXdperABCg&sclient=gwswiz&ved=0ahUKEwji75DWzY3wAhX_FDQIHW_hDa8Q4dUDCAo&uact=5, 2020). E-textiles must have electrical components. It is not the same as smart textile.

Sayol (2021) reported that e-textiles are digitized with a battery, an electronic chip, or a sensor. They are embedded into fabric through conductive fibers or multilayer 3D printing. Hayward (2021) described its uses for apparel, bed linens, specialty fabrics, "conductive fibers, stretchable electronics, and wearable technology. Innovations in advanced textiles (2021) informed that North Carolina State University has developed a sensor system for the amputees. It uses conductive yarns that are connected to a small computer. It was tested with prosthetic limbs and found that the system tracks pressure changes without adding the discomfort. MIT has developed a biodegradable patch. On meeting body tissues and organs, it changes into gel and prevents bacterial attack/growth. It degrades over time naturally. One of the Assistant Professor at the University of Rhode Island mentioned it as a smart bandage that is monitored by a wearable device to detect infection via smartphone. It seemed to help immensely with the chronic wound.

5. **Flammability**

Diaz (2021) reported that labeling requirement is added for the upholstered furniture including pillows and cushions. The following furniture is included within the scope of the new standard: sofas, chairs (dining and living room), and couches. The following articles are not part of the new standard. "Outdoor patio furniture, mattresses, foundations, bedding products, furniture used exclusively for physical fitness and exercise, or non-furniture juvenile products such as walkers, strollers, highchairs, and pillows." (Pages unnumbered) This standard will go in effect by June 25. 2021. Burkhart (2019) reported that more than 4000 burn injuries were reported per year by CPSC. Of which 150 were fatal. American Apparel recalled children's nightwear because it failed to meet the "U.S. Federal Flammability Standard." They recalled ten thousand items because they could catch fire. The standards of Canada and the United States are quite identical. Plain fabrics fail if they burn in less than 3.5 seconds. In contrast, the raised fabrics, the burn time of less than 4 seconds is not acceptable. These are based on the 45 degrees angle test. They are classified as Normal, Intermediate, and Rapid and Intense burning.

Ramsis (2014) reported that the Phase Changing Materials (PCM) reduced burns for the firefighters. Additionally, they also increased fabric thickness and thermal conductivity.

6. **Stain Removal Technology**

   Various sources provided several strategies and tools for stain removal from clothes. It is an ongoing challenge for consumers to wear stain-free clothing in everyday life. In most cases, they recommended easily available materials that are easily accessible to the consumer. With the introduction of new products and technology, there is a need to keep on exploring/learning new methods. Information below offers additional perspectives than the ones already presented in a previous chapter.

   Applications (2021) asserted that the fabrics with GreenShield can be cleaned easily and embedded with other finishes such as antimicrobial and flame-retardant finishes. It is water repellent finish that is fluorine free and removes stains also. Teflon (2021) offers Zelan™ R3 finish that lasts for 30 launderings and is water repellent and prevents rain and water-based stains. It is also approved by the United States Department of Agriculture (USDA) as bluesign®.

   Top 9 Stain Removal Techniques (4/22/2021) reported 9 techniques as blotting, brushing off the excessive dried stain, scrape off the stain, soak, wash in running water, rub with hard brush if tough and/or old, sponge with stain remover, presoak if old, and pretreat with a stain remover. Wax and gum can be removed by freezing it. Some techniques in this article read as steps rather than categories. The American Cleaning Institute (2021) offered a "Stain Removal Guide". It suggested to removing them as soon as possible, pre-treat, and follow care instructions. It offers 45 stains. For most stains, wash immediately for best results. Washing, pretreating with remover or appropriate chemicals and laundering were the three steps. Cold water was recommended for adhesives and blood. Acetone was suggested for the wood and nail polish stains, alcohol for cosmetics, and bleach for the scorch.

   Google offers several different tools and strategies for the stain removal. Kosik (2017) provides foolproof ways of removing stains. Some of the suggested materials were alcohol, bar soap, brush (soft), dishwashing detergent/liquid, shaving cream, vinegar, and warm water.

7. **Smart Textiles**

   Sayol (2021) stated that the aesthetic smart textiles use the technology that adds the multisensorial experience through lighting and sound in sneakers, as well as fabrics that change color with variations in the body heat. Other examples could be to create the textiles that protect environmental hazards and radiation. Fabrics could also impact human functions such as body temperature, breathing rate, heart rate, and sweat. Cute Circuit's sound shirts allow deaf people to enjoy music through their body movement. Jansport developed a backpack that used smart fabric with connection to social media. It allows the user to share website links, videos, and songs. Levi Strauss developed a smart denim jacket with touch sensor control built-in it. The jacket uses the Bluetooth, conductive wires, and smartphone applications. A French manufacturer has created the beachwear that has sensors to control UV and tells when additional sunscreen is needed. Both Apple and Microsoft have integrated health monitoring technology to apparel in 2019. Weight watchers, physicians, and athletes can use smart textiles to watch their vital signs.

Hu, Meng, Li, & Ibekwe (2012) described multiple uses of smart textiles. Some examples included changing aesthetics, color and responding to environmental changes. Use for shape memory fibers, fabrics, finishes, and foams; "breathable fabrics", and "phase change materials" (p. 3) were some specifics. They can make cotton fabrics wrinkle free in fiber form by changing the molecular orientation and improving conduction of fibers. Temperature changes were reported to result in increase or decrease in molecular structure and resulted in enhanced "water vapor permeability". Shape memory foams can be used for foot soles of shoes. Thermo-chromatic materials are used in microcapsules to create color changes at varying temperatures. The article also talked about the "moisture-responsive shape memory polymers" that can cause cooling for the overheated body.

Cherenack, Zusset, Kinkeldei, Munzenrieder, & Troster (2010) reported on the electronic or e-textiles is known as intelligent material that senses the environmental changes and responds to it. The electronic fibers were made from plastic substrates. E-fibers were inserted in the weft direction. The authors noted that e-fibers' thickness impacted the performance. Damaging was reported to occur in the weaving process as well wearing of a hem as a clothing item. This study used the e-textile on the tablecloth.

Gurian, M. (2007) informed regarding the use of nanotechnology as Nano-Tex-treated upholstery that had WS cleaning code. They were first used in the Houston Rockets' basketball arena in 2003. Thirty stains were tested for stain repellence of the fabric. Fantastic was reported to be the most effective solvent to get rid of the oil borne stains. Other stadiums that were upholstered with these materials with satisfactory performance were Cleveland Cavaliers, Memphis Grizzlies, and Timber wolves of Minnesota. Health industry used Nano-Tex treated nylon and polyester for upholstery in the healthcare industry. Nano-Tex treated materials used since 2003 were found to be durable, cleanable, and stain resistant for sports arena and durable against the disinfectants used in the healthcare industry. Jordan, M. (2007) focused on development from smart textiles to smart applications. Durability was critically relevant. This smart textile was created by Three layered system of sensor activation by Elek Tex suggested to have a conductive upper layer, partially conductive middle layer, and low resistance fabric for the third layer.

8. **Ultraviolet Protection**

What clothing is best for sun protection? (2021) informed that exposure to the Ultraviolet rays can cause skin damage. Use of appropriate clothing protects human beings from those damages. The article described that based on Huntsman Cancer Institute sun rays are most harmful between 10:00 a.m. to 4:00 p.m. and should be avoided. If you cannot do so, cover yourself with appropriate clothing. Closely knitted or woven fabrics, synthetic materials, dark and bright colors, less stretch, dry and newer condition, and more fabric are good choices for UV protection. Lotion with 30+ SPF at least 20 minutes prior to going out, covering the face, staying under shade, wearing sunglasses, and putting on a hat also provide good protection. They also recommended using lotion over spray that are water resistant. Sunscreen lotions are recommended for application every two hours.

Sivaramakrishnan (2021) asserted that the Sun Protection Factor (SPF) indicates how much the Sun Protection screen defends. In the textile and clothing industry, the term Ultraviolet Protection

Factor (UPF) is used more than SPF. He recommended the range of 30-50 SPF. Coating the surface with nano particles and using Zinc Oxide increases the UV protection. A garment with 50 SPF controls for 98% of radiation. Testing is done with AATCC 183. Belfasun® is a finish by Pulcra for cotton materials that used to get wet and lose UV protection. It assures 70% UVA (UV Protection for Textiles, 2021).

Chowdhary (2009) introduced it as the world's first "sun protective treatment that used nano zinc particles. It was noted to be effective at the beach, in the ocean while surfing, on the ground while playing golf, or riding the safari. It was believed to meet the UV 801 standard and tested for its effect on the skin. This finish was noted to last for 40 launderings.

The preceding information demonstrates that several companies worldwide are involved with textile improvements through special treatments that make the textiles appropriate for various end-uses. Some examples include Cognis from Germany, Clariant from Switzerland, and Delcron® Hydropur from DAK America are some examples.

Increased consumption of chemicals is reported for Asian pacific, China, Europe, and the North and South America, and middle east (https://www.grandviewresearch.com/industry-analysis/textile-chemical-market, 2021)). The specific countries presented in the article were Bangladesh, Belgium, Brazil, Canada, China, Egypt, Germany, India, Indonesia, Italy, Mexico, South Korea, Taiwan, UAE, Vietnam, United States. Involvement of companies in various geographic regions of the world reflects the impact of globalization via use of standardized tests that are used worldwide to achieve high quality products for winning the customer's confidence.

Obtaining quality is the goal. It is critical to understand that quality is not a compromise and end. It is a process of using several indicators for credibility. It can mean different things to different people. Therefore, it can be accomplished in multiple ways. It is a seal of excellence that represents available resources and their accessibility. Ultimately, it is a symbol of acceptable performance that triggers and sustains repeated use by consumers, and sale by retailers of apparel and textiles.

Summary

Quality assurance, quality control and special treatments play an important role in making the textile industry effective, productive, relevant, sustainable, and timely for new needs, times, and places. Globalization plays an important role for opening-up new opportunities and possibilities for synergized efforts to create a textile industry that does not limit itself to the geographic boundaries. This timeless process to produce quality merchandise is an ongoing flow that will exist forever in modified forms.

REFERENCES

Antoshak, R. (2016). Beyond globalization: A changing textile and apparel industry. Retrieved 4/20/2021 from https://www.linkedin.com/pulse/beyond-globalization-changing-textile-apparel-robert-antoshak/

Antimicrobial technologies for fabrics and textiles. Retrieved on 4/20/2021 from https://www.microban.com/antimicrobial-solutions/applications/antimicrobial-fabrics?creative=437120838199&keyword=%2Bantimicrobial%20%2Btextiles&matchtype=b&network=g&device=c&gclid=Cj0KCQjw9_mDBhCGARIsAN3PaFMHW_TThtYx_3Vjnl6n

Applications (2021). Retrieved 4/22/2021 from https://greenshieldfinish.com/applications/

Biostatic: Stay fresh technology. Retrieved 4/20/2021 from https://polygiene.com/biostatic/?gclid=Cj0KCQjw9_mDBhCGARIsAN3PaFM9ePHydbb_lyvMViATsYTDHXbx3GJ87If-i3PnQR7ddF8hu5j1CbEcaAsKoEALw_wcB

Burkhart, M. (2019, June 18). Flammability tests for fabric and clothing importers. Retrieved 4/22/2021 from https://www.intouch-quality.com/blog/flammability-tests-for-fabric-and-clothing-importers.

Cherenack, K., Zusset, C., Kinkeldei, Munzenrieder, N., & Troster, G. (2010). Woven electronic fibers with sensing and display functions for smart textiles. *Advanced materials, 22*, 5178-5182.

Chowdhary, U. (2009). *Textile analysis, quality control, and innovative uses.* Deer Park, NY: LINUS.

Delcron – Hydrotec Retrieved 4/20/21 from https://www.dakamericas.com/us-en/products/fibers_delcron_hydrotec.php

Diaz, J. (2021, March 23). Breaking news – New Federal law expands furniture. Customs and International Law. Retrieved 4/22/2021 from https://customsandinternationaltradelaw.com/2021/03/23/breaking-news-new-federal-law-expands-furniture-flammability-testing-standard

Gurian, M. (2007). Nanotechnology in high performance upholstery for sports arena and healthcare applications. *AATCC Review, 7*(4), 29-33.

Hayward, J. (2021). E-textiles and smart clothing 2020-2030: Technologies, markets and players.

Retrieved 4/22/2021 from https://www.idtechex.com/en/research-report/e-textiles-and-smart-clothing-2020-2030-technologies-markets-and-players/735

Hu, J., Meng, H., Li, G., & Ibekwe, S. (2012). A review of stimuli-responsive polymers for smart textile applications. *Smart Materials and Structures, 21*, 053001 (23 pp.).

Innovations in advanced textiles. (2021). *Specialty Fabrics Review*, 16-17.

Jordan, M. (2007). Real products for real life. *AATCC Review, 7*(2), 30-33.

Kosik, A. H. (2017, October 22). Foolproof ways to remove every type of stain on your clothes. Retrieved 4/22/2021 from https://www.brit.co/how-to-remove-stains/

Technology cut to perform. Retrieved on 4/19/2021 from https://weathermax.com/innovations

Globalization changes the face of textile, clothing, and footwear industries (1996). Retrieved on 4/20/2021 from https://www.ilo.org/global/about-the ilo/newsroom/news/WCMS_008075 lang--en/index.htm

Microban® partnerships provide enhanced product performance. Retrieved 4/20/21 from https://www.microban.com/partnership/who-we-work-with?creative=437120838199&keyword=%2Bantimicrobial%20%2Btextiles&matchtype=b&network=g&device=c&gclid=Cj0KCQjw9_mDBhCGARIsAN3PaFPSmDULkPlqMpCdrObdSmEeooqa_G9ogAUfaDC8qfa9QEhLMU1YBZkaAlkWEALw_wcB

Ramsis, F. (2014). Enhancing the protection performance of flame-resistant fabrics using Phase Change Materials. *AATCC Journal of Research, 1*(4), 5-10.

Sayol, I. (2021). Smart fabrics, a technology that revolutionizes experiences. Retrieved 4/22/2021 from https://ignasisayol.com/en/smart-textiles-can-be-programmed-to-monitor-things-like-biometrics-measurements-of-physical-attributes-or-behaviours-like-heart-rate-which-could-help-athletes-dieters-and-physicians-observing-pat/

Sivaramakrishnan, C. N. (2021). UV protection finishes. Retrieved 4/23/21 from https://www.fibre2fashion.com/industry-article/2328/uv-protection-finishes

Stahl, V., & Schamp, A. (2007). Cognis and Pulcra Chemicals exhibit active cooling, freshness and Pr --- (2007).

Stain Removal Guide. Retrieved 4/22/2021 from https://www.cleaninginstitute.org/cleaning-tips/clothes/stain-removal-guide.

Stay Cool in the Heat with Advanced Moisture Management (2020). Retrieved 4/20/21. https://www.apexmills.com/media_post/advanced-moisture-management/.

Thiry, M. (2008, February). A pleasing scent. *AATCC Review*, 19-25.

Top 9 Stain Removal Techniques (4/22/2021).https://www.stain-removal-101.com/stain-removal-techniques.html

UV protection for textiles (2021). Retrieved 4/23/2021 from https://www.belfasun-pulcra.com

Viswaprakash, V., & Sentamilselvan, K. (2012). Globalization and trade in the extile industry. *International Journal of Marketing and Technology*, *12*(5), 201-209.

WeatherMAX 3D. Retrieved 4/19/2021 from https://weathermax.com/innovations/.

WeatherMAX 80 Collection. Retrieved on 4/19/2021 from https://canvastraining.com/ product/weathermax-80-collection/

What clothing is best for sun protection? (2020). Retrieved 4/23/21 from https://healthcare.utah.edu/huntsmancancerinstitute/news/2017/what-clothing-is-best-for-protecting-the-skin.php

PRACTICE ACTIVITIES

1. Go through advertisements in textile magazines and journals to identify new special treatments and sources to acquire them.

2. Read journal articles and develop annotations to find the current information on quality control of various textile attributes and end-uses.

3. Review literature to identify which treatments have been introduced and which ones are discontinued.

4. Discuss what would be consumer's next expectation from the textile industry to make their lives better and its existence all pervasive?

5. Expand the list of eight categories.

APPENDIX A

Purposeful Collaboration Between Academia and Industry
Susanne Wroblewski, M.S., Research Lab Coordinator, Instructor, Central Michigan University

A research laboratory based in a university setting provides a substantial opportunity for industry and academia to partner for mutual growth and success. Grant funding enables the university to purchase, maintain and operate state-of-the-art equipment that individual companies may not be able to have on site due to the cost of the investment and the infrequent need of the unique resource. Convexly, a university can utilize the equipment for internal research where multi-disciplinary teams of undergraduates, graduates and faculty can work together to understand, optimize and validate testing strategies across a myriad of research projects. The same teams are beneficial for the external customers who are able to benefit from their research and experience. Students are able to participate in real world research and problem solving that can be applied in their future careers.

Specifically, at the Center for Merchandising and Design Technology (CMDT) we have partnered with several companies on long term development projects that help to give validation to this opportunity. One such partner is Carhartt, Inc., a Michigan-based manufacturer of high quality, durable workwear. Carhartt has partnered with CMU to help them understand the insulation provided by their outerwear so that they can communicate that clearly to their customer base to make product selection easier for the end user. For this research, the CMDT uses an NSF funded sweating thermal manikin which can be converted from the male body form to the female body form to help understand how body shape contributes to thermal comfort. Testing occurs in another NSF funded environmental chamber which enables researchers to maintain a controlled environment to ensure test repeatability under given temperature and humidity conditions.

Another research partner is Lunaler, a leading manufacturer of high-end personal care goods in China, who has partnered with CMDT to better understand how their diaper products work to help keep a baby's skin comfortable with regard to temperature and humidity. The exploratory study was initiated to allow Lunaler to further refine their products to improve the microclimate between the diaper and the skin. For this research, the CMDT uses an infant sweating thermal manikin, the first of its kind in the US. As no testing standards exist for this type of research, the two research partners developed new protocols to evaluate the microclimate. Thermal cameras, microclimate sensors, IV dispensers and thermal baths were used to ensure a wide variety of information could be collected and analyzed to determine which pieces of data were most valuable to understanding how different diaper designs effect the microclimate and therefore the baby's comfort.

These long-term collaborations allow students to see how the data collection and analysis is translated and implemented in the next generation of products designed by our partners. Manufacturers are able to utilize state of the art equipment at reasonable costs with the support of a cross-functional faculty led university research team. All parties are stronger for the collaboration.

Updated 3-5-21 with corrections from Carhartt, and again on 3-9 with corrections from Lunaler. Approved 3-10-21. Updated 3-22-21 to implement 4 of 5 recommended changes by the book author.

APPENDIX B

Reference Styles for Various Publications That Publish on Textiles

1. ***AATCC Journal of Research***

    Lee, H.; An, S. K. *AATCC Journal of Research* **2018,** *5* (2), 35-39.

2. ***APA***

    Haas, K., & Chowdhary, U. (2021). Analysis of quality indicators through fast fashion and classic brands of jeans for the apparel consumer. *Journal of Textile Science and Fashion Technology, 8*(1) DOI: 10.33552/JTSFT.2021.07.000680.

3. ***The Journal of the Textile Institute***

    Chowdhary, U., & Islam, M. R. (2019). Pre-Post Wash Wicking behavior, Moisture Transfer, and Water Repellency of Plain, Twill, and Satin Weaves. *Journal of Textile Science of Fashion Technology – JTSFT, 2(3)*. https://doi.org/10.33552/JTSFT.2019.02.000539

4. ***Journal of Textile Science and Fashion Technology***

    Malek, S., Jaouchi, B., Khedher, F., Ben Said, S., & Cheikhrouhou, M. "Influence of some sewing parameters upon the sewing efficiency of denim fabrics." *The Journal of The Textile Institute*, 108, no. 12(2017): 2079.

5. ***SSRG International Journal of Polymer and Textile Engineering***

    S. B. Marsha, and U. Chowdhary. Comparison of Selected Structural and Performance Attributes of Cotton and Cotton/Polyester Blend T-Shirts. SSRG International Journal of Polymer and Textile Engineering, vol. 5, no. 3, 40-49, 2018.

6. ***Textile Research Journal***

    Ciobanu, A. R., Ciobanu, L., Dumitras, C., & Sarghie, B. Comparative analysis of the bursting strength of knitted sandwich fabrics. *Fibres & Textiles in Eastern Europe*, 2016*; 24:* 95-101

7. ***Trends in Textile Engineering and Fashion Technology***

    Uttam D, Sethi R (2016). Impact of repeated washings on dimensional stability and fabric physical factors of woven cotton fabric. International Journal of Research in Engineering and Applied Sciences 6 (2): 126-135.

APPENDIX C

Author Index

A

Aaron, 92, 98
Abdelrahman, 113, 122, 132
Acikgoz, 150, 154
Adnan, 84, 91, 100, 111, 124, 130-131, 164, 181, 199, 202, 269, 274, 278, 279
Adolphe, 97, 102
Agarwal, 125, 131
Ahmed, 77, 83, 86, 92, 98
Akaydin, 79, 90, 98
Akgun, 67, 70, 79, 98
Alagha, 79, 98
Alcantra, 199
Ali, 92, 98, 112, 122
Alongi, 77, 98
Alpay, 79, 98
Amador, 112, 122, 131
Amirbayat, 79, 98
An, 97-98
Anitha, 110, 134
Anand, 67, 71, 125, 130
Annett-Hitchcock, 277, 280
Annis, 80, 101
Antoshak, 289
Arik, 82, 99
Araujo, 128, 132
Armstrong, 195, 202
Atalie, 58, 70
Atasagun, 85, 99, 268, 278, 279
Azoulay, 199, 202

B

Babar, 112, 122, 132
Babu, 129, 134
Bakalis, 112, 122, 131
Bao, 113, 122, 131
Bardal, 194
Barrie, 12, 13
Bardal, 204
Baumert, 82, 99, 125, 131
Beatty, 152, 154
Becerir, 79, 98
Behcet, 58, 71
Behery, 56, 70
Bellby, 54, 71
Bharani, 92, 99
Bide, 2, 58, 81, 100, 154, 215
Bishop, 67, 71, 125,130
Biswas, 69, 71, 125, 134, 208
Blanchard, 96
Bockmuhl, 150, 154
Bogdan, 90
Borak, 77, 82, 99
Borland, 6, 14
Branson, 84, 99, 185, 202, 203
Braunstein, 196, 202
Breese, 80, 101
Brownlie, 194, 204
Brzezinski, 77, 82, 99
Bueno, 112, 122, 131
Burkhart, 292, 296

C

Can, 79, 98, 99
Candan, 79, 81, 96, 99, 103, 129, 132, 199, 203
Canton , 77, 104
Cao, 84, 97,99
Cau, 203
Carp, 4,14, 216, 218
Cattermole, 217, 218
Celik, 84, 90, 100
Chandrasekran, 92, 98
Chang, 96, 99, 271, 279\

Chatterjee, 80, 104
Cerovic, 128, 134
Champion, 218
Chen, 67, 70, 83, 85, 99, 199, 203
Chena, 122, 134
Cheng, 91, 100, 130-131, 269, 270
Chen-Yu, 10, 15, 151, 154
Cheikhrouhou, 97, 102
Chernauk, 294, 296
Chiwese, 81, 89, 99, 125, 131
Choi, 92, 99
Choudhari, 110, 133
Chowdhary, 2, 5, 8 -10,14, 23,33,37, 47, 56-58, 63, 6, 69-71, 77-79, 82-84, 89, 91-92, 95, 100, 102-103, 110-112, 118, 122, 124-127, 130-131, 133, 141, 154, 162, 167, 164, 181-182, 185, 194, 195, 196, 200, 203, 208, 218, 26, 243, 267, 269, 270, 273, 279, 280
Chunjeong, 97, 105
Cimilli, 199, 203
Ciobanu, 90, 100
Cobb, 211, 21, 278,
Cohen, 54, 57, 70, 154, 185, 203, 259, 279
Collier, 2,14, 37, 47, 58, 63, 70, 78, 79, 8, 100, 154
Collins, 6, 14
Colleoni, 77, 104
Condon, 96,99, 201, 218, 271, 279
Coruh, 90, 100, 128, 132
Courtney, 195, 203
Crews, 81, 82, 99, 125, 131
Csiszar, 84,100
Cukurova, 84, 90

D

Dalbasi, 199, 203
Dallabast, 92, 101
Das, 113, 125, 128, 132
Datta, 118, 135
Davies, 6, 14, 190, 203, 210, 212, 215, 216, 218
Davis, 159, 181
Dayioglu, 96, 99, 103
Dear, 97, 101, 103
Dedhia, 277, 280
Degrimenci, 84, 90, 101, 104

Denes, 212
Desmarteau, 209, 218
Devanand, 118, 132
Dhoulb, 97, 102
Diaz, 292, 296
Dickey, 85
Dolbow, 190
Dornyi, 84, 100
Doty, 82, 101, 114-115, 125, 132, 151,209, 218
Duckett, 78, 101
Dumitras, 90
Duru, 129, 132

E

Eamon, 215, 218
Easter, 82, 101, 114-115, 125, 132, 151, 154, 209, 218, 277, 279
Edwards, 209, 218
Eladwi, 113, 122
Eldeeb, 90, 132
El-Hossini, 90, 101
Emiel, 85, 103
Erdem, 150, 154
Erdumlu, 10
Emirhanova, 77, 70, 90, 101
Epps, 37, 63, 70, 78, 79
Eryuruk, 96, 101, 270, 279
Ezazshahahi, 56, 70

F

Fahmy, 83, 85, 101
Fan, 85, 99, 203
Fen , 199
Fanguiero, 128-129, 132
Farr, 84,99, 203
Fayala, 113, 122, 133
Ferede, 58, 70
Ferreira, 118, 132
Filgueiras, 129, 132
Filiz, 83, 101
Fladeiro, 80, 103
Foisal, 118, 135
Forrest, 215, 217, 218

Freddie, 203
Freiman, 6, 15

G,
Gam, 97
Gao, 82, 104, 113, 134, 135, 199, 203
Gatterson, 151, 154
Geylk, 90, 104
Geyter, 129, 133
Ghaziantep, 84, 90
Ghith, 113, 122, 133
Gisbert, 67, 83, 99
Glasheen, 10, 15
Gocek, 150, 154
Gokarneshan, 85, 102, 267, 280
Goktepe, 80, 101
Gong, 83
Gonzales, 199, 204
Goswami, 78, 101
Gowda, 92, 99
Goyal, 125, 134
Graven, 96
Gunesoglu, 111, 133
Guo, 151, 154
Gupta, 130, 133
Gurian, 294, 296

H
Halleb, 96, 101
Hallstrom, 56, 71
Harder, 200-201, 203
Hasan, 90, 105
Hassan, 113, 122, 132
Hati, 113, 132
Haventh, 199, 203
Hayward, 292, 296
Hazavehi, 82, 101
Hearle, 79, 101
Hofer, 110, 132
Hsi, 80, 101
Holocombe, 97, 103
Hoque, 80, 100
Hori, 82, 102, 114, 133

Hossamy, 81
Hu, 80, 215, 218, 294, 296
Hussain, 56, 71, 92, 98
Hutson, 80, 100

I
Ibekwe, 215, 218, 294, 296
Ibrahim, 81, 101
Idrish, 90, 105
Illeez, 92, 101
Islam, 79, 100, 104, 126-127, 130-131, 164, 182, 273, 279

J
Jahan, 89, 102
Jasiorski, 77, 82, 99
Jeguirim, 97, 102
Jeon, 89
Jhanji, 130, 133
Jhatial, 112, 122, 133
Jin, 79
Johnson, 54, 57, 70, 154, 185, 203, 259, 279
Jonas, 127, 133
Jump, 79

K
Kabbari, 113, 122, 133
Kadolph, 57, 67, 71, 77-78, 95, 102, 208, 218, 272, 279
Kajseri, 199, 203
Kalaoglu, 96, 101, 270, 279
Kam, 82
Kang, 89, 96, 102, 270, 279
Kartal, 127, 134
Kavitha, 85, 102, 267, 280
Kavusturan, 77, 79, 90, 101
Kawabata, 56, 71
Kawamura, 98, 102
Kefsiz, 92, 104
Kelly, 195, 203
Ketema, 110, 133
Khalifa, 8, 101
Khallil, 115, 134
Khatri, 112, 122, 133

Appendix C - Author Index

Kim, 80, 82, 89. 92, 96,99, 102, 270, 279
Kinkeidei, 294, 296
Kirchhoff, 151, 154
Kislak, 83, 102
Knapp, 212
Koe, 256, 280
Koehl, 125, 131
Kosik, 293, 296
Kothari, 128, 130, 132-133
Kowalczyk, 77, 82, 99
Kretzschmar, 79, 83, 102
Kruse, 188
Kundu, 67, 69, 71, 83-84, 102, 130, 133, 267, 280
Kunkel, 196, 203
Kusterback, 209, 218
Kut, 111,133
Kuzuhara, 82, 102, 114, 133
Kwak, 89

L

Langenhove, 85, 104, 199
Langford, 208, 218, 272, 279
Lapitsky, 85, 102
Laso, 112, 122
Latifi, 80, 102
Lau, 199, 203
Lawson, 190, 204
Lazic, 128, 134
Le, 211, 218
Lee, 10, 15, 83, 89, 103, 199, 204
Leighs, 113, 132
Leys, 129, 133
Li, 67, 71, 79, 97, 102, 103, 113, 134, 215, 218, 294, 296
Lickfield, 82, 105, 114
Liddane, 204
Liouane, 113, 122, 133
Lipetz, 190
Liu, 82, 104, 114, 135
Liua, 122, 134
Long , 157, 176, 182
Lorentzen, 190, 204
Lucas, 80, 103

M

Mackay, 67, 71, 125, 130
Majumdar, 83, 103
Malengier, 85, 104, 199, 204
Mallucelli, 77, 98
Manoharan, 70
Manolache, 212
Maqsood, 56, 71, 89, 96, 105
Marooka, 97, 103
Marsha, 83, 103, 124, 130, 133
Martines, 199, 204
Mathews, 9, 14, 226, 243
Matsudaira, 56, 71
Mauer, 151, 154
Mawla, 167, 182
McCloskey, 79
McGregor, 54, 71
McKeegan, 217, 218
McKinnon, 125, 134
McQuerry, 85, 103
Medeiros, 118, 132
Meidi, 129, 132
Memon, 92, 98
Mendes, 80, 103
Menezes, 110, 133
Meng, 215, 218, 294, 296
Merkel, 23, 33, 35,37, 47, 58, 78, 103
Mesegul, 92, 104
Mia, 90, 105
Miguel, 80, 103
Mills-Senn, 209, 214, 215, 218
Mine, 58, 71
Miranda, 113, 122, 133
Mitchell, 152, 155
Mitra, 69, 71, 125, 134,208
Moiz, 113, 122, 133
Mokrzycki, 162, 182
Momotaz, 90, 105
Mondal, , 267, 280
Morent, 128, 133
Moses, 199, 202
Mousazadegan, 56. 70
Mukhopadhyay, 79, 80, 83, 103, 104

Munzenrieder, 294, 296
Murphy, 113, 122, 133

N
Nam, 84, 96, 99, 203, 271, 279
Namal, 150, 154
Nargis, 199, 203
Nawab, 56, 71
Neckar, 85, 96, 105
Niwa, 56, 71
Njeugna, 102

O
Obendorf, 83, 103, 199, 204
Oggiaro, 194. 204
Ogulata, 83, 103, 185-186, 204
Okur, 85, 99, 103, 130, 133, 268, 278-279
Oliveira, 118, 132
O'Mahoney, 217, 218
Omerglu, 58, 71, 79, 89, 103
Omeroglu, 77
Onal, 79, 81, 99
Oner , 85, 103, 130, 133
Orhan, 111, 133
Oritz, 195, 203
Orndoff, 216, 218
Ozakin, 111, 133
Ozcan, 96,99, 103
Ozdil, 79, 90, 104, 125, 134
Özgüney, 79, 84, 102
Özçelik, 79, 84, 102
Ozelik, 92. 101
Özerdem, 79, 84, 102

P
Padhye, 113, 122, 133
Pan, 82, 104, 113, 134, 135, 199, 203,
Parachura, 82, 105, 114
Parikh, 209, 218
Parthiban, 118, 132
Peiffer, 102
Peksoz, 82, 99
Peltier, 182

Perwuelz, 125, 131
Petit Pli, 209,
Phillips, 129, 162, 182
Pourdehimi, 80, 102
Poynor, 37, 47, 91, 100
Powell, 92, 99
Preus, 210, 218
Preuss, 209, 218
Price, 185
Psikuta, 85, 99, 268, 278, 279

Q
Quinn, 6, 15

R
Rabideau, 142, 153, 155
Rahman, 69, 71, 125, 134, 208
Raja, 129, 134
Rakesh, 69, 71, 125, 134, 208
Ralph Lauren, 215
Ramakrishnan, 79, 104, 129. 134
Ramaswamy, 83, 89, 103
Ramsis, 293, 297
Rana, 118, 135
Rehan, 92, 98
Rehberg, 150, 154
Reljic, 128, 134
Ritzenthaler, 153, 155
Roger, 85, 103
Rosace, 77, 104
Ross, 199
Rotich, 58-70
Roy, 125, 134
Ruppenicker, 79, 104
Russell, 79

S
Sadek, 90
Saha, 84, 267, 280
Sahin, 150, 154
Sahnoun, 97, 101, 102
Saramadi, 212
Schacher, 97, 101

Appendix C - Author Index

Satera, 194, 204
Saharkhiz, 56, 70
Sampath, 129, 134
Santos, 113, 122, 133
Saricam, 10, 15
Sarkar, 115, 134
Satrana, 194, 204
Sayol, 292, 293,297
Schamp, 291, 297
Schaqes, 150, 154
Schwartz, 125, 134
Scott, 6, 15
Seki, 83, 92, 104
Sellabona, 67, 70, 99
Senthamilselvan, 290, 297
Senthikumar, 129, 134
Sequence of laundering, 147-149
Seshadri, 215, 218
Sethi, 125, 134
Seto, 97, 103
Shahidi, 82, 101
Shaker, 56, 71, 113, 122, 132
Shalini, 110, a34
Sharkhiz, 56, 70
Sherburne, 212, 213
Shrimali, 277, 280
Shim, 128, 134
Singh, 125, 134
Siu, 199, 203
Sivaramkirishnan, 294, 296
Slater, 77, 83, 85-86, 101
Smriti, 79, 104
Soares, 113, 122, 133
Soutinho, 129, 132
Speer, 6, 15
Speijers, 54, 71
Spola, 67, 70, 83, 99
Srinivasan, 79, 104
Stahl, 291, 297Stanton, 54, 71
Steffens, 118, 132
Stepanovic, 128, 134
Stig, 56. 71
Sular, 83, 92, 104

Suna, 122, 134
Suruj-Zaman, 84
Sweeney, 185, 202

T
Takahashi, 82, 105, 114, 135
Takatera, 98, 102, 130
Tamanna, 84
Tatol, 162
Telli, 79, 90, 104, 125, 134
Tester, 54, 71
Tesfaye, 85, 104, 204
Teyeme, 85, 104, 199, 204
Thakur, 125, 132
Thiry, 6, 16, 118, 125, 134, 291, 297
Thurston, 80, 100
Tokura , 83, 105
Topalbekiroglu, 90, 104
Tornquist, 212, 218
Tortora, 2, 14, 58. 81, 100, 154
Totolin, 212
Tracz, 77, 99
Troster, 294, 296
Troynikove, 194, 204
Twafik, 81, 101
Tyndall, 97, 104

U
Ukponmwan, 80, 104
Ulku, 77, 79. 89, 103
Umair, 56, 71
Unal, 127, 134
Uttam, 125, 134
Uyanik, 90,104

V
Vanderploeg, 80, 100
Vansteenkiste, 129
Varkivani, 56, 70
Varshney, 125, 134
Vasile, 85, 104, 199, 204
Vigo, 78, 101
Vijaykumar, 125, 131

Viswaprakash, 290, 297

W
Walzer, 199, 204
Wang, 79, 82, 83, 89, 103, 104, 114, 122, 133, 135
Wei, 79, 103
Weidong, 199, 203
Wentela, 57, 70, 84, 89, 92, 100, 267, 270, 279
West, 277, 280
Wilkin, 79
Wilson, 204
Wojclechowska, 214, 218
Worku, 110, 133
Wright, 215, 218
Wroblewski, 5, 83, 105, 162, 267, 280

X
Xin, 80, 105
Xu, 113, 134

Y
Yadav, 83, 103
Yan, 80, 105
Yanai, 83, 105
Yang, 82, 105, 114
Yassen, 90, 101
Yatagai, 82, 105, 114, 135
Yesmin, 90, 105, 125, 135
Yeung, 67, 71
Yilonu, 127, 134
Youngjoo, 97, 105
Yun Jun, 113, 122, 131

Z
Zaman, 267, 280
Zerin, 118, 135
Zfenix, 80, 100
Zhang, 83, 85, 99, 199
Zhaoa, 122, 134
Zhou, 82, 114
Zhoua, 122, 134
Zhu, 67, 71, 102, 103, 130
Zimmer, 166
Zolgharnein, 82, 101
Zubair, 89, 96, 105
Zusset, 294, 296

APPENDIX D

Subject Index

A
AAFA, 29
AATCC, 1, 19, 28
Abrasion resistance, 77, 85,
Absorbency, 126
Academia and Industry, 5
AACI, 25
Accuracy, 40
Acid Dye, 178-181
ACT, 26
Additive theory, 158
Advancing color, 175
AFMA, 27
ANSI, 29
Advancing knowledge base, 9
Aesthetic attributes, 75, 110
Aesthetic finishes, 207
Air permeability, 82
Analysis of fabric failures, 5
Anatomy of hand, 196
Antibacterial, 110
Antimicrobial, 290
Apparel product development, 4
Apparel purchase criteria, 10
Appearance, 208
Appearance retention, 111
Arthritis, 197
ASTM, 1, 19, 23, 29
ATMA, 27
Average, 40

B
Ballistic protection, 211
Basic dye, 178-181
Basketball, 187, 191
Basket weave, 59
Bicycle Wear, 187, 191

Bio-polishing, 207
Bleaching, 207
Body comfort, 185, 195
Bow, 63
Breaking force, 21
Breaking strength, 86-89
Broken thread, 63
Bulletproof vest, 287
Burning test, 53
Bursting strength, 89-91

C
Calendering, 207
Care Labeling, 211
CBP, 3
Celsius, 24
Chemical testing, 54
Children, 197
CIE, 162
Cleaning, 207
Clo value, 186
CMDT, 5
Clothing comfort, 30, 185, 195
Coefficient of Variation, 40
Color, 211
Color schemes, 159-160
Color Theories, 158
Colorfastness, 114-118
   Bleaching, 114
   Burnt fumes, 114
   Chlorinated water, 114-115
   Crocking, 115
   Laundering, 115-117
   Light, 117
   Perspiration, 117
   Water, 117-118
Coloring process, 166

Comfort, 185
Comfort attributes, 75
Communication , 6
Compression therapy, 196
Compression vest, 215
Conditioning, 21-23
Conductive threads, 215
Confidence building, 5
Confidence level, 36
Consumer intentions, 13
Cord, 58
Cost reduction, 5
Cotton count, 57
Cotton Incorporated, 12
CPSC, 3, 25
Crease retention, 111
Cricket, 188, 192
Crocking, 19
CTS, 195-196
Cutting specimens, 37
Cyclofresh™, 291

D
Data analysis, 35
Decimal places, 46
Denier, 57
Diameter, 54
Digital printing, 212
Disperse dye, 178-181
DLI, 5, 27
Doby weave, 61
DOC, 25
DOD, 25
Detergent, 140
Drape, 208
Dry symbol, 139
Durable Press, 208
Durability attributes, 76
Dyes, 167, 212
  Acid, 167
  Basic, 167
  Direct, 167
  Disperse, 167
  Fluorescent brighteners, 167
  Mordant , 167
  Reactive , 167
  Sulphur, 167
  Vat, 167
DyStar, 172-173

E
Electronic textiles, 292
Electrostatic Charge, 112
Elongation, 21, 83
Enhancing predictability, 6
Environmental conditions, 23
EPA, 3, 26
Ergonomics, 195
Experimental error, 40
Evaluation, 16

F
Fabric construction, 59
Fabric defects, 63
Fabric failures, 16
Fabric , hand, 97
Fabric layout, 225
Fabric thickness, 68
Fabric weight, 67-69
Fabrics, 260-275
Face masks, 13
Fahrenheit, 24
Felting shrinkage, 208
Fiber content, 53
Fiber content analysis, 55
Fibers, 249-256
Figure skating, 188, 192
Filaments, 54
Fingerless gloves, 187
Finishes, 207, 275-278
Firefighter's uniform, 287
Flame resistance, 96
Flame-resistant fabrics, 212
Flame-resistant finishes, 208

Flammability , 96, 292
Float, 63
Florescent colors, 176
Football, 188, 193
Forensic Testing, 6,16
FPLA, 4
Fransworth Munsell's 100 hue test, 164-165
Frosting, 112
FTC, 2,3,25
Fugitive, 157
Functional, 207

G
Gamma Rays, 157
Global perspective, 12
Globalization, 288-289, 290,
Government regulations, 2,16
Gray scale of color change, 123
Gray Scale of Staining, 123-124
GreenShield, 293

H
Home laundering , 121
Hue, 158
Hypothesis, 40

I
IFAI, 27
IFI, 5
Incontinence, 197
Infrared, 157
Innovation in progress, 209
Intensity, 158
Instrumental error, 40
Interactive textiles, 215
ISO, 19, 29
ISO 9000, 29
ISO 14000, 29

J
Jacquard weave, 61
Jersey knit, 61
Jogging, 189, 194

K
Key materials in apparel, 210
Knitted denim, 210
Knitted fabric, 187
Knitting, 59

L
Laboratory sample, 40
Lab space chemistry, 163
Lab testing, 10, 16
Length, 54
Lighting, 213
Light theory , 158
Loss through abrasion, 46
Lot sample, 40
Luster, 208
Lycra, 213

M
Marine fabrics, 213
Mastectomy, 198
Mean, 40
Measurement of pills , 79
Mechanical properties, 78
Median, 40
Mercerization, 207
Metamerism, 176
Method error, 40
Microban®, 209, 290
Microscopic structure, 53
Mildew and Rot resistance, 112
Military wear, 213
Mode, 41
Moisture content, 23, 54
Moisture equilibrium, 23
Moisture Management, 214, 291
Moisture Regain, 23-24
Moisture transfer, 126,
Mosquito protection, , 291
Munsell's hue circle, 160-161
Munsell's system of color space, 161-162
Musculoskeletal discomfort, 196

N

Nanosphere, 208
NCC, 27
NCTO, 28
Neutrals, 175
Nonwovens, 62
NTC, 28

O

Objective pill classifier, 81
Oil repellency, 112
Older people, 198
OSHA, 26
Outdoor, 214
Outdoor clothing, 288
Oxford weave, 59

P

Performance attributes, 2, 16, 225-226
Performance driven pilling, 81
Permanent care labeling act, 3
PCM, 208
Personal error, 41
Pile weaves, 61
Pilling Resistance, 77
Ply, 58
Precision, 41
Preconditioning, 23
Preschooler, 198
Product development, 16
Product evaluation, 6
Professional textile care, 14
Progressive Shrinkage, 208
Purl knit, 61

Q

Quality assurance, 10, 16, 285
Quality control, 8, 14, 16, 285, 287, 288
Quality promotion, 9
Quality rainwear, 287

R

Race car driver, 287
Radar, 157
Rainwear, 7
Range, 42
Reactive dye, 178-181
Reasons for textile testing, 2, 14
Receding, 175
Recycled plastic shoes, 215
Refurbishing, 16
Refurbishing cycle, 11
Relaxation shrinkage, 208
Reliability, 42
Repeat, 59
Replicate, 42
Resins, 208
Role of clothing, 190-195
Role of textiles, 187-190, 197-198
Rounding up, 46
Running, 189, 194

S

Safety attributes, 75, 77
Sample, 42
Satin weave, 60
Scouring, 207
Seam mark, 63
Seam efficiency, 91
Seam smoothness, 113
Seam strength, 91
Seam twist, 121
Self-heated jackets, 215
Selvage, 37, 59
Sensory attributes, 75-77, 97
Service testing, 10
Shade, 158, 175
Singeing, 207
Skew, 63, 122
Single, 58
Slashing, 207
Slub, 63
Smart textiles, 215, 293
Snag, 63
Soap, 140
Soccer, 194

Soil, 140
Smart Textiles, 214
Space Clothing, 215
Special applications , 288
Special treatments, 275-278
Specialty Fabrics, 285
Specimen , 42
Sports Bra, 194
Sportswear, 190
Stain removal, 122-12
Stain removal technology, 293
Standard atmospheric conditions , 23
Standard deviation, 36, 42
Standard error, 42
Standardized tests, 14, 20
Staple fibers, 54
Stretch and Recovery, 84
Stretchy fabric, 187
Structural Attributes, 1,14, 16, 225-226
Subtractive theory, 159
Supply chain dimensions, 12
Swimwear, 189, 195

T
Tatting, 62
Technical Data Sheets (TDS), 228-231
Tear strength, 92-95
Television, 157
Tennis wear, 190, 195
Tex, 57
Textile analysis process, 6
Textile and comfort, 198
Textile Organizations, 25
Textile Testing, 1, 14, 16
TFPIA, 2
Thermal comfort, 200
Thermal insulation, 84
Thermography, 200
Tint, 175
Total Quality Satisfaction (TQS), 285
t-test, 43-45
Twill weave, 59

U
UFAC, 97
Ultraviolet protection, 294-295
UPF, 294-295

V
Value, 158
Variance, 43
Velvet , 61
Visible spectrum , 158
Visual impairment, 198

W
Wales, 61,
Warp , 62
Wash symbol, 139
Water – repellency, 19, 126
Water-repellent coat fabric, 7
Water vapor resistance, 128
Wear test, 10, 16
Weathermax, 288
Weft , 62
Weaving, 59
Wheelchair users, 198
Wicking behavior, 128
Worksheets, 232-242
Worsted count, 56
Wrinkle recovery, 82, 113-114, 208

X
X-Rays, 157

Y
Yarn crimp, 55
Yarn number, 56
Yarn twist, 57
Yarn type, 58
Yarns, 257-260

Z